D0114861

SYSTEMS ANALYSIS IN PUBLIC POLICY
A CRITIQUE

SYSTEMS ANALYSIS IN PUBLIC POLICY

A CRITIQUE

IDA R. HOOS

REVISED EDITION

UNIVERSITY OF CALIFORNIA PRESS
BERKELEY   LOS ANGELES   LONDON

This book is lovingly dedicated
to the memory of Sidney S. Hoos,
who meant everything in life to me.

University of California Press
Berkeley and Los Angeles, California

University of California Press, Ltd.
London, England

Library of Congress Catalog Card Number 82–48766
Printed in the United States of America

1 2 3 4 5 6 7 8 9

Contents

Acknowledgments

The author of a book has few privileges; one of them is the right of dedication, which I prefer to treat not as a conventional rite or a ritual convention but as an opportunity to acknowledge indebtedness to the many persons who made my research possible and enjoyable. The book is lovingly dedicated to my husband, Sidney, often devil's advocate, always faithful supporter, whose intellectual acuity and dauntless courage kept us both on course. Special thanks are due my long-suffering family, near and far, for their patience and forbearance. Like psychoanalysis, systems analysis can be a detriment to normal human and social relations.

Acknowledgment of the support of the National Aeronautics and Space Administration is not perfunctory. NASA's sponsorship of *bona fide* inquiring research is a unique and noteworthy example of the technology assessment about which other agencies of government have made so much and done so little. In this respect, Mr. James E. Webb, then Administrator, deserves credit; NASA's sponsorship of university programs in general and my research in particular resulted from his sincere dedication to public service. Professor Samuel Silver, first Director of the Space Sciences Laboratory, made that commitment an intrinsic dimension of the University of California's program. His interest assured a favorable environment for a research pursuit that might otherwise have seemed alien; his constant encouragement is gratefully acknowledged.

To Professor C. West Churchman, Director of the Social Sciences Group, I owe a long-lasting debt. The privilege of close professional association has provided me with intellectual stimulation beyond measure and tolerant understanding beyond mention. My colleagues in the kaleidoscopic history of the Social Sciences Seminar played an important role in the crystallization of my ideas. Of special value was the dialogue with Uri Hurvitz, who, in true Talmudic fashion, raised good questions and accepted only answers of the highest integrity.

Former Governor Edmund G. Brown and his top aides, especially Hale Champion, then Director of Finance, opened doors and files to primary research sources in their earnest desire to have California's experience with systems analysis studied in all its dimensions. I regret that I cannot thank by name the many State officials who graciously lent materials and gave time and counsel. In view of the shift in political winds, my expression of gratitude might constitute an embarrassing encumbrance to some of them. No such constraints prevent public acknowledgment of the valuable insights derived from discussions with two former State officials, Wilbur L. Parker, now Assistant Administrator for Program Statistics and Data Systems, U.S. Department of Health, Education, and Welfare, and John H. Stanford, now Vice President of Business and Finance, University of California. In accepting my thanks, they are under no obligation to assume responsibility.

The untold librarians who pursued elusive references and bent rules must go unnamed, but I am happy that I can acknowledge publicly the valued assistance of Mrs. Alice Sanders, who so capably managed arrangements, and Mrs. Robin Zoesch, whose willingness and meticulous attention to detail made my task easier. The chore of proofreading is no longer thankless: my heartfelt thanks for a job beautifully done in a spirit above and beyond even that of life-long friendship go to Mrs. Rose Kneznek.

Introduction:

The Past As Prologue

REASON FOR THE RETROSPECTIVE

Rarely does an author have the opportunity to analyze his or her own work retrospectively, even more rarely to present an updated perspective based on two decades of additional research and experience. Even more remarkable is it that a subject would remain timely and not only warrant but demand further study. Such, nonetheless, is the case with systems analysis, born as operations research in the Battle of Britain, spawned in the Pentagon, where, as cost/benefit analysis, "the biggest bang for the buck" became the benchmark for the management of war and peace; disseminated as PPBS (Planning Programming Budgeting System) throughout the government, applied, as policy analysis, wherever decisions were to be made, and still gaining momentum. Enshrined as the scientific and rational methodology for public and private management, the techniques are supported by an influential body of literature and an even more influential body of practitioners for whom the question is not *whether* to apply them but only *how*. Known also as technology assessment and risk analysis, the techniques are being used to calculate everything from the safety of nuclear reactors to the effects of microelectronics.

The reason that *Systems Analysis in Public Policy* comprises the central corpus of this new work is that the original, published in 1972, covers the developmental history, gives an account of instances and areas where use was occurring, contains information about the prime components of the techniques, and provides a fundamental critique of the methodology. The book has been left intact because the story it tells remains true. Its criticisms are valid and are, indeed, substantiated by time; many of its predictions have materalized; none have proved wrong. What once seemed like dour implication has become dire fact.

What was then foreseen as the future of systems analysis constitutes our present reality. Our task now is to expand the analysis, the better to understand how this paradigm governs the present and determines the shape of the future. *Systems Analysis in Public Policy* has been updated to tell us what we did not know before. An overlay of what we have learned, it may alert us to what lies ahead.

SYSTEMS ANALYSIS AS DOMINANT PARADIGM

It is necessary, as a point of departure, to review the ways in which systems analysis and the family of techniques to which it is related penetrated into and pervaded thought processes to the point that there was created a "management syndrome," i.e., the notion that all human affairs could be managed, and that by utilizing the tools of management science we would solve society's problems "rationally." Interesting to note, the universal acceptance and ubiquitous application of systems analysis are in themselves a phenomenon which merits inquiry. It is exemplified and can be explained by T. S. Kuhn's concept of the dominant paradigm, which he describes as "the entire constellation of beliefs, values, techniques . . . shared by the members of a given community."[1] That "given community" expanded and proliferated as the entire spectrum of academic disciplines from anthropology to zoology joined the engineers and economists in their embrace of systems analysis. Welcomed because of the semblance of methodical rigor it lent to fields eager to divest themselves of a "soft" image, the techniques brought an aura of respectability in an era when computerized models were becoming *de rigueur*. Welcome everywhere was a disciplinary matrix so eminently utile.

A strong supporting guild of practitioners, sometimes in universities, sometimes in government posts, sometimes in private management positions, sometimes in research organizations subsisting on federal contracts, sometimes on prestigious advisory panels, proved to be a bulwark against critical evaluation. Perhaps this explains the curious lack of advance in the state-of-the-art. The interesting paradox remains that techniques which have been bought and sold as "scientific" could continue to ignore so blatantly the rudimentary precepts of scientific procedure. Independent verification and validation are virtually nonexistent while huge expenditure continues to flow into systems studies, risk analyses, and technology assessments. Claims about "more powerful management tools" notwithstanding, there is very little difference be-

---

[1] Thomas S. Kuhn, *The Structure of Scientific Revolutions*, Chicago, Illinois: The University of Chicago Press (Second Edition, enlarged, 1970) p. 175.

tween systems studies performed a decade ago and those produced today. Nor does there seem to be an appreciable improvement in the
quality of management decisions. Rebuttal to challenge generally takes
the form of a solemn recital of the Articles of Faith: the methodology is
unexceptionable; it is only misuse that is at fault. There is nothing
wrong with the method; it is only the data that are deficient. Incidentally, the data game is generally played when advocate and adversary,
both using systems techniques, take stands on various issues.

Another paradox appears in our backward-looking mirror: how to
explain the many and dismal management failures that beset public
and private enterprise alike at the very time that they were the prime
target of opportunity for management science techniques. Other less
pretentious approaches having been scorned because they promised
neither perfection nor panacea, the dominant paradigm sanctioned the
"rational" methodology. Yet, years of dogged documentation by the
General Accounting Office show that government agencies still need to
be reminded of the most rudimentary rules of accounting and that ignorance of the most elementary management practices is rampant.
Typical is the GAO's study of computer software maintenance in government agencies, where programs were found to be overpriced and
undermanaged.

> Managers generally have neither cost accounting data on software mainte-
> nance activities and thus know little about how much maintenance really costs
> overall, or [sic] which types of maintenance cost the most. Agencies have estab-
> lished no goals and standards to measure the efficiency of their maintenance
> operation, nor criteria for acceptable maintenance costs for given situations.
> They have made only limited use of improved tools and techniques which could
> reduce the maintenance costs.[2]

That the Department of Defense should be a prime example of managerial ineptness is the crowning irony when one considers that it was
the military that was the original model. The Comptroller General reported in early 1982,[3] for example, that the Army's Automated Facilities Engineer Job Order Cost Accounting Systems, designed to manage
a work force of some 45,000 employees, was not efficient because (a) the
information it generated was not being used by management; (b) data
were not being entered promptly or accurately; (c) two design deficien-

[2] General Accounting Office, *Federal Agencies' Maintenance of Computer Programs:
Expensive and Undermanaged*, Washington, D.C., GAO/AFMD–81–25, February 26,
1981, pp. i–ii.

[3] General Accounting Office, *Improvements Needed in Operating and Using the
Army Automated Facilities Engineer Cost Accounting System*, Washington, D.C.,
GAO/AFMD–82–27, May 19, 1982, p. i.

cies pointed out by GAO five years ago had still not been corrected; (d) training of users had not been continued at an adequate level after conversion to the system; (e) it generated cumbersome reports in formats that discouraged use of the data. Nonetheless, examples of poor management abound. Many, reported by the General Accounting Office, indicate that the Army has no institutional memory. It never learns and simply repeats old mistakes. One instance[4] is that of the expenditure of tens of millions of dollars annually on material no longer needed by the requisitioners. According to the GAO report, the Defense Department, "can save an estimated $112 million over a three-year period and improve the credibility of its data base and supply readiness by strengthening its policies, procedures, and practices for periodically validating and reconciling older, outstanding orders." The staff of the House Appropriations Committee investigated the U.S. Navy's Ticonderoga, its most technically advanced, billion-dollar cruiser, and concluded that despite the vast expenditure for systems studies, the vessel would be ineffectual unless drastic corrections were made.[5]

If the emperor's closet were not bulging with vested interests determined to keep a lucrative systems game going, we might have acknowledged long ago that the folderol of "scientific" and "rational" decision-making techniques in the military and elsewhere has relevance only as *ex post facto* justification for the preferences and predilections of persons in higher places. At present, for example, "high tech fever" is the sole explanation for an investment (to date) of between $10 and $15 billion in a "Command-Control-Intelligence System" (C^3I), a radio and computer network supposed to control military maneuvers from one central location. When the system was tested in 1977, there were "abnormal terminations," the official euphemism for breakdowns, 62% of the time. Seen as useless when it fails to work and harmful when it does, because it undermines the initiative and leadership which officers must display on the field of battle, C^3I is only one in a progression of costly technological deterrents to military readiness.[6] According to testimony in Senate inquiry, "The military's pursuit of technological sophistication at any cost has caused it to ignore human contributions that account for numerous weapons failures. . . . Our bias toward short-term

4 General Accounting Office, *Better Methods for Validating and Reconciling Unfilled Materiel Orders Could Provide Substantial Economies to the Army*, Washington, D.C., GAO/PLRD–82–76, (June 2, 1982), p. i.

5 House Appropriations Committee, "Department of the Navy's CG–47 Cruiser Program," July, 1982.

6 James Fallows, "America's High-Tech Weaponry," *The Atlantic Monthly*, May 1981, pp. 21–34.

investments in weapons of increasing complexity is the cause of our long-term cost growth."[7]

The military, for all its layers of management and despite the vaunted knowhow that made it the model, continues to provide the General Accounting Office's *Monthly Bulletin* with a dismal catalogue of mismanagement practices. The story of the Pentagon updated shows it to be no more a paragon than it was in the earlier version of *Systems Analysis in Public Policy*. The wonder is that the gross inefficiencies which bedevil it and all public agencies should have persisted so tenaciously at the very time that the ranks of management experts were swelling bureaucratic hierarchies and their ministrations were becoming so widespread. One suspects, on reviewing many cases, that the mythology of methodology has caused us to take leave of common sense, a faculty lamentably undervalued. The point is illustrated by the way cost-cutting "rationalizations" were used to undercut conservation programs in the agencies concerned with U.S. energy independence. The Department of the Interior, aggressive in its promotion of development policies justified by the "need," and the Department of Energy, determined to pursue the cause of nuclear energy at all costs, dismantled the very programs designed to reduce waste in Federal buildings and operations, despite the considerable savings in resources and taxpayers' money.[8]

Many were the lessons to be learned during the past twenty years. Some which should have been learned earlier were shielded by the uncritical fealty of the fraternity of practitioners who, after all, reflect their generation's predilection for formalized decision methodologies. Other lessons were obscured by the tautological nature of systems analysis, which proceeds from (a) certain assumptions and (b) on certain premises. It defines a universe which allows or disallows certain factors and data according to their "fit," and thus produces, with disingenuous certainty, justification for (a) and (b). This process was once described by Leontief[9] as leading from sets of more or less plausible but entirely arbitrary assumptions to precisely stated but irrelevant conclusions. The crucial point is that this circular justification, a kind of incestous vali-

---

[7] Franklin Spinney, as quoted by Jeffrey Smith, "High-Cost Lemons in the U.S. Arsenal," *Science*, 17 April, 1981, p. 310.

[8] John D. Dingell, Chairman, House Energy and Commerce Committee and Subcommittee on Energy Investigations and Oversight, stated in a report, *Wasted Energy Dollars in the Federal Government*, August 4, 1982, that with the total Federal energy bill totalling some $12.5 billion annually, even a one percent decrease in consumption would save $125 million and enough power to heat many homes.

[9] Wassily Leontief, "Theoretical Assumptions and Unobserved Facts," *American Economic Review*, 1971, *op. cit.*

dation, has served as insulation from the socially important aspects of problems and has condoned flagrant distortion of them. Herein lies a danger, observed by a professor at the London School of Economics: "Deception is easily practiced from false recipes intended to simulate useful findings."[10]

ECONOMICS AND COST/BENEFIT ANALYSIS

We recognized early that the cost/benefit ratio was the linchpin of systems analysis. But we failed to anticipate its potential impact. One might have expected that in the process of sensible planning possible courses of action would be weighed in terms of their relative costs. But with costs customarily equated with the bad and benefits deemed good, criticism of cost/benefit analysis was deflected. To question the process was *pari passu* to impugn morality or motherhood. Of course, every one knew that cost/benefit analysis was a teeter-totter that tilted as it was loaded. The outcome depended on who put what on which side. What we may not have anticipated was the way the simple principle of trade-off was to be parlayed into position as the keystone of public management, to be used in regulatory deliberations, assessment of risks, and policy formulation. A favorable benefit to cost ratio came to be the *sine qua non* for most important decisions made by the powerful Office of Management and Budget. An administration whose philosophy is one of disencumbering industry of regulation as a means to stimulate production assumes a high-risk carcinogen policy, seen by some critics as having potentially tragic consequences.[11] Easing of safety rules in automotive design and of quality requirements in hospitals becomes policy justifiable on grounds of ratio of cost to return.

Should we have foreseen that herein lay the blueprint for disaster? Only one short-sighted goal was to dominate public administration: maintaining an image of cost/effectiveness—"running government in a businesslike fashion." If ever we had fancied that budgeting was the way to implement government's planning, we were to learn that the process had been reversed. Budgeting was the implement that *determined* planning. Public planning was to be subverted into a cynical numbers game played by Mammon's rules by which the richer and more powerful could count on winning. The element of economics, once conjoined with engineering in operations research to keep dollars-and-cents considerations in sight, becomes the over-riding force. Notable here is the treacherous slippage from *financial* to *economic* to *economics*. Decis-

10 David F. Hendry, "Econometrics—Alchemy or Science?" *Economica*, Vol. 47, No. 188, November, 1980, p. 390.

11 Eliot Marshall, "EPA's High-Risk Carcinogen Policy," *Science*, 3 December 1982, pp. 975–978.

ions came to be treated as economic because they involved expenditure. Hence, economists were hailed as the doctors, even though their prowess was in tampering with thermometers and not curing the fevers. But we overlooked "Goodhart's Law": *viz.*, "All economic models break down when used for policy." [12] The lesson here is clear; simply because something costs money does not automatically consign it to the bailiwick of economics as we know the discipline.

Economics is not an exact science, despite the profession's embrace of econometrics as the *Gradus ad Parnassum* to scientific respectability. Linear regression being the philosopher's stone for econometricians, we need only to turn to J.M. Keynes for an account of the deficiencies of the linear regression model.[13] His list could certainly obviate any claim to meeting "scientific" standards. He criticizes this model for (a) using an incomplete set of determining factors, i.e., containing an omitted variable bias; (b) building models with unobservable variables, such as expectations, estimated from badly measured data based on index numbers; (c) obtaining spurious correlations from the use of "proxy" variables and simultaneity; (d) being unable to separate the distinct effects of multicollinear variables; assuming linear functional forms without knowing the appropriate dimensions of the regressors; (e) mis-specifying the dynamic reactions and lag lengths; (f) incorrectly pre-filtering the data; (g) invalidly inferring "causes" from correlations; (h) predicting inaccurately, i.e., non-constant parameters; (i) confusing statistical with economic "significance" of results and failing to relate economic theory to economics. To this list, important because it undermines the methodological base of systems analysis, a British economist adds several more damning items: stochastic mis-specification, incorrect exogeneity assumptions, aggregation, lack of structural identification, and an inability to refer back uniquely firm observed results to any given initial theory.[14]

As long as a decade ago, Wassily Leontief, a Nobel prizewinner in economics, deplored his profession's growing preoccupation with mathematical modeling. More recently, he fortified his critical stance by surveying the articles published in the *American Economic Review* from 1972 through 1981. He found that the majority of the academic papers discussed only mathematical models and saw this as a "mathematical disease that has atrophied many academic economists." [15] R. Aaron

12 C.A.E. Goodhart, "Problems of Monetary Management: The UK Experience," in *Inflation, Depression and Economic Policy in the West: Lessons in the 1970's*, A.S. Counakis, ed., Oxford: Basil Blackwell, 1978.

13 John Maynard Keynes, *op. cit.*, p. 38 n. 67.

14 David F. Hendry, *op. cit.*, p. 396.

15 As quoted in "The Naked Economist," *The Economist*, July 17, 1982, p. 67.

Gordon, a noted economist, once observed that his professional colleagues had been seduced by mathematical elegance and were wont to sacrifice relevance to rigor. Then rigor mortis sets in, for abstract models and not the problems plaguing society receive attention. It may even be that the formidable front of mathematics is used to obscure the ephemeral substantive aspects that are the essence of these problems.

The observer of the current scene cannot fail to discern in the economic theorems being put forward as placebos for a sick economy a farrago of fad and fancy having a lifespan curiously commensurate with the term of an administration in office. Certainly no other academic field has produced such a plethora of prophets, some of whom have gone down in historical ignominy only to be born again with new charisma. Since politicians have a great affinity for nostrums, they anoint their favorite circle of economic seers. Thus, in the United States, the Council of Economic Advisors is comprised of an ever-changing cast of characters who first consent and then advise. They lend academic credentials, but not necessarily credibility, to whatever precepts are politically palatable.

What has been strikingly evident over the years has been the facility of the transition from the *logic* of economics to the *ideologic*. A large and conflicting body of hypotheses and theories has provided substantiation for just about any position that is politically sanctioned—radical, liberal, conservative, populist, monetarist, supply-side, libetarian, or whatever. But could we have anticipated the swing from *ideologic* to *theologic*? Certain forms of orthodoxy permeate the power structure and linger even after individual priests defect or are defrocked. It is important for purposes of our discussion to note that this process manifests itself tellingly in the cost/benefit analysis, for here is the frame of reference by which allocation and even the designation of costs and benefits are rationalized. What is to go on the teeter and what on the totter side and with what weight of data as evidence is arbitrarily predetermined and dictated by the prevailing economic religion which is, *non disputandum*, right.

We need only remind ourselves that cost/benefit analysis *per se* is nothing more than the calculated trade-off inherent in any choice. It was largely through its re-attribution in consort with systems analysis that it became imbued with a kind of mystique and accredited as one of the "powerful tools of technology"—how powerful we had yet to learn. By supplying the weapon for executing economic ideology-turned-theology, cost/benefit analysis is the fulcrum of the budgetary process. In our time, it is the numbers game played to "rationalize" relaxation of regulations and to condone reliance on the marketplace to take care of the public's health, safety, and environment. Since long-term costs or benefits to the populace-at-large rate low priority when vested interests are at stake, cost/benefit analysis contains an antisocial and insidious bias. We see now with the clarity of hindsight the way the simple principle of trade-off became the epicenter of public management. Our task at present is to ascertain how this orientation has affected some of the areas of lasting concern included in the earlier edition of *Systems Analysis in Public Policy* and how others, such as regulatory policy, risk analysis, and technology assessment are being affected.

OPTIMIZATION AND THE DECLINE OF THE BUSINESS WORLD

Reverse clairvoyance reveals that the same precepts of management science found a hospitable environment in the business world. Executives relied heavily on elegant planning models and decision-making techniques that favored analytic precision and detachment over insight and judgment based on experience. Some observers contend that slavish adherence to the "science of optimization" contributed to the deterioration of American leadership in innovativeness at home and competitiveness abroad. Jordan D. Lewis, a senior fellow at the Wharton School, explains the decline as follows and selects General Electric as an example:

The use of quantitative decision-making procedures limits a firm's ability to act on necessarily qualitative speculations about future markets and technologies. In the late 1960s, for example, General Electric used quantitative techniques to consider growth opportunities in computers, nuclear power, and semiconductor electronics. At the time, markets and technologies for the first two options were presumably closer at hand and thus easier to quantify than the third. General Electric proceeded to drop semiconductor electronics and invest heavily in computers and nuclear reactors. Since then the company has left the computer business, nuclear power sales have tumbled, and semiconductor electronics has become a major growth industry.[16]

Over the past two decades, "management by numbers" dictated short-term criteria in financial decision-making and a low-risk philosophy in corporate portfolio management.[17] Such market-driven strategies, based on profit performance calculations, have been seen as the cause for several major bank failures that had serious repercussions throughout the industry in mid-1982. There is concern that the rapacious, quick-return loan practices of some of the nation's banks may undermine the whole system. Similarly, an early profit-taking philosophy manifests

[16] Jordan D. Lewis, "Technology, Enterprise, and American Economic Growth," *Science*, 5 March 1982, p. 1207.
[17] Robert H. Hayes and William J. Abernathy, "Managing Our Way to Economic Decline," *Harvard Business Review*, July–August, 1980, pp. 67–77.

itself in the cannibalistic corporate acquisitions, merger mania, and non-productive shuffling of gains that have swept the financial sector. Profits on portfiolios may look good, but the game has proved inimical to the growth and vitality of the American economy. Instead of achieving technological superiority in products—a long, arduous task—managers cleaved to narrow bottom-line calculations. Having through such institutionalized greed lost its capability to produce goods and maintain a competitive edge over other countries, the United States now sends countless study teams to Japan and sponsors endless seminars to learn what two decades of management science dogma caused them to forget.

Heretic though it may have seemed when the original version of *Systems Analysis in Public Policy* first appeared, the contention is growing that the technico-economic management model so avidly espoused during the past decades may actually be root cause and not, as was so wishfully presumed, remedy for America's fiscal malaise. A mid-1982 Dun & Bradstreet Corporation report showed business failures at a 50-year high, with a 43 percent rise over last year's and a failure rate equalled only by that of 1932. The hypothesis that the cure contributed to the ailment gains credence when one ponders the demise of the automotive industry, where decisions have for years been dictated by the canons of cost/effectiveness. Professor William Abernathy, of the Harvard Business School, puts forward the concept of Detroit's "productivity dilemma"—its predicament rooted in pressures for cost savings that mandated greater efficiency in manufacturing but led to more standardization and rigidity at the expense of quality control, innovativeness, and technological competitiveness.[18]

Model design was driven by traditional notions of profitability: "We make more money on big cars" was General Motor's reason for eschewing smaller, more fuel-efficient vehicles. Translated into policy on product quality in general and the handling of particular defects, cost/effectiveness for the industry spelled danger to the driving public. Instead of recalling and repairing known defects, manufacturers went to court.

The transcript of a 1971 meeting between then-President Nixon and Lee Iacocca, then president of the Ford Motor Company, and Henry Ford II, then chairman of the board, was introduced in a multi-million dollar suit for damages in the death of a 15-year-old passenger in a 1975 Ford Mustang II, in which faulty gas tank design and placement were alleged. The Ford executives had met with Nixon to complain that safety regulations and the public demand for stricter automobile safety

[18] Leslie Wayne, "Management Gospel Gone Wrong," *The New York Times*, May 30, 1982.

standards were undermining their competitive position. Iacocca was heard to say: "And the Japs are in the wings ready to eat us up alive. So I'm in a position to be saying (to the Department of Transportation): 'Would you guys cool it a bit? You're gonna break us' . . . You can see that safety has really killed all of our business." Nixon agreed to investigate the DOT's regulations, so as to determine their effect on the automotive industry and the economy as a whole. "Cost/effectiveness is the word," said Nixon to the Ford executives.[19]

With high-powered legal defense, the industry won battles but lost the market. American consumers performed their own cost/benefit analysis and knew the meaning of the ominous formula $C/E = ce$ (Cost/ Effectiveness equals *caveat emptor*). "Effectiveness," for the industry, had produced uneconomic, unreliable, and sometimes dangerous vehicles for the consumer. The formula was to bring about the demise of the industry and the whole of the American economy was to pay. There may be an axiom here: decisions based on the command-performance, cost/effective model serve to satisfy vested interest, if not greed. Applied in the context of risk analysis, as will be exemplified in the final chapter, and as was suggested in the automotive industry's calculated disregard of known defects, such decisions are tantamount to technological murder.

THE CASE OF THE COSTLY MINI-DOLLAR

As an example of the kind of fiscal fiasco that can be brought about by over-reliance on cost/benefit calculations, we have the case of the Susan B. Anthony coin dollar. Put forward as "compelling reasons" in its favor by the Treasury Department were the following: (a) continuing increase of coin-operated vending machine usage; (b) higher-priced items due to rising inflation; (c) growing costs of producing and handling of the one dollar bill.[20] The Treasury compared the costs of coin as against paper as follows:

The average lives of a coin and paper dollar are estimated to be 15 years and 15 months, respectively. This is a life ratio of 12 to 1. The cost to produce a dollar bill is approximately $1\frac{1}{2}$¢ and the cost to produce a coin between the size of a quarter and half dollar made from cupro-nickel clad copper is estimated to be $2\frac{1}{2}$¢. The cost ratio is 1.6 to 1. The combined life and cost ratio $(12/1.6)$ is more than 7 to 1 in favor of the coin. In an example of potential savings, the cost of the 1.6 billion dollar bills produced last year apportioned

[19] Kevin Sack, "Nixon Tape Cited in Car Wreck Suit," *The Atlanta Journal*, November 16, 1982.

[20] U.S. Department of the Treasury, *A New Smaller Dollar Coin: Technical Considerations*, Washington, D.C., August, 1976.

for one year's use is $18 million (see calculations below). The cost of an equal number of coins apportioned for one year's use is estimated at $2.7 million. The full savings would not, of course, be realized until the dollar coin has achieved wide acceptability as a substitute for the dollar bill. This may take as long as 5 to 10 years after the introduction of the new coin.[21]

Calculation of Costs

a) Cost of dollar bill for one year's use:

$$\frac{\text{cost of bill}}{\text{year's use}} = \frac{1.5\cent}{\text{bill}} \times \frac{12 \text{ months}}{15 \text{ months life}} = \frac{1.12\cent \text{ per bill}}{\text{per year}}$$

b) Cost of one year's supply of dollar bills:

$$\frac{\text{total cost}}{\text{year's use}} = \frac{1.6 \text{ billion bills}}{\text{year}} \times \frac{1.12\cent \text{ per year}}{\text{bill}} = \$18 \text{ million}$$

c) Cost of proposed coin for one year's use:

$$\frac{\text{cost of coin}}{\text{year's use}} = \frac{2.5\cent}{\text{coin}} \times \frac{12 \text{ months}}{180 \text{ month life}} = \frac{.17\cent \text{ per coin}}{\text{per year}}$$

d) Cost of one year's supply of dollar coins:

$$\frac{\text{total cost}}{\text{year supply}} = \frac{1.6 \text{ billion coins}}{\text{year}} \times \frac{.17\cent \text{ per year}}{\text{per coin}} = \$2.72 \text{ million}$$

William H. Wallace, testifying on behalf of the Board of Governors of the Federal Reserve System,[22] provided a tabulation of that body's calculations of "the potential significant cost savings associated with substitution of a durable coin for paper money." The following is the cost/benefit analysis introduced in Congressional hearings:

COST BENEFITS OF THE ANTHONY DOLLAR

I. Comparison with $1 note

A. Production cost

Anthony dollar=$.03.
Average life=15 years.
Average annual cost (0.03÷1.5 years)=$.002.
$1 note=$.02.
Average life=1.5 years.
Average annual cost=($.02÷1.5 years)=$.013.
$1 notes in circulation=3.1 billion.
Annual cost of maintaining $1 notes in circulation=$40.3 million.
Annual cost of maintaining $1 coins in circulation=$6.2 million.
Production cost savings ($40.3 million−$6.2 million)=$34.1 million.

[21] *Ibid.*, Appendix A, p. 23.
[22] William H. Wallace, Statement, *Oversight Hearings on the Susan B. Anthony Dollar Coin and Mint Operations*, (U.S. House of Representatives, 96th Congress, First Session), Hearings before the Subcommittee on Consumer Affairs and the Subcommittee on General Oversight and Renegotiation of the Committee on Banking, Finance, and Urban Affairs, September 25 and 26, 1979, p. 47.

B. *Processing cost*

   Currency processing cost/1000 notes=$3.849.
   Coin processing cost/1000 pieces=$.381.
   Annual cost of processing $1 notes=$17.7 million.
   Annual cost of processing equivalent number of $1 coins=$1.7 million.
   Processing cost savings ($17.7 million—$1.7 million)=$16 million.

C. *Total cost*

   Currency total cost=$58.0 million per year.
   Coin total cost= —7.9 million per year.
   Total savings with $1 Coin=$50.1 million per year.

The calculated savings were impressive. If only 20% of the 2.4 billion
dollar bills outstanding were displaced by Anthony coins, the Treasury
estimated an annual production cost saving of $4.8 million and the Fed-
eral Reserve, an annual saving in handling costs of $0.8 million, for
total annual savings of $5.6 million.[23] A chart supplied by the Congres-
sional Budget Office in cooperation with the Treasury Department was
introduced in the Congressional hearings to drive the cost savings message home:

Fiscal Years, in Millions of Dollars

Savings resulting from:	1979	1980	1981	1982	1983
One-for-one substitution of new					
coins for old coins*	2.7	3.1	3.4	3.8	4.3
Displacement of $1 notes	—.4	(1)	.6	1.2	2.0
Total Savings	2.3	3.1	4.0	5.0	6.3

*Eisenhower dollar coins
(1) Less than $0.05 million

Often cited in support of the smaller dollar was a study performed
under contract with the Bureau of the Mint by the Research Triangle
Institute, in spite of its own curious disclaimer that "a statistically reliable household survey of consumer attitudes and preferences toward
coinage alternatives was not feasible within the constraints of the
study."[24] One finds it difficult to imagine what these "constraints" might
have been. If they were the perennial bane of the think tank's existence—shortage of time and money—one can only wonder at the research
team's profligate use of both in amassing the plethora of charts, tables,
and miscellaneous materials that had dubious relevance to the questions at hand. The ultimate denouement of the disastrous decision

    [23] U.S. House of Representatives, 95th Congress, Second Session, Report No. 95–
1576, *Susan B. Anthony Dollar Coin Act of 1978*, H. R. 12728.
    [24] Research Triangle Institute Center for Development and Resource Planning,
A Comprehensive Review of U.S. Coinage Requirements to 1990, Research Triangle
Park, North Carolina, RTI Project 26 U–1133, September 1976, 2 Volumes and Executive Summary.

would later demonstrate conclusively that data gathering performed under the drunkard's lamp post[25] does not shed light on the subject under study. Subsequent developments were to show that the study team's failure to conduct a proper survey of public acceptance was a fatal omission.

On every count, the Susan B. Anthony coin had been calculated to be a bargain. Not only were its costs estimated to be low compared to the paper currency it would displace but there were benefits to be gained by politicians who endorsed the legislation. At that time, even a token pro-feminist stand had pay-off value and women's groups made much ado about substituting the image of an honest-to-goodness woman, like Susan B. Anthony, for a symbolic figure like Miss Liberty. A vote against Susan B. was soon to be construed as a vote against women's rights, with the converse equally compelling. The honors due womanhood became the focus of the debate. Attention was shifted from the coin, its characteristics, and attributes (unfavorable as well as favorable) to the person whom it was to honor. Public information kits freely distributed featured a glossy picture of both sides of the coin, one side bearing a likeness of Susan B. Anthony and proclaiming, "Liberty," "In God We Trust," and the other, an eagle clutching an olive branch and, apparently, landing on the moon with a small-sized Earth tucked under the ring of 13 stars. This side was also adorned with "United States of America" in bold-faced type, "One Dollar" still larger, and "E Pluribus Unum" thrown in for good measure. Included in the kit was a six-page dissertation on the tribulations, trial, and late triumph of the intrepid lady.

Enthusiastic letters from the National Women's Political Caucus, the Gray Panthers of Metropolitan Washington, and the League of Women Voters were introduced as testimony. All of them extolled the ideals of this courageous pioneer. Their interest was not in the issues surrounding the particular coin but simply in the picture on it. For them, only the message counted; the medium was discounted. The president of the League of Women Voters wrote as follows:

After two hundred years of minting coins that honor men, buffaloes and mythological women, it's encouraging to see that at long last there is a coin that pays tribute to a real woman—the Susan B. Anthony coin. Susan B. Anthony embodied the courage and perseverance that many women have demonstrated through the ages. *It was also the type of woman who would have balked at the rapid retreat that some legislators seem to be taking from supporting the Susan B. Anthony coin.*[26] [Emphasis added]

25 See story of drunkard's search cited in Chapter 3.
26 Ruth J. Hinerfeld, President, League of Women Voters of the United States, Letter to the Honorable Mary Rose Oakar, U. S. House of Representatives, September

It should go without saying that the Susan B. Anthony campaign had the enthusiastic support of women in Congress. The Honorable Patricia Schroeder (Colorado) is quoted as exulting,[27] "We've had eagles and Indians on our coins, and live buffaloes, but we've never had a live woman. . . . We've got her now." Senator William Proxmire, from whom opprobrium might have been more likely than approbation, introduced the bill in the Senate, where he was chairman of the Committee on Banking, Housing, and Urban Affairs. The House recorded his motion twelve days later, on May 15, 1978. President Carter approved and signed S3036 as Public Law 95–447 on October 10, 1978 and Mrs. Rosalynn Carter put her stamp of approval on an Anthony mini-dollar.

Enticed by the prospect of huge savings and diverted by the false issue of feminism, otherwise perspicacious individuals and groups had for one reason or the other let loose upon the land three-quarters of a billion little white elephants. They did not travel far; no one wanted them. Frank Annunzio, chairman of the Subcommittee on Consumer Affairs, opened oversight hearings shortly after the coin was released with a statement punctuated by acrid commentary.[28] We quote from his remarks: "The new dollar coin may well go down in history as the only coin that more people wanted before it was released than after it was released." On the Treasury Department's plan to eliminate the $1 bill and promote the dollar coin through a public relations campaign that had already cost nearly $1 million, Congressman Annunzio had sharp words:[29]

The public is not the only one that has soured on the $1 coin, as can be seen by the chart showing Federal Reserve shipments of new $1 coins to commercial banks. The graph indicates weekly shipments. It looks like the final hours of Skylab, and even the Mint, the strongest defender of the new coin, is taking a second look. It has cut back its daily production of the new coin by 50 percent. It does not make sense to cut back production, but at the same time conduct a lavish public relations campaign to promote the coin. It may be all right for Colonel Sanders to spend millions of dollars a year promoting his chicken, but I don't want to see the Treasury spending tax dollars to promote its turkey.

The *Congressional Record* contained more remarks by Annunzio. Somewhat less colorful, they nonetheless disclosed important deficiencies in the data on which the decision was based. He found substantial

24, 1979, *Oversight Hearings on the Susan B. Anthony Dollar Coin and Mint operations, op. cit.,* p. 17.

27 Robert Obojski, "The Quiet Death of the Susan B. Anthony Dollar," *Collector Editions,* Spring, 1982, p. 22.

28 Frank Annunzio, Statement at *Oversight Hearings on the Susan B. Anthony Dollar Coin and Mint Operations, op. cit.,* p. 1.

29 *Ibid.,* p. 2.

error in the Federal Reserve's analysis of costs and longevity of the
dollar bill, the former overestimated by some $9.3 million annually.
Demand for the new coin was seen as overoptimistic and hence savings
from it exaggerated by 25 percent.[30] The Research Triangle Institute
had substantially underestimated costs of conversion of vending machines and, hence, prices to consumers. Review of the omissions, errors,
and discrepancies in the calculations led Congressman Annunzio to
question the validity and credibility of the very premises on which the
favorable cost/benefit ratio rested. The situation was summed up by the
Honorable Thomas B. Evans, Jr. (Delaware), long-time opponent of
the coin,[31]

> I think we were too concerned with the question of whose face was to appear
> on the dollar coin. And we failed to address the more fundamental issue of
> whether or not it was a good idea in the first place and whether or not the
> American people would accept it.

A little more *ex post facto* intelligence would reveal that the im-
broglio over the coin obscured other, more salient features, not least
among them its resemblance to the quarter. Grey Panthers, however
well-intentioned, did not speak for all elderly persons and especially
those handicapped by loss of sight or sense of feel. Their objections
were introduced into the record *after* the battle over the coin was won—
and lost.[32]

A proper cost/benefit analysis, performed in retrospect, would ask
the right, i.e., necessary, questions, such for example, as those pertaining to public acceptance, and would require that its paid research contractors supply meaningful answers. Not to be overlooked in the *post
mortem* is the vital matter of data integrity and validity of calculations.
Even in such situations as this, where figures were available, the "facts"
about costs and usage were shaky and short-lived. That the same techniques of data-gathering are used and, yes, that the same think tanks
are employed in making decisions about issues fraught with uncertainty
and involving far more than even the tens of millions of dollars and
thousands of hours of work wasted here should make the Susan B. Anthony dollar coin serve as a reminder and warning to us that cost/benefit
analysis is nothing more than a numbers game. The decisions it leads
to may be wise; they may be foolish. They may also, as we shall see in
the final chapter, be dangerous.

---

30 "New Dollar Coin Will Cost Taxpayers Millions," *Congressional Record*, Proceedings and Debates of the 96th Congress, First Session, Vol. 125, No. 156, November 7, 1979.

31 Thomas B. Evans, Jr., Testimony, *Oversight Hearings, op. cit.*, p. 11.

32 Howard E. May, President, National Federation of the Blind of Connecticut, Inc.,
Letter introduced at *Oversight Hearings, op. cit.*, pp. 4–5.

THE COST OF COST/BENEFIT ANALYSIS

The ultimate *reductio ad absurdum* is reached when cost-cutting is construed as a benefit *per se*. Such we find to be the case in mid-1982, when the Office of Management and Budget selected for drastic reduction the key agencies and services upon which the government depends for the data it will use to justify its cost-cutting! According to a report[33] by the House Government Operations Committee, the current Administration has abolished or reduced at least 50 major statistical programs once the source of basic information by which policy decisions were made and evaluated.

The Department of Defense had to delay a recruitment of manpower study because critical census data was [*sic*] not available. Delays and cancellations in tabulating census data by small areas (e.g., county ZIP codes, etc.) have forced businesses to postpone vital marketing surveys or to conduct them using outdated information. In addition, delays in the analysis and release of data have meant that block grants to local health services cannot be properly allocated, and that the Department of Education found it necessary to allocate Federal funds for the 1982–83 school year on the basis of the 1970 census information.

A study undertaken for the Committee by the Research Service of the Library of Congress is cited[34] as saying that because information is the medium of exchange in government, "changes in the amount, kind, and quality of statistical information that is collected often reflect the policy agendas [*sic*] of those in power." Eliminated with the same scimitar was the Office of Management and Budget's own Statistical Policy Branch, which had coordinated and since 1947 sought to assure the coherence and integrity of the activities and standards of more than 100 separate Federal statistical programs. The functions of that unit were turned over to four persons, two of them on a part-time basis. According to Joseph Duncan, the former director, now associated with Dun & Bradstreet,[35]

the reorganization and the cutback in staff will mean that over time the Federal programs will fragment. In the long run you'll have serious trouble with your input and output data, and thus with your information on basic economic activity.

---

[33] U.S. House of Representatives, Committee on Government Operations, *Reorganization and Budget Cutbacks May Jeopardize the Future of the Nation's Statistical System*, House Report #97–901, September 30, 1982.

[34] David Burnham, "House Panel Report Questions Cutbacks in Statistics Programs," *The New York Times*, October 4, 1982.

[35] Interview reported by Ann Crittenden, "A World With Fewer Numbers," *The New York Times*, July 11, 1982.

Lest this view reflect the understandable bias of pride-in-career, let us turn to a General Accounting Office evaluation relating to matters which once were the purlieu of the disbanded information services. A GAO review[36] found the Office of Management and Budget, which is responsible for Federal information policy, seriously deficient in a number of key areas having to do with information integrity and security. There was a marked lack of attention to the vulnerability of computerized telecommunications networks to fraudulent, wasteful, abusive, and illegal practices. A series of GAO reports over the past three years had issued warnings and guidelines, all pointing to the need for greater vigilance and concern on the part of responsible executives and agencies. In the face of these basic needs, the OMB's cost-cutting actions constitute an egregious flying-in-the-face of exigency. The situation would seem to argue for heightened attention, not officially-ordained diminution of it.

Even while deploring the data overload and lack of quality control attributable to an era in which management-by-information and management-of-information have become hopelessly confused and the "information system" is the most touted, least understood system component, one can regret the impacts and implications of the cuts. The Employment and Training Administration of the Labor Department will lose $7.7 million, or 58% of its funds; the Federal Trade Commission will suffer a reduction of 74%; the Securities and Exchange Commission, 50%.[37] Not only will the government cut off the statistics necessary for making its allocations, but the business community will lose its sources of data about gross national product, productivity levels, and trends vital to a viable economy. The point made by critics during the Congressional hearings was that this false conception of economy would, in the long run, cost the public and private sectors billions of dollars. The "benefits" of this Faustian bargain cannot now or ever be calculated. The grounds for making judgments will have been cut away.

In Great Britain, where an economy-minded government similarly singled out its statistical services for substantial reductions, concern about the theory and values behind the measures was voiced. A professor at Essex University wrote as follows:

[36] General Accounting Office, *Federal Information Systems Remain Highly Vulnerable to Fraudulent Wasteful, Abusive, and Illegal Practices*, Washington, D.C., MASAD–82–18, April 21, 1982, p. 3. General Accounting Office, "Automated System Security—Federal Agencies Should Strengthen Safeguards Over Personal and Other Sensitive Data," Washington, D.C., LCD–78–123, January 23, 1979. Also, Supplement, LCD–79–109, March 21, 1979. General Accounting Office, "Central Agencies' Compliance with Transmittal Memorandum No. 1," Washington, D.C., LCD–80–56–1, April 30, 1980.

[37] Figures supplied by the Congressional Research Service.

The Government's actions are, in effect, a direct restriction on democratic rights. In the guise of cutting manpower and saving money, the Government's proposals seem designed to divert, contain, and reduce criticisms of government policies. By restricting the free flow of information, the Government is restricting the right to free and open discussion of the industrial, economic, and social conditions of Britain.[38]

A key conclusion in the earlier version of *Systems Analysis in Public Policy* was that the systems approach in its already multifarious mutations was not a good tool with which to fashion public policy. Experience over time contradicts the standard excuse that has kept the game going, i.e., that it is *misuse* of the techniques that is culpable. On the contrary, *Systems Analysis in Public Policy* updated contends that it was, and continues to be, *use* that leads to grave blunders on the war and homefront. As to the former, evidence is farflung, from the jungles of Vietnam to the sands of Iran where lives and materiel were lost in a mission which looked good only on paper. As to the latter, i.e., the homefront, evidence is confused by its very profusion. That there has not been a wholesale rejection of the techniques as inadequate and inappropriate is due to the many disciplinary *mariages de convenance* as well as the huge vested interests. Systems analysis has assured longevity because its principles are, for all their fancy electronic trappings, simple, easy to apply, and consistent with the quick-fix, plug-in modularity of a technical era. Cost/benefit analysis and cost/effective determination are ubiquitously applicable. And anyone can use the methodology. Few credentials are required. The skills are portable and readily transported from public to private sector. The techniques of management science are an inescapable manifestation of our dominant paradigm. We are as hampered from thinking outside it as was Winnie-the-Pooh bumping down the stairs on his head and wondering whether there might not be another way if only he could stop bumping for a moment to think of it.[39]

By now, experience should have taught us that we had turned to the wrong experts—those who define problems to fit their solutions and limit the focus to the one aspect that suits their aptitude, which is technical. The result is distortion and, ultimately, superficial treatment of matters of deepest consequence. Several decades and billions of dollars expended on systems studies of everything have not moved us perceptibly up the learning curve. We still know precious little and continue to repeat past mistakes. The *now* orientation of the techniques has no memory for history and can, therefore, transmit none of its important lessons. This kind of professionally-sanctioned and institutional-

[38] Peter Townsend, "Society Tomorrow," *The Guardian*, July 5, 1981.
[39] A. A. Milne, *Winnie-The-Pooh*, New York: E. F. Dutton & Co., 1926, p. 1.

ized trained incapacity[40] has had a severely detrimental effect on our understanding of the universe in which we live. *Systems Analysis in Public Policy* in its original form offered no panacea but rather a warning signal. In the final chapter, we will review some of the fields, such as health and education, which have been subjected to systems treatment, and will move with the techniques to their future-oriented applications, such as risk analysis and technology assessment.

[40] Thorstein Veblen's much-used but rarely-acknowledged term for what later was to be known as "tunnel vision."

[1]

Survey and Perspective

INTRODUCTION

This is an inquiry into systems analysis, its origin and applications, its uses and abuses, its present impact and future implications. Systems analysis requires serious contemplation because of its central role in public planning, the vast expenditures of human and financial resources it has occasioned, and the mythology that surrounds it. Full of contradictions, a curious mixture of sweeping comprehensiveness and arbitrary eclecticism, systems analysis in its various forms has become the dominant methodology for managing the present and designing the future.

Hailed by its promoters as a Space Age product, the systems approach has also been described as "a quantitative technique with roots as old as science and management functions."[1] Acclaimed as a specialized technique for solving problems, it has nonetheless been characterized as a mere orientation or frame of reference. Accepted as a precise, logical, and scientific method, systems analysis has, in contradistinction, been called an art, without fixed rules, universally accepted principles, and criteria for quality.[2] Long a standard component of the engineering curriculum, systems analysis and related subjects are increasingly evident among course offerings in the "soft sciences," such as sociology, public health, and even architectural and environmental design. Taught

[1] C. West Churchman, Russell L. Ackoff, and E. Leonard Arnoff, *Introduction to Operations Research*, New York: John Wiley, 1957, p. 3.
[2] E. S. Quade, ed., *Analysis for Military Decisions*, Chicago: Rand McNally, 1964, p. 153.

1

in universities, bought by private business and government agencies, and sold by a growing cadre of experts, systems analysis is a commodity commanding high prices and ready acceptance at home and abroad.

Literature on the subject of systems analysis abounds. Besides articles in diverse publications and books in the various disciplines, a growing number of journals specialize in its theory, method, and applications. But contents are generally devoted to technical and theoretical aspects. Critical appraisal is missing; little attention is given to implications for the very society these exercises are supposed to improve. In the non-technical and descriptive writings found in popular magazines, systems analysis is presented as a nostrum for many problems confronting government planners at every level. Pointing to modern weapons systems as the creation of systems engineering and to spectacular feats in space as evidence of successful systems management, proponents contend that the same techniques can and should be applied to human and social affairs in almost unlimited range. The argument sounds simple: "A nation that can put a man on the moon can . . ." control air, land, and water pollution; provide safe and efficient air and surface transportation; devise workable plans for urban renewal, redevelopment, and housing; improve education; deliver adequate health and medical service; overcome crime; handle public welfare effectively. These are the areas most often deemed amenable to the systems approach and have been specifically designated as such during congressional hearings.

Some of the statements are cited here because they have been repeated frequently and paraphrased in many contexts; they underscore the yearning for the same neat ordering of human affairs that is found in the management of technical matters. They imply the arbitrary and un-challenged presumption of a successful transplant from the realm of the military or of lunar and Martian trips to man's social concerns here on earth. "We have seen how new techniques of management analysis — the so-called 'systems approach' — have streamlined our defense estab-lishment and brought the universe within man's reach. . . . The prob-lems of our urban society are growing more awesome and complicated every day. . . . There exists a technology for problem-solving and ad-ministration which seems uniquely suited for application to these pub-lic problems."[3] The facile equation underlying these pronouncements is clear: public planning becomes ever more complex; the "systems approach" has been demonstrated as the way to handle complicated tasks in military affairs and in conquering space; hence, the systems

[3] Remarks of F. Bradford Morse (Senator from Massachusetts). Hearings before the Special Subcommittee on the Utilization of Scientific Manpower of the Com-mittee on Labor and Public Welfare, United States Senate, Ninetieth Congress, First Session, *Scientific Manpower Utilization*, January 24–27, March 29 and 30, 1967, pp. 18, 19.

approach should be applied to the tangle of problems besetting mankind in the 1970s and thenceforth.

These are the claims frequently made for systems analysis, with its components and companions — operations research, cost-benefit analysis, and program budgeting. Often referred to as the modern and powerful tools of technology for managing the present scientifically and designing the future rationally, the technique draws its prestige from its defense and aerospace ancestry, its methods from engineering, mathematics, statistics, and economics. Its advocates are numerous and diverse as to discipline, background, and experience. "Systems capability" is a prime item in the stock-in-trade of aerospace and aviation firms, computer manufacturers and their multifarious subsidiaries, electronics companies, management consultants, accounting firms, and even public utility companies. The ranks of practitioners are swelled by university based or associated entrepreneurs, often in "institutes," from the fields of political science, operations research, economics, engineering, and urban planning, to mention only a few. Additional contenders for contracts are the conglomerates of brains for hire. Known as "think tanks," these private or semi-public, profit or nonprofit (albeit highly profitable) research organizations make a business of solving problems, especially those of a public nature and funded by city, county, state, and federal government. Seeking contracts for systems analyses of everything from crime in California to urban redevelopment in Maryland, from information networks in Orange County (California) to fire-fighting in New York City, these professional problem-solvers have experienced enormous growth in their business. From four $100,000 studies as a seminal experiment in California in 1964, systems contracts had, by 1967,[4] blossomed into a multimillion-dollar item, with estimates of urban civil systems for 1980 flourishing somewhere between $210 and $298 billion annually.[5]

These figures, though impressive, are unreliable. "Urban civil systems" may refer to anything from a mass transit system, which would include extensive construction and rolling stock, to a cost model for an elementary school, where a band of "systems experts" assembles a paper product through investment of man-hours and computer time. The system may include hardware, an assemblage of computers to perform designated tasks; it may be all software, i.e., the program and paper plan for the enterprise. Precisely because the *urban civil system* eludes firm definition, exact sums already spent, being spent, and likely to be

[4] John S. Gilmore, John J. Ryan, and William S. Gould, *Defense Systems Resources in the Civil Sector: An Evolving Approach, An Uncertain Market*, Washington, D.C.: U.S. Arms Control and Disarmament Agency, July, 1967, Tables C-1 and C-2, pp. 147–155.

[5] *Finance Magazine*, January, 1968.

spent are difficult to ascertain. Some few years ago, the Science Policy Research Division of the Library of Congress attempted to discover the extent to which analyses were then being carried out. The findings were far from comprehensive, for the respondents to the questionnaire were state and local officials, no attempt having been made to canvass at the federal level. Moreover, the broad range of activities covered by the term *systems analysis* rendered the accounting highly unreliable. Nonetheless, the report revealed that even by 1966 a number of states and cities were actively engaged in something called "systems analysis efforts" (see Table 1), and that in 1966 nearly $22.5 million had been expended on them (see Table 2).

TABLE 1

Number of States and Cities Engaged in
Systems Analysis Efforts by Level of Activity

Level of activities	Number of states	Number of cities
High level (20 to 25 program areas)	9	5
Moderately high level (15 to 19)	7	3
Moderate level (10 to 14)	4	7
Low level (1 to 9)	5	4

Documentation of the number of cities, counties, states, and federal agencies engaged in systems activities is interesting but the figures do not reflect the intensity of such activity. On this we have little accurate information. There being a lack of definition of terms, any contracts bearing the word *system* are grouped as though alike. Only the most astute potential bidders, scanning daily the government requests for proposal, can sort out the kind and type, and then only for their own purposes. Even when the request is for a specific service, as, for example, evaluation of a given program, the response may be in the form of a systems analysis. Largely owing to the misconceptions that have arisen and still prevail, the notion persists with many otherwise well-informed and sophisticated persons that the government's effort to apply systems analysis to civilian and social matters began and ended with the California experiment. Judgment is made on that limited and brief experience as though it were an isolated instance; as though the $400,000 spent on the endeavor represented the total amount; and as though with the completion of the four studies, the matter was closed and future applications foreclosed. Depending on the viewpoint of the observer, the attempt of a few aerospace companies to transfer their techniques to new fields was a great success or disappointment but in any case a unique event.

TABLE 2
Funds Expended in 1966 on Systems Analysis
by States and Cities (in Thousands of Dollars)

States		Cities and regional groups	
New York	4,250	Baltimore	2,675
Oklahoma	1,800	Philadelphia	2,500
Pennsylvania	1,125	Port Authority of	
Wisconsin	550	New York	1,975
Connecticut	375	Los Angeles	1,125
Maryland	350	New York City	800
Massachusetts	350	Chicago	550
Texas	350*	Mississippi Research and	
West Virginia	350	Development Center	375
Alaska	260*	Cincinnati	310*
Rhode Island	225	San Diego	225
Kentucky	225	Denver	175
Missouri	175	Phoenix	100
Florida	175	Atlanta	100
Utah	175	Detroit	100
Washington	100	Kansas City	100
South Dakota	100	New Orleans	100
North Dakota	50	Houston	66*
Wyoming	50	Cleveland	50
Delaware	50	Subtotal	11,326
Iowa	50		
Ohio	7*		
Subtotal	11,142	GRAND TOTAL	22,468.5

SOURCE: For Tables 1 and 2, *Scientific Manpower Utilization*, 1967. Hearing before the Special Subcommittee on the Utilization of Scientific Manpower of the Committee on Labor and Public Welfare, United States Senate, Ninetieth Congress, First Session, January 24, 25, 26, 27; March 29, 30, 1967, p. 368.
NOTE: Figures are estimates unless otherwise stated.
* Stated figure

Nothing could be farther from the truth. The California experience was only the beginning.[6] A trend, certainly strengthened by replication elsewhere, had been established, its growth, assured as a mythology developed, was exploited by a myriad of vested business and professional interests, and fostered by government officials eager to be identified with and to take advantage of advanced concepts of management science. Applications of systems analysis, to judge by their ubiquity, are gaining

[6] Ida R. Hoos, *Systems Analysis in Social Policy*, Research Monograph 19, London: Institute of Economic Affairs, 1969.

popular acceptance; but whether, and the extent to which, they have been usable in improving, or even altering, conventional and historically and politically established forms of public program management has not been ascertained. This is a curious anomaly when one considers that generous funding for systems analyses, which are very costly, comes from economy-minded administrators who scrutinize other expenditures closely and make a great show of adopting the very principles of cost-benefit ratios embodied in the systems technique.

Systems analysis, both as a process and as a product, has not been subjected to sufficient critical analysis. This is because of the political nature of the environment in which the technique was spawned and proliferates. Representing a considerable expenditure of public money, the completed study can be embarrassing, quite irrespective of a job well or poorly done. It may reveal long-standing inadequacy or poor management; it may recommend changes unpalatable to the power structure. It may be a piece of technical scrimshaw, a determined exercise with no discernible applicability. Expediency dictates, in all such cases, that circulation of or accessibility to the finished product be strictly limited. Discussion and evaluation are closed-door matters, for, where large sums are involved, everyone must retain a favorable image. Because political mileage, if nothing else, must be realized from the money spent, public relations statements declare the results to be useful. Consequently, systems studies, regardless of their worth, have enjoyed protection from criticism.

Until now, a *bona fide* evaluation of the finished product by an in-house staff is a rarity. Whether through lack of time or modesty about competence in the face of such high-powered contractors as RAND and Systems Development Corporation, public agencies have not shown an inclination to apply any kind of quality control standards to the "soft" products of systems analyses. They accept what is delivered and pay for it. In this respect the consulting services of other systems analysts as critics have been generally without merit. Probably less from loyalty to their fraternity and more from reluctance to damage their common cause, practitioners are remarkably gentle in their approach to the work of others. Prone to avoid challenging basic assumptions and fallacies, they usually point up a few superficial miscalculations but always concur with the recommendation that follow-on contracts, with more time and more money for more systems analysis, will help solve the problem, whatever its nature. In practically every case, the review is sympathetic to the approach and carries the veiled promise that, with continuing contracts and further refinement in methods and greater sophistication in utilization, untold benefits will result. As more, and more substantial, sums of foundation and taxpayers' money are allocated to systems studies as a means of alleviating social distress, and the legion of professional problem-solvers grows, their potential for becoming a pervasive and persuasive element in social policy-making is a matter of considerable significance for the future course of events, not only in this country but in foreign lands as the flying squad of experts for export grows.

Focus of the Research

The research reported in this book represents a critical investigation of the state-of-the-art of systems analysis. The technique is examined in theory and practice, in its own circumscribed, structured, and simulated world and in the real world, where solutions must face pragmatic test and not merely satisfy an abstract set of conditions. The assumptions implicit in the approach as it developed over time and their validity as a basis for social planning are analyzed. They are examined in the context of the specific areas in which systems analyses are being applied, *viz.*, education, crime, health, welfare, land use, transportation, and pollution of land, sea, and air. The experience with information systems as components of these areas and as entities in themselves are examined in detail. The process, procedures, and products of systems analysis are analyzed for the social, cultural, political, and economic factors that influence the adoption of this problem-solving technique in its various forms, notably cost-benefit ratios and planning-programming-budgeting.

The book is based on research which has included a wide variety of systems analyses in many contexts. Preliminary phases were devoted to an examination of the bases for, and the assumptions implicit in, the notion of using systems techniques for managing present social problems and designing the future rationally. With the pioneering California aerospace studies in 1964 as the start, the investigation traced the phenomenon of the transfer of the technique from the spheres of outer space and the military all the way to the inner city. The documentation of the transplant of systems analysis from the realm of the technological to that of the social was necessary background for understanding the significance and implications of this form of interaction between technology and society.

The book begins with an introduction to the theory and practice of systems analysis. An account of its ancestry and history is important both for an understanding of its prestige and for an appraisal of its applicability. Drawing on epistemology and the history of ideas, a discussion of the linkages of systems analysis to its philosophic forebears sheds light on congenital strengths and weaknesses. Because of the

normative, if not utopian, flavor of the systems approach, which seeks
to identify an optimum objective for a given system and so to order the
organization of the components and their interactions as to achieve a
desired and presumably desirable goal, it is useful to consider the methodology in the light of what has been called social technology.[7] Deeply
moral and ethical issues are involved here, as well as the implications for
a free society and the democratic process. On the practical level of
assessing the ultimate bounds and appropriateness of the technique,
compelling questions are raised as to whether there can be "logical" or
"rational" methods to determine "ideal" objectives for social systems,
and whether there are identifiably optimal means for achieving them.

Discussion of the theory and practice of systems analysis alerts the
reader at an early stage to the dilemmas of definition, for identical words
are found to carry divergent meanings. He soon perceives that this leads
to the possible temptation to resort to symbol manipulation when substantive knowledge is absent. With such key concepts as *system* and
model elusive of articulation and subject to marked latitude of interpretation and semantic sleight-of-hand, the ascription of "scientific precision" to the method built on them constitutes a striking paradox. Precisely because systems analysis is a technique in which form takes precedence over and even determines content, the reliance on language becomes treacherous. It encourages lack of careful formalization and
formulation. This leads to a chain reaction of poor conceptualization,
gathering of data more because they are available than indicative, and
dependence on factors only because they can be counted in the ongoing
analysis and not because they are known to be important in the final
analysis. In military applications — generally regarded as the model for
systems analyses in business, government, and elsewhere — verbal juggling is clearly evident in the high-level gamesmanship reflected in the
"scenarios" on which defense policy is planned and, perhaps, the ultimate course of human events on this planet decided.

In both military and civil applications, discrepancies between the
claims made and the product delivered are noted, not in the spirit of
carping criticism but because their persistence and prevalence illustrate again the dependence on semantic rather than substantive justification for the activity. By the same token, account is taken of the gaps
between what is preached and what is practiced. Disclaimers once offered or pitfalls once mentioned receive little further attention during
the analysis, which is carried out with apparent disregard for them. The
same expert who modestly admits that the technique can be applied
beneficially to only certain, circumscribed types of systems nonetheless
plies his trade vigorously and profitably wherever there is a likelihood

[7] Olaf Helmer, *Social Technology*, New York: Basic Books, 1966.

of contracts. At worst, the analyst who points out pitfalls is trapped by them; at best, he fails to bridge them to a professionally satisfying degree. Having done them lip service, he proceeds as though they had somehow been overcome.

It is a sad commentary on the current state-of-the-art that one does not know where to direct this shaft: toward the technique itself, toward the particular applications, or toward the practitioners. Perhaps it is in the nature of systems analysis as we observe its application that the trio is inseparable, with all three parts of a semantic web permeated with salesmanship, sometimes for the technique, sometimes for the doer, sometimes for the done for. The salesmanship may be subtle or blatant. When it is intended for selling the technique, there is likely to be a specious dialectic with many false dichotomies, in which "trial-and-error fumbling" is juxtaposed with "orderly, scientific planning." When aimed at the practitioners, there are numerous assertions of "program management capability," allusions to other contracts held, no matter how unrelated in nature and irrespective of performance quality. When the campaign is directed to the potential client, much is made of his present chaotic condition and its exponential exacerbation because of growing complexity, all of which will somehow be resolved through the application of systems techniques. The fact that such protestations of self-worth appear as part of reports, which are in many important respects indistinguishable from advertising and publicity brochures, illustrates the high incidence of salesmanship in this management game. Reading such a document, one is tempted to ask whether the objective of systems analysis is to salve, solve, or sell, especially when the prize is a contract for the winner.

Having explored the intellectual streams to which the heritage of systems analysis can be attributed, the book then traces its practical and tactical history, for herein lies the clue to its phenomenal development and acceptance. The important connection with the military once established through the relationship between operations research as a strategy in World War II and systems analysis as a management tool for the U.S. Department of Defense, it becomes necessary to ascertain the validity of the military as model for civilian and social affairs. The way in which military analysts define their techniques and assess their applicability to a different order of problems then becomes germane. How systems analysis has worked in the management of military affairs, how the conditions prevailing in the Pentagon compare with those in other agencies of government, provide background against which to review the technique and ascertain its impact on management science.

Once the systems approach was established as a potent weapon for achieving efficiency, its deployment was assured. How the methods of the military sector moved into and took over fiscal planning in the civilian is an important step in its history. The ethos of efficiency was translated into operational terms and became the prescription for all government agencies through the introduction of techniques already well-known in military planning. Cost-benefit analysis, cost-effectiveness ratios, and program budgeting became the accepted way to run the government's business. Comparable labels and isms of the past forgotten, the new, advanced concepts, purported to bring rational and systematic methods into the bureaucratic image, were the order of the day. Imposed by presidential directive on the federal level, they soon seeped down into the states, counties, and cities. And at all levels, the role of former Department of Defense systems experts is discernible, for they have been the repository of know-how and the carriers of inherited experience. To be sure, their territory has been invaded, their tools borrowed, their booty shared, but their expertness has rarely been challenged. The transplant of the techniques to nonmilitary planning, the transfer of the analysts to civilian agencies, and the impact of both on decision-making in the civil sector are examined as manifestations of the phenomenal growth and ubiquity of systems analysis.

The book then deals with systems analysis as a manifestation of technology transfer. The chapter on this subject explores the reasons underlying the transplant from military and space work to civilian systems planning, the conditions that fostered it, and the factors that influenced it. The appeal of the notion of a practical by-product of defense and aerospace expenditures appears undisputable, particularly in the Space Age. Not so unequivocal, however, is the validity of the assumptions that techniques, however well proven in one arena, could appropriately be applied elsewhere; that persons expert in applications in one field could be expected to perform equally well in others; and that transfer of the techniques would constitute a *bona fide* diversification of product that would revive severely declining defense and aerospace industries and rescue significant numbers of their employees from unemployment.

To assess the validity of the assumption that the transfer was appropriate, the archetype, defense planning, was reviewed for insights into the strengths and weaknesses of the technique as identified in its customary setting by recognized authorities in military systems analysis. Their views on the limits of applicability, and of kinds and conditions of situations which must prevail in order that a systems analysis be attempted at all, served as guidelines by which to approach analyses in new and untried areas.

For insights into the transferability of skills from the design of missiles to that of civil systems, the California experiment provided an excellent case study. The factual information it yielded has been substantiated in countless follow-on contracts and has been corroborated subsequently as systems analysis increasingly became an item for sale in many market places. The extent to which systems analysis as a form of diversification could reasonably be expected to offer job opportunities for the reservoir of engineers affected by retrenchment in the defense and aerospace industries was ascertained by exploring the quantitative and qualitative aspects of the unemployed and the manpower requirements for systems work in the civil sector. The increasing competition for contracts in civil systems analysis from a myriad of "experts" of varied origin was also taken into account.

The political environment has been an important element in hastening and implementing the process of transplant. Just as in the California instance, the notion of invoking Space Age techniques in the management of public affairs had political overtones, so later applications, used as a demonstration of a particular administration's sophistication vis-à-vis modern management science, were as much an image-making affair as a serious attempt at problem-solving. It is, then, the political climate in which the systems analysis is undertaken that must be recognized as vitally important in shaping the course of its history. Such matters as why and how systems analyses have been undertaken, by whom performed, and how they were appraised and used are politically controlled. Our research focused on the political climate, on its imprint on the entire procedure at every phase from initiation to final disposition.

The next section of the book is concerned with the methods of systems analysis. Essential features such as model construction, simulation, cost-effectiveness, and the total program concept are approached not in the customary handbook, how-to-do-it fashion that pervades the current literature, but against the background of actual experience. Critical review is necessary because so much has been made by the technique's advocates of the distinction between theory and practice. When faced with work done in this field, their stock defense is that the theory is fine but that the particular applications might have been poor or the practitioners unqualified. Our research indicates that the distinction may be spurious. *Technique*, and not *application*, must be contrasted with *theory*. And *technique*, interpreted as a method of procedure, can only be judged in its applications and uses. Model construction, simulation, and the like, when removed from the sheltered purity of textbook logic, must be tested as tools. To dismiss the accumulated evidence as work poorly done is not enough; the work may have been as well done as the tools allowed. The fact of the merit of the theory thus becomes irrelevant. Insistence on the distinction between theory and practice obscures the critical issues. It may perpetuate uses of the techniques rather than challenge their appropriateness, when the important questions to be raised are how they are used, by whom, and with what outcome.

The pragmatic problems which arise when systems techniques become the tools used in devising public programs and shaping policy come into clear view as we study the manifold instances of cost-benefit calculation as the key to decision-making, and program budgeting as the prescribed formula for management of the government's business. Specific fields, such as health and education, are singled out for thorough investigation. The trend toward development of social indicators to emulate economic indicators is critically reviewed in this framework. Finally, reliance on these techniques for establishing national goals is scrutinized in the light of the foregoing analysis of the technique and its practitioners.

Information systems are then examined with special attention because they occupy an important but anomalous position with respect to systems in general. More than a mere combination of hardware and software as found in the conventional electronic data-processing system, less than the far-reaching conception of, for example, a transportation system which would encompass various modes of travel with computerized models of the numerous interacting components, the information system is unique. Much of its methodology and many of its techniques are similar to those employed in the systems approach; its practitioners, experts, and salesmen are practically identical with those who would sell systems as solutions to management and other problems. However, there are differences which make the information system a special case within the larger study of civil systems.

Sometimes, when information systems are conceived as self-contained units, endowed with a *raison d'être* of their own, their costs calculated, their benefits estimated, they are almost indistinguishable from other systems. Often, the information system is treated as a component in the larger system, whose objectives it is expected to serve, whose efficiency of operation it is supposed to increase. In cases like this, a curious kind of subversion has often been observed. The information system, displaying the ingestive propensities of a snake, swallows up the whole enterprise. What may start out to be the design of a system of health, criminal justice, or land usage becomes a frenetic hunt for information, with a data bank the primary, and perhaps only, result. The larger objectives of the system are obscured if not obliterated; the resources devoured; the total effort begins and ends with the data-gathering and manipulation stage. The reasons for this are numerous: the predilection of the systems analysts themselves, with their assumptions about, and dependence on, "facts"; the notion that more information is somehow equated with better management; and the theory that management of the information leads to improved management of the enterprise. The development of the information system as a management tool is traced by review of a number of instances representative of the current trend. Growing sophistication in the technology of the hardware and software of information systems has had wide repercussions, for information has become an important commodity economically, socially, and politically. Therefore, the meaning of the information explosion and the way in which information has become both a private concern and a public affair are also examined.

The last chapter of the book is devoted to the long-range and wider implications of systems analysis. Here we observe the impact of the techniques on the public decision-making process, the likely effects on bureaucratic structure, the role of experts within and outside the governmental framework, and the way in which systems analysis may determine the definition of present problems and the design of the future. We consider the possibilities that systems analysis as a special tool for government by contract may weaken the civil service and divorce public officials from responsibility and accountability for their decisions. Technically derived plans, devised by experts, have deeply embedded, built-in self-justification; that this may be an important manifestation and preview of what has been called "the cybernetic state" is discussed in light of the research findings.

We ponder the hypothesis that growing reliance on extra-governmental decision making mechanisms encouraged by allocating contracts for civil systems may give rise to a "technico-corporate state," in which the contractors design, advocate, and in some cases may be the beneficiaries of, the "rationally devised" course of action. Here, the social, political, and constitutional ramifications are taken into account. Identification of the resultant constituency is all the more important in view of observations that the systems approach has had the immediate consequence of strengthening and legitimating centralized planning. Power-conscious executives and administrators have already recognized this use of the technique and have exercised it for purposes of reorganization to suit their particular motives. The usefulness of the total approach, with its inherent capacity for solidifying and rationalizing an ideological position, must not be overlooked. This could be the efficiency model for a totalitarian philosophy of government, the antidote to the inefficient, redundant bumbling of the democratic process. Historically, totalitarianism has not provided an environment in which social scientists have thrived, and yet, many of them, because of the attractiveness of the "scientific" approach, have joined the ranks of the social engineers and become imbued with the technocratic spirit.

Perhaps we are witnessing the emergence of a new breed, willing to trade its time-honored defense of open-end inquiry for the quick-and-easy returns of mission-directed research. This could be consistent and coincidental with the recent shift of government funding away from the country's universities, where academic freedom may still be valued, to the private and semi-private research institutes where experts can be expected to think as they are directed. Systems analysis may be a vehicle by which the anti-intellectualism already discernible in American society may become even more pervasive. The irony of such an eventuality would lie in the fact that the academic community has allowed itself to become so beguiled by the niceties of techniques that it has lost sight of the ultimate consequences. In so doing, it may have surrendered its treasured function of asking many, if not the right, questions, in favor of producing answers. A dimension often left out in discussion of such matters has to do with the ethics of functionaries as compared with those of professionals. At issue here may be the necessary and proper role and contribution of the social scientist. Is he more imbued with, or morally committed to, the vanishing values of the society than the technologist, who may be reflecting the *Zeitgeist* when he ignores or omits them? Can he be expected to display a higher order of morality than, for example, the professional problem solvers who take on any problem and "solve" it in their way?

The systems approach takes on a different time dimension in the hands of the fast-growing community of devotees who are constructing models to solve projected problems still in the hypothetical stage. Futures research, or futurology, where scenario writing, Delphi techniques, and far-out fancy converge, is more than mere gaming in the future tense. Because its methods are an extension of the systems approach, we must ask whether the state-of-the-art has been proven sufficiently adequate in the social planning of the present to warrant the confident use of systems analysis for forecasting and designing the future. Noting the propensities of the self-fulfilling prophecy in the models and the conceptions of the futurologists, we must ask whether their brand of determinism is any more desirable than its predecessors. The book closes with an examination of futurology and its portents, but, it is hoped, opens avenues of thought about the implications of social technology for a democratic society now and in the future.

[2]

Systems Approach
in Theoretical Perspective

Said to have "roots as old as science and the management function,"[1] and at the same time acclaimed as a product of the Space Age, the systems approach, in definition, theory, and practice, is fraught with paradox. Its dating is only the first of many inherent contradictions. For example, both strength and weakness lie in its myriad forms and manifestations, the very variety of which is encouraged by the latitude of interpretation as to what actually constitutes the systems approach. There is strength, because a concept so generously dimensioned and so encompassing in scope not only has widespread usefulness in many contexts but, through vagueness, maintains a kind of featherbed resilience against attack and, hence, a marked invulnerability to criticism. But lack of articulation conveys weakness, too, the more so because high among the attributes claimed for the systems approach is its precision, in the designation of parameters, identification of objectives, and measurement of inputs and outputs.

For a notion to have become the symbol of the "rational" and the "scientific" in management circles in business and government and yet to be so deficient as to clarity of meaning is truly anomalous. The phenomenon deserves inquiry here, not as a mere excursion into semantics but as a way to understanding the methodology that is so fundamentally influencing modes of thinking for the present and for the coming generation, at least.

Difficulties, contradictions, and complexities stem from three main

[1] C. West Churchman, Russell L. Ackoff, and E. Leonard Arnoff, *Introduction to Operations Research*, New York: John Wiley, 1957, p. 3.

sources: looseness of the word *system*; laxity as to usage of terms, with virtual interchange among *systems analysis, systems engineering,* and *systems management,* and even the occasional self-ascription of an honorific *systematic* to the analysis, engineering, management, or whatever the activity; [2] and convergence of a multiplicity of diverse disciplines and intellectual streams that have somehow been rendered congenial through semantic similitude.

DEFINITIONS OF SYSTEM

Countering the assumption of epistemological universality, Webster's *Dictionary* provides no less than fifteen different classes of meanings for *system*.[3] Number one is "an aggregation or assemblage of objects united by some form of regular interaction or interdependence; a group of diverse units so combined by nature or art as to form an integral whole, and to function, operate, or move in unison and, often, in obedience to some form of control; an organic or organized whole." Number two has several subparts, specifically: "(a) The universe; the entire known world;" "(b) The body considered as a functional unit;" and "(c) (colloquial) One's whole affective being, body, mind, or spirit." Number three shifts attention to the nonmaterial: "An organized or methodically arranged set of ideas; a complete exhibition of essential principles or facts, arranged in a rational dependence or connection." Also, "a complex of ideas, principles, doctrines, laws, etc., forming a coherent whole and recognized as the intellectual content of a particular philosophy, religion, form of government, or the like." Hence (number four): "(a) A hypothesis; a formulated theory. (b) Theory, as opposed to practice. (c) A systematic exposition of a subject; a treatise. *All now rare*" (their italics). Number five suggests structure: "A formal scheme or method governing organization, arrangement, etc., of objects or material, or a mode of procedure; a definite or set plan of ordering, operating, or proceeding; a method of classification, codification, etc." Number six carries the same notion further, *viz.*, "regular method or order; formal arrangement; orderliness." Among the meanings which precede and follow it, number seven stands out as worthy of sober contemplation: "The combination of a political machine with big financial or industrial interests for the purpose of corruptly influencing a government." Meanings numbered eight through fifteen are specialized, spanning the alphabet from *b* to *z* with a range of subjects from biological, through legal, to zoological.

[2] One example: Alice M. Rivlin, *Systematic Thinking for Social Action,* Washington, D.C., The Brookings Institution, 1971.

[3] Webster's *New International Dictionary,* Second Edition Unabridged.

Proponents of the systems approach, for all their claims to precision, have so far neglected to specify which of the above definitions they espouse. To judge by an almost universal predilection for the plural form, that is, the *systems* approach, one can only surmise that, in their ecumenism, they embrace all meanings, with the possible exception of number seven. Lack of firm definition leads persons engaged in systems analysis to indulge in a kind of solipsismal virtuosity which, contrary to the tenets of scientific method, generally yields irreproducible results. So reified and ratified, the system is what they say it is, what they conceive it to be. This they study; this they manipulate according to the rules they have set. In this way, other systems are perforce delimited, for they can only interface with, impinge upon, interact with, but never, therefore, be identical with or part of the first system.

Absence of sharp articulation creates another paradox: both arbitrary eclecticism and broad inclusiveness are possible within the rules of the game. For example, public welfare, frequently carved out as an area for system study, is approached as if it were an independent entity, apart from the economic condition, unrelated to the state of the job market, unaffected by cost and distribution of medical services, and divorced from history, geography, culture, and prevailing politics. In like fashion, its information system or, indeed, that of any enterprise, is treated as if it were a self-contained system having its own objectives and little congruence with those of the organization it is purported to serve. On the other hand, waste management — that is, pollutants in land, water, and air, and the even more comprehensive notion of resource management, or environmental quality — has been sketched as one system, with everything from farm, factory, transportation, and nuclear fission swept in.

SYSTEMS ANALYSIS, SYSTEMS ENGINEERING, AND SYSTEMS MANAGEMENT

While lexical laxity can, perhaps, account for the myriad interpretations, broad and narrow, of *system*, only casual usage can explain the virtual interchangeability among *systems analysis, systems engineering,* and *systems management*. E. S. Quade, for example, finds systems analysis closely akin to engineering because both are application rather than research oriented. He also includes *systems management* as one of a number of extensions of the body of knowledge originally called "operations analysis,"[4] and there he lets the matter remain. Attempts at distinction among the three items have not necessarily led to clarifi-

[4] E. S. Quade and W. I. Boucher, eds., *Systems Analysis and Policy Planning*, New York: American Elsevier, 1968, p. 3.

cation. One effort [5] views *systems analysis* as supplying the broad framework of the system and identifying the result wanted, *systems engineering* as creating a design that "incorporates the optimized technology,"
and *systems management* as the overall responsibility for control of
the whole procedure.

But for the practical implications of the ready substitutions of these
terms, one might dismiss assiduous examination of them as tedious ped-
antry or precious sophism. In real-life situations, we find that transfer-
ence has borne with it a convenient incognito laden with vague promises of expertness at execution. Thus, "systems competence" or "systems
capability" are often found to be ascribed without discrimination to
persons experienced in any of the three poorly defined categories of activity. This has encouraged a display of the superficial appurtenances
of each without the supporting or restraining discipline of any. Engineers who have worked on missiles or rocketry delivery systems are accredited with the capability of devising and delivering health care,
education, and welfare programs. In like fashion, persons who have
been attached to certain of the research institutes known as think tanks,
with a roving talent for contracts at home and abroad, are accepted as
qualified to set up or evaluate systems for everything from hospital
administration to urban renewal, practically irrespective of the type
of "systems work" they have previously performed. The notion of "systems capability," originated perhaps through lexicographical laziness,
has been strengthened by a number of factors and accidents of history,
economics, and politics, to be discussed later. The outcome has been a
calculated avoidance of specificity, with easy slipover from one area to
another accomplished largely by manipulation of the superficial platitudes common to all and a studied neglect of the particulars that often
comprise the essential nature of each. Current usage suggests that he
who has "systems capability" can analyze, engineer, and manage any
system.

Actually, even in the field of engineering, where the term *system* is
most at home, this is not the case. There are electrical, mechanical, fluid,
and thermal systems, in each of which knowledge is quite specialized.
Each classification has its own body of theory, its own developmental
history, as well as its analytical descriptions and idealized models. Even
though the engineering community itself, in search of a new image, is
trying to broaden its range to include all kinds of systems, the principles
and modes of thought within it remain substantially unchanged and
do not reflect the widened embrace.

Several professors of electrical engineering set forth in an authori-

[5] Guy Black, *The Application of Systems Analysis to Government Operations*, New
York: Frederick A. Praeger, 1968, pp. 6–10.

tative textbook what *system* means to them.[6] Deriving a general definition of system as "a collection of objects united by some form of interaction or dependence" from Webster's *Dictionary*, they refine it by specifying that their concern is only with the quantitative aspects of system behavior. They use mathematics extensively in order to "attain a high level of precision and clarity,"[7] and they specify that "each object which is part of a system is characterized by a finite number of measurable attributes and that the interaction between such objects as well as the interdependence between the attributes of each object can be expressed in some well-defined mathematical form."[8] The authors make no claims as to the universal applicability of their tenets. On the contrary, they are meticulous in designating the conditions, which, it may be noted, rarely if ever obtain in situations and systems where social factors and human behavior play an important part.

They point out that three fundamental questions arise in the analysis of most mechanical systems: "(1) What attributes of the objects of which the system is comprised need be considered? (2) What are the mathematical relations between the relevant attributes of each object in the system? (3) What are the mathematical relations between the attributes of different objects in the system; in other words, what are the relations representing the interactions of objects in the system?"[9] Asserting that learning how to arrive at the answers to these questions constitutes a considerable portion of the education of the engineer or physicist, the authors maintain that mathematical sophistication is essential. Also prerequisite for system design and engineering are rigorous and extensive training in circuit theory, information theory, control theory, optimization techniques, and computer programming.[10] Theorems, hypotheses, and proofs about the relations are expressed in specific mathematical formulas and equations, and all of the terms and concepts have special meaning in the context in which they are used.

The recurrence in other milieus of the language and terms used in engineering tasks is noteworthy with reference to our view of systems analysis as a conglomerate of disciplines. Although carefully set forth under strictly circumscribed conditions in its original habitat, technical terminology often degenerates into convenient jargon when transplanted. And in the transfer there is the predilection to concentrate on the quantitative aspect of processes and problems as if these were most important or as if somehow mathematical techniques could help under-

---

[6] Lotfi A. Zadeh and Charles A. Desoer, *Linear System Theory*, New York: McGraw-Hill, 1963, p. 2.
[7] *Ibid.*, p. vii.
[8] *Ibid.*, p. 2.
[9] *Ibid.*, p. 2.
[10] *Ibid.*, p. vii.

stand and balance all equations — human, social, economic, political — as they do those in engineering textbooks.

Engineers define system in more general terms as "a device, procedure, or scheme, which behaves according to some description, its function being to operate on information and/or energy and/or matter in a time reference to yield information and/or energy and/or matter." [11] Portrayed schematically, the system has been represented this way: [12]

FIGURE 1. Schema of Engineering System

It is described as follows: "a collection of matter, parts or components which are included inside a specified, often arbitrary boundary." [13] The *modus operandi* for dealing with this conception of a system often takes a sort of generalized and simplistic handbook form: [14]

(1) define the system and its components;
(2) formulate the mathematical model;
(3) determine the system equations;
(4) solve the desired output;
(5) check the solution;
(6) analyze or design.

Another example of the procedures for engineering a large, complex system is somewhat similar: [15]

(1) understanding the problem;
(2) considering the alternative solutions;
(3) choosing the optimum system;
(4) synthesis of the system;
(5) updating equipment characteristics and data;
(6) testing the system;
(7) refining the design based on a correlation of test data and requirements.

[11] David O. Ellis and Fred J. Ludwig, *Systems Philosophy*, Englewood Cliffs, New Jersey: Prentice-Hall, 1962, p. 3.

[12] J. Lowen Shearer, Arthur T. Murphy, and Herbert H. Richardson, *Introduction to System Dynamics*, Reading, Massachusetts: Addison-Wesley, 1967, p. 3.

[13] *Ibid.*, p. 103.

[14] *Ibid.*, p. 103.

[15] Stanley M. Shinners, *Technique for System Engineering*, New York: McGraw-Hill, 1967, pp. 16–17.

This ready-made structure provides a convenient framework for analysis of almost any kind of system and is to be found frequently in the preambles to many proposals for a great variety — urban, social, educational, medical, and the like.

Closer examination of the system engineer's definitions as well as his task reveals that his professional preoccupations are much narrower and more precise than the above commonly used think-and-do outlines suggest. The mathematical definition of a system indicating the specific situation as he sees it is presented in Figure 2 (see p. 22).[16]

When the systems engineering textbook refers to "analysis of a dynamic system," therefore, its use of such terms as *system definitions*, *inputs*, and *energetic interactions* relates to a specific frame of reference. The words have a special meaning in this context and convey quite a different message when they are transferred to the wider world of social systems. The following is an engineer's conception of the analysis of a dynamic system:

> The engineer must . . . *define* the system to be considered (should the ambient-temperature be considered an input? is the inertia of a connecting shaft important in this situation? etc.). He then may describe the system by means of the various dynamic system elements . . . His next step is to investigate the energetic interactions between these two elments when they are interconnected and then excited by some signal. The engineer's most important (but frequently overlooked) job is to establish a *mathematical model* of the system to be analyzed. This involves the identification and idealization of their interconnection. . . .
>
> The mathematical statement of the governing relationships between system variables is called the formation problem. Interconnection of the elements imposes constraints on the variation of system variables, and the convenient way of specifying these constraints is by a mathematical statement of the way in which the various *through-variables* are related and the way in which the various *across-variables* are related. The elemental equations then relate the through- and across-variables for each individual element. This package of equations is a complete mathematical description of the system.
>
> To investigate the *dynamic behavior* of the system, we must solve this set of equations. The input and outputs are selected and a single differential equation, called the *system equation*, relating each output and input must be determined. The initial state of the system must also be specified by a set of initial conditions. The system differential equation must be solved for the output response under the specified input signal and initial conditions. There are numerous approaches to the *solution* of the system equation, and the choice of a method will depend on the problem at hand. Briefly, these methods are (1) graphical; (2) numerical, with the possible use of a digital computer; (3) operational block diagram of the system with the eventual use of an analog computer; and (4) a purely mathematical solution.

[16] Ellis and Ludwig, *op.cit.*, pp. 129–131.

FIGURE 2. Mathematical Definition of a System

DEFINITION. A system $\mathfrak{S}$ is an object

$$\left\{ T, \tau, \Gamma, \Sigma, \Omega, \{\Gamma_R\}, \{\Sigma_R\}, \{\omega_{\gamma\sigma}\}, \{\tilde{\omega}_{\gamma\sigma}\} \right\}$$

subject to postulates 1 to 5 below :

POSTULATE 1. Γ, Σ, and Ω are sets.

POSTULATE 2. T is a directed set, $(T, \leq)$, and τ is a set of directed subsets of T.

CONVENTION: Names are assigned as follows :

Symbol	Name of Set	Name of Element
T	Chronology	Time
τ	Staging space	Run
Γ	Input space	Input argument
Σ	Phase space	State
Ω	Output space	Output argument

CONVENTION: If $R \in \tau$, certain nets over R are named as follows :

Net	Name
$\gamma : R \longrightarrow \Gamma$	Input
$\sigma : R \longrightarrow \Sigma$	Staging
$\omega : R \longrightarrow \Omega$	Output

POSTULATE 3. For each $R \in \tau$,
$$\Gamma_R \subset \Gamma^R \text{ and } \Sigma_R \subset \Sigma^R.$$

CONVENTION: The sets Γ_R and Σ_R are called the spaces of R-admissible inputs and R-admissible stagings, respectively.

CONVENTION: If $R \in \tau$ and $t \in R$, we denote by R_t the set $\{s \in R \mid s \leq t\}$.

CONVENTION: If $R \in \tau$, $\gamma \in \Gamma_R$, the sets R_γ and R_σ are understood to bear the quasi-orderings induced from R by γ and σ, respectively. Subsets of R_γ, for example, are understood to inherit this quasi-ordering.

POSTULATE 4. If $R \in \tau$, and $\gamma \in \Gamma_R$, and $\sigma \in \Sigma_R$, there is a mapping

$$\tilde{\omega}_{\gamma\sigma} : \Gamma \otimes \Sigma \longrightarrow \Omega$$

defined and called the $\gamma\sigma$ correlatant.

CONVENTION: If $R \in \tau$, and $\gamma \in \Gamma_R$, and $\sigma \in \Sigma_R$, the mapping

$$\omega_{\gamma\sigma} : R \longrightarrow \Omega$$

defined by

$$\omega_{\gamma\sigma} = \left(\frac{\gamma}{R_t} , \frac{\sigma}{R_t} \right) \tilde{\omega}_{\gamma\sigma} ,$$

is called the $\gamma\sigma$ resultant.

POSTULATE 5. If $\in \tau$, $S \in \tau$, $f : R \longrightarrow S$ is an order isomorphism, $\gamma \in \Gamma_R$, $\sigma \in \Sigma_R$, $\hat{\gamma} \in \Gamma_S$, $\hat{\sigma} \in \Sigma_S$, $\hat{\gamma} = f^{-1}\gamma$ and $\sigma = f^{-1}\sigma$, then

$$\omega_{\hat{\gamma}\hat{\sigma}} = f^{-1}\omega_{\gamma\sigma}.$$

22

After obtaining a solution for the response, the engineer has another major job. The tasks of initial modeling and final analyzing or designing are functions which *clearly* distinguish the engineer from the mathematician. The engineer must *check* his solution (is it correct dimensionally? does it correspond to physical reality? does it check for simplified situations which can be easily analyzed? etc.). His interest in the whole matter of dynamic systems is to eventually analyze to determine whether a certain performance is obtained and is satisfactory, or more generally, he must design the system so that it will meet certain performance specifications.

The process of designing is usually an iterative analysis. The results of one analysis point toward a change in the system which may improve the performance, etc. The design aspects distinguish the engineer from the scientist. The engineer is ultimately interested in building a system which will perform a useful function for the benefit of mankind.[17]

The notion of doing the public good, as expressed in the final sentence above, reflects the engineering community's quest for a social role. One observes it emerging on college campuses as well as in the corporate-industrial milieu. The provost of the Polytechnic Institute of Brooklyn, for example, reported "an astonishing increase in student dedication to the idea of utilizing technology for social and individual benefit."[18] The dean of the College of Engineering, University of California at Berkeley, deplored the "diffuse public image of the engineer as the man peering through a transit, slouched over a drawing board, or wiring resistors on an electronic breadboard." Instead, he cited as a range of possibilities for new social tasks a list presented by the dean of Engineering and Applied Physics at Harvard: "the technology of education, the technology of the delivery of medical care, the technology of urban planning; new transportation technologies; a new information technology evolving towards what one might term a social or collective brain; new technologies of environmental management such as weather modification or waste disposal; oceanic engineering."[19]

Protestations of benevolence to mankind as an underlying philosophy for teaching and learning systems engineering stand in juxtaposition, however, to the pedagogical content of educational materials and exercises in standard curricula at the present time. One finds such tasks as instrumentation tracking radar and command-and-control systems in antisubmarine warfare offered as practical uses for the techniques. A book prefaced by such generally irreproachable sentiments as the desire to construct "a system which will perform a useful func-

---

[17] Shearer, Murphy, and Richardson, *op.cit.*, pp. 102–103.

[18] Shinners, *op.cit.*, Foreword by John G. Truxal, p. v.

[19] George J. Maslach, "In Search of a New Image," *The California Engineer*, Vol. 46, No. 2, December, 1967, p. 7.

tion for the benefit of mankind" [20] concentrates on such matters as ascertaining the performance of missile systems. This, the students are taught, may be measured in terms of two probabilistic considerations: the "miss distance" of the missile and the "probability of kill" for a given miss distance.[21]

In contradistinction to precise formulas and in-depth exposition of procedures for calculating the design of mechanical systems, engineering texts and teachers lump social systems together in a happy hodgepodge and treat them cavalierly in "Technology and Society" curricula, the new look in engineering course planning. Organized as a response to what have been interpreted to be social exigencies, such courses are offered as "interdisciplinary" and are usually a parade of social scientists, with an anthropologist, a sociologist, a psychologist, an economist, and an urban planner, each giving a two-hour lecture. This kaleidoscopic gallimaufry of discrete offerings is supposed to convey the fundamentals of accumulated wisdom and experience in each field in sufficient measure to serve as input to the engineer's socialization process. Armed with this exposure, he goes forth to do battle with society's major problems: education, delivery of medical care, urban planning, and social welfare. Among the lessons which he has still to learn, however, is that many of society's pressing problems, which may have been generated or aggravated by technological change and development, are basically social in nature. Calling upon an engineer to cure them is much like asking an economist to treat a heart ailment because the patient became ill over money matters!

Like the curricula, current textbooks in systems engineering contain no specific methods for assessing the performance of the social, biomedical, educational, and other non-space and non-military arenas. Nor is there instruction as to how engineers might include in their cost-estimating the expenses involved in protecting the environment from the effects of the process or product they have devised. Moreover, we soon find that, belying the aura of precision lent by a plethora of formulas, charts, and diagrams, even in the engineer's territory of the calculable and ponderable, exactitude is not always attainable. Experience and judgment in the given field are vital. Many approximations and estimations must be made. With the engineered system the outcome of compromise among such factors as performance, reliability, cost, schedule, maintainability, power consumption, weight, and life expectancy, to mention only a few of the mechanically but not necessarily socially important matters, the process is a good deal less foolproof than the naive are led and inclined to believe.

[20] Shearer, Murphy, and Richardson, *op.cit.*
[21] Shinners, *op.cit.*, p. 38.

In the Panglossian * glow surrounding systems engineering as the optimum method for approaching life's complexities, all but overlooked is the possibility that, even on its home ground, the technique cannot claim unqualified success. Some of the very systems cited as exemplars are, in fact, prime examples of miscalculation and mismanagement. In the development of many of them, "costs and times tend to be grossly underestimated and performance tends to be mercifully unmeasured." [22] SAGE, the Semi-Automatic Ground Environment system for air defense, is a case in point. Here, the number of man-hours of required programing was underestimated by six thousand, at a time when the total number of programmers in the world was hardly more than one thousand. Actual installation-wide tests found the program on schedule at first but it soon slipped one year and then another year. Contrary to assumptions of uniformity, each location was discovered to behave idiosyncratically and, therefore, to require its own custom-tailored, lengthy, and costly program. Obsolete before it was completed and long before it was paid for, SAGE was successful only because our enemies failed to attack.

BMEWS, the Ballistic Missile Early Warning System, was engineered to detect incoming ballistic missiles through the electronic sensing of the energy they reflected. But its designers apparently forgot that large, distant objects, such as the moon, can reflect as much energy as do lesser, nearer ones. When, early in its operational life, BMEWS detected "incoming ballistic missiles," only a lack of confidence in the system blocked the reflex of counterstrike, which would have precipitated one of the greatest tragedies in history — all because an untested electronic system had been relied on to launch nuclear missiles as a reaction to moonbeams.[23] After study of these and a number of other well-publicized systems, Dr. J. C. R. Licklider, professor of Electrical Engineering at the Massachusetts Institute of Technology, issued some impressive caveats about the dangers of dependence on an anti-ballistic missile system in particular and technologically contrived and controlled systems in general. Even in tasks which may, in comparison to the DEW Line (Distant Early Warning system) and SACCS (Strategic Air Command Control System), seem modest, conventional, and undebatable, predominance of systems engineering as the accepted procedure may have obscured other, perhaps more promising, approaches. There may

*Pangloss was the character in Voltaire's *Candide* whose philosophy was "all is for the best in this best of all possible worlds."
[22] J. C. R. Licklider, "Underestimates and Overestimations," *Computers and Automation*, August, 1969, p. 48. From Abram Chayes and Jerome B. Wiesner, eds., *ABM: An Evaluation of the Decision to Deploy an Antiballistic Missile System*, New York Harper & Row, 1969.
[23] *Ibid.*, p. 50.

be more advantageous ways, with respect to cost, quality, and manpower utilization, to mention only a few of the standard checkpoints, to accomplish even the customary engineering tasks.

The unique contributions of the engineering community to the mythology and confusion surrounding the systems approach have been dealt with at length for several reasons. First, much of what now comprises the systems approach, whether practiced by economists, political scientists, or sociologists, is rooted in the heritage from engineering and is permeated by the same basic philosophy. Second, the ascription of universal transferability and applicability has been iterated and re-iterated by engineers until it has taken on a kind of reality, as it emerges in concrete form in the world of contract-getting. This is evident in the preamble to — and also generously lards the body of — almost every proposal crafted in response to government requests, practically irrespective of subject area. To judge from statements emanating from national meetings, the professional electrical engineering society, heady with their command and control over computers and mesmerized as to their capability of handling large masses of data, no matter what their substance, conceive that they have a mandate not only to *solve* social problems but actually to *formulate* them.[24] Such hubris is not universal among engineers, but there is widespread evidence of methodological arrogance, which has potential danger. As our research corroborates, a technological conception of a problem limits the focus to those aspects which can be expressed quantitatively and which fit certain models. The technological solution which results may be satisfactory from the engineering point of view but, because it has encompassed only selected facets, vital dimensions may have been neglected. Such violation of the essence of problems may, in the long run, exacerbate rather than ameliorate the troublesome condition.

GENERAL SYSTEM THEORY

The fact that the systems approach is closely identified with engineering is not mere happenstance; many basic tools and procedures stem directly from that context: the centrality of measurement and mathematics, the structured organization of materials and ideas, the methodological conceptualization of the task. Basic to engineering science, these factors have found ready acceptance in, and are especially compatible with, many other disciplines affected by computer availability. Devotees of technology's promise are persuaded that quanti-

[24] Assistant Secretary of Commerce Myron Tribus, Speech at IEEE Meeting, Washington, D.C., as quoted in *Modern Data*, Vol. 3, No. 1, January, 1970, p. 40.

fication will render their methods rigorous, too, and thus enhance their claim to being scientific.

Although current procedures in the systems approach strongly reflect the influence of engineering science, its intellectual heritage has deeper and wider dimensions. In fact, the approach, as we now encounter it, resembles the geological phenomenon known as "Roxbury pudding-stone" in both history and constitution. This formation, located in a suburb of Boston, Massachusetts, resulted from glacial movement, which over the miles and the centuries dragged with it, accumulated, and then incorporated a vast heterogeny of types of rock, all set in a matrix and solidified in an agglomerate mass. Many fragments still retain their original identity and character; some have undergone meta-morphosis in varying degrees. In like manner, the systems approach is a kind of mosaic, made up of bits and pieces of ideas, theories, and methodology from a number of disciplines, discernible among which are — in addition to engineering — sociology, biology, philosophy, psy-chology, and economics.

Each discipline has its own intrinsic and fundamental conception of system, along with its own definitions, principles, assumptions, and hypotheses. But there is a dynamic which pulls them together, makes them *gemütlich*, and provides them with a mutually supportive kin-ship. This consists of their orientation to and emphasis on the *totality* of the experience, entity, or phenomenon under consideration. Com-mon emphasis on wholes rather than parts has encouraged a sort of methodological superstructure to be built on a "Cottleston Pie" anal-ogy [25] that serves to sustain a superficial but spurious impression of epistemological universality and consensus. From there, the next step is to the development of quantified measures, computerized computa-tions, and the mass assembling and manipulation of data. While not necessarily germane to the philosophy underlying the total systems concept, these procedures have become practically *de rigueur*.

In Sociology

When we review the history of sociology, we find that the con-ception of society as a total social system has gone in and out of style several times. In its early forms, the approach was bio-organismic.

---

[25] "Cottleston Pie," a song sung by Winnie-the-Pooh, makes unlikes analogous through simple linkages:

> A fish can't whistle and neither can I.
> Ask me a riddle and I reply:
> "Cottleston, Cottleston, Cottleston Pie."

A. A. Milne, *Winnie-the-Pooh*, 1926, in *The World of Pooh*, New York: E. P. Dutton, 1957, p. 72.

Spencer,[26] a pioneer proponent of this viewpoint, saw society as an organism, similar to biological organisms in a number of essential ways. Both, he claimed, experience growth and, in the process, undergo differentiation in structure and function. Both are composed of units, the one having cells, the other, individuals. Both have special sustaining systems, vasculatory and circulatory in the organism, arteries of commerce for society. Both have special regulatory systems, nervous in the organism, governmental in society. Perceiving in both a mutual dependence of parts, he based the case for his analogy on "the unquestionable community" between them.[27] Many theorists following Spencer espoused his conception of the human society as a homologue of the natural organism and carried it even further. Their social morphology went so far as to equate the epidermal tissue of animals with the protective network of army and police, and to ascribe sex to various social organisms, masculinity to the state, femininity to the church.

To the extent that the hypothesizing was based on a recognition that human society represents a kind of living unity different from a mere sum of the isolated individuals, this approach early demonstrated its usefulness and has continued to do so through its intermittent revivals and recurrences in the history of ideas. To be sure, the logical adequacy of many of the analogies was severely questioned and undermined even before the turn of the century.[28] But in general the resilience of the approach is demonstrated in the fact that it has managed to survive devastating criticism of its basic premises. P. A. Sorokin[29] long ago pointed up the speciousness of the syllogism underlying the fundamental inferences.

Just because human society may be considered a kind of unity in which the members are interdependent, and an organism is a unity of interrelated parts, it does not follow, he argued, that society is an organism. By the same token, the solar system, an automobile, a plant, an animal, a river, or a man represent a kind of unity with interdependent parts, but this does not mean that they are identical. Nor does establishment of their truismatic relationship imply that their intrinsic substance, or the rules governing their behavior or performance, or the methods best applicable to an understanding of the dy-

[26] Herbert Spencer, *The Principles of Sociology*, Vol. 1, Part II, New York: Appleton, 1910.

[27] *The Works of Herbert Spencer*, Germany: Osnabrück, 1871, in *Specialized Administration*, Vol. 15, p. 411.

[28] See especially Gabriel Tarde, "La theorie organique des sociétés," *Annals Institut International de Sociologie*, Vol. IV, pp. 238–239, or Gabriel Tarde, *La Logique Sociale*, Paris: Alcan., 1895.

[29] P. A. Sorokin, *Contemporary Sociological Theories*, New York: Harper & Brothers, 1928, especially chapter IV, pp. 195 ff.

namics of one are proper with respect to another. Criticizing the bio-organismic analogical methods as a prime example of a fallacy in analogical reasoning, Sorokin also pointed up the practical inferences made by various theorists of this persuasion. Some used their bio-organismic premises as an argument in favor of monarchy, adminis-trative centralization, absolutism, or socialism as a form of the greatest integration of social organism.[30] Any pedagogical value likely to be gained from bio-organismic analogies which supply concrete images to help visualize the abstract and complex structure of society was, in Sorokin's view, greatly overweighted by their misuse and their scien-tific fallacies.[31]

Interpreting Sorokin's observations in light of the current defini-tions and use of systems concepts, we realize that his criticism is as appropriate and applicable to modern manifestations of the systems approach as it was a generation ago to bio-organismic theories. In the swing of the pendulum between the generalized and the specialized orientations, it is not surprising that Sorokin's criticisms, however cogent, have been all but ignored or forgotten. It is noteworthy that the systems approach, periodically dismissed and rejected as unscien-tific, has now been revived and is revered on the ground that it is ra-tional and scientific. Its present quantitative underpinnings and tech-nical trappings make it the all-purpose scientific methodology. It is acclaimed a Space Age phenomenon.

Modern sociologists, anxious to render their discipline more re-spectable and scientific, are tending toward quantification. Many have made the computer the keystone of their research activity and are more preoccupied with amassing and manipulating information than with conducting meaningful research. In response to what has been per-ceived as a need for rapprochement among theory and method, col-lege curricula are now training the new generation of sociologists in the use of more sophisticated analytical tools; course offerings include symbolic logic, set theory, probability, and other methods derived from mathematics and statistics. The professional journals reflect this orienta-tion, with a preponderance of articles concerned with technical niceties. If one were to rely on superficial review of respective tables of contents, sociology and econometrics journals would be almost undistinguish-able. What is important is that beneath the apparent similarity, the common use of symbolic language, and even the technical calculations, there are deep-seated ideological differences.

In quest of more sophisticated analytical tools, modern sociologists

---

[30] *Ibid.*, p. 210.
[31] *Ibid.*, p. 211.

have also embraced the systems approach as they construe it. A supporting frame of reference comes from Talcott Parsons' "systematic general theory," [32] which has been sketched as follows: "'System' is the concept that refers both to a complex of interdependencies between parts, components, and processes that involves discernible regularities of relationship, and to a similar type of interdependency between such a complex and its surrounding environment." [33] Furthermore, "the social system is . . . a very complex entity. As an organization of human interests, activities and commitments, it must be viewed as a system and in functional perspective." [34] An attempt at translating the total approach into operational terms was made by Walter Buckley,[35] who finds a striking similarity between society and an organism. He defines a system as "a whole which functions as a whole by virtue of the interdependence of its parts." [36] General system theory, for him, is a method intended to ascertain how the relationships are brought about, organized, and maintained. Developing the thesis that overemphasis on the scientific in various disciplines has led to an avalanche of findings but little knowledge, he argues a case for a "modern system point of view" as necessary counteragent.[37] Such an approach will, he assumes, embrace and combine a number of divergent disciplines. His earnest assertions that the modern system point of view shows promise of reestablishing holistic approaches without abandoning scientific rigor and his apologia that analogies are not mere metaphors [38] have served more as a booster of the current trend toward indiscriminate application of something called systems analysis to all manner of social phenomena than to development of much needed analytic procedures. Despite the common-sense logic and philosophic congeniality of Buckley's criticism of splinter-minded psychologists and sociologists, his conception of the "modern system point of view" neither stems the avalanche of unrelated findings nor provides an insightful framework for the interpretation of the output of the disciplines and subdisciplines.

IN PSYCHOLOGY

In psychology, the total approach emerged in the early 1920s as a reaction against the tendency — then fashionable and subsequently

[32] Talcott Parsons, *The Social System*, Glencoe: Free Press, 1951.

[33] Talcott Parsons, "Systems Analysis: Social Systems," *International Encyclopedia of the Social Sciences*, Vol. 15, 1968, p. 458.

[34] *Ibid.*, p. 472.

[35] Walter Buckley, ed., Foreword to *Modern Systems Research for the Behavioral Scientist*, Chicago: Aldine, 1968, p. xxi.

[36] *Ibid.*, p. xv.

[37] *Ibid.*, p. 493.

[38] *Ibid.*, p. xxi.

never eclipsed — to achieve a scientific method of analyzing its subject matter into constituent elements. The formulations of *Gestalt-theorie* were first developed and tested in perceptual organization, a field of systematic psychology where atomistic reductionism had been entrenched. Wolfgang Köhler, one of the founders of Gestalt psychology,[39] observed striking similarities between certain aspects of field physics and facts of perceptual grouping and coherence. He argued that, just as there are in physics certain instances of functional wholes that cannot be compounded from the action of their separate parts, so also are there counterparts in such human experiences as, for example, memory and understanding.[40] In contrast to the neuron and dendrite counters who were wont to reduce psychology to its least biological denominator, proponents of Gestalt, sometimes translated as the "configurational" theory, chose to recognize form, sense, and value as striking characteristics of mental life.

Gestalt-theorie might have been eclipsed by the increasing force of the very techiques it sought to counteract. Because of its vulnerability to attack for being intuitive, the theory as developed by Köhler and his followers could have been short-lived but for the contributions of Kurt Lewin,[41] who reconciled it with the emergent trend toward symbolic mathematical conceptualization and scientific method generally. For Lewin, the total situation was paramount, with the psychological field or life space his fundamental construct. He created topological psychology or "field theory," interpreting all psychological events as functions of the life span, which consists of the individual and his environment in dynamic interaction. According to his theory, living systems tend to maintain labile equilibrium with their environments; need-tensions, level of aspiration, goal-directed action, and release of tension are the motivational processes in the restoration of equilibrium.

Lewin maintained that with the trend toward progressive narrowing of attention to a limited number of variables, the complexity of real-life situations could only be represented and interpreted by the broadening and continual crossing of the traditional boundaries between the social sciences. His field theory, an extension of the Gestalt approach, had considerable impact because of its focus on the interrelationships between psychological events, between individual and group, and between groups and the wider social environment. Rarely

[39] The other two men identified with the development of Gestalt psychology are Max Wertheimer (1880–1943) and Kurt Koffka (1886–1941).

[40] Wolfgang Köhler, "Perception: An Introduction to the Gestalt-theorie," *Psychological Bulletin*, Vol. 19, 1922, pp. 531–585, and *Principles of Gestalt Psychology*, New York: Harcourt and Brace, 1935.

[41] Kurt Lewin, *Field Theory in Social Science: Selected Theoretical Papers*, Dorwin Cartwright, ed., London: Tavistock, 1963.

acknowledged, Lewin's legacy is especially important because he was the spiritual godfather of much of the current activity in group dynamics, from T-groups in industrial relations, to encounter groups in race relations, to *ersatz* primary groups engaged in behavior modification and attitude manipulation. In 1943, far in advance of the vogue of the 1970s, he put forward the notion of "psychological ecology," which embraced the social channels and gatekeepers that account for the way in which technological, cultural, and economic factors combine to influence choices and decisions.

With the possible exception of Lewin's topological concepts, which lend themselves to manipulation by modern technological tools, Gestalt theory eludes counting and measurement and is, consequently, more useful to psychiatrists and psychologists with a total environment orientation than to those whose methods reflect the current quantitative emphasis. Lack of popularity should not, however, be allowed to obscure the place of Gestalt theory in the historical development of the systems approach, which, by 1955, had already been revived by psychologists. The then accepted definition was: [42] "Systems are bounded regions in space-time, involving energy interchange among their parts, which are associated in functional relationships and with their environments."

Like Gestalt theory a generation earlier, systems theory in psychology was an antidote to the idea of simple stimulus-and-response behavior patterns, in which are posited "penny-in-the-slot reactions by virtual automatons." [43] To the extent that the systems approach offered a framework for less mechanistic theories, it was welcomed. Less well received, however, were its organismic overtones. Entirely rejected was the attempt, probably in the name of methodological refinement and control, to make a case for the operation of closed systems. Parsons asserted that a social system, like all living systems, was inherently an open system, "engaged in processes of interchange (or 'input-output relations') with its environment, as well as consisting of interchanges among its internal units." [44] Having distinguished four levels of openness in psychological systems, Gordon W. Allport advised that closed systems be left to the realm of physics where they may be more appropriate, although even there, he maintained, "a question exists as to whether Einstein's formula for the release of matter into energy does not finally demonstrate the futility of positing a closed system." [45]

[42] James G. Miller, "Toward a General Theory for the Behavioral Sciences," *American Psychologist*, Vol. 10, 1955, pp. 513–531.
[43] Gordon W. Allport, "The Open System in Personality Theory," *Journal of Abnormal and Social Psychology*, Vol. 61, 1960, pp. 301–311.
[44] Talcott Parsons, "Systems Analysis: Social Systems," *International Encyclopedia of the Social Sciences, op.cit.*, p. 460.
[45] Gordon W. Allport, *op.cit.*

In Economics

System concepts in various aspects and forms occupy an important place in the history and development of economic thought. A significant starting point appears to be the Physiocrats, a group known in their day as *Les économistes*, who enjoyed considerable influence in France from 1760 to 1770 and whose long-range imprint is indelible. François Quesnay and his disciples developed an analytic scheme with agriculture at is fulcrum and with *l'ordre naturel* the ideal dictate of human nature as revealed by human reason. Reorganizing the general interdependence of all sectors and all elements of the economic process, Quesnay developed an overall description, known as the *tableau économique*, which displayed the universal compatibility and even complementarity of individual interests in competitive society. The *tableau* is credited as the first method ever devised to convey an explicit conception of the nature of economic equilibrium.[46]

Recognition of an all-pervading interdependence, though a meaningful first step, did not supply answers to the question whether analysis of the interdependence would yield accurate and specific relations, so that prices and quantities of products and productive services that constitute the economic system could be calculated. A significant move forward was made by Leon Walras, who, using theoretical physics as his guide, formulated a mathematical mode of analysis to formulate a system of equations about economic relationships. So great was this achievement that Schumpeter called it "the Magna Carta of economic theory."[47] Convinced that quantitative, mathematical techniques were needed to assure the application of scientific method to economic matters, Walras set economics on a path from which it has not yet departed.[48] His theory of general equilibrium encompassed the fields of exchange, production, capital, and money in a unified formulation, and he assumed a closed system which, although ideal (in Weber's sense[49]), described the normal state toward which the economy spontaneously moves under free competition. With the logic of the system based on the logic of simultaneous equations, there was the implicit

[46] Joseph A. Schumpeter, *History of Economic Analysis*, edited from manuscript by Elizabeth Boody Schumpete, New York: Oxford University Press, 1968 (seventh printing), p. 242.

[47] *Ibid.*, p. 242.

[48] Ben B. Seligman, *Main Currents in Modern Economics*, Glencoe: Free Press, 1962, p. 367. Milton Friedman is quoted in the article on Walras (in the *International Encyclopedia of the Social Sciences*, Vol. 16, p. 452): "We curtsy to Marshall, but we walk with Walras."

[49] *Max Weber on the Methodology of the Social Sciences*, translated and edited by Edward Shils and Henry A. Finch, Glencoe: Free Press, 1949.

suggestion that a set of given conditions could inevitably determine its consequences.

Walras' monumental contributions to economic thought include several which are crucial to modern systems approaches. These are his painstaking application of quantitative methods and use of mathematical equations and his refinement of Quesnay's general equilibrium concept of a century earlier into a heroic abstraction encompassing the entire economic system. While in no way disputing the importance of Walras' work, it is necessary to take note of professional economists' evaluations of these two contributions. On the subject of his use of mathematics, Seligman makes the following observation:

> In Walras' system, for example, each good and productive service was to have its own equation, so that with 10,000 goods and 1,000 factors there would have to be 21,999 equations. For the whole economy the number of equations would be immense: empirical research, consequently, would have to group data in order to make economic investigation manageable. . . . Even more important was the fact that the analysis had little to say about joint and multiple products, *an almost fatal defect*. It may very well be that the institutionalists are right: perhaps more psychology and history and sociology are necessary if we are to grasp the true nature of the human animal. *Mathematics, queen of the sciences, had been shown to need some additional workers.*[50] (My italics.)

The purity of his model of the economic system was a simulated abstraction from its institutional setting. "It was a system devoid of human beings functioning in a complex social matrix. The factors of production remained what they had been throughout all such systems — abstract categories unmoved by the forces that give an economy its characteristic motion. . . . Economics thus became a science of exchange, buttressed by a mechanical technique of maximizing satisfactions. As Milton Friedman has said, the Walrasian model was a form of analysis without much substance."[51]

Nonetheless, economists continue to "walk with Walras,"[52] the field of economic theory continues to become more and more the province of the mathematically anointed,[53] and refinements of the system equilibrium hypothesis have rendered it highly respectable. Nothing less than an encyclopedic work like Schumpeter's[54] would adequately trace the growth and development of mathematical techniques in concep-

[50] Ben B. Seligman, *op.cit.*, p. 385.
[51] *Ibid.*, p. 385.
[52] Cf. footnote 48.
[53] Paul A. Samuelson, "Economic Theory and Mathematics — An Appraisal," *American Economic Review*, Vol. XLII, No. 2, May, 1952, pp. 56–66.
[54] Schumpeter, *op.cit.*

tualizing economic relationships. Walras had worthy followers too numerous to list in this context. Perhaps proof of the prevailing and continuing trend toward recognition of this orientation has been persuasively established by the Swedish Academy of Science's selections in 1969 for the first two Nobel Prizes in Economic Science. Honored were Dr. Ragnar Frisch of Norway and Dr. Jan Tinbergen of the Netherlands for their development of mathematical models for the analysis of economic processes. The high level recognition of the econometric aspect has been interpreted as endorsement of the emphasis on quantitative methodology, possibly even at a sacrifice of theoretical and philosophical considerations. A manifestation of the quest for more precise tools in all of the social sciences, new and improved quantitative techniques in econometrics have also been readily accepted and adopted by other disciplines. Among them are game theory, linear programing, and input-output analysis. With roots in Walras' mathematical conceptions and theory of mutual independence and with branches reaching into the very core of operations research and systems analysis, these closely related techniques are being widely used and should be included in this historical review.

Game theory, linear programing, and input-output analysis, although related in origin, orientation, and application, came into being separately and merged gradually in economics, where they were developed and widely used.[55] Game theory, developed by John von Neumann [56] in 1928, rests on the hypothesis that there is a similarity between parlor games of skill and conflict situations in economic, political, and military life. Under certain assumptions, each participant can act so as to be guaranteed at least a certain minimum gain or maximum loss. By each participant's acting to secure his minimum guaranteed return, opponents are prevented from attaining anything more than their minimum guaranteeable gains. As a result, the minimum gains become the actual gains, and the actions and returns for all participants are determinate. Game theory has provided a framework in which to devise strategy under competitive circumstances. It has had important implications for economics, military decisions, and statistical theory.[57]

[55] The concepts are listed in the chronology suggested by Robert Dorfman, Paul A. Samuelson, and Robert M. Solow, *Linear Programming and Economic Analysis*, New York: McGraw-Hill, 1958. There may be some disagreement over the actual order of appearance. J. R. Hicks apparently has some other time relationship in mind in his essay, "Linear Theory," *Surveys of Economic Theory*. Prepared for the American Economic Association and The Royal Economic Society, Vol. III, Surveys IX–XIII, pp. 75–114.

[56] John von Neumann, "Zur Theorie der Gesellschafts-spiele," *Mathematische Annalen*, Vol. 100, 1928, pp. 295–320, and John von Neumann and Oskar Morgenstern, *Theory of Games and Economic Behavior*, Princeton University Press, 1944.

[57] Dorfman, Samuelson, and Solow, *op.cit.*, p. 2.

Input-output analysis, developed by Wassily W. Leontief in 1936,[58] is based on the notion that a large part of the dynamics of a modern economy is devoted to the production of intermediate goods, and the output of intermediate goods is closely associated with output of final products. In this closed system of economic activity, there is an inter-relationship linking all sectors of the economy. Equilibrium exists when the outputs of the various products are such that just enough of each is produced to meet the input requirements of all others. Leontief's primary objective is specification of this balance through aggregation, analysis, and interpretation of vast amounts of empirical data.[59] An input-output table, laying out the flows of goods and services, can por-tray the structure of an industry or an entire economy at any desired level of detail and, by revealing their dynamic inner characteristics, can serve underdeveloped countries in their planning for industrialization.[60]

Linear programming, like calculus, is primarily a mathematical tool, and not, strictly speaking, the province of the economist. Nonetheless, because a substantial class of economic problems fulfills its postulates, and because the technique has been considerably developed and re-fined by economists, it may appropriately be included here. Defined as "a deterministic model which assumes linear behavioral relationships and in which an optimal solution is sought (maximizing or minimizing) subject to one or more limiting restraints," this method is used to de-termine the best or optimum use of resources to achieve a desired re-sult when the limitations on available resources can be expressed by simultaneous linear equations.[61] In other words, linear programming concerns itself with the allocation of limited resources in such fashion as to maximize a product or minimize its cost.[62] The method, devel-oped by George B. Dantzig in 1947 for planning the diversified activi-ties of the U.S. Air Force, stimulated two subsequent streams of activ-ity — applications to managerial planning in industry and exploration of the implications for economic theory in general.[63]

Inclusion of game theory, input-output analysis, and linear pro-graming under the rubric of economics is not to be construed as a suggestion that these methods are the private preserve of economists and that all other users are poachers. Perhaps it is because an equally

[58] Wassily W. Leontief, *The Structure of American Economy 1919–1929*, Cambridge: Harvard University Press, 1941.

[59] Dorfman, Samuelson, and Solow, *op.cit.*, p. 3.

[60] Wassily W. Leontief, "The Structure of Development," *The Scientific American*, Vol. 209, No. 3, September, 1963, pp. 148–166.

[61] U.S. General Accounting Office, *Glossary for Systems Analysis and Planning-Programming-Budgeting*, Washington, D.C.: U.S. Government Printing Office, 1969, p. 32.

[62] Ben B. Seligman, *op.cit.*, p. 781.

[63] Dorfman, Samuelson, and Solow, *op.cit.*, p. 4.

persuasive case could have been made for placing them in the earlier discussion of engineering that we perceive the extent to which operations research and systems analysis, of which they form the essential core, represent a confluence and convergence of ideas. It is noteworthy that in fields as widely separated as engineering and economics there exists such commonality of tools, a phenomenon which merely underscores the ubiquity and widening reliance on mathematics. In many disciplines, the use of mathematical methods, logic, and symbols exemplifies the zenith of technical advance. This is a manifestation of the prevailing *Zeitgeist*, in which "mathematical precision" is accepted as a term that brooks no internal division — though mathematicians do not profess such faith in the infallibility of their methods. These methods, then, as an intrinsic part of systems analysis and applied by practitioners of widely disparate background to problems of public concern, signify the coincidence of the engineers' desire to apply their tools to peaceful, socially useful pursuits with the behavioral and social scientists' quest for more rigorous techniques.

Practice in the use of mathematical tools has not attained perfection nor even consensus that quantitative approaches have helped adjust the economy, improve public planning at home, or devise a livable strategy abroad. If, in any of these areas, refinements can be claimed, they are largely in the nature of nicer abstraction, always more comfortably remote from concrete reality. The more mathematics has been invoked in a particular problem, the greater the emphasis on technical aspects and the less accessible to scrutiny and understanding by persons outside the fraternal order. Interest has centered on building and rebuilding the toolboxes, described in the virtually incomprehensible language of symbols and formulas.[64] The longer and more widespread the experience with the quantitative approach, the longer grows the list of cautions and caveats.

On this subject, Leontief's views are apropos and telling. In his review of *Perspectives on Economic Growth*,[65] he wrote:

> Construction of abstract "models" intended to describe in mathematical terms the complex interrelationships governing the process of economic growth has become one of the favorite occupations of economic theorists. *Unfortunately, the lack of factual knowledge of conditions existing in the real world forces the model builder to base many if not all of his general conclusions on all kinds of a priori assumptions, chosen for their convenience rather than for their correspondence to observed facts.* (My italics.)

[64] Seligman, *op.cit.*, p. 790.
[65] Wassily Leontief, Review of *Perspectives on Economic Growth*, Walter Heller, editor, New York: Random House, 1968, in *The New York Review*, October 10, 1968, p. 32.

Commenting more recently on the fundamental imbalance of the present state of economics, Leontief scored the emphasis on hypothetical situations rather than with observable reality, with formal mathematical reasoning rating higher among his colleagues and their disciples than empirical analysis. "Uncritical enthusiasm for mathematical formulation tends often to conceal the ephemeral substantive content of the argument behind the formidable front of algebraic signs." [66]

These remarkable criticisms come from Leontief, whose work for many years has been regarded as the crucial link between Walras and modern users of input-output models. The point he makes is reminiscent of the message conveyed in the now classic review of Tinbergen's econometric accomplishments.[67] A commentary on a volume of papers in appreciation of Tinbergen reflects the criticisms: "While some might admire the technical ingenuity and elegance of the contributions, others might reply that if something is not worth doing, it is not worth doing well." [68]

Now, in many milieus, preoccupation with technicalities has been observed to deflect attention from assumptions and issues. Expressing trends and influences in figures tends to introduce a bias in favor of the calculable; that which cannot be weighed or measured is not taken into account. Crucial intangibles are neglected.[69] Concern for purity of model and rules of the game may impose so many constraints that the result is little more than a tautological exercise, satisfying only to the precious. Models which have gained acceptance because they complied with rules and postulates have been shown to have incorporated unsophisticated assumptions and hidden biases. Work on the same problem, with the same tools, can yield a model which is the exact opposite of one in general use.[70] Sober examination of some methodological disagreements now appearing as articles and book reviews in the professional journals causes one to reflect that it may not be an altogether unmixed blessing that the technique still remains to a considerable extent at an abstract level and has not been embraced as the planning tool to quite the total extent recommended by its creators.

The hazards of dependence on this kind of approach to public affairs

[66] Wassily Leontief, "Theoretical Assumptions and Nonobserved Facts," *The American Economic Review*, Vol. LXI, No. 1, March, 1971, pp. 1–2.

[67] J. M. Keynes, "Professor Tinbergen's Method," Review in *The Economic Journal*, Vol. XLIX, No. 195, September, 1939, pp. 558–569.

[68] Paul Streeten, Review of *Towards Balanced International Growth, Essays Presented to J. Tinbergen*, H. C. Bos, ed., Amsterdam and London: North-Holland, 1969, *The Economic Journal*, Vol. LXXX, No. 319, September, 1970, pp. 679–681.

[69] John Brunner, "The New Idolatry," in *Rebirth of Britain*, London: Pan Books, in association with The Institute of Economic Affairs, 1964, p. 38.

[70] Harvey Leibenstein, "Pitfalls in Benefit-Cost Analysis of Birth Prevention," *Population Studies*, Vol. XXIII, No. 2, July, 1969, pp. 161–171.

have been outlined by Don K. Price. His main objection was that they made no allowance for humane sentiments or moral judgments. Kenneth E. Boulding, within the framework of a discussion of the impossibility of applying rational standards to public decision making, articulated the dangers of quantification as the way of assigning a rank order to goals in order to establish priorities.

The quantification of value functions into value indices, whether this is money or whether it is more subtle and complicated measures of pay-off, introduces elements of ethical danger into the decision-making process, *simply because the clarity and apparent objectivity of quantitatively measurable subordinate goals can easily lead to failure to bear in mind that they are in fact subordinate.*[71] (My italics.)

GENERAL SYSTEM THEORY AS SYNERGY

Identification and analysis of the individual pebbles trapped in the puddingstone have provided clues to the intellectual precedents of the systems approach. Through review of them, we have been able to ascertain their status, strengths, and weaknesses within their home disciplines. Brought together, they exemplify Boulding's observation about the ease with which the interdisciplinary deteriorates into the undisciplined.[72] How the synthetic agglomeration has been rationalized into a general theory must properly be considered against this backdrop. Arguments put forward by Ludwig von Bertalanffy, who claims to be among the first to introduce the notion, are based on a number of interrelated and nebulous postulates: a general tendency, in the various sciences, physical and social, toward integration; convergence of this tendency into a general theory of systems; possibility that such theory might be a likely means for approaching exact theory in nonphysical science fields; promise of a unity of science through development of unifying principles running through the individual disciplines.[73] By way of defense for a science of wholeness, he juxtaposes "molecular" against organismic biology, stimulus-response behaviorism against Gestalt psychology, social atoms against social systems. Observation of many phenomena in biology and in the social and behavioral sciences have convinced von Bertalanffy that not only are mathematical expressions and models applicable to them all but that these display remarkable structural similarity and isomorphism. On

[71] Kenneth E. Boulding, "The Ethics of Rational Decision," *Management Science,* Vol. 12, No. 6, February, 1966, p. B-165.
[72] Kenneth E. Boulding, "General Systems Theory — The Skeleton of Science," *Management Science,* Vol. 2, No. 3, April, 1956, pp. 197–209.
[73] Ludwig von Bertalanffy, *General System Theory,* New York: George Braziller, 1968, p. 37.

the argument that probability theory is applicable to such diverse fields as thermodynamics, biological and medical experimentation, and life insurance statistics, von Bertalanffy proposes a logico-mathematical methodology which uses computerization, simulation, and cybernetics. Information theory, theory of automata, games, decisions, and queuing are utilized.

Objections to the approach as perceived or imagined by Bertalanffy are threefold. One, the so-called isomorphisms are said to be nothing more than tired truisms about the universal applicability of mathematics; thus, $2 + 2 = 4$ prevails whether chicks, cheese, soap, or the solar system are under consideration. Two, superficial analogies may mislead, for they camouflage crucial differences and can lead to erroneous conclusions. Three, adherence to an alleged "irreducibility" doctrine renders the approach philosophically and methodologically unsound in that it could impede analytic advances, a dubious loss in Bertalanffy's estimation because they have effected the reduction of chemistry to physical principles and life phenomena to molecular biology. His counter-arguments depend more on iteration than on evidence, however. He is wont to repeat that his isomorphisms are not mere analogy and that his new organismic biology is not a revival of the long-discredited bio-organismic theories of old. Using the current jargon, he claims that his is a new conception of organized complexity, in which the general model, applicable to physiological, neurophysiological, behavioral, and social phenomena, is of the feedback system, elaborated mathematically or as a quantitative scheme, however the case allows.[74]

Bertalanffy has tempered his endorsement of the systems approach by a few thoughtful caveats. He warns against "incautious expansion to fields for which its concepts are not made"; dangers of distortion of reality through "forcible imposition" of mathematical models; detriment to scientific progress of a return to "vague analogies." But the warnings are too general to serve as useful guidelines and too weak to stem the flood of enthusiasm for quantitative methods and the systems approach. By its attribute of being all things to all people, the methodology has provided a vehicle for all who would ride. Perhaps not to so complete a *reductio ad ultimum* as the *Report from Iron Mountain*[75] but far along the road to hastening such negative

[74] Ludwig von Bertalanffy, "General Systems Theory and a New View of the Nature of Man," paper given at American Psychiatric Association Annual Meeting, 1968, pp. 5 and 6.

[75] *Report from Iron Mountain on the Possibility and Desirability of Peace*, with Introductory Material by Leonard C. Lewin, New York: Dial Press, 1967.

utopianism as Huxley's *Brave New World* [76] and Orwell's *1984*, [77] von Bertalanffy saw the system orientation as serving and hastening "the process of mechanization, automation, and devaluation of man." [78]

[76] Aldous Huxley, *Brave New World*, New York: Harper and Brothers, 1946.
[77] George Orwell, *1984*, London: Secker and Warburg, 1949.
[78] Von Bertalanffy, "General Systems Theory and a New View of the Nature of Man," *op.cit.*, p. 5.

[3]

Systems Approach
in Practical Perspective

TACTICAL DEVELOPMENT OF THE TECHNIQUES

Review of the intellectual forebears of the systems approach, though necessary for an understanding of its theoretical antecedents, is not sufficient as an explanation of its growth and development. The account of its practical and tactical history — how it came into being, its use, its transfer from military to civilian affairs, and how it appears in a social setting — is missing.

The systems approach is a lineal descendent of, and shares a common heritage with, operations research. As it relates to the man-machine relationship, the technique dates back to the Industrial Revolution, if not earlier. For military planning specifically, it emerged in its present form during World War II, when the British High Command sought the help of teams of physicists, biologists, mathematicians, and other specialists to devise strategy for incorporating advanced and unconventional equipment into the air defense system. The new weapons and weapons systems, of which radar was an early example, were so radically different in concept from anything previously known that traditional military experience had no relevance. The new methods of operations analysis which were developed formed the core of the technique called "operations analysis" at the time. Subsequently, as it was refined and expanded, it came to be known as, or was almost indistinguishable from, operations research, systems engineering, management science, cost-effective analysis, and systems analysis.[1]

[1] E. S. Quade, "Introduction," *Analysis for Military Decisions, E. S. Quade,* editor, Chicago: Rand McNally, 1967, p. 3.

42

Distinctions among these terms are nebulous and arbitrary, with purpose and context of the analysis indicating more the desiderata than any differences in methods used. E. S. Quade, an authority in the field, provides differentiations which, though not definitive, are at least indicative of the hazy conceptualization in the area where the techniques supposedly achieved their greatest triumph. Quade describes operations research in its narrow sense as analysis to increase efficient functioning of man-machine systems and in its broader view as practically all quantitative analysis. In his exposition, Quade emphasizes the point that the notion of increasing efficiency is practically meaningless when applied to matters concerning national and institutional policy. He regards operations research, systems analysis, and related techniques as tools useful in particular, circumscribed circumstances. For example, he finds "systems design," "systems research," and "systems engineering" generally applied to the performance and implementation of existing or new military or industrial systems. "Management science" pertains to the efficient management and control of existing systems and is most often used interchangeably with "operations research" in a business milieu. "Cost-effectiveness analysis" is the assessment of differences in cost or resource requirements among the various available alternatives for achieving some specified goal.[2] Elsewhere, it has been suggested that systems analysis differs in scope from the other approaches and that its distinctive attributes are a more distant future environment, with greater flexibility of choices; more interdependent variables; greater uncertainties; and less obvious objectives and rules of choice.[3]

These efforts at elucidation, though commendable, are not particularly fruitful. The terms and concepts are used interchangeably by the very experts who have attempted the verbal refinement. Quade, for example, virtually negates the distinctions he has so carefully made when he describes the process by which conceptualization in military usage came about. "It was not the systematic character of these studies but rather the nature of the subjects being investigated that originally suggested the name. The first postwar military studies were primarily concerned with weapon systems." "When used in a military context, the label 'systems analysis' is applied very broadly to any systematic approach to the comparison of alternatives."[4] In the next paragraph, Quade broadens his conception of systems analysis to include the very ideas embodied in and labelled on the previous page of his book as "systems research" and "cost-effectiveness analysis."

[2] *Ibid.*, p. 3.

[3] Albert Wohlstetter, "Scientists, Seers, and Strategy," unpublished paper (Council for Atomic Age Studies), Columbia University, 1962, pp. 36–37.

[4] Quade, *op.cit.*, p. 4.

Systems analysis might be defined as an inquiry to aid a decision-maker choose a course of action by systematically investigating his proper objectives, comparing quantitatively where possible the costs, effectiveness, and risks associated with the alternative policies or strategies for achieving them, *and formulating additional alternatives if those examined are found wanting.*[5]

In these statements a semantic slippage, common to many advocates of the systems approach, emerges. Note the intimation that there is a necessary connection between the systems approach, which is a specific technique, and "any systematic approach." In becoming "systems analysis," the analysis of systems conveys the flavor of being systematic, by some unspecified set of norms. This honorific endowment has carried over into the wider use of systems analysis and, in fact, serves as one of its major selling points. Another has been its military record. Through its link with operational research, the systems approach gains credit for having ordered the exploitation of radar and other weapons systems when traditional combat experience proved inadequate. Not only did it help save Britain from German air attacks but it aided in plotting strategy on and under the seas. Thus, the parlor game of war became institutionalized and dignified to a technique of staggering proportions.

Its methodology included mathematical models of conflict (of which the Monte Carlo is perhaps best known); logistic simulations (of which SAMSON, or Support-Availability Multi-System Operations Model, is often cited as an example); probability, risk, and uncertainty theory (sometimes using the Delphi technique, frequently used in political analyses, and generally depending on cost-effectiveness analyses); and tactical war gaming, based mainly on the RAND Corporation's Strategic Operations Model (STRAW, for Strategic War Games; SAFE for Strategy-and-Force-Evaluation; CWO, for Cold War Games; and MAGIC, for Manual Assisted Gaming of Integrated Combat). From these exercises came a cornucopia of procedures, concepts, and methods. Trade-off and cost-effectiveness (or cost-benefit analysis), planning-programming-budgeting, Monte Carlo models, and scenario construction became part of the language and literature, not solely in military planning but in ever widening areas of public affairs.

When first applied in Washington, this arsenal of sophisticated tools became a potent weapon against prevailing defense management styles. Inadequacy of military experience as a guide to the development of and protection against radically changing weapons systems was the entering wedge for reorganization and realignment of the decision-making structure. In addition, there was always an ample supply of

[5] *Ibid.*, p. 4.

damning evidence of "profligate waste" and "inept managerial practices" to convince the White House, Congress, and the public that sweeping reform was in order. A new philosophy retired the war lords and elevated the management scientists. With war and defense regarded as business too big to be left to the generals and admirals, the problem of national security was, in theory, construed as "one big economic problem," with strategy and cost seen "as interdependent as the front and rear sights of a rifle." [6] The argument that what was needed in the defense establishment was efficiency of management was persuasive, and the rapidly mushrooming syndrome of efficiency soon embraced not only strategic and tactical matters in the field but procurement, policy, and political matters at home and abroad.

To expedite and implement the reformation, President Kennedy in 1961 appointed as Secretary of Defense Robert S. McNamara, former president of the Ford Motor Company. Generally acclaimed as a genius in industrial management himself, McNamara placed in key positions a number of former RAND economists,[7] with Charles J. Hitch as Assistant Secretary of Defense (Comptroller). The program format they devised became the Five-Year Force Structure and Financial Program, a set of tables once called "the Secretary's Book," that in all important aspects controlled the defense program.[8] Military planning and budgeting, previously handled as independent activities by the Joint Chiefs of Staff and the civilian Comptroller, respectively, were now consolidated under one authority. In place of the accustomed projections for troop strength and weaponry for several years and line-item budgeting for one year at a time, Secretary of Defense McNamara instituted "program packages," which grouped all function-related budget items, from the research and development stage to operational activities and procurement.

The new approach to fiscal management was defended loyally by its Department of Defense practitioners in congressional hearings, frozen into college textbooks and curricula, and reported in the form of "appreciations" [9] by some of its designers. The catechism was simple but

[6] Charles J. Hitch and Roland N. McKean, *The Economics of Defense in the Nuclear Age*, Cambridge: Harvard University Press, 1961, p. 3.

[7] Bruce L. R. Smith, *The RAND Corporation: Case Study of a Nonprofit Advisory Corporation*, Cambridge: Harvard University Press, 1966.

[8] William A. Niskanen, "The Defense Resource Allocation Process," pp. 3–23, in *Defense Management*, Stephen Enke, ed., Englewood Cliffs, New Jersey: Prentice-Hall, 1967, p. 18.

[9] Charles J. Hitch, "An Appreciation of Systems Analysis," paper read at meeting of Operations Research Society of America, Los Angeles, California, August 15, 1955; and E. S. Quade, ed., *An Appreciation of Analysis for Military Decisions*, Chicago: Rand McNally, 1966.

strong. The system would force the military to identify and justify its objectives; indicate various alternatives for achieving them; compute the cost and effectiveness of every alternative; and provide greater certainty as to scope, objectives, technical characteristics, management arrangements, and probable costs through research and development (R&D) programing in instances where unknowns or new technology were involved. An otherwise critical observer of bureaucracy praised the procedure on the ground that, by avoiding "concealed, parochial, and *de facto* decisions in the lower echelons, and misdirected control by arbitrary budget ceilings," it "boils out real policy choices and exposes them to top-level decision" and thus "gives military expertise and judgment sharper focus and greater pertinence." "By phasing the level of commitment from low-budget, widely diversified preliminary and program definition studies, the government can contain the blind tendencies of a runaway technology fueled by service rivalries and by the Contract State. It can retain flexibility and choice at every point of the process at lowest possible cost." [10]

As proof positive that scientific management of the fiscal side of the military establishment was good strategy, Charles J. Hitch cited the USSR's translation of his *Economics of Defense in the Nuclear Age* [11] into Russian. [12] Rare indeed amidst the paeans of praise for the techniques was even the suggestion that scientific management as applied in Department of Defense affairs might not quite live up to expectation. A former RAND economist and Director of Special Studies in the Office of the Secretary of Defense voiced some doubt which could have been construed as prophetic if it had not passed unheeded. He acknowledged the value of the Department of Defense programming system as an effective instrument for program control but questioned whether it could serve as an effective instrument of program change. Test of this could come, he felt, only by subjection to a period of external pressure like the Vietnam War. [13] Subsequent events having to do with military strategy in Vietnam and Pentagon practices at home indicate that scientific management had still to prove itself.

Long before proof, or even adequate trial, could establish the validity of the military as model for further and wider application, the technique in its various forms became rigidified and entrenched as required

---

[10] H. L. Nieburg, *In the Name of Science*, Chicago: Quadrangle Books, 1966, pp. 358 and 359.

[11] Hitch, *op. cit.*

[12] Charles J. Hitch, *Decision-Making for Defense*, Berkeley and Los Angeles: University of California Press, 1965, p. 46.

[13] William A. Niskanen, *op.cit.*, p. 10.

procedure in agencies at all levels of government. It rationalized and became the staff of life of new bureaucratic structures; it acquired a constituency of and advocacy by professionals of all stripe. It attracted and commanded huge expenditures of public funds; and it gave further impetus to already flourishing government-by-contract activities. Above all, it deeply implanted the notion that what government affairs needed was better management, and the more "scientific," the better, at that. So great has been the persuasion inherited from the military, that the techniques spawned in the Pentagon by RAND economists became transferred to the war on poverty and to many other battles on the home front through the subsequent movement, in the perpetual Washington game of musical high-chairs, of the former Department of Defense Whiz Kids into civilian agencies. Now similarly rationalized as economic matters because they, too, require allocation and use of resources, non-military affairs of all kinds became the target for the "powerful tools of technology." Cost-effectiveness, program budgeting, elaborate software for the gathering, processing, and manipulating of information, and systems studies traveled into the civilian arena under the systematic banner and on the seldom articulated but pervasive notion that, in order to function well, the body politic, social, or economic needed only better management. The systems way was the way to run the business of government and the logic was clear: big government is big business. Big business owes its success to efficient operation through scientific management. Ergo, the government has only to apply the principles of scientific management as practiced in the military and its problems will be solved.

The Pentagon as Paragon

The military cannot be offered as a model for emulation by civilian planners, however, without attention to two important considerations: the peculiar bureaucratic, political, and social environment in which defense budget decisions are made; and the validity of the success story of Pentagon management practices on their own home territory. The former should serve to demonstrate that the constraints and conditions surrounding military decision-making differ in many important respects from those prevailing in other departments and agencies of government. The latter will anticipate and refute the frequently iterated claim that the systems approach worked wonders in the military and that if it proved less satisfactory in other areas, the fault lay with improper, inept use; that the theory is excellent, but that its applications were poor. What is always lacking in these arguments is the recognition that what is at issue is not the *theory*. That, we learned in an earlier chapter, is a heterogeneous hodgepodge that can claim little scientific purity anyway. Systems analysis has been touted as a *technique*, a method of procedure, of getting a job done, and it is on this ground that it must be assessed and evaluated.

As for the conditions under which budgetary decisions for the military are made, it must be noted that the structural and political environment of defense allocations has been, even within the framework of government decision-making, unique unto itself. Some important differences between the Department of Defense and other departments have been sketched as follows: The Department of Defense has traditionally enjoyed a greater degree of autonomy and freedom from congressional control than other agencies or branches of government. Its "products," in the way of services to the community, are, despite their high cost, low on the priority list of the electorate, as evidenced by political campaign issues and voter behavior. Little mention is made of multi-billion-dollar weapons systems whereas issues like funds for a medical program or a sewer system capture headlines. Most important allocative decisions in the military are based on guidelines generated internally and with little reference to other agencies or departments. Consequently, the Department of Defense, in contrast to other sectors of government, has provided "an abnormally easy place" to apply the techniques of program budgeting, cost-effectiveness analysis, and systems analysis.[14] Three additional facets of the environment in which defense budget allocations are made need mention in this context: size, secrecy, and stereotypes. And they are thoroughly intertwined and interrelated. (1) No other government agency in history has ever commanded an expense account of such magnitude. In the face of an 80-billion-dollar budget, the questioning of million- and even hundred-million-dollar expenditures, even though equivalent to the total expenditures of a smaller state, department, or country, is made to seem paltry. (2) Inquiry into military affairs has been discouraged if not deterred by restricted access. Strategic use of the term *classified* has protected many transactions from scrutiny. (3) The prevalence of stereotypes, that the military can do no wrong, what is good for the Department of Defense is good for the country, and that criticism of military matters is unpatriotic, have made the military planners practically immune from the attacks to which other officials are regularly exposed. In the face of increasing complexity and horrendous destructive capability of weaponry systems, there has been a growing faith that science and

---

[14] James R. Schlesinger, *Systems Analysis and the Political Process*, Santa Monica: RAND Corporation, P-3464, June, 1967, pp. 14–17.

sophistication, felicitously wedded in the "Academic Strategists," would save us, if not all humanity.[15]

The U.S. defense complex, an awesome institution, is the ultimate expression of national policy. Its objectives are almost automatically translated into national priorities and determine the relative weights of all other endeavors. It is vital, therefore, that we understand the bases on which decisions are made. The rationale for spending billions of dollars comes mainly from system analyses, cost-effectiveness ratios, and scenarios of "experts" whose decisions about defense and security have only recently come under public scrutiny through congressional hearings. Through Senate and House investigations, the interaction between these decisions and the dynamics of the arms race as a whole has become clear. Because of an expected action-reaction phenomenon (see Fig. 3), even though stimulated in large part by uncertainty about the adversary's capabilities and intentions, there has been enormous proliferation of nuclear missile defense systems, and each development, taken as an entity in itself, has been rationalized and made to seem "cost-effective," if not in monetary terms, at least in terms of "overkill." In every decision, the scenarios of RAND and similar experts justified the objectives; the costs, whether in dollars or human lives, were estimated on a speculative, arbitrary basis. Thanks to war games played and won on the blackboards of these experts, the United States, in fiscal year 1970, allocated 7,599.7 million dollars (see Table 3 — Final Fiscal) to the technical means of assuming successful defense or offense, whatever the simulation called for. And, in the case of either, the result has been the same — a rapidly escalating arms race and an ever more precarious balance of terror. According to the calculated risks plotted by analysts in well-insulated think tanks, these were the decisions to take, or, put in their parlance, this was "the way to go."

The red herring of tactical supremacy through sophisticated concepts of weaponry has satisfied the economic rationale of the Department of Defense but has diverted attention from the steady advances in the techniques of chemical and biological warfare. In the discussion about the relative merits of the Sentinel anti-ballistic missile system, as a safeguard against Red China as compared to the Safeguard missile system as a means of making the U.S. threat more credible to potential enemies,[16] the ongoing developments in chemical and biological warfare are almost forgotten. Gases to paralyze the nervous system, incapacitating agents to block normal sensory and thought processes,

[15] Philip Green, *Deadly Logic, The Theory of Nuclear Deterrence*, Columbus: Ohio State University Press, 1966.

[16] American Enterprise Institute for Public Policy Research, *The Safeguard ABM System*, Special Analysis No. 9, Ninety-first Congress, First Session, June 2, 1969.

FIGURE 3. Expected Action-Reaction Phenomenon

U.S. FATALITIES in a variety of hypothetical nuclear exchanges in the mid-1970's are rounded off to the nearest five million in this bar chart. U.S.S.R. force I is basically an extrapolation of current Russian forces reflecting some future growth in both offensive and defensive capability; force II assumes a major Russian response to our deployment of an ABM system. Two of the four U.S. damage-limiting programs, pos- tures A and B, are tailored against U.S.S.R. force I; the other two, postures C and D, are tailored against U.S.S.R. force II. The chart illustrates the basic incompatibility between a policy of attempting to minimize the consequences of nuclear war and a policy of attempting to minimize the probability of nuclear war. If war seemed imminent, with the strategic balances as hypothesized in this chart, there would be tremendous pressure on both sides to strike first, and as a result of this added incentive the chances of escalation would be enhanced. The chart is based on information contained in former Secretary McNamara's posture statement for fiscal 1967.

TABLE 3
Final Appropriations for Major Weapon Systems for 1970

Contractor or Systems Manager	Weapon	Funding (Millions)	Remarks
Army	Safeguard anti-ballistic missile system	$786.3	Includes $400.9 million for research & development; $76.6 million for McDonnell Douglas Spartan and $26.5 million for Martin Sprint missiles.
Air Force	Minuteman 2/3	718.0	Includes $75 million for research & development.
Air Force	Manned Orbiting Laboratory	125.3	Termination and closedown.
Navy	Shrike	16.6	Includes $9.5 million for Navy and $7.1 million for Air Force missiles.
Navy	Sidewinder 1C	32.0	Procurement.
Navy	Condor	8.0	Research & development.
Navy	Underwater-launched missile system	10.0	Research & development.
Lockheed	Poseidon	846.2	Includes $354.7 million for four Polaris submarine conversions.
Lockheed	C-5A	872.6	Includes $225 million for prior-year overruns; $132.4 million for spares and repair parts, and $34.2 million for research and development.
Lockheed	P-3C	220.6	Procure 23 aircraft; total includes $22.1 million Fiscal 1969 carryover.

TABLE 3 — Continued

Contractor or Systems Manager	Weapon	Funding (Millions)	Remarks
Lockheed	Polaris A-3	26.4	Components, support and reliability maintenance only.
Lockheed	C-130E	51.7	Procure 18 aircraft.
Lockheed	SR-71	3.0	Research & development.
General Dynamics	F-111D/F	817.2	Includes $73.7 million for research & development, $71.4 million prior-year overruns, $70 million for spares and $56 million for long-lead items to support planned Fiscal '71 funding; procurement level is eight F-111D and 60 F-111F.
General Dynamics	FB-111	40.0	Procurement.
General Dynamics	Redeye	22.9	Procurement.
General Dynamics	Standard ARM Missile	4.0	Research & development.
General Dynamics	Standard RIM Missile	67.7	Includes $32.1 million for RIM-67A procurement; $25.6 million for RIM-66A procurement, and $10 million research.
Grumman	F-14A	441.5	Includes research and development, procurement of nine R&D aircraft.
Grumman	A-6A	860.0	Includes $19.5 million for modification to KA-6D and KA-6D spares and $4 million Fiscal 1969 carryover.

TABLE 3 — Continued

Contractor or Systems Manager	Weapon	Funding (Millions)	Remarks
Grumman	EA-6B	200.3	Procure 12 aircraft; total includes $19.7 million Fiscal 1969 carryover.
Grumman	C-2A	36.8	Procure eight aircraft.
Grumman	OV-1C	5.3	Ground avionics support equipment.
McDonnell Douglas	F-15	175.1	Research & development.
McDonnell Douglas	F-4	187.4	Includes $25.7 million for F-4E and $5.9 million for RF-4C long-lead items to support planned Fiscal 1971 procurement; $155.8 million for 34 F-4Js.
McDonnell Douglas	Nike-Hercules	19.6	Modifications only.
McDonnell Douglas	A-4M	68.6	Procure 49 aircraft.
McDonnell Douglas	TA-4J	96.4	Procure 75 aircraft; includes $6.6 million Fiscal 1969 carryover and $2.9 million long-lead items to support planned Fiscal '71 procurement.
Ling-Temco-Vought	A-7E	113.1	Procure 27 aircraft; includes $9.1 million Fiscal 1969 carryover and $4.4 million long-lead items for planned Fiscal 1971 procurement.
Ling-Temco-Vought	A-7D	399.8	Procure 128 aircraft; includes $25.9 million Fiscal 1969

TABLE 3 — Continued

Contractor or Systems Manager	Weapon	Funding (Millions)	Remarks
			carryover and $26.5 million long-lead items for planned Fiscal 1971 procurement.
Bell Helicopter	AH-1G	86.0	Procure 170 helicopters.
Bell Helicopter	UH-1H	102.9	Includes 175 helicopters for Air Force and 160 for Army.
Bell Helicopter	OH-58A	68.4	Procure 600 helicopters.
Bell Helicopter	UH-1N	34.1	Procure 62 helicopters.
Boeing Vertol	CH-47C	56.3	Procure 36 helicopters.
Boeing Vertol	CH-46E/F	30.3	Procure 34 helicopters. Includes $5 million Fiscal 1969 carryover.
Boeing	SRAM	85.1	Research & development funding is $75.1 million.
Sikorsky	CH-54A	13.0	Procure six helicopters.
Sikorsky	CH-53C	18.4	Procure eight helicopters.
Philco-Ford	Chaparral	86.0	Missile procurement.
Philco-Ford	Shillelagh	50.5	Missile procurement.
Raytheon	Hawk	75.3	Missile procurement.
Raytheon	Sparrow-3	73.3	Includes $41.7 million for Air Force and $31.6 million for Navy missiles.
Hughes Tool Co.	TOW	100.0	Missile procurement.
Hughes Tool Co.	Maverick	39.6	Missile procurement.
North American Rockwell	RA-5C	15.3	For special support equipment.
North American Rockwell	T-2C	16.5	Procure 24 aircraft.

TABLE 3 — Continued

Contractor or Systems Manager	Weapon	Funding (Millions)	Remarks
Northrop	T-38A	36.6	Procure 38 trainers.
Northrop	F-5A	11.2	Procure 10 aircraft.
Cessna	O-2A	3.6	Procure 34 aircraft. Includes $1 million Fiscal 1969 carryover.
Cessna	A-37B	16.0	Procure 36 aircraft.
Beech	U-21	15.0	Includes $7.5 million for 22 U-21A aircraft and $7.5 million for seven RU-21s.
Goodyear	Subroc	25.6	Missile procurement.
Hawker-Siddeley	AV-6B	42.3	Procure 12 VTOL fighters.

SOURCE: *Aviation Week & Space Technology*, January 5, 1970, p. 25.

harassing chemicals to control or kill, and the modern counterpart of age-old scorched earth methods — defoliants and herbicides — contribute to a growing arsenal of chemical agents. Biological agents, lethal or debilitating, are being developed in cooperation with friendly and erstwhile hostile nations alike. Britain, Sweden, Japan, and West Germany have been reported to have conducted some form of research in biological warfare for the U.S. Army.[17] The effort, referred to as "public health in reverse," has been directed to explore a number of bacterial and viral diseases as potential enemy-destroyers. Their list includes: anthrax, brucellosis, encephalomyelitis, plague, psittacosis, q-fever, Rift Valley fever, Rocky Mountain spotted fever, and tularemia.[18] After sober review of the history of modern warfare, one wonders not so much that these dread weapons have been and are being conceived by humans for use against humans but that, in this day of the strategy seminar, they have not been developed and deployed more assiduously. With Mother Nature working to insure cheap and easy production, technology to assure supersonic delivery,[19] and the

[17] Seymour M. Hersh, *Chemical and Biological Warfare*, Garden City, New York: Doubleday, 1969, p. 234.

[18] *Ibid.*, pp. xi and xii.

[19] Litton Industries, Inc., Applied Science Division, for example, has worked on the design and fabrication of a self-contained, externally-mounted tank, suitable for attachment to the F100, F105 and F4C, as a dispenser unit for dry biologicals, according to documented reports by Hersh, *op.cit.*, pp. 69–70.

techniques of systems analysis to provide them with justification as the most cost-effective, most rational method of disposing of an enemy, one wonders why the Department of Defense has persisted in making such a case for what appears to be, by comparison, the modest potential of anti-ballistic-missile (ABM) and multiple-independently-targeted-reentry-vehicle (MIRV) concepts. Not surprising, but nevertheless unnerving, is the realization not only that the more horrendous methods are not yet being fully exploited but that it is the *technological* approach to national security that has been deliberately and rationally chosen. The model devised by the Department of Defense experts has created in the minds of the bemused public the myth that there are technological solutions, even though the problems may be essentially political, economic, or social.

In their approach to national security, military analysts first scan the horizons of time and space for threats. Quick to acknowledge that uncertainties in the world complicate the decision-making process, they plot their responses in terms of military strategy. In fact, their very mission precludes any other kind of approach.[20] When the Department of Defense engages in intelligence gathering about troop build-ups, nuclear sophistication, and *Wehrmacht* capability abroad, contentment reigns at home. When Congress and the public uncover evidence of Department-of-Defense-sponsored research into the social, economic, and political conditions of a particular country, even though these circumstances might have important bearing on the military posture of its government, pandemonium reigns. This situation is cited not as an argument in favor of having the Department of Defense conduct non-military research but rather as an illustration of the institutionally circumscribed uni-dimensional world of the military analyst. According to a RAND analyst, experts' estimates of "probabilities pertaining to various states of the world" [21] are the proper desiderata for choice of force structure and strategy. If the "probabilities" are construed to be hostile and violent, then, by application of the principles of "behavioral cybernetics," the "deterrence theory," [22] with all its ramifications and repercussions, becomes inevitable. A defensive posture toward the world and a foreign policy designed primarily as protection from potential attack guarantees perpetuation of a syndrome that virtually excludes serious consideration of social, economic, and politi-

[20] Melvin R. Laird, "Toward a Strategy of Realistic Deterrence," *Defense Industry Bulletin*, Vol. 7, No. 2, Spring, 1971, pp. 3 ff.

[21] James R. Schlesinger, "The Changing Environment for Systems Analysis," in Stephen Enke, ed., *Defense Management*, Englewood Cliffs, New Jersey: Prentice-Hall, 1967, p. 110.

[22] Philip Green, *op.cit.*, p. 242.

cal avenues through which to achieve long range and longer lasting international relationships. Military analysts, by definition and by direction, follow the warpath and their techniques reinforce their closed-loop version of events now and in the future.

A favorite device by which the military analyst reaches his conception of the world is through creation of a scenario. The scenario, as its name implies, is a sketch of the make-believe. The term, perhaps regrettably borrowed from Hollywood, has as many definitions as it has experts and champions. It is the logical extreme of a series of trend projections, the result of extrapolations made from conjectural answers to *what if* questions about the state of the world. A sequence of speculative outcomes to hypothetical queries, the scenario is intended to describe the various possible conditions under which the system being studied may be assumed to operate at the present or some future date. Resort to such techniques is necessary and desirable, we are assured, because in the military, planners require, at some stage of their work, "pictures, imaginings, fictions, if you will, of the circumstances under which the military systems they are concerned with will have to operate."[23] This is the scenario, the tale spun by the military analyst. It may be full of fury, with strategic nuclear war spreading destruction and destroying neatly calculated portions of the human population; it may reflect only the scenario writer's strange love of horror stories. It may signify nothing so far as a sound basis for military planning is concerned. But persuasive it is, for it has been arrived at through "systematic solicitation of expert opinions," *expert* here being the honorific term bestowed on all who would play the particular war game.[24]

A prime example of the scenario at work is the current controversy over the development and deployment of offensive and defensive nuclear weapons. Scenarios produced by experts make a case for or against anti-ballistic-missile systems and thus convey the impression that herein lies the answer to national security. At the very time that public attention is being attracted by authoritative sounding but entirely conjectural debate on the USSR's *first strike capacity* as compared with our *assured destruction* capability, scientists on both sides of the Iron Curtain and in between are busily engaged in the pursuit of chemical and biological agents against which Minuteman, Safeguard, Sentinel, and other such systems could not offer even the *short safe periods* calculated by the war game strategists. Moreover, even if the scenarios were to take into account the possibility of nerve gas, anthrax, and the like as

---

[23] Seyom Brown, "Schenarios in Systems Analyses," in *Systems Analysis and Policy Planning*, Quade and Boucher, eds., *op. cit.*, p. 299.

[24] Olaf Helmer, *Social Technology*, New York: Basic Books, 1966, p. 48.

the coming generation of agents of war, they would still represent a disservice to a country concerned with dealing with the problem of national security in a rational manner. Concentration on the military and technical aspects carries the built-in assumption of the feasibility of a purely technological approach. More perfect command and control, more or less overkill through multiple independently targeted reentry vehicles — these are made to appear as the central issues, when, in reality, the problem of national security may be largely political. The defense hardware focus of military-oriented technicians diverts resources, intellectual and financial, from the basic issues, which are economic and political and on a worldwide scale.

Nonetheless, despite their obvious shortcomings, some scenarios exude such an aura of authenticity that, at one time called "sophisticated analyses of potential political-military conflicts" and contingencies, several were presented to a congressional investigating committee [25] by the then Secretary of Defense Robert S. McNamara as the basis for planning troop strength. Interesting to note in this instance was the lack of clarification as to whether the Secretary derived the force requirements from an "ideal" or a "real process" at that! [26]

The gap between the simulated and the real may yet be learned through bitter experience in Vietnam and Cambodia, where an irrational enemy that plays by its own rules has so far displayed remarkable resilience against exposure to America's advanced technology and strategy. Short of eradicating him from the face of his own map by the use of readily available technological means, as some military advisers and politicians have urged, there appears to be little hope of total victory. The claims made for villages pacified here, enemy sanctuaries captured there, and supply trails bombed everywhere only reinforce the credibility trap designed for the gullible at home. They have little effect on the recalcitrant nations or on the course of the war. New scenarios will have to be written, but not by the old authors. And to the surprise of no one, dissatisfaction with present Southeast Asia policy has taken the form of a strengthening by the Nixon Administration of the role of military officers, as against civilian personnel, in the planning and execution of even economic and social programs in Laos and South Vietnam. While the contemplated shift was, in many important respects, a transfer of authority within Congress, from the Foreign Relations to the Armed Services Committee, the implication was clear. The move reflected an internal reorganization within the

[25] Subcommittee on Department of Defense Appropriations, Committee on Appropriations, House of Representatives, *Department of Defense Appropriations for 1965*, February 17, 1964, pp. 304–305.
[26] Seyom Brown, *op.cit.*, p. 298.

Defense Department, with Army men retrieving some of their pre-empted, pre-McNamara power.

The successes of systems analysis as a method for achieving peace and security seem to be purely fictitious. The scenarios, designed by blackboard warriors turned expert, are logical extrapolations from poorly conceived premises. The rationale by which important programs have been justified differ hardly at all from the *reductio ad horrendum* of the *Report from Iron Mountain*, which, in the name of sweet reason, offers the following conclusions:

It is uncertain, at this time, whether peace will ever be possible. It is far more questionable, by the objective standard of continued social survival rather than that of emotional pacifism, that it would be desirable even if it were demonstrably attainable. The war system, for all its subjective repugnance to important sections of "public opinion," has demonstrated its effectiveness since the beginning of recorded history; it has provided the basis for development of many impressively durable civilizations, including that which is dominant today. It has consistently provided unambiguous social priorities. It is, on the whole, a known quantity.[27]

Because of the chameleon-like attributes that render the systems approach all things to all people and, therefore, impervious to criticism on any specific count, failings and shortcomings such as those noted have not seriously impaired the prestigious image of the technique as high-level management science at work. Far from becoming a casualty in the shift from a Democratic to a Republican high command in Washington in 1968, systems analysis, cost-effective ratios, and program budgeting have remained deeply entrenched. Although, consistent with tradition, the Nixon Administration rode into office and continued to make much political mileage on the failings, follies, and foibles of its predecessor, some of the earlier innovations, particularly the systems approach, survived. The Secretary of Defense, Melvin R. Laird, singled it out for praise.

[Systems analysis, or program review] is a very important tool within the Defense Department for helping David Packard (the Deputy Secretary) and me to make hard choices in acquiring weapons and establishing force goals. There has been criticism of this function, or of its misuse in the past. Some of the criticism has been justified. In my view, however, *systems analysis, when properly used, is an essential management tool.* There are no absolute answers to the kinds of questions we face in Defense Department decision-making. *Systems analysis, properly used, elevates the level of judgment and helps decision makers to sort out fact and opinion.*[28] (My italics.)

[27] *Report from Iron Mountain on the Possibility and Desirability of Peace*, with Introductory Material by Leonard C. Lewin, New York: Dial Press, 1967, pp. 89–90.
[28] Summary of Statement by Secretary Melvin R. Laird on Fiscal Year (FY) 1971

The notion of systems analysis as an efficient management tool, once endemic to the Department of Defense, spread in various forms into all branches and permeated all layers of government, down to the least township. Most interesting in this phenomenon is the eager acceptance of scientific management concepts as developed in the military as a model for emulation without critical examination of their performance on their own proving ground. This brings us to the second point made in the introduction of this section, namely, the successes of Pentagon management practices within their own bailiwick.

In actuality, contrary to and negating claims to efficiency of procedure and operation, the Department of Defense has been proven guilty of so much mismanagement that *inefficiency* is now said to be one of its hallmarks [29] and, worse still, *scientific management* has been the device used to rationalize and camouflage the abuses. Investigations by the General Accounting Office and various House and Senate committees provide so extensive a bill of documented particulars, of waste running to billions of dollars, of slipshod procurement practices, of elusive and imprecise accounting procedures (for all the 2,897 computers used by the Department of Defense for other than specific weapons systems [30]), that the Department stands out, not as exemplar, but as a horrible example of management practices. In a congressional report, "extensive and pervasive economic inefficiency and waste" were directly attributed to the Department's "practices and circumstances." [31] Specifically cited were the absence of effective inventory controls and management practices over government-owned property; billions of dollars spent on weapons systems that had to be abandoned because they performed below contract specifications or not at all; actual costs of extremely expensive programs exceeding estimated costs by several hundred percent; negotiated, instead of competitive, contract procedures, permitting egregiously high prices to begin with, while "most procurement dollars are spent in the environment of negotiation." [32]

Defense Program and Budget, delivered on February 20, 1970 to a joint session of the Senate Armed Services Committee and the Senate Subcommittee on Department of Defense Appropriations, as reported in *Defense Industry Bulletin*, Vol. 6, No. 4, April, 1970, p. 6.

[29] Senator William Proxmire, Letter of Transmittal, *The Economics of Military Procurement*, Report of the Subcommittee on Economy in Government of the Joint Economic Committee, Congress of the United States, Washington, D.C.: U.S. Government Printing Office, May, 1969, p. v.

[30] Lee Metcalf (Senator from Montana), "The Computer Age is Dawning on Capitol Hill," *Congressional Record*, June 11, 1970, p. E5464.

[31] *The Economics of Military Procurement*, Report of the Subcommittee on Economy in Government of the Joint Economic Committee, Congress of the United States, Washington, D.C.: U.S. Government Printing Office, May, 1969, p. 3.

[32] *Ibid.*, p. 3.

Charged with the responsibility for obtaining the best military equipment and supplies at the least possible price, or, in the parlance of cost-effectiveness analysts, "getting the biggest bang for the buck," the Department of Defense has been severely criticized, its budget deemed "bloated and inflated far beyond what an *economy minded and efficient* Department of Defense could and should attain." [33] (My italics.) "Loose and flagrantly negligent" were the terms applied to management practices related to government-owned property and working capital supplied to defense contractors. With a disproportionate amount of the $13.3 billion worth of money and equipment held by the larger contractors, Congressmen saw evidence of the forces that have helped weld the military-industrial complex into what has been called a semi-independent corporate state.[34]

Another is the system of progress payments, which reimburse contractors for up to 90 percent of incurred cost. Not dependent on progress, in the sense of work completed, costs often exceed original estimates; a contractor can collect 75 percent of the contract price without having completed half the job. Moreover, by receiving the payments interest-free, the contractor can operate on capital supplied by the U.S. government and thus enjoy a tremendous advantage over potential competitors. In effect, the procedures are really no-interest loans which encourage the favored contractors to submit unrealistically low bids which further entrench their economic position and power. These practices have contributed to some of the most flagrant examples of cost overruns ever reported in industry history.

The following table indicates cost growth of weapon systems now underway; the figures, gathered by Defense Secretary Melvin R. Laird in response to specific requests by the House Appropriations and the Senate Armed Services Committees, are neither complete nor entirely accurate, various discrepancies having appeared between the tabulations. For example, the Lockheed AH-56A armed helicopter system, at $203.9 million, an increase of $125.9 million over the original estimate, did not appear at all, because the figures were under litigation.

There are documented cost overruns in naval procurement, as for example a 25.6 percent increase over the original $427.5 million for a nuclear-powered carrier, a 60.6 percent increase over the $1.1 billion for a destroyer, and a rise of 40.7 percent for a Navy landing helicopter ship which was approved at $957 million. But none is so spectacular as the C-5A, notable here not only for the $2 billion increase in cost but even more because it was selected as the first application of

[33] *Ibid.*, p. 4.
[34] Seymour Melman, *Pentagon Capitalism*, New York: McGraw-Hill, 1970.

TABLE 4
The Defense Program: Financial Summary by Fiscal Year
In Billions of Dollars

	Fiscal year '62 original	Fiscal year '62 final	Fiscal year '63	Fiscal year '64	Fiscal year '65	Fiscal year '66 proposed
Strategic forces						
Offense	7.6	9.0	8.4	7.3	5.3	4.5
Air and missile defense	2.2	2.0	1.9	2.0	1.7	1.6
Civil defense		0.3	0.1	0.1	0.1	0.2
TOTAL	9.8	11.3	10.4	9.4	7.1	6.3
Tactical forces						
General purpose	14.5	17.4	17.6	17.7	18.1	19.0
Airlift and sealift	.9	1.2	1.4	1.3	1.5	1.6
Reserves	1.7	1.8	1.8	2.0	2.1	2.0
Military assistance	1.8	1.8	1.6	1.2	1.2	1.3
TOTAL	18.9	22.2	22.4	22.2	22.9	23.9
Support activities						
General support	11.4	12.1	13.0	13.7	14.3	14.6
Research and development	3.9	4.2	5.1	5.3	5.1	5.4
Retired pay	0.9	0.9	1.0	1.2	1.4	1.5
TOTAL	16.2	17.2	19.1	20.2	20.8	21.5
Total Obligation Authority	44.9	50.7	51.9	51.8	50.8	51.7

SOURCE: Adapted from William A. Niskanen, "The Defense Resource Allocation Process" in *Defense Management*, Stephen Enke, ed., Englewood Cliffs, New Jersey: Prentice-Hall, 1967, p. 8.

the total package procurement concept (TPPC). On September 30, 1965, the U.S. Air Force selected Lockheed Aircraft Corporation as the airframe prime contractor for 120 C-5A airplanes to cost $3.4 billion. In November, 1968, testimony received during congressional hearings revealed that actual costs would total $5.3 billion.[35] This was the manifestation of advanced management that was specifically designed to serve as a deterrent to cost overruns and below-specification performance.

Justifying the huge increase, the Air Force attributed the cost growth to normal development problems associated with "complex weapons and inflation." But the congressional committee rejected this claim on the ground that the C-5A had been deliberately selected for the first application of the total package procurement concept because it was *not* a highly complex weapon system requiring technological advances beyond the state-of-the-art, and future inflation for at least three years had already been included in the negotiated price and could not legitimately be added again. Testimony also revealed a repricing formula, built into the contract and described by the subcommittee as "one of the most blatant reverse incentives ever encountered." Contrary to a claim made in the Air Force Manual on the total program procurement concept that the procedures would insure economy,[36] the facts showed inflated cost at every unit in the production of the C-5A, with a virtual guarantee to the contractor for payment of excess costs.[37] Lack of sufficient control in crucial stages of the development process of the C-5A was attributed, in a subsequent review by a panel of experts, to the total procurement package plan. In a complete reversal of opinion about what had previously been hailed as advanced management at its best, the present Secretary of the Air Force, Robert C. Seamans, Jr., called it the wrong way to buy new military equipment.

Rarely weighed in the balance of wrong or right, the ready-to-use methodology of the total approach is undeniably handy. Cost-effectiveness has had to demonstrate neither reduced governmental expense nor enhanced performance; it still is highly regarded as the way to arrive at decisions; the total package concept, despite conspicuous failure, has gained widespread acceptance in the guise of planning-programming-budgeting; systems analysis has become the "rational" and "scientific" way to approach all manner of problems, public or private. The military, having gone into successful business by itself, whether associated with the industrial complex or in the form of the state capitalism described by Melman,[38] still serves as a persuasive model.

[35] *The Economics of Military Procurement, op.cit.*, p. 18.
[36] May 10, 1966.
[37] *The Economics of Military Procurement, op.cit.*, pp. 20–21.
[38] Melman, *Pentagon Capitalism, op.cit.*

DEPLOYMENT OF THE TECHNIQUES

The ethos of efficiency dominates the political, business, and social scene. Compatible with and an expression of that ethos is the predilection for scientific and systematic management of all affairs, military, civil, and human. The systems approach, as a manifestation of advanced techniques and in its widening dimension, engenders considerable appeal, perhaps even the more for having survived attack on Capitol Hill. For politically astute observers at all levels of government, the syndrome of success had practical value and the techniques were seized upon as useful, if not for *solving* persisting problems, at least for making them look better. The tools were, perhaps, more useful politically than usable in any social sense, but this did not detract from their appeal. They could be used for rationalizing almost any course of action or ideological position. They could be used to buttress decisions by "analysis," a ploy used in Sacramento and other seats of government to execute drastic change. Mission-oriented "studies" could be used to determine the destinies of programs and even agencies. As a tool for increasing centralization of authority, systems analysis and its arsenal of techniques had demonstrated enormous capability in the reorganization and re-alignment of the Department of Defense to strengthen the hand of the administrator. That example was not lost on power-hungry officials throughout the land. Consequently, even though specific aspects of the systems approach to defense management had not fared well under congressional scrutiny, total package procurement, for example, having failed to perform well, the major tenets remained unscathed and intact.

Management — of policies, planning, programs, and problems — has become the style of, and is manifestly the prevailing philosophy in, the present administration in Washington. It permeates the entire web of government, with efficiency the perennially popular watchword and rational methods the politically palatable means to achieving it. That current bureaucratic reorganization proposals should contribute to greatly increased centralization of power in the White House should, therefore, be expected, for it reflects the trend of the times. Recommendations for the change emanate from an Advisory Council on Executive Reorganization under the leadership of Roy L. Ash of Litton Industries, a firm which has, among its diversified activities, specialized in systems for domestic and foreign consumption.[39] In announcing the creation of a Domestic Council "to plan domestic policy" and an Office of Management and Budget "to see that the policy and the programs that flow from it are successfully carried out," the President indicated

[39] "Greece: Government by Subcontract," *The Economist*, June 3, 1967. pp. 1039–1040.

that his intent was to bring "real business management into Government at the very highest level." The restructuring entails an erosion of the status of such nominally nonpolitical entities as the Bureau of the Budget and the Council of Economic Advisers, threatens to bypass the Cabinet, and promises protection from congressional inquiry. But the rationale, and, remarkably, the language provided by its architects come through clearly in the President's adoption of the super management concept: "A President whose programs are carefully coordinated, whose information system keeps him adequately informed, and whose organizational assignments are plainly set out, can delegate authority with security and confidence."

High level espousal of the notion that greater efficiency in government will be achieved through management of bureaucratic and other problems practically assures continued use of techniques inherited from an earlier administration. Already firmly entrenched and not likely to be affected by the change in the political climate are the specific procedures related to the systems approach, namely, cost-effectiveness (often called cost-benefit) analysis and planning-programming-budgeting system (PPBS). As their phenomenal rapidity and scope of dissemination and adoption are clearly attributable to the fact that their history is intertwined with that of the Department of Defense, it is interesting to conjecture whether the dénouement is still ahead, how long it will take, and what will precipitate it.

For the present, we find it necessary only to re-emphasize the relationship of these techniques with the Department of Defense because it was on this basis that President Lyndon B. Johnson made his decision to prescribe PPBS for adoption by all major federal agencies.[40] In his message to Congress on the quality of American government (March 17, 1967), he stated, "This system — *which proved its worth many times over in the Defense Department* — now brings to each department and agency the *most advanced techniques of modern business management.*" [41] (My italics.) Having observed earlier that from within the classified confines of the Department of Defense these methods had exuded an aura of scientific certainty, of precision planning, one can, perhaps, understand the President's enthusiasm, albeit premature, for so enticing an antidote to traditional budgetary bumbling. What is harder to understand is his triumphant claim of having achieved, two years after introducing the new methods, results not then attained and nowhere in sight six years later. One cannot but

---

[40] August 25, 1965.

[41] *Planning-Programming-Budgeting*, Official Documents, prepared by the Subcommittee on National Security and International Operations of the Committee on Government Operations, Washington, D.C.: U.S. Government Printing Office, 1967, p. 6.

wonder who supplied the rosy reports which caused the President's euphoria.

Some clue might be derived from systematic study of the career patterns of the Department of Defense experts when they disbanded and dispersed into highly placed positions within government or in influential advisory relationship to it. Even a cursory tracing of the whereabouts of the Department-of-Defense-bred specialists corroborates the surmise that they were in position to have perpetrated an artificially created closed loop, first through impressing the President with the potency of their tools and later by feeding back progress reports that reflected more wishful thinking than accomplishment. Eager witnesses to the potential of PPBS, they appear at congressional hearings, present papers at professional gatherings, and publish voluminously. And the greater the confusion when national, state, county, and local agencies attempt to translate the facile platitudes of the PPBS format into operating procedures, the greater the market for their expert consulting services.

Expertness in the new managerial techniques is nebulous and elusive of definition, however. And the ranks of specialists are swelled with accountants, economists, econometricians, systems engineers, and business analysts who have seized the opportunity to offer themselves as consultants, presumably capable of introducing and implementing PPBS at any level of government, from local to national. Notable here is the lack of specificity with respect to qualification; the major requisites appear to be self-imputed and honorific. Thus, "professional ability" is rarely mentioned. "Expertness" is the term used. And the new experts on managing the affairs of the nation tend to reinforce propagation of what has been called "the fallacy of management as technical gadgetry," [42] for they come to their task with little understanding, less interest, and no experience in the political and policy implications of cost-benefit calculations and program-budgeted objectives in the public sector.[43] The label of expert is self-attached, honored by divisions within the "club" — econometricians recognizing econometricians as legitimate practitioners of the art, systems engineers recognizing systems engineers, and the like — and acquired in diverse ways.

The most common career progression is the one based on a college degree in electrical engineering with postgraduate work in business administration, somewhere punctuated by a slight exposure to politi-

---

[42] United Nations, Department of Economic and Social Affairs, Public Administration Branch, *The Administration of Economic Development Planning: Principles and Fallacies*, New York: United Nations, 1966, ST/TAO/M/32, p. 12.

[43] Bertram M. Gross, "The New Systems Budgeting," paper prepared for delivery at Annual Meeting of The American Political Science Association, Washington, D.C., September 5, 1968, p. 4.

cal science or sociology. The aspiring expert would have offered as his project or thesis a modest cost-benefit analysis of something — a library system, a program to assess the effectiveness of a dropout prevention program, a proposed park, a waste treatment plant. Necessarily simplified and limited in scope because of the constraints of time and funds, the model would contain only a few selected variables, the data base would be shallow. But the exercise, having satisfied the rules of the game and the requirements for the degree, would serve as leverage, or, more frequently, as catapult, to "expertness." By virtue of the cost-benefit analysis on the park situation, for example, the aspiring specialist offers his "model of sub-organizational decision-making with respect to an open space program" as evidence of prowess, becomes consultant to federal or any other agencies, and establishes himself as a specialist in program budgeting for recreation. He may even develop his own research institute, with a team of experts like himself, so as to widen his sphere of activity. Similarly, there are now experts planning educational programs because they once did an input-output analysis of a local high school, specialists advising on the location and organization of a public library system because they once "modeled" the operation of a local branch library.

In each successive paper and book, the model constructed by this expert takes on more authority as he and his followers refer to it. Even though there are statements buried under pages of formulas in appendixes that a variety of improvements will have to be made before the methods can be used in actual planning, the expert now confidently exports his blueprint for "systematic planning" to the developed and developing countries. Always alert to the universality of scarcity of funds for health, education, or whatever, he makes much of his optimization or sub-optimization procedures, dear to the hearts of the technically oriented fraternity now international but often far from the real world. On the home front, his employment and steady advance have been virtually assured with the widespread adoption of PPBS. Ready to advise the uninitiated on program budgeting and the information system and cost-benefit studies that are an intrinsic part of it, the cadre of emergent experts often graduate to the ranks of "public planners," where they perpetuate the kind of management philosophy their techniques stand for.

The Techniques at Work in the Civilian Sector

In the form of planning-programming-budgeting system, the techniques of the military invaded the civilian sector and became firmly entrenched. Planning-Programming-Budgeting System (PPBS), as borrowed from the Department of Defense, was projected to all major federal departments and agencies of the U.S. Government on August 25, 1965, by presidential directive. The imposition of PPBS on civilian agencies was supposed to introduce into fiscal planning generally the scientific management still viewed as successful in military planning. The subsequent *dénouement* wrought by time and experience in the Department of Defense has already been discussed, as has the inappropriateness of the military as model for the civilian sector. Nonetheless, President Johnson, persuaded that the planning and programming budgeting system would "present us with the alternatives and the information on the basis of which we can, together, make better decisions," launched an operation which brought the techniques of systems analysis into every facet and level of government.

Without test or trial, PPBS became mandatory procedure and spread rapidly throughout the hundreds of bureaus and divisions of the federal government. State governors, mayors, and minor politicians introduced "total reform of the budget policy through PPBS" [44] and rode the slogans of "rational decision making" and "sharper policy focus" to victory. The format of objectives and costs and benefits judiciously charted became requisite for success in the game of grantsmanship with Washington, especially with Department of Defense graduates now setting policy in many departments. High ratings were earned for compatibility of layout, terms, and language. It must be noticed, however, that the illusion of careful or analytical conceptualization rests more on form than on content. Overall benefits derived may reside solely in economy of handling and processing requests for grants at the Washington level and not in the intrinsic and substantive value of the programs submitted.

Nonetheless, like the military successes in Vietnam, the fictitious accomplishments of PPBS are still put forward as though actual. And, as with the former, so in the case of the latter, the myths prevail in high places. Two years after the introduction of the methodology, PPBS' *achievements* were listed as follows:

(1) Identify our national goals with precision and on a continuing basis;
(2) Choose among those goals the ones that are most urgent;
(3) Search for alternative means for reaching those goals most effectively at the least cost;

[44] Ronald Pelosi (Member, San Francisco Board of Supervisors), "Budget Reform," series of talks on Radio Station KCBS, San Francisco, California, June 12 and 13, 1969.

(4) Inform ourselves not merely on next year's costs, but on the second, and third, and subsequent years' costs of our programs;

(5) Measure the performance of our programs to insure a dollar's worth of service for each dollar spent.[45]

These five items typify the confusion between what PPBS *is* and what it *does*, what it has accomplished and what someone hopes it will accomplish. An enchanted President once voiced the same jumble of fact and wishful fancy in his assurance that "the system," that is, planning-programming-budgeting system, would "illuminate our choices" of programs to bring the Great Society closer to all the people.

For example, how can we best help an underprivileged child break out of poverty and become a productive citizen? Should we concentrate on improving his education? Would it help more to spend the same funds for his food, or clothing, or medical care? Does the real answer lie in training his father for a job, or perhaps teaching his mother the principles of nutrition? Or is some combination of approaches most effective? [46]

The suggestion that program budgeting could provide answers to such questions indicates a measure of faith further iterated by the President in his Message to Congress on the Quality of the American Government. On that occasion, he eulogized PPBS for having "proved its worth many times over in the Defense Department" and for now bringing "to each department and agency the most advanced techniques of modern business management." This system, he claimed, "forces us to ask the fundamental questions that illuminate our choices." The list of chores assigned were remarkably similar, if not identical in intent, to the *achievements* itemized in another context.

(1) Develop its objectives and goals, precisely and carefully;

(2) Evaluate each of its programs to meet these objectives, weighing the benefits against the costs;

(3) Examine, in every case, alternative means of achieving these objectives;

(4) Shape its budget request on the basis of this analysis, and justify that request in the context of a long-range program and financial plan.[47]

[45] *Planning-Programming-Budgeting System: Progress and Potentials.* Hearings before the Subcommittee on Economy in Government of the Joint Economic Committee, Ninetieth Congress, First Session, September 14, 19, 20, and 21, 1967, p. 1.

[46] Excerpt from The President's Message to Congress, "The Quality of American Government," March 17, 1967, *Weekly Compilation of Presidential Documents,* March 20, 1967, Vol. 3, No. 11.

[47] Excerpt from The President's Message to Congress, "The Quality of American Government," March 17, 1967, *Weekly Compilation of Presidential Documents,* March 20, 1967, Vol. 3, No. 11, as reprinted in *Planning-Programming-Budgeting, op cit.,* p. 6.

By some kind of logical or procedural sleight-of-hand, this exercise in the *quest for justifiable objectives* was expected to contribute to the ability to *achieve a higher level set of objectives, viz.*

(1) Identify our national goals with greater precision;
(2) Determine which of those goals are the most urgent;
(3) Develop and analyze alternative means of reaching those goals most effectively;
(4) Inform ourselves accurately of the probable costs of our programs.[48]

Notable here is the iteration which appears in the President's statements. Slavish repetition without clarification has only served to compound the confusion which has accompanied blanket imposition of program budgeting. Never in all the oft-paraphrased list of particulars is it made clear how PPBS would both force us to ask and, curiously, help us at the same time to answer such questions as whether we should concentrate on an underprivileged child's education, health, or parents' welfare. Actually, persons less bedazzled than White House speech writers should have known that PPBS methods can neither identify nor solve such problems. In fact, because the techniques of PPBS are quantitative, they can deal with only the measurable aspects of programs underway or under consideration — dollars spent in relation to pupils taught, housing units built, miles of road laid, or whatever. Due to its nature, the method of analysis forces the question into the form that it can answer. The result, in terms of what is learned and what is achieved, is much like the horse-and-rabbit stew described so ably by Anthony Downs. The variables that are selected because of their tractability (the rabbit) are treated meticulously, but there is almost total neglect of the incommensurable aspects, which are enormous (the horse).[49] The great appeal of PPBS is that its concentration on the scientifically prepared rabbit lends such an aura of technical precision and such a useful basis for straw man building.

An example of the bounty offered the tired or lazy bureaucrat or the administrator eager to grasp at any technique that appears promising or that makes him look good is implicit in the Department of Health, Education and Welfare exhortative recipe for preparing the rabbit for stew. It is cited here not because of its intrinsic importance nor for the insights it provides into PPBS, but more because it typifies the form-

[48]Memorandum from the President to the Heads of Departments and Agencies in the Government-Wide Planning, Programming, Budgeting System, November 17, 1966, *Weekly Compilation of Presidential Documents*, November 21, 1966, Vol. 2, No. 46, as reprinted in *Planning-Programming-Budgeting, op. cit.*, p. 3.

[49] Anthony Downs, "Comments on Urban Renewal Programs," in *Measuring Benefits of Government Investments*, Robert Dorfman, ed., Washington, D.C.: The Brookings Institution, 1965, pp. 342–351.

without-content display so frequently used by purveyors of systems techniques to give the semblance of systematic treatment to whatever subject may be at hand.

1. Decisions will be better if you know what you are trying to do — if objectives are stated and resources devoted to the accomplishment of a particular objective are grouped together.
2. Decisions will be better if information is available on how resources are presently being used — by major objectives, ways in which objectives are being carried out, types of people being served, and so forth.
3. Decisions will be better if the effectiveness of present programs is evaluated
4. Decisions will be better if alternative ways of accomplishing objectives are considered and analyzed.
5. It makes sense to plan ahead — to decide first what the Department should be doing several years in the future, and then what immediate legislative and budgetary changes are needed to move in the desired direction.
6. It is good to be systematic about decision-making — to follow an explicit procedure for reviewing long-range plans periodically in the light of new information, evaluation, and analysis, and translating changes of plans into budgetary and legislative consequences.[50]

If this array of platitudes offered as a guide to public officials is meaningful at all, it should be commonplace and obvious. Review of the individual items illustrates the point.

(1) If "you don't know what you are trying to do," then you are certainly not the right person for the job. PPBS will not help you and a technical expert cannot.

(2) If you gather information in the frame of reference of objectives, you follow the principle of what Kaplan has called "the drunkard's search," in which, according to the story he tells, a drunkard, hunting under a lamppost for keys which he had dropped some distance away, is asked why he did not look where he had lost them. His reply: "It's lighter here." [51] Much of the information-gathering in the execution of PPBS is of this quality, calibre, and intent. With its purposes established before it is collected, it has to be commensurable and compatible with certain set units of measurement. As will be further discussed in a later chapter, the assembling of the data base and the development of management information systems have taken on important dimensions in the context of PPBS because of their very mission-oriented character.

[50] Alice M. Rivlin, "The Planning, Programming, and Budgeting System in the Department of Health, Education, and Welfare: Some Lessons from Experience," in *The Analysis and Evaluation of Public Expenditures: The PPB System*, a compendium of papers submitted to the Subcommittee on Economy in Government of the Joint Economic Committee, Ninety-first Congress, First Session, Vol. 3, Washington, D.C.: U.S. Government Printing Office, 1969, p. 910.

[51] Abraham Kaplan, *The Conduct of Inquiry*, San Francisco: Chandler, 1964, p. 11.

Like the drunkard in the story, we go where we can see and not where the keys are. Facts are accepted as relevant only if they fit into the preconceived scheme and relate to the predetermined goal. And, to be considered, they must be in quantitative form, either by nature or by arbitrary assignment of a price. If, as has been claimed by PPBS promotors, the technique forces the decision maker to seek information on how resources are being used, then one wonders what kind of accounting system he used previously. If he did not know what was going on in his organization before the advent of PPBS, he must be a poor administrator. Perhaps in actual fact, the technique and its accompanying band of technicians succeeded only in supplying him with a new vocabulary, for example, inputs, outputs, cost-benefit ratios, and so on, in which to cast concepts with which he had dealt all along. In that case, he was just another *bourgeois gentilhomme,* talking prose.

(3) If the public administrator could prove "effectiveness," his perennial struggle for a *raison d'être* would be forever eased. Unfortunately, the definition of "effectiveness" is a slippery, sliding word game, played every time with *ad hoc* rules. When "effectiveness" of a Job Corps training program, for example, was being calculated by the contractor, "completions" were the mark of success; "dropouts" were the failures. When the latter appeared to be on the increase, "certificates of completion" were issued every other Saturday instead of the diploma originally given at the end of some previously designated period, such as six months. Immediately, the number of "completions" rose; "dropouts" declined; the "effectiveness" of the enterprise was assured, and so was its continued funding.[52] The "effectiveness" of a prepackaged reading program sold to a school district was assayed by psychologists in the employ of the company whose tests, tied into the programed course of instruction, elicited a kind of TV quiz response. Now proven to be "educationally effective," the canned curriculum is being promoted nationally.

(4) The search and analysis of an alternative way to accomplish objectives occurs strictly within the limits of the particular program. The result could be an undermining of the very foundations of interrelatedness on which systems analysis and program budgeting are based. For example, suppose the identified objective was to restore cleanliness and purity to the shores of Gitchee Gumee. One way would be to alter surrounding community patterns of dumping and sewage treatment and disposal. But this is a highly political matter; each township is jealous of its jurisdictional sovereignty. One might value an aesthetically pleasing waterfront; another might favor the heavily industrial

---

[52] Ida R. Hoos, *Retraining the Workforce: Analysis of Current Experience,* Berkeley and Los Angeles: University of California Press, 1967, p. 173.

development that strengthens its tax base. And while the city councils debate on the pros and cons, their efforts are vitiated by the washing up of deadly chemical residues: from fertilizers whose use was once rationalized in *its* own program, that is, increased production on the farm; oil from offshore drilling authorized because of its revenue; or nuclear waste, the generation of which was justified by the economic, scientific, or military end it was supposed to accomplish. To single out a particular program for suboptimization involves enormous assumptions about the larger whole of which it is a part and about the total society as well. It assumes that the program's objectives are *ipso facto* good and that the important question is merely how best to achieve them. In presuming that they are worthy of attainment, the analyst has also made the judgment that they do not negate some other comparably virtuous but competing purpose.

For example, by what scale of values does the Army Corps of Engineers base its calculations in diverting waters from and, therefore, destroying Louisiana's Atchafalaya Swamp, the nation's second largest wetland of its kind? Farmers faced with flood losses support the plan to build the gigantic levee and dam; conservationists and sportsmen contend that the water being carried to the Gulf of Mexico is essential to maintenance of the trees and plants, fish and birds, its alligators and snakes, and countless other forms of life. Should the shores of Gitchee Gumee be used for nuclear plant sites? Thermal pollution of the "shiny big sea water" may be no worse than nasty oil spills and leaks; the power generated would serve many more families than could possibly avail themselves of the aesthetic and recreational pleasures of pristine littoral purity. Because the tools of analysis are applicable only to the alternative that lends itself or can be subjected to a Procrustean treatment of quantification, a convincing "costing out" is bound to favor the damming diversion and power plant over preservation of natural beauty. At the micro-level, it is this kind of cost-benefit analysis that encourages industrial polluters to "let the punishment fit the crime," that is, pay the fines levied on them, and continue their operations as before. No doubt, the offenders can even write off such charges as "business expenses." This is another "business expense," taken by the very corporations which are simultaneously spending millions on creating, through advertising, another business expense, an image of ecological piety and public service.

(5) The common-sense assertion that "it makes sense to plan ahead" is irrefutable. It is also commonplace. Benjamin Franklin and his prudent forefathers practiced this wisdom long before PPBS and its advocates were conceived. The implied suggestion that PPBS has had a salutary influence on the executive and legislative budgetary process

has not been borne out by experience. On the operating level, it has created a state of upheaval and confusion, with every section of city, county, and state, as well as federal government, busily engaged in the quest of an *apologia pro sua vita*. Departments whose primary function was research or public development have diverted personnel to the task of distilling from the myriad purposes of the organization that which can be assessed and justified in cost-benefit terms so as to avoid being traded off at some higher level for some program more convincingly rationalized than theirs. The better to participate in this fiscal numbers game, agencies anxiously seek and eagerly accept the assistance of "experts," who supposedly know how to apply the "systematic tools" to any old outfit or problem.

Far from providing guidelines for "legislative and budgetary changes," PPBS seems to have failed to achieve any improvements in the executive budgetary process or to respond to the needs of Congress. Belying the façade of methodological precision and nicety, various structural and conceptual weaknesses persist and undermine the very foundations of PPBS. Some of the problems, pinpointed in a congressional committee report, are crucial.[53]

> The lack of professional agreement on certain basic analytical issues, such as the appropriate public interest rate for discounting long-lived public investments; the development of shadow prices when outputs are not marketed, the evaluation of expenditures with multiple objectives, and the evaluation of public expenditures in regions or periods of less than full employment; and the lack of adequate data from which to develop measures of the social benefits of outputs and social costs of inputs.

(6) "It is good to be systematic about decision making," the final item in the catechism, is a profession of faith in PPBS, which has been described by an experienced government official as "the fatal triumph of financial management over economics.[54] Deeper insight suggests that PPBS may represent the even more disastrous triumph of economic rationality over the political and social rationality which reasonably, logically, and necessarily belong in government decisions on resource allocation. Comprehensive review of a large number of attempts to impose program budgeting on ongoing operations has led to the con-

[53] *Economic Analysis and the Efficiency of Government*, Report of the Subcommittee on Economy in Government of the Joint Economic Committee, U.S. Congress, Ninety-first Congress, Second Session, Washington, D.C.: U.S. Government Printing Office, February 9, 1970, pp. 8–9.

[54] Samuel M. Greenhouse, "Today's PPBS: The Fatal Triumph of Financial Management over Economics," in *The Analysis and Evaluation of Public Expenditures: The PPB System*, a Compendium of Papers submitted to the Subcommittee on Economy in Government, U.S. Congress, Ninety-first Congress, First Session, Vol. 3, Washington, D.C.: U.S. Government Printing Office, 1969, pp. 886–898.

clusion that inappropriately applied economics has resulted in mis-directed economies. Wildavsky makes the compelling point that in the encroachment of economics into such intrinsically political processes as budget-making, the perspective, assumptions, and value judgments of the economist have been allowed to prevail.[55] He indicates that this is not necessarily in the best, long-range interests of the country and persuasively defends his position by critical and systematic review of the preconceptions, definitions, methods, and effects of cost-benefit and systems analysis as related to and inextricably bound up with PPBS. It may well be, as he implies, that it is the lack of theoretical discipline of political science that has created the vacuum into which economics has moved and expanded. This would explain, but certainly not excuse, the sudden blossoming of the economist as the expert in all aspects of public planning, whether the area be health, education, urban redevelopment, or construction of low-cost housing.

While there is no disputing the assertion that "it is good to be syste-matic," the question still remains: By whose standards is the decision-making to be judged systematic? Apparently, for the economists now engaged in public policy-making through cost engineering, the answer is simple and the rationale clear. The business of government costs money; programs use scarce resources. Therefore, these are economic matters and require the expert attention of economists. As we shall see later in the review of cost-benefit analysis of education and health — two favorite "target" areas — program recommendations, development, and evaluation made solely on the basis of economics can lead to a number of reductions to extreme absurdity and to the likely conclu-sion that we are looking to the wrong experts for help.

The adequacy of the professional economists as society's physicians and the appropriateness of their favored tools for fashioning the opti-mum model of governmental budgeting have not gone unnoticed by political scientists. Allen Schick, for example, described the limitations of the particular kind of economics now being applied and criticized "the provincialism in general of economic reasoning." He noted that "its isolation from border disciplines has hindered the progress of budgetary improvement." The apparent rigor and certitude of economic analysis have, he contends, been allowed to outweigh other outlooks and meth-ods more pertinent to the real world of budgeting and politics.[56] Wildavsky has long warned against the fallacious reasoning of equat-

[55] Aaron Wildavsky, "The Political Economy of Efficiency: Cost-Benefit Analysis, Systems Analysis, and Program Budgeting," *Public Administration Review*, Vol. XXVI, No. 4, December, 1966, pp. 292–311.

[56] Allen Schick, "Systems Politics and Systems Budgeting," paper prepared for delivery at Annual Meeting, The American Political Science Association, Washing-ton, D.C., September 5, 1968, p. 23.

ing budgetary reform with budgetary practices.[57] He has repeatedly underscored the basic contradictions residing in a model — no matter how rational from an economic point of view — for budgeting, which is an essentially political process. His point that the budget is a way of implementing political decisions and not arriving at them is, however, more often quoted than heeded.

Bertram M. Gross, generally more tolerant of PPBS, foresaw some dangers, which are linked firmly with the technological orientation that both defines and solves (in its own terms) our social problems.[58] He observed that in the political sphere PPBS had already affected structure and style and he saw a new breed of "technipols" emerging as important elements in the network of power elites. Monopoly by technocratic politics, achieved through the rationality of efficiency, could, according to Gross, ultimately promote disorder and discontinuity instead of the societal systematization and order purported to be the objectives. With respect to theoretical implications, he warned against the seductive potential of systems techniques and the possibility that preoccupation with the fractionated subspecialty of micro-analysis in the public sector would encourage "free-wheeling speculation" without anchorage in appropriate discipline and theory and lead to trivialization of the study of man and his place in the social universe.

Despite a certain amount of enlightenment tinged with disenchantment among bureaucrats, PPBS remains the prescribed form. Although Washington officials have already begun to talk of "policy planning" instead of "program planning," PPBS is not on the decline. In many sectors and at various levels a mythology is still in the making. The notion, dignified by presidential authority, that program budgeting could illuminate choices of programs to upgrade the quality of life has been allowed to distort the real-life processes of budget-making. To be sure, some program budgeters and cost-benefit analysts dismiss as the grandiosity of political oratory the more extravagant claims. But they are not averse to playing this management game. By the same logic that cast military planning in the mold of "economic rationality," health, education, welfare, housing, and transportation, to mention but a few social concerns, have now been reduced to their least common denominator, the dollar, and are treated as though exclusively economic. As a result, planning in these areas has become largely an exercise in cost-benefit analysis, with quantification the means and no end to the models rationally contrived and technically satisfying but irreproduc-

[57] Aaron Wildavsky, *op.cit.*

[58] Bertram M. Gross, "The New Systems Budgeting," paper prepared for delivery at Annual Meeting, The American Political Science Association, Washington, D.C., September 5, 1968, pp. 18 ff.

ible and untestable, arbitrarily selective, and dangerous in the value judgments they incorporate but conceal.

In the zeal to embrace quantification, and, incidentally, perpetuate their own status as experts, many advocates of program budgeting and cost-benefit analysis have elected to overlook qualifications, sometimes expressed by the analyst himself, sometimes pointed out by critical observers. As a consequence, these matters, although potentially significant if not crucial, are given only a brief footnote, passing mention in an appendix, or receive "in-depth treatment" in a "think piece," thoughtfully placed in a journal far from the scene of the action. It is interesting to note the extent to which the plethora of little journals has become the repository for the conveniently shelved conscience of today's experts.

The predilection to impose on the real world the technical artifice, to translate reality into a sort of tractable management game continues, and public planning from county to Congress shows it. The caveats have not been paid the attention that has been accorded the kudos and, as a result, the techniques and the technicians continue to domi nate the government scene even though there is no record of efficiency to prove their prowess. The extent of this domination becomes evident in the current push toward a "system of national accounting." [59] Apparently, the mirage of success has so deluded some administrators that they believe that such a system is feasible and attainable, and that the way to achieve social systems accounting is through identification of social indicators.

Social Indicators

By the standard definitions, social indicators appear to be little more and no better than, and fully as quantitative as any old statistics. Nonetheless, they have been confidently described as "statistics, statistical series, and other forms of evidence that enable us to assess where we stand and where we are going with respect to our values and goals, and to evaluate specific programs and determine their impacts." [60] Notable here is the extension of cost-benefit techniques to such unwonted areas as *values* and *goals*. The enthusiasm of those social scientists who recognize the need for more "systematic" approaches to public planning policy has carried their wishful thoughts beyond the primitive state-of-the-art as they themselves perceive it in their more

[59] Bertram M. Gross, "The State of the Nation: Social Systems Accounting," in Raymond A. Bauer, ed., *Social Indicators*, Cambridge, Massachusetts: MIT Press, 1967, pp. 154–271.

[60] Raymond A. Bauer, "Detection and Anticipation of Impact," in *Social Indicators*, *op.cit.*, p. 1.

realistic moments. Through the rosy promise of "rich work with partial system models," they look to "more powerful models that bring economic, political, sociological, and cultural variables together into a general systems theory." [61] Achievement of these ambitious goals will presumably come about from current work on social indicators, of which *Toward a Social Report* is the prime example.[62]

Our research uncovered little evidence to support the attribution of richness in the models available for study. Conceptualization appears always to be arbitrarily restricted by the methodology and limitations imposed by the technique are rationalized but not overcome. While mention is made of "political, sociological, and cultural variables," such factors have proven elusive of capture and control by the "systematic" approach. Consequently, they have been omitted. Only those variables which could be handled quantitatively have been taken into account, and the accounting has remained largely economic. The "general systems theory," supposed to provide the unifying principle, is actually too general in focus and vague in scope to constitute a theoretical framework and is too eclectic to merit consideration as a discipline. Although philosophically it draws from many intellectual streams, it leaves out the crucial historical and theoretical developments that govern proper use and application. So enticing has been the prospect of a "social balance sheet," however, that social scientists, who should know better, and bureaucrats and politicians, who cannot be expected to know better, have allowed themselves to overlook the shortcomings and inadequacies of the systems approach to present problems and to espouse it as the way to managing social affairs.

For this task, all claims of multi-disciplinary and qualitative dimensions to the contrary, social indicators are the means and economic indicators the model. In fact, the idea of a national balance sheet is modeled after economic practices, Gross having rated national economic accounting as "one of the greatest social inventions of the modern world." Adulation embraces the *Economic Report of the President* as well:

> This report finds its way to the desks of the major élites of the country. Thus, in addition to the free copies sent to members of Congress, government officials, the press, and depositary libraries, the Superintendent of Documents sold more than fifty thousand copies of the *Economic Report* and this figure has risen every year. In addition, the Council's monthly *Economic Indicators,* a carefully organized set of thirty-seven charts with tables, has become the basis whereby people "in the know" keep their fingers on the pulse of the economy.[63]

[61] Gross, *op.cit.,* p. 157.
[62] U.S. Department of Health, Education, and Welfare, *Toward a Social Report,* Washington, D.C.: U.S. Government Printing Office, 1969.
[63] Gross, "Preface," in *Social Indicators, op.cit.,* p. xii.

Never denying nor for a moment gainsaying the importance of statistics properly gathered and interpreted, we still must address realistically the fact that there is considerable disagreement among economists as to the reliability and significance of the pulse beats thus monitored. Moreover, the erratic behavior of the economy as it resists conventional doctoring indicates that there is no magic formula that can control its present state, let alone predict its future condition. Although the best-selling *Economic Report of the President* and *Economic Indicators* are used by many experienced economic analysts to study the past and as a basis for modest and cautious extrapolation of specific trends, their limitations are well documented. They provide no macro-model for future planning, economic or social. Most social scientists, economists included, are aware of these facts. Bauer, revealing an interesting ambivalence characteristic of enthusiasts for social indicators, has pointed out that statistics are seductive in their persuasiveness but fickle in that they represent only the articulateness and power of the interest group; the susceptibility of the phenomenon to being measured; the extent to which the phenomenon is socially visible; and the preferences and skills of the agency personnel who gather the statistics.[64]

Similarly, ambivalence is displayed by other members of a panel brought together in 1966 by the U.S. Department of Health, Education, and Welfare as experts on the measurement of social change to develop "necessary social statistics and indicators." [65] While stressing the need for non-economic statistics and evoking the analogy to economics, many of the "weekend scholars" who participated in the "Social Report" exercise have written earnest dissertations on the inappropriateness of the economic experience as a model for the social.[66] Although enthusiastic in their support of the social counterpart of economic statistics, many of the authorities who convened several times to develop the "Social Report" have published statements that lend strength to the counter-argument, *viz.*, that objective measures of the public good are — by their very qualitative, relative, value-laden, culturally defined and subjectively conceptualized nature — simply unattainable. This being the case, what may pass as and be accepted for social indicators may be so prejudiced, so biased, and so contrived as to be downright dangerous.

[64] Raymond A. Bauer, "Detection and Anticipation of Impact: The Nature of the Task," *op.cit.*, p. 26.

[65] Letter of Transmittal, Wilbur J. Cohen, Secretary of Health, Education and Welfare to the President of the United States, January 11, 1969, *Toward a Social Report*, U.S. Department of Health, Education, and Welfare, Washington, D.C.: U.S. Government Printing Office, 1969.

[66] Eleanor Bernert Sheldon and Howard E. Freemen, "Social Indicators: Promises and Potential," *Policy Sciences*, Vol. 1, No. 1, Spring, 1970, p. 106.

Even before participating in the "Social Report" endeavor, Biderman had attempted a sociological assessment of non-economic statistics, with more negative than positive conclusions. Having documented the pitfalls, he could recommend only that the phenomenology of social indicators be examined, that they be approached from the point of view of the sociology of knowledge as the institutional and social products they are.[67]

One of the main selling points of the social indicators movement was that herein lay the mechanism for cost-benefit analysis of specific social action programs. In the Report, under Chapter II's formal title, "Social Mobility," the question is posed, "How Much Opportunity is There?" and, presumably, the answer will be found in "evaluative research," through statistical controls or "systems analysis." The use of indicators to assess program effectiveness has been sharply criticized by Sheldon and Freeman in a definitive paper.[68] The use of "social indicators" to measure outcomes of programs could lead to the most egregious statistical manipulation, for herein lie the arbitrary selection and control of variables that could virtually prescribe results without reference to important determining factors and causal interrelationships.

In addition, and as further evidence of the ambivalence of the Panel, is the plea by Moynihan for a move *away* from the "program approach to public planning," which he called a "McNamara colonization of domestic departments" and a failure at that, toward the development, instead, of a "true policy" orientation, a frankly normative, value-laden, compassionate judgment.[69] Another Panel member, emphasizing the linkage of social reporting with social forecasting, reported in another context on the deliberations of the Panel as well as several other symposia dealing with indicators of social change. He asserted that participants, for the most part, agreed that the problem was at least as much that we have no idea what *we ought to be measuring* as that we are *failing to gather the kind of information we know how to collect.*[70]

Despite the obvious shortcomings and deficiencies of economic indicators, as well as the reservations about the feasibility and advisability of social indices, an oversold Administration, in March, 1966, directed

[67] Albert D. Biderman, "Social Indicators and Goals," pp. 68–154, in *Social Indicators, op.cit.*

[68] Sheldon and Freeman, *op.cit.*

[69] Daniel P. Moynihan, "Policy vs. Program in the '70's," *The Public Interest,* No. 20, Summer, 1970, pp. 90–101.

[70] Otis Dudley Duncan, "Social Forecasting: The State of the Art," *The Public Interest,* No. 17, Fall, 1969, p. 111.

the Secretary of Health, Education, and Welfare "to search for ways in which to improve the nation's ability to chart its social progress." The specific charge was "to develop the necessary social statistics and indicators to supplement those prepared by the Bureau of Labor Statistics and the Council of Economic Advisers." The self-deception embodied in this directive lies in its final, non-sequential but highly consequential sentence: "With these yardsticks, we can better measure the distance we have come and plan for the way ahead." [71] Notable here is the still-pervasive influence of the "cargo cult," the notion that a technique that conceivably worked satisfactorily in one situation would perform equally well in another. Journalistic oratory aside, the President's statement that there existed measuring devices for program evaluation and planning revealed that he was still dwelling on the promises of program budgeting (PPBS) without having been apprised of its debacle as a policy-making instrument.

The document, *Toward a Social Report,* which emerged from the occasional deliberations of the forty-odd academicians and administrators, claims to be "a step in the direction of a social report and the development of a comprehensive set of social indicators." [72] If this compendium is to be taken as a step in the direction of the "systematic approach" so earnestly promoted by the architects of the Social Report enterprise, then we seem to be headed straight for the past. The amorphous state of conceptualization reflected in the higgledy-piggledy of seven assorted areas of concern puts us far behind the social pathologists of a half-century ago. They, too, focused on crime, poverty, and health and in terms no less normative. When they raised value-laden questions, however, they recognized that they could not expect definitive answers; underlying the current advocacy of social indices there is the insidious lure of techniques attainable but not yet harnessed. As for methods used in amassing the data on which the Social Report was built, there is no evidence that progress has been made since Durkheim. [73] In fact, nothing presented between the Introduction and the Appendix rivals his insights and systematic collection of data to support explicit hypotheses. *Toward a Social Report,* itself a poor indicator of the state-of-the-art in sociology, stands as a persuasive argument against artificially contrived and inappropriate measures of the human and social condition.

[71] As quoted in January 11, 1969, letter of transmittal from Wilbur J. Cohen, then Secretary of Health, Education, and Welfare, to the President of the United States, as Preface to *Toward a Social Report, op.cit.*

[72] *Ibid.,* p. xiv.

[73] Emile Durkheim, *Suicide: A Study in Sociology,* translated by John A. Spaulding and George Simpson, Glencoe: Free Press, 1958.

NATIONAL GOALS

So pervasive has been the predilection to apply management techniques to all facets of public planning that not only present problems but even future policy become the target. Organized by the White House was a special task force to set national goals and priorities. And social data and social indicators were to be the basis upon which these were to be built. In his introduction to the report of the National Goals Research Staff, Moynihan stressed the usefulness of a social report in the move from program to policy oriented government, a change which he had perceived so recently as being "one of the formative ideas of the 1970s" [74] and which, miraculously, by Washington time standards, was apparently under way by July 4, 1970.[75] President Nixon established the National Goals Research Staff on July 13, 1970 and designated as their first assignment the assembling of data "that can help illumine the possible range of national goals for 1976 — our 200th anniversary." [76] The staff assembled to perform the illumination was described in the President's statement as "small, highly technical, made up of experts in the collection, correlation, and processing of data relating to social needs, and in the projection of social trends." In light of our review of the nebulousness of social data, whether related to needs or trends, one cannot but wonder by what standards expertness was bestowed. Having learned through the debacle of *Toward a Social Report* that no one had succeeded in identifying the determining factors that establish trends, we find little basis for ascribing so generously competence in "social bookkeeping." Moreover, in the face of existing specialization and division of labor in the field of information handling, are we to believe that these experts were indeed generalists who not only collected but correlated; not only collected and correlated but processed as well; and in addition to the "collection, correlation, and processing," were qualified to project social trends?

These questions are raised not to impugn the capabilities or motives of the individuals who participated in the goals research but to point up the propensity toward myth making and image building inherent in such an endeavor. As with *Toward a Social Report*, *Toward Balanced Growth* was an exercise in futility overlaid with journalistic rhetoric and bedecked with political self-justification. The administration, it seems, aspires to direct and control the process of social

[74] Daniel P. Moynihan, "Policy vs. Program in the '70's," *op.cit.*, p. 91.

[75] Counsellor's Statement, Report of the National Goals Research Staff, *Toward Balanced Growth: Quantity with Quality*, Washington, D.C.: U.S. Government Printing Office, July 4, 1970, p. 5.

[76] Statement of the President announcing establishment of National Goals Research Staff, July 13, 1969, in Report of the National Goals Research Staff, *op.cit.*, p. 223.

change through what the President calls "the extraordinary array of tools and techniques" which he has been led to believe are used "successfully in business and the social and physical sciences." [77]

That instances of success reside more in the selling of the technique than in applications of it is now clear. Moreover, there appears to be growing disarray and disenchantment among the economists themselves over the technical scholasticism and mathematical preoccupation dominating their profession. Leontief, himself a pioneer in analytical techniques,[78] took the occasion of his retirement as president of the American Economics Association to criticize his profession for having bestowed its honors on the abstract theorists and builders of beautiful mathematical models which contributed little to the solution of actual problems. The selection by the Association of Professor John Kenneth Galbraith as president-elect and program chairman for 1971 has been interpreted as a belated expression of approval for his long-time effort to restore "richer, social, moral, and aesthetic qualities to a profession that shows signs of becoming dessicated by technical scholasticism and an ostentatious display of mathematical rigor."

Ignorant of or ignoring the dearth of evidence to support the ascription of successful applications of the "extraordinary tools and techniques" elsewhere in time and space, the President's statement writers chose to overlook the lack of consensus among professional economists. The functions they prescribed for the National Goals Staff contained a kind of jactation that could only undermine further the credibility and professional credibility of the goals search venture:

(1) forecasting future developments, and assessing the longer-range consequences of present social trends;
(2) measuring the probable future impact of alternative courses of action, including measuring the degree to which change in one area would be likely to affect another.[79]

The resulting report, *Toward Balanced Growth: Quantity with Quality*, was built on the quicksand of *Toward a Social Report*, its predecessor by a scant six months but already fallaciously accorded by its designers the status of *fait accompli* of "providing some social indicators that are designed to help Americans evaluate the performance of the society." [80] A compilation of the pet peeves of its authors,

[77] Statement of the President announcing establishment of National Goals Research Staff, in *Toward Balanced Growth, op.cit.*, p. 221.
[78] Wassily W. Leontief, *The Structure of American Economy, 1919–1929*, Cambridge: Harvard University Press, 1941.
[79] Statement of the President announcing establishment of National Goals Research Staff.
[80] *Toward Balanced Growth, op.cit.*, p. 23.

it serves more as a vehicle for disseminating their views than as a model for any kind of systematic conceptualization and reasonable approach to the dilemmas of reconciling quality with quantity, technology with humanity. Failing completely to explore whether the publicized functions were attainable or even desirable, the *Growth* report only perpetuates the prevailing myths that future developments can be forecast with any degree of reliability, that longer range consequences of present social trends can be assessed, that probable future impact of alternative courses of action, to say nothing of the degree to which change in one area would be likely to affect another, can be measured at all. The state-of-the-art is nowhere nearly developed enough to make even the assignment of such tasks realistic.

Through propagandistic promotion, iteration and reiteration, and top echelon anointment, the tools borrowed from technology and the techniques derived from a heterogeny of sources have become *de rigueur* in government circles. Cost-benefit analysis, program budgeting, social indicators "scientifically" conceived, and social goals precisely determined have been accorded a reality and prestige far exceeding their accomplishment. Serious questioning of these methods as instruments of responsible accounting and stewardship has not occurred, despite the possibility that substitution of neat program categories, that is, the ready-to-use program package approach inherited from the military, for nettlesome line items may actually sacrifice checks and balances without delivering the efficiency promised by the "costing engineers."

For the time being and at least for the near future, PPBS will continue to dominate the budgeting process. What started out to be a philosophical orientation, a mode of thinking, became the prescribed course in the Department of Defense and resulted in the "McNamara colonization of domestic departments."[81] Tied in with the general wave of enthusiasm for rational approaches, systematic methods, and scientific management, program budgeting techniques are likely to influence the form of public fiscal planning at various levels. We may have yet to rediscover the truism that budget-making is not an exact science but a highly political art, where even arithmetical processes undergo interesting metamorphosis.

The course of PPBS' future may be altered by Moynihan's new emphasis on policy as against program planning. Legal considerations may ultimately have bearing on the fate of program budgeting in the civilian sector. In New York, for example, legislators and non-political budget analysts have challenged its constitutionality on grounds that lump sum appropriations denied their right, under the State constitu-

---

[81] Daniel P. Moynihan, "Policy vs. Program in the '70's," *op.cit.*

tion, to strike out, reduce, or add items. The decision by the State Supreme Court Justice was overruled by the Appellate Division, but the appeal was strictly on a legal technicality. The fundamental objections were never addressed. With the troublesome issues still untouched, program budgeting may yet face challenge in the U.S. Supreme Court, if not on the specific objections raised by the New York officials, then possibly under such laws as Access to Public Information. Program budgeting may be the latest fad in fiscal management, but it is certainly not the last word.

[4]

Systems Analysis as Technological Transfer

Systems analysis has been variously hailed, sometimes as valuable "fallout" from the national defense effort, often as perhaps the most useful "spinoff" from space endeavors. Hopefully regarded as a vehicle to convey the advances of technology and science directly into channels for mankind's benefit and betterment, systems analysis has attracted considerable support, especially because instant utilization is understandably agreeable to government agencies such as the Department of Defense or the National Aeronautics and Space Administration, whose huge budgets must periodically be rendered palatable to Congress and the public. Superficially, at least, the conditions for successful transplant of systems techniques from the military and outer space to social problems are ideal. The technology is ready-made, "proved" in the arena of warfare and space exploration as the scientific way to manage the large-scale enterprise. The environment is hospitable; "Space Age concepts" are generally *gemütlich* in the latter twentieth century, when a plenitude of complex social problems demand some kind of orderly treatment. Strong political and economic influences foster wide adoption of the techniques, ready to be applied by a large and growing number of "systems experts" armed with solutions and in search of problems. Because systems analysis is a way of defining and handling problems, it may yet have to be reckoned with as the technology that will most profoundly change our society. It is important, therefore, that we trace the process of transfer from military and space to civil affairs, the better to assess and evaluate the assumptions, the logistics, and the perceived outcome of specific applications.

THE "MAN ON THE MOON" MAGIC

On October 18, 1965, Senator Gaylord Nelson introduced a Scientific Manpower Utilization Bill (S.2662) in the U.S. Senate. The proposed legislation reflected the then nascent notion that the nation that could put a man on the moon could, by application of the same methods, cure any and all of its terrestrial ailments. Its stated purpose was: "to mobilize and utilize the scientific and engineering manpower of the Nation to employ systems analysis and systems engineering to help to fully employ the Nation's manpower resources to solve national problems." [1] The forensic of the speech of introduction titled, "A Space Age Trajectory to the Great Society," became familiar through subsequent repetition and was expanded, elaborated, and embroidered with each iteration.

Mr. President, why can not the same specialist who can figure out a way to put a man in space figure out a way to keep him out of jail?

Why can not the engineers who can move a rocket to Mars figure out a way to move people through our cities and across the country without the horrors of modern traffic and the concrete desert of our highway system?

Why can not the scientists who can cleanse instruments to spend germ-free years in space devise a method to end the present pollution of air and water here on earth?

Why can not highly trained manpower, which can calculate a way to transmit pictures for millions of miles in space, also show us a way to transmit enough simple information to keep track of our criminals?

Why can not we use computers to deal with the down-to-earth special problems of modern America?

The answer is we can — if we have the wit to apply our scientific know-how to the analysis and solution of social problems with the same creativity we have applied it to space problems. The purpose of the proposed Scientific Manpower Utilization Act of 1965 is to test new ways to use the scientific manpower and know-how of the space age to solve a great variety of social problems.[2]

The transfer of "intellectual technology" from the arena of the military and the outer reaches of space to the decaying city has always been bathed in moonglow. In calling on the aerospace industry to apply systems techniques to civil problems in 1964, Governor Edmund G. Brown had already launched the lunar analogy, "We can use the know-

---

[1] S.2662, Eighty-ninth Congress, First Session, October 18, 1965.
[2] Statement by Senator Gaylord Nelson in *Congressional Record*, October 18, 1965.

how that will get a man to the moon to get Dad to work on time." A presidential State of the Union address challenged the nation which could aspire to put a man on the moon to direct the same genius to solving its urgent social problems.[3] Vice-presidential speeches were cast in the same light.

The techniques that are going to put a man on the Moon are going to be *exactly* (my italics) the techniques that we are going to need to clean up our cities; the management techniques that are involved, the coordination of government and business, of scientist and engineer. We're not going to make these cities over just by a speech. And we're not going to do it either just because we have a hundred billion dollars that somebody wants to put into it. I get on my favorite topic: It takes more than just money to do anything. It requires knowledge, planning; it requires the technology, the ability to get things done. There is no checkbook answer to the problems of America. There are some human answers and the *system analysis approach* (his italics) that we have used in our Defense Department; the systems analysis that we have used in our space and aeronautic program — that is the approach that the modern city of America is going to need if it's going to become a livable social institution. So maybe we're pioneering in space only to save ourselves on Earth. As a matter of fact, maybe the nation that puts a man on the Moon is a nation that will put man on his feet right here on Earth. I think so.[4]

Congressional hearings on several Scientific Manpower Utilization bills[5] provided an ideal platform from which proponents of systems analysis could implicitly or explicitly promote the idea that techniques that had worked in space and defense should be applied to civilian affairs and that systems capability was a talent movable from one arena to another. Representatives of the aerospace industry maintained that their sophisticated systems skills and broad technological base would be useful in solving the problems of slums, poverty, pollution, education, and transportation just as they had dramatically and successfully sent men to the moon and preserved national security. They pointed to the essentially similar characteristics of the problems, *viz.*, large-scale, complex, full of unknowns. The varied backgrounds of the panel of witnesses indicate that purveyors of systems analysis were by no means limited to aircraft companies.

[3] President Lyndon B. Johnson, State of the Union Address, January, 1968.
[4] Vice President Hubert H. Humphrey, speech at Smithsonian Institution, quoted in *Aerospace Technology*, Vol. 21, No. 24, May 20, 1968, p. 19.
[5] Hearings before the Special Committee on the Utilization of Scientific Manpower of the Committee on Labor and Public Welfare, *Scientific Manpower Utilization, 1965–66*, U.S. Senate, Eighty-ninth Congress, First and Second Sessions on S.2662, November 19, 1965; May 15 and 18, 1966. Hearings before the Special Subcommittee on the Utilization of Scientific Manpower of the Committee on Labor and Public Welfare, *Scientific Manpower Utilization, 1967*, U.S. Senate, Ninetieth Congress, First Session, on S.430 and S.467, January 24, 25, 26, 27; March 29 and 30, 1967.

Testifying in favor of the bill were advocates from government, universities, and business, as well as the general public. In the latter category were Mr. Robert A. Mang, a spokesman for the Friends Committee on Legislation, and Mrs. Patricia Arnold, a member of the Economic Committee of Women for Peace. The reasons given for their support reveal many of the popular clichés and misconceptions about systems analysis. Mr. Mang explained that his group saw great potential in "the integration of technical competence" that the aerospace companies could bring to the civilian sector. "We recognized the value of applying this kind of approach to some of the basic problems confronting our Nation, problems such as education, transportation, waste management, and others as mentioned in this bill." [6] Mrs. Arnold's group favored the Nelson proposal because they believed in peaceful settlement of world problems and construed this act as a move in the direction of "the peaceful solution of economic conversion." [7] The parade of sellers, eager to exploit the market for their wares, and of buyers, anxious to explore new ways to solve what they considered to be the nation's most urgent problems, added impetus to the man-on-the-moon mythology, the transfer of the techniques of problem-solving. This was further buttressed by inclusion in the report of the hearings of certain selected articles, in all of which the theme of the management of public affairs by "business lessons from the Pentagon" and by "Space Age concepts" prevailed.[8]

THE DOLEFUL DIALECTIC

In many instances, the inapposite juxtaposition, the doleful dichotomy was the theme: neatness and order *versus* social disorder; technical precision *versus* confusion; grappling with wholes *versus* piecemeal fragmentation; efficient management *versus* bumbling bureaucracy. "City riots, poverty and race problems, urban decay, medical care, housing, traffic, crime, smog — all of these now have reached the level where they constitute a major issue of our time." These were the trouble spots designated by the vice president of TRW, Inc., a firm which competes actively for contracts in most of these areas, as appropriate for systems approach — a "powerful methodology" in military and space work and now "also suited to attacking the civil-systems type of problems." [9] In the perennial dialectic between strife and harmony, poverty

---

[6] Robert A. Mang, testimony at Hearings on S.2662, November 19, 1965, p. 140.

[7] Mrs. Patricia Arnold, testimony at Hearings, *ibid.*, pp. 142–143.

[8] Hearings on S.430 and S.467, January 24, 25, 26, 27; March 29 and 30, 1967, *op.cit.*, "Additional Information," p. V.

[9] Simon Ramo, *Cure for Chaos, Fresh Solutions to Social Problems through the Systems Approach*, New York: Iland McKay, 1969, pp. 9–10.

and prosperity, chaos and order, simple logic is always on the positive side, and the positivist persuasion promulgates the proposition that scientific, technological methods are *ipso facto* better than any that can be put in antithetical relation to them. Is it conceivable that anyone would logically opt for anachronistic inefficiency through horse-and-buggy means when, instead, he can invoke an arsenal of sophisticated tools which will bring efficiency? The answer to this almost rhetorical question draws strength from and strengthens the already existent ethos of efficiency, automatically accredits efficiency as a social good, and practically assures easement into the next step of the syllogism, *viz.*, that city riots and race problems, urban decay, and the other helter-skelter ingredients of the potpourri constituting "a major issue of our time" need better management. It is through this logic that systems analysis has been transplanted from the realm of the military and the moon-bound to the social scene.

LANGUAGE AS EXPEDITER

In remarkable contrast to the usual language barriers impeding movement of ideas among the various disciplines, the process of transfer of systems analysis has been considerably aided by language. This is primarily because of the rapid and widespread diffusion of the same symbols and words, among which *system, parameter, interface, model,* and *simulation* are perhaps the most commonly shared. They have become jejune parlance in every field from anthropology to zoology, from the most abstruse and abstract mathematics to the most concrete engineering, in the soft sciences as well as the hard. In fact, the softer the science, the greater the inclination to adopt the jargon of the hard, those disciplines which lack a strong theoretical framework being among the most avid to adopt and rely on the terminology. But in the process of linguistic dissemination, rigor of definition vanishes and verbiage remains. As terms merge with and become popular *argot*, similarity rests more in the phenotypes, the superficial appurtenances, than in the genotypes, the basic characteristics; there is much *a capriccio* interpretation and conceptualization. Substitution of language for substantive knowledge, of logic for experience, has encouraged a kind of semantic solution to social problems, an artificial and symbolic treatment that fails to address troubling and troublesome factors and dimensions. The common glossary is attractive, nonetheless, for it has created a virtual open-sesame market situation. With familiarity with the language a prime requisite, systems capability becomes a movable talent and systems analysis everyone's business.

No longer the private preserve of the aerospace industry, urban, civil, or social studies attract a diverse and variegated array of contenders for contracts. Aviation and aerospace firms are certainly active, but they have been joined by computer manufacturers and their subsidiaries, electronics companies, accounting firms, management consultants, directory publishers, and merged and conglomerated software vendors of every stripe. There are also university-based entrepreneurs, research organizations such as the RAND Corporation, Systems Development Corporation, Stanford Research Institute, and the Hudson Institute, Inc. In addition, there is a proliferation of experts for hire with unpronounceable acronyms, post-office boxes in Santa Monica, San Mateo, and Silver Spring as addresses, and a zeal to apply the powerful new management tools to the public order.

ECONOMIC AND POLITICAL FACTORS IN THE TRANSFER

Improvement of governmental planning through modernization of techniques was only one factor in the transfer. Of equal importance was the national concern, heightened in certain local regions, to cushion the impacts of retrenchments in the aerospace and defense industries and find promising avenues for their diversification. Completion of defense projects or aerospace missions has always caused considerable disruption in communities. Prosperity in Seattle and San Diego, in Huntsville and at Cape Kennedy, has always been a fragile matter, dependent in large part on the state of the contracts. Cutback, even in the name of national economy, is a spectre dreaded by employees within the industries directly involved and the townspeople at large. According to some estimates, for every worker laid off, seven in other businesses and services, private and public, are adversely affected. When the Boeing Company cut its workforce from a high of 101,000 in January, 1968, to 45,000, unemployment in the entire Puget Sound Area burgeoned; hotel business dropped 25 percent; automobile sales declined by 35 percent; real estate sales decreased by about 40 percent. Using the economic multiplier concept, a business economist calculated that the Boeing reduction in 1970 alone caused a loss within the state of income of $1.25 billion to $1.43 billion, the latter considered a conservative estimate based on inclusion of reduced and local government expenditures due to loss of revenue associated with decreased income.[10]

The federal government has long been aware of the impacts of massive dislocation, and legislation has encouraged ameliorative steps. The

[10] Richard G. O'Lone, "Boeing Cutbacks Shake Economy of Seattle Area," *Aviation Week & Space Technology*, June 29, 1970, pp. 14–17.

Employment Act of 1946, the Manpower Development and Training Acts of the 1960s, and the Public Works and Economic Development Act of 1965 all sought in their time to provide means by which to achieve labor force adjustment. Particularly interesting in this context is the Arms Control and Disarmament Act of 1961,[11] which specifically committed the U.S. Arms Control and Disarmament Agency, as one of its responsibilities, to explore "the economic . . . consequences of arms control and disarmament, including the problems of readjustment arising in industry and the reallocation of national resources." Accordingly, various research teams were deployed to assess technological innovation in civilian public areas [12] and, above all, as diversification or conversion in case of cutbacks in federal funding, to evaluate the non-defense, non-aerospace public sector market for the systems capability of defense firms.[13] Clearly discernible in the task assigned the investigators was the assumption that, by bringing its talents to bear on domestic problems, threatened defense industry could find new outlets for its manpower and, at the same time, raise the level of governance through the application of science and technology.

Largely because of the tendency for firms in the defense-space category to cluster on the West Coast, California in particular felt threatened when retrenchment loomed. Officials in the Department of Finance were all the more receptive, therefore, to the idea that the systems approach which had worked so well in missile and aerospace missions could be applied to crime, welfare, transportation, waste management, and other persistent problems. There was great appeal in the notion of addressing each problem area as a total system, with "systematic" identification of its objectives, "rational" analysis of its component parts and contributing factors, and "precise" evaluation of the outcome of ameliorative programs. The aerospace companies that responded to the State of California's requests for proposal reviewed the social scene and found the conventional procedures associated with bureaucracy in a democracy an easy target for criticism. Duplication, piecemeal fragmentation, and general inefficiency could, they claimed, be overcome by utilization of their systems talents. They would take crime, transportation, or whatever else needed improvement, subject it to their analysis, express its dynamics in terms of models, simulate its

[11] Public Law 87–297, *Arms Control and Disarmament Act*, 75 Stat. 633, September 26, 1961.

[12] Ronald P. Black and Charles W. Foreman, *Technological Innovation in Civilian Public Areas*, U.S. Arms Control and Disarmament Agency, ACDA/E-118, September, 1967.

[13] John S. Gilmore, John J. Regan, and William S. Gould, *Defense Systems Resources in the Civil Sector: An Evolving Approach, An Uncertain Market*, U.S. Arms Control and Disarmament Agency, ACDA/E-103, July, 1967.

activity so as to ascertain and take immediate advantage of the feedback effect of changes, and thus render government more efficient and effective.

Like newly-arrived Columbuses, they approached each problem area as though it had never been visited before and cast its common knowledge into forms familiar to them. Actually, they contributed little new; they merely expressed it differently — in the systems jargon. Platitudes appeared as though uncovered through earnest technical investigation. Proposed studies, revealing more the bias of the analysts than insights into the problem, looked almost identical, quite irrespective of the subject under scrutiny. Willing to overlook the methodological arrogance and substantive limitations, however, the State of California, anxious to employ its displaced engineers and improve its governance, displayed its pioneering spirit by the utilization of Space Age techniques for the commonweal.

Another facet of the quest for new markets as a hedge against unemployment was the desirability of locating new channels for diversification of the manpower talent residing in military and space installations. In 1964, with half of all the engineers and scientists trained in research and development concentrated in California, and in certain defined areas at that, local concern for continued utilization of this reservoir was understandably urgent. Loss of persons of this intellectual calibre would, it was feared, have severe repercussions not only on the local economy but throughout community life, in terms of civic leadership and participation. From the viewpoint of society at large, redirection of the *Wehrmacht* to peaceful pursuits won almost universal support, the wide extent of which is suggested in proposed congressional legislation [14] and commission reports,[15] as well as in the enthusiasm voiced by Quakers and diverse other groups.[16]

Not to be overlooked as a factor favoring conversion were employee attitudes toward non-defense diversification. Some technical experts, apt to regard defense work as a prostitution of their profession, perceived the possibility of applying their systems expertness to civilian problems as a way of restoring integrity to their somewhat tainted image. Germane here is the phenomenon known as "weapon maker's guilt." Case studies of some large corporations such as E. I. du Pont de Nemours, Inc., indicate that the label, "merchants of death," that was attached to them during the 1930s had apparently disturbed a

[14] Scientific Manpower Utilization Acts, S.2662, S.430, and S.467.
[15] National Commission on Technology, Automation, and Economic Progress, *Applying Technology to Unmet Needs*, The Report of the Commission, Appendix, Vol. V, Washington, D.C.: U.S. Government Printing Office, February, 1966.
[16] Testimony, Hearings on Scientific Manpower Utilization, 1965, *op.cit.*

number of senior scientists and engineers.[17] Welcoming non-weapons work, such persons reported that a burden had been lifted from their conscience when they could "tell the wife and kids what Dad does for a living." Consistent with the release from guilt was the earnest desire to benefit society, a phenomenon noted earlier as a strong force diverting attention among professional engineers in general — that is, not alone those engaged in missiles and rocketry — from their traditional occupations to those associated with doing the public good. Morally satisfying and socially acceptable peace work held out the prospect of challenge and opportunity, with emphasis on the desirable and not the deplorable aspects of technology at work.

A final factor encouraging development of civilian outlets for defense manpower was the tapering off in Pentagon spending, with a decline in military prime contract awards, from $8.8 billion in the third quarter of 1969 down more than $2 billion from the same period in 1968. Figure 4 shows the concomitant drop in defense-related jobs, probably about 400,000 in 1969.[18] The local trauma and travail generated by the cutbacks had convinced at least some Congressmen that a healthier state of economic affairs could be achieved if there were less dependence of private industry on government. Accordingly, they favored a friendly separation, if not divorce, between industry and government whose mutual interdependence had begotten the hyphenated opprobrium known as the military-industrial complex.

Political, no less than economic, circumstances promoted the technological transfer. In California, for example, the governor and his advisers recognized that any plan that offered a possible cushion against unemployment would appeal to the electorate, potentially vulnerable workers, and firms facing retrenchment. Preserving prosperity has always been good political strategy; protecting payrolls while at the same time harnessing Space Age techniques to improve the management of public affairs proved to be such a potent formula that it survived even after the governor lost the election.

If it demonstrated nothing else, the California experience proved that, *regardless of their intrinsic worth,* systems studies are an extremely handy political tool, in the application of which reside both advantage and protection. First, the systems study promises to be a useful mechanism for postponement of action. Better than the research committee it is dislodging, the systems study, through the rigmarole attendant on the awarding of the contract, conduct of the busy work, and form and

[17] John S. Gilmore and Dean C. Coddington, *Defense Industry Diversification, An Analysis with 12 Case Studies,* U.S. Arms Control and Disarmament Agency, Publication 30, Washington, D.C.: U.S. Government Printing Office, January, 1966, p. 22.

[18] *Manpower Report of the President,* prepared by the U.S. Department of Labor, Washington, D.C.: U.S. Government Printing Office, March, 1970, p. 33.

FIGURE 4. Decline of Defense-Generated
Employment in 1969

**After 3 years of steady expansion
defense-generated employment
declined in 1969.**

Defense-generated employment[1]

[1] Includes the Atomic Energy Commission.

[2] Includes government enterprises selling products and services
to the public.

[3] Preliminary.

SOURCE: U.S. Department of Labor, *Manpower Report
of the President*, Washington, D.C., U.S. Government
Printing Office, March, 1970, p. 34.

disposition of the final report, provides evidence of activity, quite irrespective of action. As high-level, legitimated procrastination, the systems study may already have surpassed the Blue Ribbon Commission,
itself a well-tried delaying device.[19] The more this tactic is employed,
the more it ultimately contributes to a state popularly known as "paraly-
sis by analysis."

Second, the systems study is a strategic weapon, sometimes offensive,
sometimes defensive. For example, the government agency or department that takes the initiative in instituting an analysis is in much safer
position vis-à-vis its hegemony and operational authority than the one

[19] Elizabeth B. Drew, "On Giving Oneself a Hotfoot: Government by Commission,"
The Atlantic Monthly, Vol. 221, No. 4, May, 1968, pp. 45–50.

subjected to such study by another, usually superior, level. To the extent that the contractor can exert influence over, participate in, and monitor the project, the philosophy and thinking of the affected agency will be reflected in the final outcome. Thus the bounds, the variables, and the selection of program alternatives and objectives are prescribed and predetermined. Consequently, results and recommendations are likely to be far more palatable than any superimposed from above. If, through the medium of the study, the client's conception of his organizational *raison d'être* is substantiated or enhanced, he may use it as "scientific" justification for pursuit of a particular course of action. If he finds the report inimical, he is in a position to ignore it. By his order, the completed study can be either implemented or classified as state secret and relegated to a bottom drawer or back shelf. Rarely does it become available for scrutiny or review by any except the carefully designated few.

Systems analysis has a great future as a means to justify or to shake up the bureaucratic *status quo*. The kind of case made for maintaining or abandoning the existing organizational structure depends on the way objectives and performance measures have been devised. Functional and jurisdictional re-alignments, supported by "rational" and "logical" arguments and crafted in the name of more efficient operation, can be proposed and defended. "Scientific" corroboration can be cited as reason for attacking a problem not only across traditional bureaus and divisions but also outside jurisdictional units and boundaries. In effect, here is a tool for circumventing traditional checks and balances and undermining, for better or worse, the bureaucratic structure. Moreover, the techniques of systems analysis can, if used astutely, remove highly charged political issues from the arena of public debate by relegating them to "scientific" appraisal. They can, by the same token, enable public officials to examine questions implicit in many problems but avoided because of their politically sensitive nature. The introduction of rational tools has already effected a kind of metamorphosis in public administration. Governmental planning, once tinged with the brush of socialism, has been divested of its historical stigmata, with political science, the science of government policy making, ambitiously concerning itself with rational planning for now and the future.

Validity of Reasons and Assumptions Underlying the Transfer

The mélange of economic and political factors underlying the transplant of systems techniques onto the social scene warrants critical review because contained in it is a large measure of wishful thinking, public relations, and sheer ignorance. With respect to the economic reasons put forth above, there is no denying that changing concepts, completed contracts, and new priorities in defense and space work are having a drastic effect on employment levels. Despite the commendability of the effort to diversify, it is patently unrealistic, however, to regard systems analysis as an activity which will absorb significant portions of redundant manpower. To begin with, systems analysis, in contrast to production work, is not labor intensive. The total number of analysts employed in all of the original California studies barely exceeded fifty, and if the most enthusiastic extrapolations for future activities were to materialize, the employment opportunities thus generated could not accommodate the numbers displaced by cutbacks in defense and aerospace. A single layoff in Seattle or San Diego can throw 2,000 persons out of work at any given time; the typical team of systems analysts may consist of twenty-five members at most. There seems to be no basis for the assumption that under the same economic conditions that contributed to substantial retrenchment this kind of enterprise would create jobs for the redundant. Moreover, even superficial acquaintance with industrial history and experience indicates that whenever mass unemployment occurs, there is always considerable structural maladjustment. That is to say, the skills required on new jobs do not correspond with those thrown on the market. This is apparent in the case of the Boeing layoffs, for example, where a substantial percentage of those rendered jobless by cutbacks are hourly workers, that is, machinists, assemblers, tool-and-die makers, and clerical personnel. For them, systems analysis offers no solution.

Even for personnel in the scientific and engineering categories of the affected industries, civil systems work presents no assured future. Its absorptive capacity must be assessed both with respect to quantity and qualification. Table 5 shows the distribution of scientists and engineers employed in 1967. Of the total 1,849,000 listed, 17,650 were estimated to be systems analysts, a category defined in rather broad terms. An exercise to reach an order-of-magnitude estimate of civil sector systems activity among defense-related industries found that in the twenty-five firms doing $13 billion worth of defense work in 1966, the average size of the civil systems-oriented team was fifteen. At most, 375 professionals in these companies could claim specific experience of a kind suitable for transfer.[20] Narrowing the focus to one aerospace corporation, the Boeing Company, which probably has a larger percentage of systems analysts than the average industrial firm, we find that of their 26,500 scientific and engineering personnel, 250 to 300, or about 1 percent, are systems analysts.[21] And we have no reason to assume that even this

[20] Hearings on *Scientific Manpower Utilization, op.cit.,* p. 293.
[21] John S. Gilmore, *et al., Defense Systems Resources in the Civil Sector,* pp. 73–74.

TABLE 5

Distribution of Scientists and Engineers and Estimate of Systems Analysts,[1] by Type of Employer, 1967

Type of employer	Engineers[2]	Scientists[3]	Total	Systems analysts percentage of total[4]	Estimated number of systems analysts
Business service firm, for profit[5]	14,000	7,300[6]	21,300	15.0	3,200[7]
All other industry and business	1,012,100	297,400	1,309,500	0.6[8]	7,860
Nonprofits	7,600[8]	24,900	32,500	12.0	3,900[9]
Educational institutions	39,500[10]	222,000	261,500	0.4[11]	1,040
Federal Government	73,000	67,000	140,000	1.0	1,400
Other government	62,800	21,400	84,200	0.3	250
TOTAL	1,209,000	640,000	1,849,000		17,650[12]

SOURCE: *Scientific Manpower Utilization*, 1967, Hearings before the Special Subcommittee on the Utilization of Scientific Manpower of the Committee on Labor and Public Welfare, United States Senate, Ninetieth Congress, First Session, on S.430 and S.467, January 24, 25, 26, 27; March 29 and 30, 1967.

[1] The definition of systems analysts as used herein are those scientists and engineers who are concerned with a search for preferred designs of systems by logical comparison of a variety of combinations and uses of the equipment, personnel, and procedures that comprise the alternative systems. The systems analysis includes the investigation necessary to determine the criteria by which the system may be judged. The functions of these systems analysts include:

Identify functional and operational performance requirements for new systems from analyses of defined goals, objectives, policies, and potential operational environments.

Synthesize alternative systems and operational concepts capable of meeting the identified system requirements.

Analyze the alternative systems and operations to provide the decision with comparative data on the consequences (benefits and penalties) associated with the implementation of each alternative.

Derive and evaluate initial design requirements for the preferred system to provide basic systems engineering criteria for subsystem performance selection.

[2] Source is *Scientists, Engineers, and Technicians* in the 1960's. National Science Foundation, NSF 63–64. Figures for 1960 and NSF's estimate for 1970 requirements have been interpolated linearly to arrive at an estimate for 1967.

[3] The number of scientists employed by each type of employer in the United States was derived from *American Science Manpower*, published by the National Science Foundation in 1966. Document No. 66–29, Government Printing Office.

This document indicates that 415,000 in the natural and selected social science fields in 1964 were included in the National Register and NSF believes that about 75 percent of those qualified are included (thus indicating a total of 554,000 in the United States in 1964). A compound growth rate of 5 percent per year was applied to all categories to obtain the estimates for 1967 of 640,000. The sub-breakdown of industry and business — into systems analysis and softwear firms on one hand and all other for-profit industry on the other — are planning research estimates.

[4] These percentage estimates are based on the educated judgment of planning research personnel except where otherwise noted. However, since an approximate independent check is made on the total in 12 below these estimates are considered to be reasonable approximations.

[5] Includes firms in categories such as systems analysis, computer software, and management consultants; does not include architects and engineers.

[6] Used scientist data in source document *Scientists, Engineers, and Technicians* in the 1960's and interpolated to 1967 as was done for engineers; see note 2. Since these data include only the "hard" sciences, we have doubled the number to include the "soft" (social) sciences, including economists, psychologists, etc.

[7] Twenty-one major companies engaged primarily in systems analysis and software business were estimated to have 6,576 engineers and scientists and 2,025 systems analysts in 1967. It was assumed that all other systems analysis and software firms had another 2,824 engineers and scientists and 575 systems analysts, giving grand totals of 9,400 and 2,600, respectively. An additional 600 systems analysts could be attributed to business service firms other than the systems analysis and computer software types.

[8] An analysis performed by the Boeing Co. indicates that it has 26,500 scientific and engineering personnel and 250 to 300 systems analysts; this is about 1 percent. Boeing probably has a larger percentage of systems analysts than the average U.S. industrial firm. Therefore, on this basis, a value of 0.6 percent is estimated for the average U.S. industrial firm; it might in fact be 0.4 or 0.8 percent.

[9] Six captive nonprofit companies (Aerospace, Center for Naval Analysis, Institute for Defense Analyses, MITRE, Research Analysis Corporation, and RAND) have some 4,110 engineering and scientific personnel and about 1,620 systems analysts. This percentage of systems analysts is 39.4 percent. These companies would have a larger percentage of systems analysts than the other nonprofit corporations. (Other nonprofits would have about 8.5 percent systems analysts, based on the total number of systems analysts in all nonprofits, which is calculated to be 3,900).

[10] Data for educational institutions in the source document probably includes some nonprofit organizations associated with universities, such as Lincoln Labs and Willow Run Research Center. An adjustment to shift 5,000 from the educational institutions to nonprofits has been made in data from the source document.

[11] This percentage estimate includes only those academic personnel who practice in the multidisciplined systems analysis more than half of their time. It excludes their relevant teaching time.

[12] The two largest professional societies that represent systems analysts are Operations Research Society of America (ORSA) and The Institute of Management Sciences (TIMS). ORSA has about 3,200 members and TIMS has about 3,100 members. It is estimated that 40 percent of these 6,300 memberships represents personnel who belong to both groups; therefore, there are 5,040 individuals represented. It is further estimated that about 50 percent of the nonduplicate society members qualify as systems analysts. Based on a small sample of organizations, it is estimated that about 1 in 8 (12.5 percent) belong to one of these two organizations. This would indicate about 20,000 systems analysts in the United States. (This exhibit indicates about 17,650.)

small group ever engaged in civil systems work. Approaching re-employment in aggregate and gross terms glosses over the realities of the situation, *viz.,* that the large mass of workers affected by cutbacks cannot
possibly be absorbed by the new "intellectual" industry and that even
among those persons counted as professional systems analysts, the number who can claim experience with civil systems work is miniscule.

On the micro-level, there are interesting sidelights to be derived from
examining the way in which analysts assigned to the California studies
thought they had been selected for the projects. The following table
lists the reasons they gave.

TABLE 6

Reasons Given by Personnel for Reassignment

Reasons Given	*Number of Persons*
Experienced in the area	8
Experienced in an area needed for study	20
Interviewee requested to be on project	8
Between projects	6
Knew project leader	4
Other[a]	5
	51

SOURCE: Ronald P. Black and Charles W. Foreman, "Transferability
of Research and Development Skills in the Aerospace Industry," in
Applying Technology to Unmet Needs, Report of the National Commission on Technology, Automation, and Economic Progress, p. V-128.
[a] Acquaintanceship with another team member, graduate school training, possible link between team and State personnel, outside interests,
hard worker.

The sample, although extremely limited, is worth pondering. Scarcely half of the participants could claim competence in the specific or
related study areas; the rest offered a diversity of reasons that had no
bearing on the particular work at hand. It might be apropos to note,
without pejorative intent, that in a showcase demonstration such as
the California experiment, it might reasonably have been expected that
personnel of the highest competence and calibre would have been
selected. Such does not appear to have been the case. The actual pattern
of re-assignment paralleled that of any reduction in force, in which the
workers available for immediate redeployment are often the most
relinquishable. Review of the qualifications of the particular persons
assigned by industry contractors to government projects shows that
there may be room for doubt as to their superior ability, either with
respect to customary engineering tasks or the new public projects. One

might conclude on the basis of this sample at least that giant corporations do not as a matter of practice or as a practical matter allocate their most talented scientists and engineers to the public works contracts. Perhaps the explanation for a man's relocation is more his expendability than his ability.

Undoubtedly, an unanticipated bonus was reaped, by those selected, from an undergraduate minor in economics or a chance course in sociology or education. Depending on the system to be analyzed, an interesting assortment of titles blossomed. "Manager of Socio-Economic Systems," "Educational Systems Analyst," "Specialist in Socio-Tech Systems," or even "Advanced Concepts Specialist" were among those which appeared. The practice of *ad hoc* title bestowal upon the persons delegated to perform the transplant raises compelling questions about prevailing personnel practices in the systems work done on familiar ground and home territory; the possibility that civil systems, which defy quality control and yet involve so significant an element of public trust, are being handled in cavalier fashion; the jeopardy into which public planning could be placed were it to rely on systems designed by Nanki-Poos who "tune their supple song" to the "changing humor" of the occasion, or, in other words, by inappropriate experts masquerading as specialists. Clearly, the roster of responsible public planners needs persons with a certain kind of education, experience, and competence. There is nothing in the California demonstration nor in subsequent systems studies that would substantiate the hypothesis that such skills are especially or even noticeably resident in the mass of workers in aerospace and defense, in their scientific and engineering personnel, nor even, from among the ranks of the latter, in those who can lay claim to some familiarity with systems work.

Systems work in the realm of public affairs is not only different as to number and types of workers needed but also totally dissimilar in the type of work to be performed and the conditions which prevail. These are so essential and fundamental as to nullify the illusion and negate the assertion, encouraged by superficial semantic analogy, of transfer of skills. Working on systems for defense and aerospace, the engineer functions in a highly structured environment. Here, the system *is* the intricate organization that synchronizes and calibrates components to acheive a specific end. The fact that the system is *also* the end that is *achieved*, such, for example, as the MIRV (Multiple Independently Targeted Re-entry Vehicle), only serves to underscore the confusion generated by verbal impoverishment that allows for such a multitude of uses for the one word, *system*. The engineer works on clearly defined tasks; the tolerances are close. As a member of a strictly programed component of a highly organized system, he is subject to constant checking and control. All of his activities must dovetail with those of the rest of the huge enterprise.

By contrast, the circumstances governing and the criteria for judging performance in defense and aerospace missions bear little resemblance to those prevailing in social accounting. In the realm of public affairs, the "social engineer's" course has been virtually uncharted. He has been accorded a degree of autonomy not only absent in his usual work but far exceeding that given to responsible professionals in the field in which he now finds himself. The aerospace team studying waste management in California, for example, recommended a centralized authority with virtual dictatorial powers over all resources as though they were dealing with virgin territory, unsullied by counties, townships, and cities, each with entrenched interests about land use and zoning. The group designing a system of criminal justice arbitrarily defined and disposed of a population-at-risk as though this existed in a social vacuum. This *carte blanche* permitted the contracting teams to disregard existing bureaucratic and jurisdictional boundaries and propose "logical" arrangements that failed to take the realities into account. These and countless repetitions of the California experience strengthen the postulate that it is easy, simple, and simplistic to posit an ideal situation, for the simulation often excludes the troublesome real-life factors that aggravate the problem. The techniques of systems analysis seem to be better suited to solution of *ersatz* social ailments than to those which actually persist.

Similar latitude and freedom from constraint were allowed with respect to the time frame, even though public planning takes place with an eye on the calendar. Alexis de Tocqueville remarked, as long ago as 1831, that the four-year cycle of presidential campaigns had a visible effect on policy-making in the United States.[22] At state and local levels, elected officials must synchronize their activities with elections in order to survive. And the electorate expects the periodic program review and accounting, no matter how deeply couched in the self-congratulatory euphemisms of the political contest. To dwell in the post-1984, never-never land of the year 2000 and on is, therefore, a good deal easier than to cope with the slough of the 1970s, and systems designers seize the opportunity. The *California Integrated Transportation Study*, for example, held forth the tantalizing prospects of "trains gliding through tubes at speeds of today's jetliners, possibly far below surface streets and countryside," "ships that 'fly' a few feet over the waves at several hundred miles per hour, only to nestle gently to a dock where they will exchange hundreds of thousands of pounds of containerized cargo in

[22] Alexis de Tocqueville, *Democracy in America*, the Henry Reeve text, revised by Phillips Bradley, New York: Alfred A. Knopf, 1963, Vol. I, pp. 127 ff.

short times comparable to today's airplanes," "trucks or buses that ride a cushion of air on guideways, moving between cities at several times today's cruising speeds and within cities at slow speeds." [23] Significantly, however, the transplanted experts, in designing the brave new world for posterity, never come to grips with the dilemmas facing the planner today. Ignored in the transportation study was the complex of crucial interacting causes and effects contributing to the state of creeping concrete that has robbed the countryside of open space and the city of living room. Overlooked was the imminent head-on collision between a rapidly growing society acculturated to its private motorized mode of travel and a culture suddenly alerted to and alarmed over ecological degradation.

Instead, the study team gamboled in Elysian fields, where, thanks to the blessings still to come from automation, "the office employee of tomorrow may well be able to schedule his five hours of work anytime during a twelve-hour period, perhaps within the confines of his own home in the foothills of the Sierras or on the coast of Northern California." [24] Notably lacking in the idyllic scenario was concern for the blue collar or day worker who lived not in the sylvan shade of the mountains but in the lurking shadow of a slum, where bus service was poor and after-dark travel a peril. Completely forgotten was the original charge, viz,, a plan to get Dad through the traffic tangles or onto a form of transit that would, as California's governor had requested, get him to work on time.

To assess further the credibility of systems analysis as a vehicle for the re-employment of workers displaced from defense and aerospace, one might add to the discussion about qualifications of transferees and their ability to inject a new technique into new problem areas the observation that the territory which they seek to enter is far from undisputed. Government contracts for systems studies and designs attract the avid attention of not only an assortment of companies besides aerospace and defense, but also of specialists from a heterogeny of disciplines and with great diversity as to background and experience. The ranks of consultants for hire grow daily, a fact which suggests that systems-work, for whatever it is worth, cannot be accorded the job-making potential for redundant employees once wishfully thought.

Nor can the activity be reasonably judged a promising way of breaking the dependence of industry upon government. Table 7, which lists federal agency support of systems analysis by function, gives a clue to the market attracting the various practitioners and their wares. Based

[23] North American Aviation, Inc., *California Integrated Transportation Study*, September, 1965, Vol. I, p. 4.

[24] *Ibid.*, p. 8.

TABLE 7

Federal Agencies Support of System Analysis Activity (States and Cities) by Function

	Planning and policies (1)	Personnel management (2)	Interagency activity (3)	Management standards control (4)	Equipment selection (5)	Procurement activity (6)	Legislatures (7)	Courts (8)	Financial (9)	Taxation (10)	Education (11)	Health and hospitals (12)	Crime and corrections (13)	Transportation (14)	Urban renewal and growth (15)	Science and research promotion (16)	Natural resources (17)	Pollution control (18)	Parks and recreation (19)	Regulation of commerce, etc. (20)	Labor and man-power services (21)	Utilities and enterprises (22)	Welfare and anti-poverty (23)	Social security and veterans (24)	Other (25)
Alaska	HUD										HEW	HEW	DOJ	DOT			Int.		Int.		DOL		HEW	HEW	
Arkansas				HUD								HEW		DOT											
California											HEW	(1)	(1)	DOT											
Colorado												(2)	(2)												
Connecticut[3]																									
Idaho														DOT											
Illinois[3]																									
Indiana[3]																									
Iowa	HUD		HUD								HEW	HEW		DOT							DOL				
Kansas	(4)								OEO		HEW	HEW		DOT	(5)	(6)			(7)			HUD			
Maine[3]			HUD																						
Maryland[3]																									
Massachusetts	HUD		HUD		DOL						HEW	HEW		DOT							DOL		(2)		
Missouri												HEW			(2)			(2)							
Nebraska												HEW													
New Mexico[3,8]																									
New York[3]														DOT											
North Carolina														DOT											
Ohio														DOT		HEW									
Oregon				(2)							HEW	HEW		DOT							(2)		HEW		
Pennsylvania[3]											HEW	HEW			(10)	(6)	(4)						(2)		
Rhode Island	(9)		HUD														Int.				(11)		(12)		

	HUD	OEO	HEW HEW DOJ	DOC HEW Int.	DOC HEW Int.	NSF DOT HUD	DOC DOL	DOC DOL DOC HEW[13]
South Carolina								
South Dakota[3]								
Texas	HEW / HUD							
Utah	HUD							
Vermont								
Washington	BOB							
West Virginia[3]			HUD[14]					
Wisconsin[3]								
CITIES								
Atlanta[3]								
Buffalo[3]								
Cincinnati			HEW HEW DOJ DOJ (2) (2)					(2) OEO (2)
Chicago				HEW		DOT HUD		
Cleveland		(2)	(2) (2)			(2)	(2)	
Dallas[3]								
Denver[3]								
Detroit	(15)	(15)						
Kansas City[3]								
Los Angeles[3]								
New Orleans[3]				HEW		HUD		
New York City			(1⁰) (2)	HEW		HUD		HEW
Philadelphia								
Phoenix[3]								
San Diego[3]								
San Francisco[3]								

[1] NIMH.
[2] Did not specify source.
[3] Did not indicate Federal support.
[4] HEW, OEO, HUD, DOT.
[5] HEW, HUD.
[6] HEW, NSF, HUD.
[7] HUD, Int. (Bureau of Reclamation).
[8] HUD will support PPBS.
[9] HUD, DOD, DOT, EDA.
[10] HUD, DOT.
[11] Int. (Federal Water Pollution Control Adm.).
[12] HEW, OEO.
[13] HEW, V.A.
[14] DOT, Interior.
[15] HUD, OEO.

SOURCE: Systems Technology Applied to Social and Community Problems, Committee print prepared for the Subcommittee on Employment, Manpower, and Poverty of the Committee on Labor and Public Welfare, 91st Congress 1st Session, U.S. Senate, June, 1969, pp. 173-174.

TABLE 8

Indications of Systems Analysis Capability by Function 1968

I X—in-house capability; Y—out-of-house capability; Z—out-of-house and in-house capability I

STATES	(1) Planning and policies	(2) Personnel management	(3) Interagency activity	(4) Management standards control	(5) Equipment selection	(6) Procurement activity	(7) Legislatures	(8) Courts	(9) Financial	(10) Taxation	(11) Education	(12) Health and hospitals	(13) Crime and corrections	(14) Transportation	(15) Urban renewal and growth	(16) Science and research promotion	(17) Natural resources	(18) Pollution control	(19) Parks and recreation	(20) Regulation of commerce, etc.	(21) Labor and manpower services	(22) Utilities and enterprises	(23) Welfare and anti-poverty	(24) Social security and veterans	(25) Other
Alaska	X	X	X	X	X	X			X	X	Y	Y	Y	Y			Y		Y		Y		Y	X	
Arkansas	Y	X	X	Y	X				X	X	Y	Y	Y	X	Y	Y	Y	Y	Y		Y		Y	Y	X
California	Y	Y	Y	Y	Y	Y	X		Y	Y	Y	Y	Y	Y	Y	Y	Y	Y	Y	Y	Y	X	X	Y	
Colorado	Y	Y	X	Y	Y	Y		X	Y	Y	Y	Y	X	X	X	Y	X		X	X		X	Y	X	
Connecticut	X	Y	X	X	X	X	X		X	X	X	X		X					X				X		
Idaho	Z	Y	X	Y	X	X	Z		X	X	Y	Y		Y	X	Y	Y		X		X		Y		
Illinois	X	X	Y	X	X	X	X		X	X	Y	X		Y	X	Z	X	X	X	X	Y		X	X	
Indiana	X	X	X	X	X	X	Y		X	Y	X	Y	X	Y	X	Z	Y	Y	Y	Y	Y		Z	Y	
Iowa	Y	X	Y	Y	Y	Y		Z	Z			Y		X					Z		Z			Y	
Kansas	Y				X				Y	Y	Z	Z	Z	Z	Z	Z		Z			N	N			Y1
Maine									Y														Y		
Maryland	X	X	X		X	Z	Z		X	X	Y	Y	Y	X	Z		Y	X	X	X	X	X	Y	X	
Massachusetts	Z	X	Z	X	Y	Z	X		X	X	Y	Y	Y	Y	Z	Y	Y	Y	Z	X	Y	Z	Z	Z	
Missouri	X	X	Z	X	X	X		Z	Z	Z	Z	Y	Z	Z	Z		Y	X		Y	Y		Y	Y	
Nebraska		Y	X						Y	Y				Z	X								X		
New Mexico	X	X	X	X	Z	Z	X	X	X	X	X	X	X	X	X	X	X	Z	X	X	Y	X	Y	X	
New York	Y	Y	X	N	Y	Y	Y	Z	X	Y	Y	Y	Y	Y	Y	Y	Y	N	Y	Y	X	Y	X	X	Y1
North Carolina	Y	Y	Y	X	X	X	X	X	X	X	Y	Y	X	Y	X	Z	X		X		Y		X		
Ohio	X	X	Y	Y	Y	X	X		X	Y	Y	Y	Y	Y	Y	Y	Y	Y	X	X	X	X	X	X	X
Oregon	X	Y	Y	Y	Y	X	Y		X	Y	Y	Y	X	Y		Y	X	Y	X	X	Y	X	X	X	
Pennsylvania	Y	Y	Y	Y	Y	X	Y	Y	X	Y	Y	Y	Y	Y	Y	Y	Y	Y	X	X	X	X	Y	X	X
Rhode Island	Y	N	Y	Y	X	X	Y	Y	X	Y	Y	Y	X	Y	Y	N	Y	Y	X	X	Y	Y	Y	X	Y2

South Carolina
South Dakota
Texas
Utah
Vermont
Washington
West Virginia
Wisconsin

Atlanta, Ga
Buffalo, N.Y.
Chicago, Ill.
Cincinnati, Ohio
Cleveland, Ohio
Denver, Colo.
Detroit, Mich.
Houston, Tex.
Kansas City, Mo.
Los Angeles, Calif.
New Orleans, La.
New York, N.Y.
Philadelphia, Pa.
Phoenix, Ariz.
San Diego, Calif.
San Francisco

REGIONAL DEVELOPMENT ORGANIZATIONS AND U.S. Territories
Port Authority of
New York
Guam
Puerto Rico

1 Motor vehicle, liquor accounting and inventory.
2 Liquor control board.
3 Limited application at city level, nonprofit Southern California Transit District.
4 Limited.
5 Other: Sanitation, fire prevention, library services.

SOURCE: Systems Technology Applied to Social and Community Problems, Committee print prepared for the Subcommittee on Employment, Manpower, and Poverty of the Committee on Labor and Public Welfare, 91st Congress 1st Session, U.S. Senate, June, 1969, pp. 170-171.

on a questionnaire, the information gathered is neither complete nor definitive. The figures, taken in conjunction with Table 8 (which shows the distribution of systems analysis capability, out-of-house and in-house) do, however, indicate the incidence of outside contracting, which amounted to an estimated $27.3 million for the period 1965-1969.[25] This amount is on the rise as the tendency of government agencies to draw on outside talent increases. With it, there will occur a crescendo of the public-private interaction that perpetuates rather than eliminates dependence.

This concrescence of interests leads to an intense degree of commensality, where the condition of mutual sustenance thrives in the environment surrounding systems analyses. Public funds are involved and public issues are at stake. Therefore, this high level management game is a politically sensitive matter, with "musical chairs" the pattern of movement of the players. Once large sums are expended, the outcome, whatever its value, must be adjudged worthwhile, and everyone associated with the enterprise must come out looking good. When the contractor delivers a doubtful product, the astute administrator appoints a carefully selected task force to review the findings (*pianissimo* if useless) and make recommendations that may bear little relationship to the completed study. No one in political life, except him possessed of a death wish, would admit that he had acted unwisely in having such a study done or in the choice of contractor. Monitors hired to ensure an acceptable result or, perhaps, to evaluate the report have not supplied outstanding service. Likely to be fellow-analysts from competing organizations, these consultants take a "sum quod eris" [26] posture, which clearly indicates the fraternal loyalty that shields them and their work from public scrutiny. Sharing the same technical approach to the problem as the team conducting the systems study, the monitor fails to discern fallacious assumptions or neglected variables. Instead, he is inclined to question only innocuous minutiae and hint sympathetically that any deficiencies are due to (a) limitations of funds and (b) time. He therefore recommends more of (a) for follow-on contracts, to which he will have access as prime or sub-contractor, and extended (b), which will benefit him under either circumstance. Free-floating criticism or evaluation, which could in most of the cases observed result in an emperor's-new-clothes debacle, is studiously avoided. Finished studies, consequently, become protected property, access to which is severely limited.

[25] U.S. Senate Subcommittee on Employment, Manpower, and Poverty of the Committee on Labor and Public Welfare, *Systems Technology Applied to Social and Community Problems*, Washington, D.C.: U.S. Government Printing Office, June, 1969, p. 176.
[26] Legend found on old tombstones, "I am what you will be."

In New York City, for example, tight security was imposed to keep a $500,000 NYC-RAND Institute report from public view. When *The New York Times* obtained a draft of the first volume and published an article on it, the city's Housing and Development Administration undertook an investigation to identify and bring criminal charges against the person who supplied the document. Only "public papers" must, by New York State law, be open to inspection; "investigations" and "studies" are exempt by New York City Charter. Ten City Councilmen had earlier instituted legal action to force the city to make public the controversial housing report which, they claimed, had already circulated in private banking circles, and of which the chairman of the housing committee had not even been given a copy.

In other instances, contracting agencies have circumspectly doled out numbered copies. Sometimes distribution is in the hands of the contractor and subject to his discretion, which may or may not coincide with the greater public interest. Usually, the "out-of-print" situation is soon mercifully reached. Proof positive of the dangers courted by high visibility and of the distinct advantages of self-effacement on the part of those responsible for systems studies in the public sector can be found in the reactions of the aroused public when, in New York, they learned that their nearly bankrupt and perennially hard-up city had paid out six-figure sums to discover facts that were common knowledge, skirted controversial issues, and postponed in high public relations style clear-cut policy commitments and decisions.

A catalogue of the political factors which guarantee the hothouse environment for systems techniques should include the advantages of non-responsible decision making. Public officials who, by virtue of having invoked the powerful tools of technology can claim credit or enjoy exoneration, whichever is politic, are in an especially favorable position. The mayor of a large city, for example, wins his election by pledging to do something about the bad conditions of housing, transportation, health, crime, and so on. Among his first official acts is the signing of contracts with consultants to do "urban analysis" and "plan rationally." From then on, he has a ready-made rationalization for any position taken, any decision made or avoided. In New York City, for example, where $75 million was paid to outside consultants in 1969, it was discovered, late in the game, that ten different studies of one bridge had been made since 1948, that the current Transportation Administrator was unaware of six of them, and that not one of them was implementable or implemented. A sequence of administrations had reaped the benefits of public display of concern over the situation without making a further attempt at its amelioration. But, even more important, if action *had* been taken, its results could, if politically strategic, have been blamed on outsiders. Far from insensitive to the many fruitful dimensions to be derived from systems work, the City of New York bought the entire back cover of an issue of the Institute of Management Science's journal [27] to broadcast "an opportunity to be at the center of complex urban systems analyses." The advertisement, unwonted in nature, called for any number of "talented individuals" with experience in "problem formulation, modelling, computer systems design and programming," to work at salaries from $15,000 to $25,000. Proclaimed in the text was the intelligence, somewhat counter to current disclosures on the subject, that ". . . the mayoral staff of the Lindsay Administration is creatively utilizing quantitative analyses and computer technology with support from NYC-RAND Institute and consulting services such as McKinsey & Company. But all the problems are not solved and we need more talented individuals capable of project leadership and analysis." [28]

With New York as model, the lesser cities of the nation cannot be far behind. The political advantages are evident, the temptations are great. Contracts with outside experts could become another ingredient in the familiar old pork-barrel recipe. Wherever there are funds, there are consultants for hire, and there are no professional standards to distinguish the "carpetbagger," castigated by a *New York Times* editorial, from the "legitimate specialist," to whom they do obeisance.[29]

THE PROCESS OF TECHNOLOGICAL TRANSFER

The procedures through which government agencies brought aerospace, defense, and, later, miscellaneous systems specialists into public planning have had considerable bearing on the ultimate magnitude, dynamics, and direction of this manifestation of technology transfer. Previous industry-government transactions concerned specific goods and services. With clearly identified and generally understood objects and entities, there could be explicitly articulated and enforceable standards. If, for example, the Department of Defense asked for a Titan 3D space booster, specifications for design, fabrication, and testing were designated and mutually understood by all parties to the agreement. The responding firms could produce evidence of similar missions successfully accomplished, capability palpably demonstrated. In sharp

---

[27] *Management Science*, Vol. 16, No. 11, July, 1970 (Theory Series), back cover.

[28] An article on New York City's use of consultants was prepared by *The New York Times* and appeared in a series, starting on July 1, 1970. In it, questions were raised as to who the consultants were, how they were selected, what was their impact on the city, how expenditures for them were justified, and whether their management solutions to basically political problems were effective.

[29] "The City's Consultants," *The New York Times* editorial, July 11, 1970.

contrast, arrangements for civil systems studies deal with intangible concepts and symbols. Throughout every phase of the operation, nothing but words and figures are exchanged. What is crucial, therefore, is how and what language is used.

When the State of California formulated the original requests to the aerospace industry for proposals for systems designs of information, care of the mentally ill and the criminals, waste management, and transportation, there was no precedent to follow. The standard format of request for proposal was utilized, the usual ritual of proposal submission observed. There was, to begin with, the request for proposal (RFP), to be disseminated among the large aerospace companies with talent to spare. But the formulation of such an RFP posed a dilemma, never subsequently resolved. In calling for bids, the state had stressed its intention to "draw upon the imagination of the contractor in approaching the optimal solution to the problem at hand through an overall analysis of the total program with effective suboptimization of the component parts." [30] How to formulate an RFP that conveys to the prospective contractor the essence of the problem, the objectives of the system, and the political, economic, and social costs and benefits of certain courses of action or nonaction is an art not yet mastered. Government still finds itself in a situation of being sold solutions in the absence of a a clear understanding of the problems at hand, of being presented with prefabricated answers before the full dimensions of the questions have been grasped.

The tendency in phrasing the RFP has been toward over-specificity or over-generality. If the terms are set forth in detail, the response is likely to be an item-by-item proposal that precludes the very innovativeness that the enterprise was supposed to introduce. The too-specific RFP does the contractor's work for him, in a sense; it denies him latitude and is practically bound to defeat its own purpose. The intentionally loose, vague, and general RFP, so framed as "to draw upon the imagination of the contractor," encourages an equally generalized and vague response. The latter procedure places the responsibility of defining the problem in the hands of persons who may be inexperienced with the substantive essentials, naïve politically, overly dependent on the mechanical and technical aspects of their task, and insensitive to its social dimensions.

The proposal itself is another key instrument in the dealings between public agency and contractor, for it is the means by which the latter conveys his claim to competence. It also conceivably could provide a checkpoint for subsequent reference and comparison between promise

[30] State of California, Department of Finance, Sacramento, California, "Requests for Proposals," November 18, 1964.

and product, but we find no evidence of such systematic evaluation. Because the proposal must carry the message of the superiority of its creator, it is primarily a selling device, in which substantiation of the assertions of prowess takes the form of a mixture of salesmanship; promotion of the technique and the particular corporate image, as much as the particular aptitude of either; and technical jargon, used more to impress the reader than to shed light. There is usually heavy reliance on linguistic status symbols — a pandering to the pervasive propensity to revere whatever is "scientific," the more so the less comprehensible it is!

Despite the heterogeny of contenders and the diversity of their backgrounds, proposals are remarkably stereotyped, not only as to structure but also content. Almost invariably, they start with a platitudinous statement of the matter at hand. Often this is little more than a paraphrase of a simplistic view.

Mental illness and crime are major social problems faced by all nations of the world. In the United States, however, the problem takes on a unique complexity because of the interdependent structure of the city, county, state and federal government agencies which are assigned the tasks of administration, legislation and enforcement of laws designed to cope with the many and varied aspects of the problem.[31]

Then comes an introduction to the methodology in general. This, interesting to note, reveals a considerable lack of the very objectivity and freedom from bias attributed to the technical approach. The description of systems analysis tries to convey the notion that the state-of-the-art has been developed to such a high degree as to be the answer to society's ailing systems and that the particular competing company has the artists best equipped to ply their skills. The following is a typical example.

General Planning Corporation and its associates propose to use a rigorous methodological approach to derive precise understandings of the optimal allocation of resources required to improve the functions of the welfare system. One such approach, born out of the U.S. Department of Defense's Systems Analysis activities, is variously referred to as "Program Packaging," or the "PPB" (Planning, Programming, and Budgeting) approach. This approach has proved invaluable in the design of our national security/defense force by providing clear "program definition" to the weapon system requirement. General Planning Corporation has successfully applied this approach to other non-military problems as, e.g., to problems of regional area economic development. We feel this powerful set of systems analysis tools will prove equally efficient in assisting the State Welfare Board in its seeking for a significantly

---

[31] *Criminal and Mentally Ill Populations*, Technical Proposal T-04418, TEMPO, General Electric Company, Santa Barbara, California, December 18, 1964, p. 2.

better solution to the problem of hard core poverty and the rising costs of welfare.[32]

Another proposal for the same contract by a different company contains a similar message and implications.

Systems analysis is a term which, as yet, lacks a precise definition. It can, however, be characterized as follows: It provides an *overall scientific* look at the problems, thus ensuring that all elements are covered.

It is *interdisciplinary*, bringing to bear the expertize [sic] of many skills to discover and measure complex interrelationships perhaps not realized previously.

It is *formal*, in following a systematic procedure, formally stating objectives and requirements, and analyzing alternate solutions.

It is completely *objective* in assessing elements of the problem, developing alternative solutions, and evaluating their cost and benefit.

Lockheed, entrusted with the management of major NASA and Department of Defense projects, uses such techniques of systems analysis as mathematics, operations research, linear programming, and the like. It can bring to the solution of social problems the unique combination of prudence and imagination, both of which are prerequisites to the design of sophisticated space-age systems.[33]

There is, implicit in proposals, a kind of *post hoc, ergo propter hoc* sales message. Through declaration, association, and iteration, the prospective customer is first innoculated with the suggestion that systems analysis has been proven invaluable in important missions. This weapon, effective in conquering space, is now set forth as ready for successful war on crime, poverty, pollution, or whatever else ails society. The next stage of the promotion ties the corporate image into the success syndrome. Like the several instances cited above, all of the fifty-odd proposals submitted in response to the State of California's original call dwelt long on defense and aerospace contracts and subcontracts held, by the applicant, as though designing and building a

[32] General Planning Corporation, "A Proposal for a Study of the Welfare System in Terms of Program Services Development and Information System Design," April 14, 1966, p. 1.

[33] *Proposal for a System Analysis Study of the California Welfare System*, Lockheed Missiles & Space Company, A Group Division of Lockheed Aircraft Corporation, Sunnyvale, California, LMSC-894504, April 15, 1966, pp. 1–2. Lockheed's claims to managerial prowess, like those of its prime customer, the Pentagon, have been subjected to congressional scrutiny and found severely lacking in substantiation. During the June, 1971, hearings of the Senate Banking and Currency Committee, the company has been accused of gross mismanagement of its own affairs. Its request for a $250 million federal government guaranteed loan to save it from bankruptcy occasioned the proposal of the stipulation that this might be considered only if Daniel J. Haughton, chairman, and all members of the Lockheed board resign.

rocket's launch system were an indicator of ability to ascertain the relevant factors contributing to welfare loads, dependency, or crime.

To bolster the particular company's prestige further, a large section of the proposal is always devoted to biographical materials relating both to the organizational roster as a whole and the experts to be assigned to the task. But scrutiny of these pages of *curricula vitae* soon reveals that the first portion is probably irrelevant and the second unreliable as a clue to special competence. The company, research institute, or management consulting firm may truthfully count thousands of advanced degrees among its employees. But the panegyrics of publicizing this fact, often set forth in advertisements as well as in formal proposals, do little to substantiate the claims being made. The corps of scientists and engineers may be tremendous; they may have carried out complicated projects. But respect for their accomplishments need not catalyze instant apotheosis. They are not supermen, nor, to judge from their records, are they even Renaissance men. The schools they attended, the posts they held, the papers they published show more specialization than scope. Even the team of "socio-technical experts" designated for the prospective project displayed a remarkable dearth of the dimensions one might have considered as requisite.

This shortcoming was often overcome by the promise to complement "inhouse capability" with outside consultants. Even this became an opportunity for self-eulogy. One document proclaimed that the company had "long carried on a policy of drawing upon the keenest minds available." Another stated that "eminent consultants are also available from outside the . . . organization to act as contributors in researching projects requiring specialized capabilities." This form of ellipsis is popular and familiar in systems proposal and report writing, for its crypticism allows considerable latitude of interpretation. It is common knowledge that there are "eminent consultants"; does mentioning their existence in this context imply that they will be hired, that their services will be used, their advice heeded? In the face of such stellar capability on the horizon, is there any reason why the government agency should contract for the services of the Johnnies-come-lately?

Many proposals list the names and titles of their consultants. Three main categories are evident: outside experts hired to advise, guide, or evaluate the effort; specialists from within the contracting organization, perhaps attached to another branch in the case of a giant corporation; independent professionals, usually from the academic community, who perform such tasks as a public service and not primarily as an entrepreneurial venture. The first two groups are virtually captive; the first, because, once bought and paid for, their contribution can be put to use or on the shelf. The second may be deprived of meaningful participation because of the pecking order that prevails in the large firms. In one of the studies, to lend the enterprise a social science orientation, a member of the company's personnel department was borrowed. With a Ph.D. in psychology and a forte in personality testing, he apparently enjoyed less status than the leader of the team and played about the same role in the mission as the Dormouse at the Hatter's Mad Tea-Party. The third group is serviceable in the activity popularly and tastelessly called "brainpicking," in which professional research and faculty persons are visited for a session of quick orientation or at least the gathering of useful terminology in the field under study.

The experience of one aerospace team in California demonstrated that, from the strategic point of view of getting a system study done and the report bound and delivered, the participation of an unpaid resource committee could be a source of embarrassment and delay. The group, made up of authorities in the area, took its duties seriously, questioned fallacious assumptions, challenged improper data manipulation, and revealed dangerous implications of work done and undone. The project leader resolved all these problems by suspending the regular meetings of the resource people and by judiciously avoiding the exercise of his option to call them together again.

Another item often included for credit in the proposal is "conference participation." With the growing interest in systems analyses, more and more professional societies, government agencies, and, especially, social planning groups schedule at their conferences special sessions devoted to quantitative techniques and their potential applications. Almost always, the rostrum of speakers includes representatives from the "think industry," be it in the form of an aerospace company, a RAND-type organization, or an entrepreneurial consultant. Presentation of papers at such meetings is listed as though evidence of some kind of superior competence when, in actual fact, little credit is due anyone, the speaker who delivered the thinly disguised sales promotion or the association so naïve as to invite a hungry fox into its henhouse. The papers, whether the conference be concerned with health, welfare, education, or crime, are designed to convince the particular profession of the need for a "systematic" approach to its fiscal, operational, and perennial chaos. With subtle finesse and not much elucidation, the "systematic" approach, about which there is no dispute, becomes "the systems approach," with its accompanying tale of accomplishment in the Department of Defense and outer space. And deftly inserted in the sales package is the notion of the "systems capability" of the speaker and his company.

Tremendous advantage, far out of proportion to service rendered or competence demonstrated, accrues to being able to refer in the proposal to civil systems analyses done under previous contract. The citing of completed studies as proof of capability appears to be a shrewdly calculated trading on the supposition that there will be no challenge about their value. Under the political circumstances surrounding the whole transaction, this ploy carries low risk and high returns. Paraded as evidence are plastic-bound agglomerations of charts, overlay maps, and computer printouts with text that belabors the obvious, ignores the critical, and leaves virtually untouched the problems at hand. Nonetheless, while there may exist reasonable doubt about their worth, their usefulness is indisputable, for they constitute leverage for all concerned in obtaining more grant money for more studies of the same kind and calibre.

An integral and vital part of the transplant of systems analysis, the ritual of the proposal has been recognized and exploited assiduously by vendors as a way of getting their message across. So highly developed, in fact, is the state-of-the-art of proposal composition that some firms augment their in-house writing staff by engaging the talents of outside specialists whose forte is the preparation of such documents. Thus far, the buyers, that is, government bodies, have not developed sophisticated strategies for using the proposal procedures to further their own objectives. They still ask the impossible, accept the improbable, and provide protective cover against exposure. In the California transportation study, for example, it was patently preposterous to have asked for a transportation system "which the state will need 30 to 50 years from now to provide efficient movement" and to ask systems engineers "who should pay for it; who should run it." [84] The Space Age response of lettuce shot through tubes from field to market and work transmitted electronically to far-flung homes of non-commuting employees was appropriate to the RFP, not to the problems besetting public planners. And asking the systems engineers who should pay implied that they were possessed with clairvoyance denied professionals in the field. Poor questions generate poor answers, and fuzzy conceptualization embodied in the RFP is the first link in a causal chain of events.

Clear thinking on problems, issues, and policies is a *sine qua non* for responsible decision makers seeking assistance. And, if their RFPs were unequivocal as to tasks, terms, and expectations, contracting agencies would have some basis for evaluating the finished product. In the absence of a universally accepted set of criteria for a good anal-

---

[84] Edmund G. Brown, address given at University of California (Los Angeles) Extension Symposium Luncheon, Los Angeles, California, November 14, 1964.

ysis,[35] the ethics of the marketplace prevail and the contract is fulfilled when the study is delivered as scheduled.

The instances in which questions regarding usefulness have been raised are rare but noteworthy. In California, when the outcome of a $225,000 study was scrutinized and found wanting, the contractor adopted a *caveat emptor* posture and blamed the agency for asking the wrong questions, failing to clarify its goals, and imposing too many bureaucratic roadblocks to allow for the brave new technical approach to work its benefits. Sensing the embarrassment that might spring from disclosure of having asked too much, gotten too little, and paid exorbitantly, the state discreetly paid the bill.

On the federal level, criticism of systems analysis contracts has been rare and, therefore, all the more noteworthy. The Comptroller General of the United States reviewed the administration by the Office of Civil Defense, Department of the Army, of three research study contracts, totalling about $600,000, awarded to Hudson Institute, Inc. The results of the investigation were reported to the Congress "because they illustrate the need for exercising careful control over contractors engaged to make independent research studies so as to provide greater assurance that the reports obtained are truly useful." [36] The effort was estimated to have cost the government firm about $45,000 to $52,000 per man-year of work in its execution. One study was judged to have "added no new thoughts and failed to provide any information not previously known." Another appeared to be "a rehash of old, if not tired, ideas." A third lacked "sufficient depth to warrant general distribution." Herman J. Kahn, the director of the Hudson Institute, used the criticism as an occasion for self-justification of his organization and its methods. Instead of addressing the issues and trying to rectify shortcomings, he used the occasion to extol the practices of his establishment. Contending that a research organization engaged in "rather speculative areas of study" needed an unusual degree of freedom "to develop its thinking as it goes along," he asserted that his institute would not accept contracts unless such scope were permitted. He declared: "This kind of speculative research must be evaluated on the kind of 'batting average' basis, and if the batting average gets too high, we believe that one should be suspicious that the work is not being imaginative and adventurous enough." [37]

[35] E. S. Quade, ed., *Analysis for Military Decisions*, Chicago: Rand McNally, 1967, p. 149.

[36] Elmer R. Staats, Comptroller General of the United States, Report to the Congress, *Observations on the Administration by the Office of Civil Defense of Research Study Contracts Awarded to Hudson Institute, Inc.*, B-133209, Washington, D.C., March 25, 1968, p. 2.

[37] *Ibid.*, Appendix IV, p. 39.

Apparently, high-level criticism has not appreciably affected high-pressure salesmanship, for the latter is capable of mutation to match the mood of the moment. The very dilemma of the contracting agency in choosing between the specific work statement, which "may inhibit creativity and prevent the researcher from freely using his ingenuity in making his studies," and the too general, in which "the government may be subjected to the risk of paying for a study which is totally or partially useless,"[38] presents a self-serving opportunity and justification for work poorly done and more of the same.

The General Accounting Office emphasized the need for work objectives made more specific and suggested that the contractor be told in specific terms what the agency hoped to learn from the study without telling the contractor how to make the study.[39] But this looks better on paper than in practice, for it could lead to the narrow mission-oriented, ideology-justifying type of systems analysis known in government circles as the "hang 'em type," in which outside experts are called upon to provide "scientific" rationalization for a politically expedient course of action.

In making proposal procedures less perfunctory and more a control point, government agencies will be taking a necessary step. But it is not sufficient to insure a useful and usable product. Other phases in the conduct of the systems analysis transaction have important bearing on the outcome and must be taken into account, quite apart from the methodology and questions as to its intrinsic appropriateness, adequacy, and applicability. The stages of the study, whether of welfare or waste management, whether by major "think tank" or minor satellite, follow a certain stereotyped pattern, and this appears to be one which stifles rather than stimulates comprehension in depth of the problem to be addressed.

Most studies are initiated with a series of interviews. Selection of the persons with whom contact is to be made is crucial, for their viewpoints are likely to be inculcated in the design. Members of the team are deployed to ascertain through contact with key individuals the high-level thinking on the subject. It is often their orientation which becomes the *leitmotif* of the whole endeavor, which is justified and strengthened by it, and which almost assures self-preservation and perpetuation. In the area of crime, for example, where vast sums of money are being allocated through legislation for "safe streets," the prevailing mood among city, county, state, and federal officials is one of law enforcement. With apprehension of miscreants its prime objective, the system of criminal justice likely to be regarded with favor is the finely

[38] *Ibid.*, p. 21.
[39] *Ibid.*, p. 22.

meshed trap; the more offenders it catches, the more effective it is. This conception of crime has encouraged many hundreds of thousands of dollars' worth of systems designed to catch a criminal, as though that were tantamount to reducing crime.

The predominant official attitude having been assayed, the analysts now know the ideological lay of the land and can map their course accordingly. In many instances, they will permit this point of view to influence the model they construct, the variables they include as pertinent, the data they select as relevant. There are cases, to be sure, in which the outside experts have elected to proceed on a path of their own devising. If unfamiliar with the field, they are inclined to mistake their ignorance for objectivity, display naïvete, and take their own preconceptions as guidelines. In the California Welfare Study, for example, the analysts based their conclusions on a severely limited and not too closely related sample, projected a target population through prediction techniques that reflected their own bias about welfare recipients more than a knowledge of the substantive problems, and produced little more than an overpowering electronic information system. Whatever the philosophy, the system designed is an expression and externalization of a particular bias, for, paradoxically enough, the personal and subjective play a more decisive role in these "scientific" and "rational" approaches than in the less sophisticated methods they are intended to supersede. The implications of this observation are the more insidious when we realize how deeply the bias is imbedded in the whole process and how completely it may be camouflaged by methodological purfling and technical footling.

The stage of the systems analysis known as data gathering begins early and supplies a convenient accounting for time spent or tasks left undone. The frenetic display of activity in the amassing of a quantity of facts and figures which become the data base is often so *gemütlich* to systems designers that many of them never progress beyond it. The information about a system becomes the system itself. Thus, many systems analyses, purportedly undertaken to improve programs in health, education, welfare, or whatever, concentrate on data-flow and result in complex and elaborate data-processing systems which drain rather than enhance development. So prevalent is the tendency to give the information system a *raison d'être* of its own, to make it an end in itself, that the subject requires special consideration within the framework of this book. A later chapter is devoted to information systems. For the time being, it should be sufficient to note that data-gathering, undertaken as means, frequently becomes the end. This may account, to a large extent, for the phenomenon we are now witnessing of the metamorphosis of so many government agencies and educational institutions into counting houses, where the work is busy, electronic techniques improving, but understanding and amelioration of real-life conditions more and more attenuated. Bringing in experts from outside the discipline has encouraged tinkering with the technical superficialities in avoidance of, and as substitute for, purposeful study and amelioration of the malaise growing in the vitals of society.

The standard techniques employed throughout the process of systems analysis belie the service orientation of which so much is made in institutional advertisements and professional statements of intent. Quite irrespective of the objectives of the system under study, the aim is to get the job done quickly and the report packaged and delivered. Meaningful participation from professional authorities in the field or from the government agencies being served is construed as interference and there is a set of tactics for deliberate and systematic avoidance of involvement. Some were mentioned earlier in connection with the resource committee who took their advisory role too seriously for the comfort of the aerospace team designing a welfare system. There are other evasive practices occurring so frequently and consistently that they seem to form a pattern, which may have eluded recognition because of the isolated circumstances of the individual projects. The logistics of non-engagement are rather subtle but so pervasive as to suggest that they are an intrinsic part of the procedure, a reflection of the state-of-the-art, and a clue to the self rather than the social orientation of this approach to public planning.

A mechanism popularly used is the "progress report," in which content and time are the key means of preventing "interference." For example, in the Office of Civil Defense dealings with the Hudson Institute, the Comptroller General examined the reports and found that they described the studies under way but provided no information on the work Hudson had done or what had been accomplished. Notably absent was sufficient information to permit an evaluation of Hudson's progress.[40] In the California studies, interim reports usually took the form of paraphrases and restatements of items listed in the proposal. "Progress" was indistinguishable from mere show of activity, which detailed such trivia as number of persons interviewed, field visits made. The reports provided no basis upon which to assess progress. Nor, to judge from the timing of their submittal, were they intended to.

Hudson furnished its first report on contract 64-116 about seven months after work was authorized to start and when two-thirds of the research originally estimated had been completed. Under a second contract, the first progress report appeared five months later, with three-quarters of the estimated job done. The Comptroller General's

[40] *Ibid.*, p. 16.

observation of progress reports "submitted so late that it would have been difficult to change the direction of the work even if the information provided had indicated that such a change was warranted" [41] may, to the conscientious social planner, seem like damning criticism. To the entrepreneur with a technique to sell, it is a clear guideline — the way to pursue systems analysis on his own terms. Tardiness, in the hands of a systems craftsman, can even be transformed into a virtue. In one of the California studies, the progress reports, which were supposed to elicit helpful response from a resource committee, reached the members the very day of the scheduled meeting, sometimes right at the conference table. The project leader countered the complaint that such timing precluded proper digestion of the documents with the earnest and pious assertion that the delay was due to the fact that his group wanted to give the State of California its money's worth by "working right down to the deadline," without "wasting time" on report writing. With content meager and doubtful and time a parrying weapon, the progress report, instead of providing an effective means for the government agency to monitor the analysis, becomes another device used by systems analysts to perpetuate the current state-of-the-art and flow of contracts by shielding the work-in-progress from critical evaluation.

Reason might suggest that, with interim reports so inadequate, the final report would be the crucial instrument in assessing the outcome of the systems analysis. But this has not happened. Despite the General Accounting Office's disclosures and sporadic attempts at investigations, systems analyses go on unchecked. Reports like Hudson's, "lacking in depth or sufficient value to warrant the loading of bookshelves," [42] proliferate. Almost every federal, state, county, and municipal body is in the process of acquiring a costly collection of analytic studies, neither for access nor to assess. Their numbers will grow with the accelerating trend toward "rational planning," aided by such built-in self-serving mechanisms. Systems analyses will persist as the accepted approach so long as the myth prevails that techniques can substitute for thoughtful inquiry and that management of problems can supplant amelioration of contributing circumstances.

Paradoxically enough, non-feasibility and non-implementation may be the most important growth factors, for systems studies are likely to proliferate until they are challenged by application. Perhaps their devastating effect lies in the fact that they have not really been tried, tested, and found wanting. Instead, they remain as entities, unevaluated

[41] *Ibid.*, p. 17.
[42] *Ibid.*, Appendix II, p. 8.

and unchallenged.[43] Sitting on a shelf, they rest and thrive on the old cliché that the theory is great, an argument that obscures the fact that systems techniques (as a package) are bought and sold as a practical method. Even if the theory, which review in Chapter II reveals to be less rigorous and precise than advocates would have us believe, were more perfect, our concern is still for real-life problems and not the simulated facsimiles thereof.

Critical assessment has been made of the reasons for and forces behind the transfer of systems analysis from aerospace and defense work to social concerns. The processes by which the transfer is being effected have been subjected to review. These factors, almost as much as the problem-solving techniques themselves, not only have considerable bearing on the outcome of any particular study but, more important, influence the very role of systems analysis as the methodology of the present and future.

[43] This observation was made, during the course of a personal interview, by Mr. François Duchêne, Director of the Institute for Strategic Studies, London.

[5]

The Techniques at Work in Waste Management and Supersonic Transport

In a world seemingly more beset with chaos at every turn, the yearning for cosmos appears almost universal. This longing is reflected in the conscious or unconscious idealization of the well-ordered system, wherein uncertainty is managed and controlled rationally. Just as young children like to believe that somewhere in the realm of adulthood there exist wellsprings of protection and surety, so a confused and perplexed society is wont to look beyond its immediate experience to the vast reaches of science for answers. And, in the spirit of the times, the expectation is that these will come in the form of new techniques, perhaps not fully understood but great in their promise. The phenomenon is not new. In other ages, anxious peoples turned in matters martial and civil to seers and sybils; they accepted the pronouncements and prophecies that emanated from mystical rites with all the greater credence because they understood them poorly. In the Space Age, the methodology of systems analysis is the new mythology. To be sure, the means of divination are more sophisticated than observation of the flight formations of birds or examination of the viscera of beasts, but otherwise the process is much the same. There are standard set procedures, used in all cases; there is a symbolic language. For the uninitiated, understanding is less important than believing.

Earlier chapters were devoted to the systems approach in theoretical and practical perspective. This chapter focuses on the methods at work. Here we explore some of the essential features of systems analysis — models, simulations, and cost-effectiveness. The fact that some of these items are concepts while others are procedures, that there are overlaps between them and inconsistencies among them, dismays only the meticulous. The typical practitioner, dwelling in his man-machine-made universe, merely adds another definition to an already agglomerated glossary and proceeds as though on a pre-magnetized course.

METHODOLOGY, METHODS, AND MODELS

Although frequently set forth as two separate procedures, modeling and simulation are cross-referenced to the point of being redundant. Let us first consider *model* and then proceed to *simulation*, much in the manner of those for whom these concepts are stock in trade. The word *model* is second only to *system* in ambiguity of meaning and ubiquity of usage. The literature on the subject abounds with definitions, most of which are cannibalized from one or two key sources. The simplest, "A model is that which is analyzed," [1] is in the tradition of Gertrude Stein's "rose is a rose" and no more useful. Somewhat more to the point is the conception of the model as a representation of something. Attempts have been made to clarify and attain somewhat sharper focus. E. S. Quade,[2] perhaps the most quoted, albeit not necessarily credited, authority in the field, offers the following insights:

A model is a representation of reality which abstracts the features of the situation relevant to the question being studied. The means of representation may vary from a set of mathematical equations or a computer program to a purely verbal description of the situation, in which judgment alone is used to assess the consequences of various choices.

There are other definitions and many attempts at classification. Everything from facetious reference to the traditional 36-24-36 as model of female pulchritude to a scenario for strategy in a war game have been included, with a considerable expenditure of effort to purify them.[3] A government handbook sets forth some definitions and distinctions, with deterministic and probabilistic types of models given separate listings.[4] Despite the wide disperson of definitions and the increasing complexity of classification as subsequent waves of econometricians, operations researchers, and the like try to improve upon and refine the simpler

[1] H. Kahn and I. Mann, "Techniques of Systems Analysis," Santa Monica: RAND Corporation, Memorandum RM-1829-1-PR, June, 1957, p. 13.

[2] E. S. Quade and W. I. Boucher, eds. *Systems Analysis and Policy Planning*, New York: American Elsevier, 1968, p. 12.

[3] R. D. Specht, "The Nature of Models," in Quade and Boucher, *op.cit.*, pp. 211 ff.

[4] U.S. General Accounting Office, *Glossary for Systems Analysis and Planning-Programming-Budgeting*, October, 1969, p. 38.

models of an earlier era, one generalization appears warranted. The model is a symbolic representation of something, and, like all representations, it is subject to the distortions, prejudgments, and limitations of vision and wisdom of its creator. It is based on a stereotype, a concept developed with great prescience by Walter Lippmann [5] many years ago, and subject to the same caveats as any such representation of reality.

But, as the last word in current symbology, *model* is useful and has been assigned a purposive role. In sociologistic jargon, it "structures" a situation, that is, establishes some semblance of order through articulating a frame of reference, rules, and the like. Quade accords the model the primary function of organizing thought in such fashion as ultimately to lead to a set of mathematical equations. It is presumed that, by permitting manipulation of variables, these will represent the likely outcome of the exercise of various options. For Quade, this is the point where the *simulation* technique is useful. In instances where a mathematical model is unattainable, imitation of the essential features and behavior of a system through simulation offers a way of dealing with (or, in popular argot, "getting a handle on") the problem.

Lauded as a promising problem-solving device is the game structure, itself a model of a certain kind. This, we are informed, "furnishes the participants with an artificial, simulated environment within which they can jointly and simultaneously experiment, acquiring through feedback the insights necessary to make successful predictions within the gaming context and thus indirectly about the real world." [6] The reference to experimentation is, unfortunately, never made clear, and the reader is faced with a choice as to whether the experiment has to do with real-life experiences under controlled conditions, or, as is so often the case, "fooling around with the computer" in an effort to "tease out" something usable. What is clear is that the simulation, a game of "what-iffiness," relies on further abstraction to prove hypotheses which are at best expressions of only certain types of *Weltanschauungen*, that is, views of the world. [7] There is in their very conception a tautology and circularity of reasoning in the form of incestuous reinforcement, if not validation of sense or nonsense, whichever constituted the model being tried.

Proponents and practitioners cannot be accused of ignorance in this matter. Their books always contain a section on pitfalls and caveats. Going far beyond mere taxonomy and into the philosophical conceptualization of models and their makers, Boguslaw has discussed "ritual

[5] Walter Lippmann, *Public Opinion*, New York: Harcourt, Brace, 1922.

[6] Quade and Boucher, *op.cit.*, p. 44.

[7] C. West Churchman, *The Systems Approach*, New York: Delacorte Press, 1968, p. 121.

modeling" as the ultimate exercise in logic and mathematics — a manifestation of techniques invoked as a substitute for problem-solving.[8] What Kahn called "modelism"[9] and others have called "modelitis" is apparently an occupational disease. Kahn and Mann described the symptoms as being more interested in the model than in the real world and studying only the portions of questions that are amenable to quantitative treatment. Quade and Boucher's specific manifestations of the malady form the core around which the following commentary is built.[10]

Overconcentration on the model, a situation in which technically oriented and trained analysts focus attention on the mechanics of computation or on the technical relationships in the model, rather than on important questions raised in the study. Kaplan has warned against the tendency toward such absorption with perfecting the instrument that sight is lost of the material with which it must work.[11]

Excessive attention to detail, a preoccupation which can lead to a plethora of complicated formulas which may convey little meaning or even mask, through the complexity of formulation, major errors.

Neglect of the question, through attempting to set up a model that treats simultaneously every aspect of a complex problem. Quade's curious antidote is "to design the model around the questions to be answered, rather than as an imitation of the real world." And from this purified and rarefied environment will emanate the "successful predictions" about the "real world," promised earlier.[12]

Incorrect use of the model, exemplified as the acceptance as useful output of the results of a computation not central to the question which the model was designed to answer. Quade's illustrations come from military experience, but this ailment, which could be described as a grasping at technically-contrived straws, could be classed as equally dangerous, if not fatal, in civil matters as well.

Disregard of the limitations, especially those imposed on the ranges over which some of the approximate relationships in the model were expected to hold. The example used by Quade has to do with scale, in an exercise in the strategy of atom bomb dropping. Perhaps even more telling is the time factor. Forrester's computer simulation model of the central city[13] specified "rate variables," which reflected different

[8] Robert Boguslaw, *The New Utopians,* Englewood Cliffs, New Jersey: Prentice-Hall, pp. 65, 66.

[9] H. Kahn and I. Mann, *Ten Common Pitfalls,* Santa Monica: RAND Corporation, RM-1937, ASTIA document number AD 133035, July 17, 1957, p. 1.

[10] Quade and Boucher, *op.cit.,* pp. 353 ff.

[11] Abraham Kaplan, *The Conduct of Inquiry,* San Francisco: Chandler, 1964, p. 11.

[12] Quade and Boucher, *op.cit.,* p. 44.

[13] Jay W. Forrester, *Urban Dynamics,* Cambridge: MIT Press, 1969.

parameters. If these worked together, they helped one another. If not, they cancelled each other out. And there is no knowing which will occur. But, despite these and many other limitations of the Forrester model, whose nature is acknowledged as preliminary by the author himself, the qualifications are ignored and firm policy recommendations regarding urban planning emerge. The problem of forecasting manpower from time series has been posed as especially perplexing, with standard approaches based on assumptions rarely present in real-life situations like, for example, independence of successive observations, normality of distribution of the residuals about a line of regression, and unchanging variances over the observed time domain. Instead, because of incompleteness of the model, the heroic assumption must be made that the time series is a sample from a hyperpopulation of all possible relevant time series.[14]

Neglect of the subjective elements. The techniques of systems analysis, the very process of modeling, despite disclaimers to the contrary, effectively rule out consideration of the subjective, the intangible, the immeasurable and unaccountable factors that prevail in real life. Therefore, although it is fashionable for textbook writers to warn against over-preoccupation with quantitative aspects, it is conventional wisdom that these are the only ones that are included in the model. Consequently, to exhort the model-maker to abandon his single-mindedness is, in itself, a kind of social window dressing. It is tantamount to advising him to forsake his cherished tool kit, leave his carefully contrived world where games are played according to set rules, and face the problems of real life where and as they occur. The supreme caveat here is embedded in Quade's comment, ". . . if we insist on a completely quantitative treatment, we may have to simplify the problem so drastically that it loses all realism,"[15] with "almost meaningless results."[16]

Just as in the process of psychoanalysis, identification of the source of maladjustment does not cure, so in systems analysis, disclosure of weaknesses has not overcome them. Once having in appendix, footnote, or special section acknowledged the possible pitfalls, many analysts are prone to explain away deficiencies in their model in terms of the technique itself and without reference to or regard for the subject matter at hand. By cleaving to the new orthodoxy,[17] they find a refuge from what may be necessary critical evaluation. Conforming to the rules of

[14] J. E. Morton, *On Manpower Forecasting*, Kalamazoo, Michigan: The W. E. Upjohn Institute for Employment Research, Methods for Manpower Analysis No. 2, September, 1968, p. 41.

[15] Quade and Boucher, *op.cit.*, p. 359.

[16] *Ibid.*, p. 40.

[17] Kaplan, *op.cit.*, p. 276.

their own idealized logic, they can account for omission of important aspects of a situation by claiming that theirs is a "sub-optimized" model, with further optimization to come in a sort of "Perils of Pauline" sequence. In practice, such refinements rarely contribute to significant alterations but instead add to the preciosity of the exercise.

And herein lies one of the greatest dangers of the technical approach to social problems. The professional, stylized façade is accorded the status of a thoughtful paradigm, the manipulation of masses of data yields proof merely through the "mystique of quantity." [18] Because of the nature of the enterprise, first-order consequences are accepted as though eternal verities, because deeper understanding eludes a technique which approaches life as a game, with its payoff strategies calculated according to minimax or maximin criteria or, perhaps, conceived as an exercise in satisficing. What may be a thoroughly satisfying model in the technical sense may be completely unacceptable as a guide to real-life planning. The lack of congruence between the model that satisfies and the problem that baffles is not new. Keynes expressed it clearly in his famous critique, "Professor Tinbergen's Method," in 1939 [19]: "If only he [Professor Tinbergen] is allowed to carry on, he is quite ready and happy at the end of it to go a long way towards admitting with an engaging modesty, that the results probably have no value. The worst of him is that he is much more interested in getting on with the job than in spending time in deciding whether the job is worth getting on with."

The model-building step is the fulcrum of systems analysis, for embedded in it is the fundamental assumption that the essence of the system under consideration can be captured quantitatively and expressed meaningfully in mathematical terms or equations. How the model is conceived influences the emphasis and direction of the analysis and, consequently, its conclusions. The fact that professional problem solvers, such as social engineers, operations researchers, and the like, display an increasing propensity to rely on models of their own making as though definitive of real world processes and phenomena must be viewed as a serious development for herein lies the symptom of the new orthodoxy, deplorable insofar as it may lead to ignoring important, nonquantifiable factors and dangerous in that it may obscure premises with doubtful validity. Manipulation of the model and preoccupation with refinement of its computational niceties characterize the activities of those experts whose claim to competence rests primarily on technical

[18] *Ibid.*, p. 172.

[19] J. M. Keynes, "Professor Tinbergen's Method," review of J. Tinbergen, *A Method and its Application to Investment Activity* (Statistical Testing of Business-Cycle Theories I), Geneva: League of Nations, 1939, in *The Economic Journal*, Vol. XLIX, No. 195, September, 1939, p. 559.

virtuosity. Forgotten in the exercise is the empirical validity of the assumptions, without assessment and verification of which the whole performance takes on the appearance of a vainglorious game.[20]

Likely to be similarly sterile is the process of simulation unless the basically essential features of the system have been incorporated in the model. Simulation, it must be recalled, is the procedure in which possible hypotheses are tested by manipulation of the model. If the elements of the original model are inadequate, inappropriate, or improper, simulation contributes nothing worthwhile. The temptation at this stage has been to construct an "ideal" representation, to run elaborate calculations to ascertain possible outcomes if certain variables were changed in some fashion, and to forget that the entire "explanation" was predicated on at best unvalidated and at worst invalid assumptions. Although military analysts, who use simulation extensively in their strategy recommendations, acknowledge the absence of rigorous rules and discipline and, instead, admit a heavy reliance on "art," [21] the technique advances into the social sphere with such an aura of authority as to imply firm foundation and precision and, thus, lead to a false concretization of evidence for recommendations.

In systems analyses in health, education, and welfare, to mention but a few, simulation appears as though it were a necessary procedure. The juggling of variables through computer exercises is accorded status as the new and technologically perfected substitute for real-life experimentation and observation. Mathematical and symbolic manipulation has thus displaced the test tube and the laboratory. Reflecting all the strengths and weaknesses of the model on which it is based and, consequently, suffering from the same obfuscation of assumption and reification of conjecture, the simulation, an abstract and limited representation of reality, has become a decisive step in planning delivery of medical services, educational policy, and intervention strategy in public welfare.

Objectives Defined and Redefined

Quite apart from the validity of the model and yet intrinsically embedded in it are considerations of objectives. When the techniques of systems analysis were first applied to public planning in California, it was on the wistful hope that, if they succeeded in accomplishing nothing else, they would force public administrators to make explicit

---

[20] Wassily Leontief, "Theoretical Assumptions and Nonobserved Facts," *The American Economic Review*, Vol. LXI, No. 1, March, 1971.

[21] Norman C. Dalkey, "Simulation," Chapter 12 in *Systems Analysis and Policy Planning*, Quade and Boucher, eds., New York: American Elsevier, 1968, p. 247.

their objectives. In fact, this has been a strong selling point for systems analysis and program budgeting in government at all levels and in all places where the associated techniques have been applied. Embodied here is the notion that an identified and identifiable goal is the essence of the systems analysis. This view is not universally held, however. Charles J. Hitch, an eminent authority on the subject, maintains that *uncertainty* about objectives is the quintessence of systems analysis. Labelling as a "tiresome bromide" the injunction that the analyst start with an objective, and displaying a bit of straw-man destructiveness in directing his attack to "the *right* objectives," he claims that the RAND Corporation, with which he was associated, never undertook a major system study at the beginning of which satisfactory objectives could be defined.[22] The very purpose of an analysis, in his opinion, is the learning about objectives.

> Systems analysis at the national level . . . involves a continuous cycle of defining military objectives, designing alternative systems to achieve these objectives, evaluating these alternatives in terms of their effectiveness and cost, questioning the objectives and other assumptions underlying the analysis, opening new alternatives, and establishing new military objectives, and so on.[23]

In this case, as in others cited in Chapter III, the military serves as a poor model for civilian planning. While the former can indulge in heuristic exercises to ascertain objectives, the latter proceeds on a kind of pot-of-gold-at-the-end-of-every-rainbow serendipity. In the realm of civilian affairs, there simply could not be a system design unless and until objectives were made explicit, because it is for their achievement that the system operates, that the internal web of component parts interrelate. The very concept of *system* implies an interaction between means and ends. It is to be expected, therefore, that in conventional practice, objectives play a determining role in the model and, of course, the system which it represents. They affect its temporal and spatial boundaries, the varibles taken into and left out of account, and how its "interfacing" with contiguous and impinging environments is handled.

It becomes apparent, then, that the analyst's conception of the system and its goals is crucial. And it should be remembered that most analysts are technically oriented. This means that they view the situation in terms of their tools and trade. Operating on the presumption that theirs is the *systematic* way, they have focused on the tangible and the measurable and have pursued an arbitrary and eclectic course, all in the name

---

[22] Charles J. Hitch, *On the Choice of Objectives in Systems Studies*, Santa Monica: RAND Corporation, P-1955, March 30, 1960, p. 11.
[23] Charles J. Hitch, *Decision Making for Defense*, Berkeley and Los Angeles: University of California Press, 1965, p. 52.

of systematic analysis. The analyst's delineation of the objectives has been seen to influence profoundly his model and to affect his choices, assignment of weights, and even so seemingly quantitative a procedure as his allocation of costs and benefits.

The point cannot be stressed enough that *discriminatory value judgements prevail throughout systems analytic procedures.* Who is the Paul being paid and the Peter getting robbed, whose benefit becomes whose cost is not a question of indisputable accounting but rather a highly subjective interpretation. The hidden imprint starts with the selection of goals, itself a normative matter, and goes on to bias the direction of the study through designation or neglect of alternatives, ascription of relevance to the various possible factors, and development of criteria for the reliability of the data base.

In connection with this point, it might be well to note that, without being so catalogued officially, Roland N. McKean's RAND research study of water resources, a sort of Bible for cost-effectiveness calculators, is one of the most normative treatises in print.[24] While the structure displays methodological rigor, the substance is full of value judgments. His enumeration of goals, for example, is a listing of someone's or some group's priorities, e.g., *adequate* pollution control; *reasonable* irrigation development; *proper* erosion and sediment reduction; *suitable* flood control; *optimum* contribution in alleviating the impact of drought; *full* development of the basin's resources for recreational purposes. Choice among alternative courses of action entails use of criteria, which in themselves imply value judgments already made. His examples of external economies and diseconomies, or, as he calls them, "spillovers," can be more properly construed as situations in which social ethics rather than economics should be applied.

The case of water resource allocation has created a nice bit of whimsy. Once the pioneer model for cost-benefit analysis, it was the first to face serious public challenge over conflicting objectives as ascertained by divergent interests.[25] With more than a billion dollars devoted annually by the federal government to dams, irrigation, and navigation projects and with a projected expenditure of $70–100 billion over the next generation,[26] the need to establish guidelines for public policy is obvious. Starting with a statement of national objectives for water resource development, a high level government task force set about an evaluation of the costs and benefits of various water and related land

[24] Ronald H. McKean, *Efficiency in Government through Systems Analysis,* New York: John Wiley, 1963.

[25] U.S. Water Resources Council, Report to the Water Resources Council by the Special Task Force, *Procedures for Evaluation of Water and Related Land Resource Projects,* June, 1969, p. 54.

[26] Ronald N. McKean, *op.cit.*

projects. The objectives were impeccable: national income, regional development, environmental enhancement, and the well-being of people.[27] Despite stalwart assertions that "it is both possible and necessary to apply systematic and quantitative methods to a considerable portion of the evaluation process," [28] allocation, assessment, and measurement of all project costs and benefits with their tangible and intangible components posed great methodological difficulties. Jurisdictional tangles among the Army Corps of Engineers, Department of the Interior, the Federal Power Commission, the Department of Agriculture, the Bureau of Reclamation, the Department of Health, Education, and Welfare, to say nothing of Transportation and other agencies, have made for a bureaucratic maze particularly vulnerable to the regional and political pressures of special interest groups.

Nonetheless, after much sober consideration and even with candid recognition of the limitations of the state of knowledge and the consequent shortcomings of the analyses, the task force made a number of definite recommendations. They favored a change in evaluation procedures, one in which greater weight would be given to secondary benefits, such as improvement of recreational facilities and wildlife preservation. Quite aside from the possibility that the proposed revisions would affect the federally prescribed interest rate in calculating costs and so provide justification for selected projects, the distinct likelihood emerged that including erstwhile neglected, intangible side effects to which an arbitrary dollar value had been assigned, would produce a favorable cost-benefit ratio for programs otherwise not economically feasible. The official nod of the task force in the direction of the social dimensions of their problems brought further administrative complication as well as confrontation with aroused citizens. The National Wildlife Federation had already challenged the theoretical price tag assigned by the Army Corps of Engineers to fish resources. And conservation groups expressed opposition to having their interests arbitrarily rung in or out, to credit or discredit a particular project by tipping the balance.

In the vicinity of San Francisco, "Save the Bay" is a popular slogan, but whether the Bay should be saved for reasons of health, business, aesthetics, transportation, or security will make a considerable difference in the estimation of benefits and costs. The lesson here is clearly evident for all who will read. Just so long as assessment of economic feasibility remains in the hands of agencies with vested interest in the outcome of such studies, cost-benefit analyses will be a useful vehicle for substantiating a particular position. It will be all the more persuasive because

[27] U.S. Water Resources Council, Report, *op.cit.*, June, 1969, p. 3.
[28] *Ibid.*, p. 75.

of its semblance of disingenuous guilelessness and impartiality, achieved through "modern advanced management concepts."

With due deference to the Hitch model, the total system design in the civilian sphere reflects the analyst's conception of the goals, objectives, or purpose of the system. And this conception stems directly from his *Weltanschauung*. Therefore, an appreciation of the implications of objective identification calls for an appraisal of the qualifications of the analyst. His attitudes and aptitudes should be brought into sharp focus and questioned precisely because objectives are not unequivocal entities about which there is universal consensus. Subjective and normative, objectives are a matter for interpretation which can be accomplished properly only through comprehension of the subject at hand. To treat them as a mere procedural step in an analytic scheme is to trivialize the whole endeavor into mere technical game playing. Full consideration of the objectives is all the more urgent because, within the framework of systems analysis techniques, they are cast in quantitative terms.

Contrary to disclaimers by apologists, objectives are assessed only through the available tools, for they are the measure of the system's output. In the calculations, various factors must be taken into account and their costs and benefits weighed. This assessment, because it must be compatible and comparable with other measures applied, is, of course, quantitative, and almost invariably in dollar terms. Only those factors which have a price or can be arbitrarily assigned a dollar value are included; excluded are intangibles and, with them, all the qualifying nuances and attributes that represent social values, costs, and benefits in the never ending tug-of-war with the economic. In some team-executed systems analyses, an attempt to overcome this serious deficiency is made by consultation with authorities in subject-matter fields. But their "inputs" are ignored unless they are in usable form. And often they are not. Sometimes, a "house sociologist" participates. But if his intent is to broaden the dimensions, the effect is imperceptible. Perhaps his very willingness to be allied with this group indicates a *Gemütlichkeit* of methodological leaning. There is in sociology, as in most other fields, the strong tendency to regard quantification as the means to achieving rigor, and, therefore, becoming "scientific." [29]

Just so long as systems analysis remained a sort of pencil-and-paper game played for whatever reasons by whomsoever in and out of the public sector, the question of objectives and their definition remained largely an academic matter. With the adoption of program planning and budgeting (PPBS) as official procedure for all government agencies,

[29] Alvin W. Gouldner, *The Coming Crisis of Western Sociology*, New York: Basic Books, 1970.

many real problems associated with objective identification and specification have come to light. Far from being a perfunctory step in a process, stated objectives are at the core of all planning. Who identifies them and by what yardsticks the costs and benefits of achieving them are calculated become matters of deep social consequence.

Thus, when the analyst called upon to design an efficient system of delivery of medical care to the needy regards "efficiency of operation" as a hardware matter, he develops an elaborate electronic data-processing setup intended to produce more and faster records. The creators of a waste management system see public attitudes as crucial and concentrate on manipulating them rather than on the messy political and economic factors contributing to the problem. Designers of a system of rapid transit regard fast movement of people between certain points as their primary mandate. Even though the public has become accustomed to the convenience of one-man, one-car mobility, they assume that it will quietly acquiesce to paying far from low fares to be taken where the fixed-bed tracks lead. The Bay Area Rapid Transit System, for example, built lines through and to many places, so laid waste by the protracted and inept construction stages that it may be years before former use patterns will be restored, if ever. Terminals are out in the fields and way stations stand as sole occupants of once prosperous and now desolate neighborhood business sections.

The spread of the notion that the better business management practices developed by the Department of Defense could be used in the war on poverty to improve efficiency and to promote eligibility for federal grants has contributed to a proliferation of cost-benefit studies of welfare. Some of them are intended to modernize and improve record-keeping and paper work procedures. Analyses of this type come under the heading of Information Systems and will be discussed later. In this context we need only mention the curious logic that justifies the design of elaborate electronic systems which will add further to already staggering costs in order to prevent "abuse." Noteworthy here is the inconsistent image of the recipient, at one and the same time a hapless sluggard and yet an entrepreneurial perpetrator of clever fraud.

Another kind of cost-benefit study seeks to establish "rational" choices between possible intervention strategies, that is, to select the most "cost-effective" programs. Inherent in this approach is the basic paradox prevalent in the systems attack on welfare: it is the acceptance of welfare as a system the function of which is to run itself better, through more updated information systems, or to get people off it, or both. And in this view of welfare as a system, these missions apparently must be accomplished without a visible mechanism for perturbing other systems of the society, even though, almost invariably, the preventive, corrective, and ameliorative avenues lie outside and beyond the baili-wick of the welfare system. In fact, one might observe that the welfare system is a kind of social response or expression of public concern for the malfunctioning of other systems within the society — education, health, housing, employment, social security, and the like. It is all the more contradictory, therefore, that efficiency of welfare operation should be expected to prove itself by its self-purging capability.[30] And yet, this is precisely how cost-benefit measures are being applied.

Architects of a public welfare system betray their stereotype of the recipient as a ne'er-do-well offender against the Protestant Ethic. Re-flecting the orientation of the analysts, especially those recruited from the ranks of successful defense-related business and industry, many cost-benefit analyses are, consequently, based on a specious dichotomy between *work* and *welfare*, as though each represented a voluntary op-tion, to be exercised at will. In the display of figure juggling that occurs here, the advantages to the society of payrolls as compared with relief rolls are, of course, made very clear. But the case would be more con-vincing if the availability of low-skilled but decent paying jobs could be demonstrated and if the employability of the major proportion of welfare recipients could be established. Even if all the problems asso-ciated with getting the vocationally handicapped to work were some-how waved away by a magic wand, there would very likely be the musi-cal chairs aspect to the solution. Placement of such persons in the labor force would contribute to the displacement of workers of marginal em-ployable status. Pushed down the economic ladder and out of their jobs, they would move off the work rolls and onto welfare rolls. A re-habilitation program that could meet the tests of cost-efficiency for one system in the short run could be seriously disruptive to that and to other systems over a longer time span.

In the design of criminal justice systems, the "police mentality" ap-proach prevails. Law enforcement at the street level is stressed and serves as *raison d'être* for more and more comprehensive information networks, designed to catch persons who rightfully or wrongfully have been tabbed "potential offenders." When detection and control are construed as the prime objectives of a criminal justice system, there is instant "rational" justification for the acquisition of "hard" technology, in the form of helicopters for surveillance and crowd control. It may well be that, with the growing trend toward thought-and-behavior-modifying devices and drugs, such systematic designs will include the implanting of electrodes in the brains of offenders or the administra-

[30] Ida R. Hoos, "When California System-Analyzed the Welfare Problem," in *In-formation Technology in a Democracy*, Alan F. Westin, editor, Cambridge: Harvard University Press, 1971, pp. 409–419.

tion of drugs to assure the peace and harmony of the community. Designed more with regard to the current cliché of law-and-order than
with respect to lawful and orderly administration of justice, such systems leave out such crucial considerations as the social environment,
police activities, the state of the court calendar, and the functions and
functioning of penal institutions.

Cost-Benefit Analysis for War and Peace

Among the management techniques closely associated with and
stemming from virtually the same roots as systems analysis, cost-benefit
analysis, or the quantitative assessment of the ratio between costs measured and effectiveness achieved, is in perhaps widest usage. Universally
appealing for its common-sense aspects, this method of public planning
is rarely questioned. It is, however, subject to the same challenges and
requires the same critical review as to assumptions, factors considered,
and facets excluded as the analysis of the larger system, of which the
cost-benefit ratios may form significant decision points.

The process of systems analysis of present or future, in military or
civil matters, always requires a choice among various possible courses
of action. Comparison between alternatives is generally in terms of
their costs as related to effectiveness of outcome. Sometimes, concern
with this portion of program selection is so great that other considerations are intentionally set aside. The cost-benefit ratio, if it is to be
meaningful at all, calls for calculation of the costs and the benefits in
the same terms. Because the coin of the realm is the most accessible
measure, variables are almost always reckoned in dollar terms. The
inevitable consequence is the tendency to treat the matter under study
as though it were primarily, if not exclusively, economic. We find here
a kind of tautological justification that says that programs in health,
education, or whatever cost money; therefore, they are economic and,
accordingly, can best be judged and allocations made through cost-
benefit analysis. Because the variables likely to be taken into account
are either those which have dollar value or those to which price tags
may be affixed, no matter how arbitrarily, human and social costs and
benefits, which elude measurement on a dollar scale, are assigned values
which reflect the preconceived notions or bias of the analyst, or they
are simply not considered at all.

Cost-benefit analysis in military affairs is said to be an old concept,
familiar even to Julius Caesar, Napoleon Bonaparte, and other martial
figures in history. Nonetheless, its advent in the U.S. Department of
Defense when Robert S. McNamara was Secretary was regarded as a
kind of milestone, the second major step after the operations analysis

of World War II. It is generally averred that "sophisticated instruments of management" brought about a "revolution" in strategic defense planning in 1961–1962, and, that with the establishment in 1965 of the position of Assistant Secretary of Defense for Systems Analysis, military cost-benefit analysis "came of age."[31] Hailed as an important accounting innovation, the technique is often contrasted invidiously with "horse-and-buggy" bookkeeping practices in general use.

Modernization of cost-allocation procedures, in civilian or military planning, needs no defense in this context. Even though in this, as in numerous instances of advocacy of the systems approach, the game being played is apparently one in which there are many straw men, there is little to be gained by refuting *ad hominem* arguments against anachronistic methods. What must be questioned now, as in the earlier discussion of systems analysis in the military, are the *particular* methods, the assumptions on which they are based, the aura of precision surrounding them, and the consequences of reliance on them. In our review of this technique in the management of public affairs, we find a need for greater attention to the intangible costs for which this method provides little accommodation. Authorities in the field have been candid in their caveats. For example, a number of years ago, Dr. Henry A. Kissinger declared that cost-effectiveness had already been carried too far.[32] In the development of federal water resource projects, the field of civil planning in which cost-benefit procedures received early acceptance, disaffection has become evident.

Nonetheless, cost-benefit analysis remains the keystone of much public planning. As an entity in itself, as part of the systems approach, and especially as an element in program budgeting, cost-benefit analysis has spread from the military into most of the civilian agencies and departments of federal government and has been adopted by planners of every level down to the states, counties, and cities. There, it will continue to influence the approach to public administration long after the glamour of Mr. McNamara's "Whiz Kids," already dispersed among the Under Secretariat in Washington, will have dimmed and the infallibility attributed to the "sophisticated management tools" will have been shattered.

Already, as was noted earlier, the model of military planning based on cost-benefit calculations has been seriously challenged by disclosures by congressional investigators. A subcommittee on Economy in Government found, in sharp contradiction of claims to efficiency, that "wasteful, inefficient practices" raised "basic questions concerning the

[31] Stephen Enke, *Defense Management*, Englewood Cliffs, New Jersey: Prentice-Hall, 1967, p. vi.

[32] *Missile/Space Daily*, April 9, 1964, p. 173.

Defense Department's management of its own affairs." Well documented in the reports of this and of other House and Senate committees as well as of the General Accounting Office were instances of the waste and misuse of billions of dollars, with absence of effective management practices repeatedly cited as the cause.[33]

The value of the legacy of cost-benefit techniques, willed to the civilian agencies and permeating thinking all the way down to town and county planners, hungry for new techniques, is, therefore, open to discussion. Most government agencies embark on cost-benefit studies with economy as their objective. Few of them are able to indulge with impunity in the fanciful cost estimating and profligate contract-letting that has characterized defense spending. Even in the military, prognostications about the possible responses of an imagined or imaginary enemy were necessary but not sufficient to establish public confidence in the grand rationalization of huge expenditures. Just who, in such areas as outdoor recreation, urban renewal, education, public health, crime, and welfare, is the antagonist to justify this kind of cost-benefit legerdemain is far from clear. The protagonists would have us believe that the economic calculus can and must be utilized and, in fact, that rational public planning is impossible without it. This persuasion has brought about a kind of circular reasoning. In order to proceed logically, one must weigh, measure, quantify. Certain elements are amenable to this type of treatment. Thus, they become the crucial items in the calculation, even though they do not encompass or are not relevant to the real-life questions that should be faced.

Despite all these visible drawbacks, we find that there has been rapid diffusion of cost-benefit analysis into all branches of government. We observe that this is due in large part to the fact that "evidence of rational planning" is a condition for grants from federal agencies, a policy promoted by former Department of Defense personnel now located in positions of importance in civilian agencies, as well as by their bedazzled emulators.

Critical review suggests that the approach has generated numerous problems, perhaps more than it has settled. Identifying, quantifying, and relating service objectives with the costs and benefits of various courses of action have forced concentration on the measurable elements rather than the whole. Called "piece-meal fragmentation" when old-line bureaucrats approached their task this way, the technique is called "sub-optimization" when professional analysts juggle the parts they can handle. It is often likely that these portions are relatively less impor-

---

[33] Report of the Subcommittee on Economy in Government of the Joint Economic Committee, "The Economics of Procurement," November 11, 12, 13, and 14, 1968, and January 16, 1969.

tant than those which could not be objectively weighed or meaningfully weighted. After an investigation of a wide variety of experiences with cost-benefit analysis, our findings suggest that although the desire to introduce a semblance of rationality into public spending is commendable, it appears to excite the urge to "scientific objectivity," which turns out to be neither scientific nor objective. In many instances, it has encouraged the casting of subjective value judgments as to cost and benefits in hard terms. Through the show of formulas and calculations, there has been conveyed to the unenlightened not only an impression of accuracy that does not exist but also the notion that solely that which is quantifiable is significant. Overconfidence in cost-benefit analysis in the planning process in many areas of public administration has led to such preoccupation with the quantifiable trivia and minutiae that broad and basic issues are obscured. Several selected applications of the technique illustrate this point and demonstrate how snugly advocacy can be cloaked in the accouterments of scientific methodology.

WASTE MANAGEMENT

A cost-benefit model of solid waste management, designed for the Fresno, California area but reusable elsewhere, was developed by Aerojet-General Corporation with Engineering Science, Inc. as its subcontractor under a $175,000 contract with the California State Department of Public Health.[34] The model was supposed to link objectives, alternatives, and resources so as "(a) to determine an optimum system for the management of solid wastes in the Fresno Region and (b) to develop a technology for that determination that would be applicable to other similar regions throughout California and the nation." [35] Eighteen different systems for managing municipal and industrial wastes and four methods for agricultural wastes were set forth, with the costs, expressed in 1967 dollars, projected to the year 2000. Calculation of the total cost for each proposed system was derived from estimates of unit costs of carrying out the five steps in handling solid waste, viz., storage, collection, transportation, processing, and disposal. The total of these five stages was multiplied by projected amounts of waste to yield the final cost figures. The matter of simple arithmetic by which comparative costs were derived is, however, of relatively little moment. One might

[34] The project was underway from September 15, 1966 to March 31, 1968 and was funded in large part by a Public Health Service Demonstration Grant (No. DO1-UI-00028-01), National Center for Urban and Industrial Health, Solid Wastes Program, U.S. Department of Health, Education, and Welfare.

[35] State of California, Department of Public Health, Bureau of Vector Control, *California Integrated Solid Wastes Management Project, A Systems Study of Solid Wastes Management in the Fresno Area,* 1968, p. A-1.

more meaningfully question a system that fails to take into account the social, cultural, and economic factors, to say nothing of rapidly changing philosophies about environmental quality, that impinge on the very generation of waste.

Of still greater significance as well as relevance to our considerations is the way in which benefits were conceived, concretized in quantitative terms, and weighted for future use. Aware that with respect to solid waste management there exist no firm output standards, the engineers set out to craft some. Through what they called a "forced decision-making method," they developed a "Performance Scoring Procedure," which postulated that "effectiveness can be expressed or measured in terms of the degree to which the system decreases the environmental or bad effects of solid wastes." "The performance-scoring procedure . . . identifies a series of bad effects (B.E.) and quantifies these bad effects for various wastes in various conditions to produce a table of solid waste B.E. scores." [36] First, Aerojet-General and Engineering Science discussed environmental bad effects with state and county health department personnel and set up thirteen categories: (1) flies; (2) water pollution; (3) air pollution; (4) rodents; (5) human disease; (6) animal disease; (7) insects other than flies; (8) safety hazards; (9) odor; (10) plant disease; (11) land pollution; (12) unsightliness; and (13) toxicity.[37] Next they conducted interviews with thirty-nine persons, roughly about three apiece for each bad effect, and thus obtained a rating scale from zero to five of the relative contribution of a given waste. Each respondent arrived at his score independently, no effort having been made by the investigators to ascertain whether the number scale had the same meaning for all participants. Then, the number assignments were averaged, and, although actually resulting in an ordinal scale, were henceforth treated and manipulated as though they had been obtained through measurement methods that would have achieved a ratio scale.[38] The "hard data" were nothing but a crystallizing of the hastily contrived catalogue of unpleasantries into arbitrary and overlapping categories through an artificial weighting procedure in which three individuals, no matter how expert, were taken to represent the total community attitude.

This was patently a parody on public opinion polling, itself not an undisputed means to gathering data. The perpetrators of this methodologically nonsensical approach to a serious problem apparently

---

[36] *Ibid.*, p. IV-1.

[37] *Ibid.*, p. IV-2.

[38] David R. Stimson and Irwin Price, "An Evaluation of the Use of Systems Analysis to Solve a Waste Management Problem," paper at Joint Meeting, American Astronautical Society and Operations Research Society, Denver, Colorado, June 17–20, 1969, p. 14.

failed to recognize either the simplistic solutions they were inviting, that is, clothespins to protect against olfactory affront, or the invitation to Madison Avenue and public relations style treatment of the matter, that is, to manipulate people's attitudes and ignore the problem. The consulting engineers' own scoring of their performance sounded more like Little Jack Horner than sober professionals dedicated to advancing the state-of-the-art:

> The performance scoring procedure, developed by utilizing systems analysis techniques, provides a technical-economic selection process *far superior to that of individual judgment.* While the mathematical routines used in the scoring procedure are quite simple, the number of wastes, bad effects, and conditions of wastes resulted in the necessity for *handling and manipulating some 25,000 bits of numerical data. Hence, a computer program was developed and a digital computer used to perform the calculations and provide printed tabulations of the results."* (My italics.) [39]

This method, rated by its creators as "a significant step in the direction of the development of performance standards," has at its core the table of B.E. scores, purported to be so refined and precise that, in the words of its designers, "any waste management's performance effectiveness can be gaged by the degree of reduction of these environmental or bad effects." [40]

A review of the Fresno demonstration reveals that the fabrication of benefits and attendant manufacture of data (25,000 bits), thenceforth to be handled, manipulated, and spewed out in yards of tabulations, satisfied the intent of the systems designers better, perhaps, than the needs of society. As will be recalled, the engineers had set out "(a) to determine an optimum system for the management of solid wastes in the Fresno Region and (b) to develop a technology for that determination that would be applicable to other similar regions throughout California and the nation." [41] From their point of view, "an optimum system" for the management of solid wastes was largely a matter of public attitude, and their popularity poll in reverse was the technology by which determination of that optimality could be achieved. The techniques of the rating scale rigged on the basis of interviews and numerical data made to measure were undeniably as applicable to other regions of California and the nation as to Fresno. By the same logic they might be equally applicable to other problem areas, such as health, welfare, transportation, or education. But they studiously avoided the essential problems in any of the areas of concern.

[39] State of California, Department of Public Health, *California Integrated Solid Wastes Management Project, op.cit.,* p. A-8.

[40] *Ibid.,* p. IV-1.

[41] *Ibid.,* p. A-1.

The calculation of benefits or costs is, apparently, simple in cases where simplistic, arbitrary assumptions have been made. Conclusions can be made to seem ever more valid in the distance of time. Consequently, the target date for the waste management system was the year 2000. This predilection for the twenty-first century as the time for full fruition of their designs is common among systems analysts in many fields, notably transportation, urban planning, and land use, and in other lands as well.[42] The positive correlation between distance into the future and comfortable confidence is due to three obvious factors: (1) enhanced opportunity for amassing greater quantities of data out of projections and extrapolations; (2) benign postponement of the day of reckoning; (3) likelihood of realization of the self-fulfilling prophecy.

SUPERSONIC TRANSPORT

The *Weltanschauung* of the analyst emerges as the dominant factor in the cost-benefit study, a fact which casts doubts on the objectivity on which the approach bases its claim to usefulness in the planning process. Another severely critical bias stems from the mission-orientation of the particular analysis. Frequently, the objective is to justify a particular point of view or institutional premise. Such, for example, was the analysis of "the economics of the supersonic transport."[43] Here, advocacy could be seen in the selective handling of costs, the ascription of putative benefits. On the monetary cost side, the figures were fairly firm, enormously high, and rarely mentioned except as argument in favor of continued appropriations. With $700 million spent since 1966, an amount exceeding the maximum outlay then stipulated by President Kennedy, the project had by 1971 already dropped years behind schedule. In order to salvage the project and maintain the program pace, congressional funding requests were estimated at $189 million for fiscal 1972, $48 million for fiscal 1973, and $15 million for fiscal 1974. Total cost of the program, through the first prototype flight, supposed to occur near the end of 1972, was at one time expected to be $1.5 billion, 85 percent from U.S. government, 11 percent from contractor (mainly Boeing for airframe and General Electric for engine development), and 4 percent from airlines funding. Later, a cost increase of nearly $1 billion was estimated by William M. Allen, chairman of the board of the Boeing Company for the building

[42] W. Steingenga, "Recent Planning Problems of the Netherlands," *Regional Studies*, Vol. 2, No. 1, Pergamon Press, September, 1968, pp. 105–113.
[43] Allen H. Skaggs, "Economics of the SST Program," in *Analysis for Planning-Programming-Budgeting*, Mark Alfandary-Alexander, ed., Washington, D.C.: Washington Operations Research Council, 1968, pp. 117–128.

and testing of two prototype planes. Costs of actual production phases were once expected to reach $3 billion, with delivery of certificated aircraft set for mid-1978, a delay of four years over the target date set in June, 1967.[44] Each subsequent report showed a rise in costs and lag in time.

Because speed is the major, if not the sole, contribution to the traveler of this controversial and costly aircraft, one of the research contractors participating in the study of the economics of the SST program unearthed the intelligence that a $20,000 per year executive would be willing to pay $10 for each hour of travel saved. Incidentally, none of the calculations included time lost as 1800 mile-per-hour giants circled over crowded airport runways or when, after landing, the 275 incoming passengers sought to retrieve their luggage and secure surface transportation. When the airlines failed to accept the travel-time-saved figure as assurance of sufficient revenue to invest in supersonic planes, the researchers had to find other justification for the SST. The growth rate of the airline industry, comparison of the operating economies of the United States version with the Soviet TU-144, the British/French Concorde, and the competitive subsonic Boeing 747 were drawn upon to build the case for supersonic transport.

Omitted from the cost calculations were such items as the sonic boom, noise pollution, and the possible degradation of environmental quality. And yet, the planners knew that the inevitable sonic boom would represent an increase of orders of magnitude in the amount of noise and in numbers of persons exposed to it. One estimate, based on the proposed British/French Concorde and Boeing supersonic transports, anticipated that in the late 1970s about 65 million people in the United States could be exposed to about ten sonic booms per day (26 million receiving ten to fifty booms and 39 million receiving one to nine).[45] No one knows the likely effect of the booms on those exposed to it. Studies have been made and tests of acceptability conducted, but the simulated situation does not carry the full impact under normal living conditions and the tests, performed in St. Louis in 1961, in Oklahoma City in 1964, in Chicago in 1965, and at Edwards Air Force Base, California, in 1966, were carried out by engineers and without the participation of physicians, psychologists, or psychiatrists.[46] Taken into account were solely the least crucial circumstances. The human subjects were

[44] Harold D. Watkins, "SST Faces Congressional Hurdle," *Aviation Week & Space Technology*, September 29, 1969, pp. 16–19.

[45] Karl D. Kryter, "Sonic Booms from Supersonic Transport," *Science*, Vol. 163, January 24, 1969, pp. 359–367.

[46] K. Pearsons and K. D. Kryter, "Laboratory Tests of Subjective Reactions to Sonic Booms," Report No. CR-187 (National Aeronautics and Space Administration), Washington, D.C., 1964.

young, healthy, and prepared. The startle effect was not assessed. There was no consideration for infants, the aged, or the nervous. The claim that only poorly constructed buildings are affected by sonic booms provides little comfort to the owners and occupants. And in this respect, it might be worthwhile to mention that many schools and hospitals are included in this category. The fact that only $20 million in claims reached the government during the period 1956–1967 and that only a small percentage was approved is often paraded as reassuring evidence of only minor damage.[47] More realistic appraisals place an estimate of about $85 million annually for "Great Circle" SST routes and $37 million for the circuitous routes. But even these amounts may be low, for they are based on damages caused by B-58 aircraft. The SST would create sonic booms averaging 5 to 25 percent higher in intensity and have about twice the duration of booms generated by B-58s.[48] The figures do not reflect the extent to which booms weaken structures, a possibility that may elude precise calculation but certainly does not escape the sober consideration of persons living in tornado belts and along mighty geological fault lines.

In its selective quest for supportive evidence, the Department of Transportation dismissed categorically the health hazards that might be aggravated by a full fleet of supersonic planes. Scientists serving on the National Academy of Sciences panel on weather and climate modification had warned that there would occur a depletion of the protective layer of ozone in the stratosphere that shields the earth from solar ultraviolet radiation. This could account for 23,000 to 103,000 additional cases of skin cancer per year, according to Dr. Gio Gori, an associate director of the National Cancer Institute. The scientific soundness of this ominous projection was endorsed by the National Institutes of Health.

Despite high level and high sounding dedication to rational national priorities and even "preservation of environmental quality" in its various manifestations, three successive administrations nonetheless succeeded in plotting costs and benefits in such fashion as to justify continuance of the SST. Development and production costs were admittedly vague, but they were used as inputs into the "basic economic projections," which were definitely favorable for industry, national defense, and even international relations. One cannot but regret that details on the latter item were absent. One wonders what evidence for

[47] U.S. Department of Transportation, "Summary of Sonic Boom Claims Presented in the U.S. to the Air Force, Fiscal Years 1956–1967," Washington, D.C., 1967.

[48] Cornell Aeronautical Laboratory, "Analysis of Population Size in the Sonic Effects Zone along Likely SST Routes," *SST Memo No. 507*, Contract FA-WA-4297, Federal Aviation Administration, Washington, D.C., 1964.

peace and prosperity was available to the analysts in view of the heightened competition with even erstwhile friendly nations, the distinct possibility of speedier transport of soldiers as well as civilians, and the lack of historical justification for the proposition that making the world smaller has made it cozier or safer for its inhabitants.

With dollar costs minimized, opportunity costs omitted, and social costs ignored, the balance with respect to benefits was made to appear so overwhelming that opponents were regarded as latter-day Luddites, pitiable in their feeble attempt to stay the mighty advance of the state-of-the-art, or benighted traitors, advocating that their country voluntarily surrender its enviable position of technical leadership in the air transport world. The arithmetic of the benefits was based on a simulation of remarkably low fidelity in that it posited an $18 billion deficit in balance of payments, during the decade of the 1970s, about $5.5 billion of which United States airlines would be spending on the purchase of British/French Concordes and $12.5 billion of which would represent the estimated loss in SST sales to foreign airlines.[49] Moreover, the calculations were built on the premises of technological success, economic soundness, and commercial acceptability questioned and found wanting by members of the presidential panel of experts. The reasoning through which the SST program was promoted to the status of major national goal and thereby automatically given weighted benefits was paradoxical to the point of self-contradiction.

Pushed as a competitor to undercut the advantages enjoyed by the Concorde or the Russian Tu-144, the SST at the same time won enthusiastic praise as a vital factor in "communications technology that shrinks global distances and knits the world together." The benefits of such an international goodwill mission have not been supported by historical experience. Conventional jet aircraft have already reduced the Atlantic to a river without perceptible improvement in our relations with overseas neighbors. In fact, relative ease and economy of movements of goods such as automobiles, textiles, and footwear have contributed to such a flooding of domestic markets and such severe competition with home-manufactured products that protective trade barriers have been imposed by the United States. This isolationism will certainly have repercussions in the nations discriminated against, and retaliatory measures against American goods will be the logical response. Here lies the classic case of international trade competition that has led to serious conflict in times past. And, the better to insure disenchantment between the United States and erstwhile distant countries, friendly and hostile, the design of the American SST is larger, faster, and longer-ranged than

[49] Robert Hotz, "The Supersonic 'Go,'" editorial, *Aviation Week & Space Technology*, September 29, 1969, p. 11.

that of its foreign competitors, its prime economic objective being to render the Concorde and the Tu-144 obsolete and push them off the main traffic arteries.

After seven years and about $700 million worth of support for the development of the supersonic transport, the U.S. Senate in late March, 1971, voted fifty-one to forty-six to discontinue its funding. The debates accompanying the demise of the venture were no less acrimonious than those which had kept it alive. The fury of the economic argument, now centering on markets foregone, jobs lost, technological prowess stymied, was severe. In fact, there was a dramatic but abortive attempt to revive the project through a kind of fiscal subterfuge in which a pro-SST group tried to convince Congress that the $678 million estimated for terminating the program would exceed the $478 million it claimed would complete the prototypes. The figures were disputed, the logic excoriated. In the *post-mortem* period, there have been interesting and thought-provoking disclosures. Senator William Proxmire revealed that in 1969 the U.S. Department of Transportation had spent $12,872 on a children's story book called *The Supersonic Pussy Cat*, in which a lucky feline flew to Paris in two and one-eighth hours. An accompanying teacher's manual suggested "exercises which can excite interest in supersonic flight." [50]

The Senate, pondering the request to appropriate $97.3 million to terminating the SST, may have put only a temporary *finis* to this chapter in aviation history. A new generation, with its own pre-set rationalizations, may have to face similar decisions in the 1990s with the advent of hypersonic aircraft. With configuration and propulsion studies reportedly under way, the public still has much in store in the wide world of travel.[51]

Instances of footling with figures or of finagling with facts are far from isolated. In fact, the more cost-benefit analysis is accepted as synonymous with, and a *sine qua non* of, rational planning, the more likely is the technique to dominate the social scene. Examples of applications in public health and education are discussed in the next chapter.

[51] Richard G. O'Lone, "Hypersonic Transport Study Grows," *Aviation Week & Space Technology*, June 22, 1970, pp. 44–50.

[6]

The Techniques at Work in Education and Health

THE SYSTEMS APPROACH TO EDUCATION

It is important, in discussing systems analysis and program budgeting as tools in planning public services, to recall that the systems approach has had as a major selling point its comprehensiveness and integrativeness. In the growing literature on the systems approach in the field of education, the concept of totality is generally juxtaposed against the piecemeal and fragmented in a dialectic contrived to convey the notion that the latter has now been rendered obsolete.[1] In actual practice, the systems approach allows for fully as much fractionation as ever occurred before. Little has changed in this respect but the language, which provides convenient terminology to justify focusing on arbitrarily and eclectically devised problem areas. Cost-benefit analysis encourages preoccupation with bits and pieces; suboptimization serves as useful rationalization for failure or inability to grasp and grapple with large wholes. The fact that, short of dealing with the entire universe as the whole, *any* system becomes a subwhole is apparently forgotten. Whether the subwhole is the entire web of social institutions, a subsection of them, or some microcosmic unit within one of them is a matter of degree or definition. The designation of some models as *macro* and others as *micro* is intended to clarify, but the distinction is entirely relative, the line of demarcation cut with pinking shears rather than a precision tool. For example, the education program of the United States as a whole

[1] Organization for Economic Cooperation and Development, Centre for Educational Research and Innovation, *Basic Paper on Educational Planning, Policy and Administration*, Paris, August 20, 1970.

147

would call for a macro-model, but considerably less macro than for the entire operational scope of the Department of Health, Education and Welfare, of which it is only a part and which in itself, under some circumstances created by imposition of program budgeting at the top levels of government planning, must account for its own activities when, in the context of a larger macro-model, they may be traded off against some higher priority agency's funding needs. In the field of educational planning, Tinbergen's macro-models of education and labor market needs have become an important reference point. His planning models were designed to "describe the demand flow for various types of qualified manpower to be expected from the organizers of production and of education." Their purpose was "to aid in the process of planning for education and for labor market policies, tacitly assuming that ways and means can be found to induce the population to seek the desirable education."[2] Imitated and applied, Tinbergen's models have been used internationally in the calculation of educational requirements for the economic development of various countries.

A macro-model of more modest proportions might be represented in the conception of a nationwide two-year junior college program such as was recommended by the Educational Policies Commission of the National Education Association.[3] The focus could be narrowed still further. One could develop a model for the vocational education system of a designated school district, or a particular curriculum within a school as, for example, the experimental program in St. Louis for preventing high school dropping-out.[4] Where — in the downward slide from the Olympian heights of Greece, where Tinbergen's models showed near-saturation in third-level students,[5] to the mud flats of Missouri, where the model showed the dropout prevention program to be unprofitable[6] — the *macro* becomes *micro* is not clear. And it would matter little except to underscore the points that imprecisions prevail even in such purely quantitative aspects of the systems approach as size specification, and neither breadth nor scope is necessarily guaranteed by the methodology. On the contrary, through jingoistic terminology, all kinds

[2] Jan Tinbergen and H. C. Bos, "A Planning Model for the Educational Requirements of Economic Development," *Econometric Models of Education*, Organization for Economic Cooperation and Development, Education and Development, Paris, 1965, p. 10.

[3] Werner Z. Hirsch and Morton J. Marcus, "Some Benefit-Cost Considerations of Universal Junior College Education," *National Tax Journal*, Vol. XIX, No. 1, March, 1966.

[4] Burton A. Weisbrod, "Preventing High School Dropouts," in *Measuring the Benefits of Government Investments*, Robert Dorfman, ed., Washington, D.C.: The Brookings Institution, 1965, pp. 117–149.

[5] G. Williams, "Planning Models for the Calculation of Educational Requirements for Economic Development — Greece," *Econometric Models of Education, op.cit.*

[6] Weisbrod, *op.cit.*

of piecemeal fragmentation are countenanced and each piece is accorded a *raison d'être* of its own. Moreover, the procedures, especially those associated with cost-benefit analysis, contribute to artificial splintering for the sake of extracting from the whole that which is quantifiable.

In the field of education, cost-benefit analysis and program budgeting pass for the new look in planning. Public school administrators, who traditionally have been the subject of criticism and the object of calumny for what they have and have not done, have long occupied a low position on the professional totem pole. Their activities and "inventory" always highly visible, they have long been vulnerable to attack. It is small wonder that they have been attracted by the polemics about "sophisticated" and "systematic" tools. Cowed into believing that their ways are inefficient, that establishment of and adherence to "performance standards" will endear them to legislative budget-makers and the public at large, school administrators have become easy prey to the persuasive propaganda. Professional planning societies' meetings and journals are now replete with technical refinements on educational models; input-output analyses of school systems abound. Many of them are in essence "technical" explorations of conventional wisdom with considerable emphasis on a few knowns, elaborate statement of limitations and margins for error, tables and appendixes in abundance — all in evidence of doggedly persistent application of the method.[7]

The imposition of program budgeting has become the prime cause for the transformation of the educational establishment into a counting house, where busy number work has replaced the once-honored thinking cap. Required to justify their activities and, possibly, their very existence in terms of objectives achieved, public school officials are engaged in cost-benefit juggling which will affect the course of public education for years to come. In this endeavor, they are aided by grants from the federal government as well as from private foundations, the provision being "to improve planning and budgetary procedures," and abetted by the "intellectual carpetbaggers," always game to apply their "technical expertness" to green fields.

California's experience illustrates some of the problems associated with program budgeting in education. During the 1967 session of the State Legislature,[8] an Advisory Commission on School District Budgeting was instituted; its mandate, to develop a program budgeting

[7] Robert G. Spiegelman, "A Benefit-Cost Model to Evaluate Education Programs," *Socio-Economic Planning Sciences*, Vol. I, No. 4, August, 1968, pp. 443–460.

C. Selby Smith, "Costs and Benefits in Further Education: Some Evidence from a Pilot Study," *The Economic Journal*, Vol. LXXX, No. 319, September, 1970, pp. 583–604.

[8] The Advisory Commission on School District Budgeting and Accounting, *Report on Planning, Programming, Budgeting System for California School Districts*, presented to the California State Board of Education, June 14, 1968.

system; its model, the Department of Defense; its mentors, a flying squadron of "program budgeting experts"; [9] its funding from national sources.[10] The prime contract for implementing PPBS went to Peat, Marwick, and Mitchell, a nation-wide accounting firm. Something over $500,000 was allocated for a fifteen-district, four-year pilot project. The time and the money have been spent and extensions of both sought, but workable procedures are not yet in sight. Although a RAND format supplied them (see Fig. 5), was faithfully studied, many schoolmen cannot get beyond the starting box on the diagram, *viz., problem definition*. To be sure, no school administrator lacks problems but he need

FIGURE 5. Components of a Program-Budgeting System

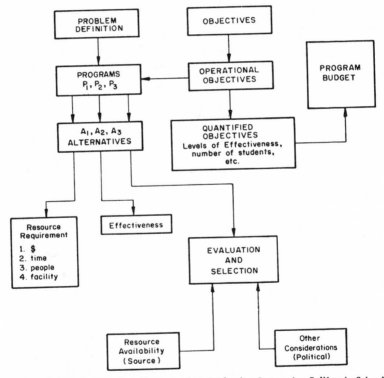

SOURCE: *Report on Planning, Programming, Budgeting System for California School Districts*. Presentation by the Rand Corporation to the Advisory Commission on School District Budgeting and Accounting, June 14, 1968.

[9] State-Local Finances Project of George Washington University, Washington, D.C.
[10] U.S. Office of Education, Department of Health, Education and Welfare, Elementary and Secondary Education Act of 1965, Title V.

only follow the arrows on the chart to discover that his particular plethora of problems does not fit into the prefabricated procedures for solution. Once he has stated his problem, he must proceed to the next box, where he is expected to propose possible programs (P_1, P_2, P_3), and then, like Uncle Wiggly, hop to the next stop with "Alternatives" (A_1, A_2, A_3). These inevitably lead him to considerations of cost (Resource Requirement), where the salient items are listed as "$, time, people, and facility." Arrows also go from "Alternatives" to "Effectiveness" and "Evaluation and Selection." Presumably, calculations in these two boxes will correspond to the cost box, for there can be no cost-benefit analysis without compatibility. For some curious reason, "Evaluation and Selection" is connected to "Alternatives" but not to "Effectiveness." "Objectives," like the cheese in the children's game, stands alone, but an arrow draws it to something separated out as "Operational Objectives," which, in turn, is hooked into the box called "Quantified Objectives." Dubious elucidation here is provided by the subscripted legend, "Levels of Effectiveness, number of students, etc." Here, the one-way arrows stop; the end of the trail is reached. The road that started at "Problem Definition" comes to no such dead end, however. Having reached "Evaluation and Selection," where two unexplained and inexplicable forces impinge on them, viz., "Resource Availability (Source)" and "Other Considerations (Political)," the incomprehensibly embellished "Evaluation and Selection" lead triumphantly by one-way irreversible arrow to "Program Budget," conceived as the grand finale with, contrary to all the publicity and promises, no feedback on program formulation in its vital, formative stages.

The RAND diagram exemplifies and intensifies the difficulties of program budgeting, but it does not help overcome them. Even with high priced talent from outside, California educators are having trouble carrying out the mandate to develop program budgeting. Some of them, possibly inspired by the array of consultants assembled to guide them, have skipped lightly over the preliminary box of "Problem Definition," arbitrarily selected several ongoing programs, and moved into the "Resources Requirement" (1. $ 2. time 3. people 4. facility). Costs-chasing, although a comfortable occupation, is not likely, however, to yield the kind of information that could meaningfully be related to instructional techniques, pupil performance, and similar matters which rightfully engage the attention of educators.[11] The typical response to frustration at failure to achieve a workable cost-effectiveness formula in education

[11] Legislative Analyst, State of California, *Fiscal Review and Analysis of Selected Categorical Aid Education Programs in California* (Final Report), May 17, 1971, pp. 125 ff.

as elsewhere leads to preoccupation with and fixation at the level of development of a cost model.

Review of cost models, even those constructed by the most prestigious "think tanks" in the state, serves only to strengthen the conviction that this kind of model, unrelated to proper consideration of performance or effectiveness or whatever it is that is being striven for or achieved, is merely another form of expense accounting, less desirable in fiscal planning than conventional methods because it is arbitrarily selective. What is left out is generally more crucial to the educational process than that which is included. Corollary to the determined gathering of figures is the pursuit of data. When outside experts take on the task of improving the management of public affairs, they make a great show of their discovery that data gaps are rife and data unreliability is rampant. This invariably leads to the recommendation that there be designed an elaborate information system. As will be seen in the next chapter, the information system has become the *sine qua non* in public planning and serves equally well as an excuse for action and for inaction. Until there is explicit elucidation as to the kind of information that is needed in order to achieve the highest purposes of education, the expenditure of money and time at this stage of the process is a delaying tactic and a rationalization by consultants for not completing the tasks they knowingly and wittingly contracted to perform.

In California, an expensive education cost model, in the development of which paucity of data was claimed by the team of hired experts, failed to include the often crippling costs, direct and indirect, of maintaining data banks. Nor did it account adequately in its elaborate costing procedures for the already extensive information-gathering activities going on in the Department of Education. Designed with the assistance of Aerojet-General Corporation engineers, the multi-million dollar electronic data-processing system already in operation stores vast quantities of information on every facet of the State's educational establishment. Besides keeping track of the children, their age, address, school location, grade, I.Q. and achievement records, and the like, it can report for any given day how many children were sent home for reasons of illness. This Sorceror's Apprentice approach to statistics gathering had its beginnings in the need for data for Average Daily Attendance reporting and reimbursement but may have outrun its usefulness. Unresponsive to most user needs, it could not properly justify its expensive existence when subjected to official interrogation by a committee of the State Assembly.

Oblivious to the doubtful value of the information system already in operation or, perhaps, choosing to ignore it, "Space Age technologists" from the National Aeronautics and Space Administration's Office of

Advanced Research and Technology and California Institute of Technology's Jet Propulsion Laboratory have developed a computerized attendance system for a high school in Sacramento, California. Intended to "free teachers from the tedium of calling the roll and recording tardy and absent students," the $100,000 system, which was adapted from one used in the Mariner interplanetary missions, works through a compact transmitter in each classroom.[12] Instant readouts of class attendance for each period appear in the accounting office, where the receiving system requires the full time of a clerk-typist. This abundance of technologically derived intelligence is being amassed in a state where educational budgets have been the target for drastic surgery resulting in unfavorable teacher-pupil ratios, severe cutting back of special programs, and no funds for the earthquake-proofing of antiquated buildings. What earthly use there is in monitoring high school students hourly is not asked by the Space Age designers nor the purchasers of this doubtful bounty. Moreover, a cost model that would ignore this $100,000 item plus the fulltime salary to tend it is a poor instrument for planning and for any kind of responsible stewardship of public resources.

Preoccupation with the cost input side of the analysis and with the school bookkeeping chores postpones the day of real reckoning, when not only the economic costs but the social costs of pursuing a course of action or not pursuing it are entered into the ledger. On that day, systems planners will also have to assay the benefit side. They will have to answer the question that underlies the entire educational enterprise: *cui bono*, for whose good? Neither cost models nor a "goal oriented" budget can have meaning unless the objectives are clearly articulated. But by virtue of the technique and its rules, goals must be stated in terms comparable to the input side; they must be quantifiable. This, for educators, is a dangerous course, for it forces unrealistic assumptions, encourages unwarranted presumptions, and devalues the larger dimensions and purpose of education in society.

EDUCATION PLANNING AND MANPOWER NEEDS

Education planning, construed by systems analysts to be a form of "policy intervention" or "manipulation of the future," [13] thus becomes another game, played according to its own rules. Some of these were set down by Tinbergen when he fended off anticipated criticism

---

[12] "School Control, Statistical Aids Devised from Space Technology," *Aviation Week & Space Technology*, May 24, 1971, p. 19.
[13] Olaf Helmer, "The Delphi Technique and Educational Innovation," in Werner Z. Hirsch, et al., *Inventing Education for the Future*, San Francisco: Chandler, 1967, pp. 74–99.

of his models. Aware that "educationalists, economists, and other social scientists" might challenge his tying education planning with labor market policies, he invited "improved" models, but he specified that they had to "meet the practical conditions imposed." These included using "measurable variables and coefficients" and having a possible solution.[14] How well Tinbergen satisfies his own conditions is not above dispute. His assumption that "ways and means can be found to induce the population to seek the desirable education" reverberates with dictatorial and totalitarian overtones. Ignoring the social and psychological factors and the political framework, confusing cause and effect in the educational process, and forgetting lessons of history and geography, he and his followers have devised a kind of "iron law of education," [15] inimical to the growth it was purported to foster.

Without presuming to challenge the technical correctness of Tinbergen's models, we must, nonetheless, examine their implications for educational planning. In Spain and Turkey, the analysis revealed too few third-level students for attainment of "the desired growth rate of the economy"; in Greece, possibly too many.[16] If, as the authors warn, the models are not intended for short-term planning of the final phases of education, are we then to conclude that they should be used for the long term? If this is the case, the findings would encourage the Greek government to order its third-level institutions to declare a moratorium until the demand and supply balance. Or they could institute more stringent screening procedures than already exist in the elementary schools and thus thin out the flow in the pipeline. In Southern Italy, where this has been customary, although possibly for different reasons, the practice has resulted in an abundance of shoeshine boys, not counted in labor force calculations and not considered in any one's models.

Whether made explicit or not, the notion of measuring the rewards of education through labor force participation underlies most of the cost-benefit literature. For economists, wages earned are the measure of success. The wedding of educational planning to manpower needs is an enticing one for it offers the conveniences of quantifiable inputs and outputs. The counting of students and teachers, the enumerating of jobs, the matching of one with the other, all have appeal because they lend themselves readily to "systematic" treatment. They also carry certain assumptions: that manpower forecasting is an exact science; that the values of education lie vocationally in the after-school life; that

[14] Jan Tinbergen and H. C. Bos, op.cit., p. 10.

[15] Thomas Balogh, "Comments on the Paper by Messrs. Tinbergen and Bos," in *The Residual Factor and Economic Growth*, Paris: Organisation for Economic Co-operation and Development, Study Group in Economics of Education, 1964, p. 181.

[16] *Ibid.*, pp. 98, 99.

education is a kind of escalator that rides upward from rags to riches; and that the student population (and their parents) will willingly comply with the dictates of a system that, like the Queen in *Alice in Wonderland*, sets one painter to paint some roses red and another to paint some white.

These assumptions are built on shaky premises. The state-of-the-art in manpower forecasting is not nearly well enough developed to provide a secure basis on which to plan. Moreover, with the job market in flux as a result of social, political, historical, and technological factors, any orderly tableau of inputs and outputs would have such short-lived validity that deductions made from it for the educational process, which of necessity requires a longer span of time, could be grossly inappropriate. Rash, indeed, would be the analyst whose data base was income distribution during this period. Consider, for example, the unemployment situation of the 1970s, with the electronics engineers hired so enthusiastically fifteen years ago laid off by the thousands, the teachers needed so desperately five years ago lucky to find an occasional temporary assignment, hundreds of Ph.D.'s in science unemployed or underemployed.[17] With postgraduate students in college requiring public assistance in the form of food stamps if not outright welfare grants, young doctors doing volunteer duty in migrant labor camps instead of making their way up the traditional American medical ladder, and teachers donating their services to deprived and underprivileged sectors, tying education to income could lead to some strange projections for the years ahead.

Using today's unemployment figures as the basis for curriculum planning, the case made through cost-benefit analysis for a universal junior college [18] would, by its own fundamental assumption, be denied. Such a two-year post-high-school program was proposed and its benefits calculated on the incremental income such higher education would command. The authors recognized that their "tangible benefit" criterion did pose a special problem with respect to the education of women. Carried to its extreme, it could deprive little girls of instruction even in reading and writing just as it did their great-great-grandmothers in the Old World. Moreover, emphasis on earnings, popular in benefit analysis, could lead to many courses for plumbers, whose training pays off early and well, and few for physicians, who spend at least twenty years in school before earning a penny.

The assumption underlying the notion that education is an effective

[17] Deborah Shapley, "Job Prospects: Science Graduates Face Worst Year in Two Decades," *Science*, Vol. 172, May 21, 1971, pp. 823–824.

[18] Werner Z. Hirsch and Morton J. Marcus, "Some Benefit-Cost Considerations of Universal Junior College Education," *op.cit.*

means of generating earning capability is far from indisputable. The one-way causality between education and income has yet to be proven. It is far more likely that the "poverty syndrome," which includes poor health, bad housing, and poverty-derived congenital handicaps that have affected capacity to learn and earn, is such a powerful determinant of and deterrent to vocational success that focus on education alone is myopic. For example, medical testing of children in the Head Start program showed that about one-third of them had physical defects ranging from infected tonsils to long-term deficiency diseases.[19] Many of the ailments have been found to affect mental development and acuity. A study of training programs for persons on welfare revealed that dental and optical problems, recurring illnesses, and inaccessibility of medical care caused tardiness and absenteeism, nullified positive results from the classes, and made job-hunting and holding a near impossibility.[20] A cost-benefit analysis of several education programs mounted as part of the War on Poverty revealed that poverty and education were not clearly linked and that dollar gains from special educational benefits were hard to find.[21] The economic benefits of training and education, therefore, have yet to be demonstrated. Despite the creditable efforts to show evidence that even such limited-goal endeavors as projects undertaken through the Manpower Development and Training Act have succeeded, the overall benefits and payoffs are nebulous.[22]

Professional research has so far failed to establish clear-cut causal relationships or to distinguish between cause and effect in the complex circumstances surrounding the vocational career.

The Goals of Education

A brief review of the history of public education in the United States discloses how ephemeral various stipulated goals have been. In the early days, the prime objective was the inculcation of certain patterns of conduct, with emphasis on the virtues of self-control and self-discipline. The public school was the institution expected to preserve morality and promote the social order.[23] Growing urbanization and

[19] Julius B. Richmond, "For the Child of Poverty," *The American Child*, Vol. 48, No. 2, Spring, 1966, p. 8.

[20] Ida R. Hoos, *Retraining the Workforce*, Berkeley and Los Angeles: University of California Press, 1967, pp. 179 ff.

[21] Thomas Ribick, *Education and Poverty*, Washington, D.C.: The Brookings Institution, 1968.

[22] U.S. Department of Labor Manpower Administration, *Manpower Evaluation Report*, "Earnings Mobility of MDTA Trainees," No. 7, April, 1967, p. 16, and *Manpower Evaluation Report*, No. 8, December, 1968, p. 35.

[23] R. J. Wiebe, "The Social Functions of Public Education," *American Quarterly*, Vol. 21, Summer, 1969, pp. 147–164.

industrialization in the latter half of the nineteenth century forged the link between schooling and employment. Persons with a high school diploma could aspire to white-collar status; a normal school certificate assured entry into the teaching profession. For wave after wave of immigrants, the American dream became a reality through the educational system and, incidentally, gave proof to the hypothesis that its proper goal was successful preparation for the world of work. Vocational education legislation brought about development of special secondary school curricula in the trades and establishment of "practical arts" high schools. Herein lay tacit acknowledgment of the diversity of pupil endowment, talent, and motivation, and the realities of the division of labor in the market place. Repeating the all-too-familiar pattern of reform, however, the principle as conceived in the top echelons of the bureaucracy was promising, the practice, a travesty, denying instead of providing opportunity to the less capable students. So great a temporal lag occurred that a large percentage of the funds were spent on anachronistic agricultural courses.[24]

As the glow of America's great melting pot became dimmed by an upsurge of ethnic self-determination, with demands for more equality in education and employment opportunity, much of the invidious discrimination inherent in the system that welded school to work became visible. Assignment to vocational courses had become a stigma, a visible symbol of academic inferiority and permanent relegation to second class status. The trade and shop classes, used as a repository for the less motivated and the less talented, were regarded as a means of foreclosing instead of creating equal opportunity, especially among students of minority races. Within a quarter century, so much resentment was generated that the pendulum of public opinion swung all the way back to the point that many school districts eliminated their special curriculum high schools and returned to the comprehensive type which had generated the dissatisfaction in the first place. The question of how democratic is equal remains unresolved.

In becoming a target for protest and demands for redress for wrongs in the social and economic order, the school system, no longer the simple reflection, repository, and perpetuator of the society's values, has taken on wider and paradoxical dimensions. It is now seen as both cause and consequence of societal ills and thus has become incubator for, as well as object of, bitter criticism and disillusionment. And as the public attitude toward schools has changed, so also has the conception of their proper goals. The attempt in the 1970s to distill out of the boiling mass of divergent conceptions some neat

---

[24] U.S. Department of Health, Education, and Welfare, Office of Education, *Education for a Changing World*, Washington, D.C.: U.S. Government Printing Office, 1963.

measurable objective may stem from faith in the "modern tools of technology," but they seem to be based on nostalgic reference to the simpler life of a century ago. By forcing identification of objectives which can be reduced to readily acquired and handled quantitative units, the techniques of program budgeting actually deny and violate the multiplicity of goals that should characterize a broad-gauged educational system. Concerned only with the done and not constructed even to address what ought to be done, the "new tools," contrary to the claim of their being innovative, are reactionary in the extreme.

Gearing education to the proximate needs of the economy represents not only a skewed view of the society's value system; it also is a serious distortion of the role of education in civilized society. The "customer oriented" goal of supplying a labor force disregards individual needs, interests, opportunity, and rights. A regressive step on the scale of civilization, it comes at the very time when advancing technology has dwarfed man's role in the production process, when automation has deprived him of whatever emotional and psychological satisfaction he once could have derived from work, and when reduction of hours and mandatory retirement have already provided him with more leisure than he knows how to enjoy.[25] If the goal of education were construed to be nothing more than successful labor force participation, our institutions could do no better than to produce machine tenders and stamped out robots, pre-selected by computer to fit into the pre-programed slots. What appears very likely is that the full and productive life of the future will have to be achieved with little reference to, if not in spite of, the means by which the daily bread is earned. Unless our vision of and expectations from the educational system are broadened, the avenues of self-fulfillment will at best be booby-trapped by the canned culture of television and at worst will deteriorate into escape routes into the drug culture, already beckoning a welcome to the bored and disenchanted of all ages and position.

> The real problems of education are going to center on the need to develop people capable of living the fullest possible lives in an age of plenty. We shall have to produce men and women who are able to understand the significance of the past, who are in the stream of current ideas and who can make use of them, and who have the quality of imagination that is capable of foreseeing and welcoming the future.[26]

Tailoring the educational system to suit the economy can only be accomplished through strengthening the central powers of decision-

[25] Ida R. Hoos, *Automation in the Office*, Washington, D.C.: Public Affairs Press, 1961, p. 109.
[26] Sir Leon Bogrit, *The Age of Automation*, New York: Mentor Books, 1965, p. 77.

making. Just as program budgeting in the Department of Defense concentrated more authority in the hands of the Secretary, naming the goal and then directing the efforts of the entire organization to achieve it could bring about authoritarianism in the state of education. Ideologically distasteful though such a trend may be, it is perceptible. In England, where an academic consultative conference agreed that manpower considerations should play a greater part in university decisions, it was also recognized that this situation would force the establishment and centralization of controls.[27] How this would affect the cherished academic freedom of professors and the students' rights to choose a career was not made known then or subsequently. "Program performance" could be virtually assured by a college administration that engineered a curriculum of instant relevance to the economy and selected a student body to accommodate such goals.

PROGRAM PERFORMANCE IN EDUCATION

Always in the name of rationally allocating scarce resources, a college administration could build a cost model, relating the various disciplines respectively to their expenses, for example, faculty salaries, payroll of supporting personnel, square feet of space occupied, prorated campus-wide overhead and upkeep. It would no doubt demonstrate the obvious. On the campuses of the University of California, for example, it would reveal that high-energy physics, with a small number of students per class, high faculty-student ratio, enormous needs for space for accelerators, peripheral apparatus, laboratories, extremely expensive computers, and other equipment, showed relatively low "output," calculated in number of graduates and their employment under conditions of severe retrenchment in science. Would such findings suggest that enrollment in this field should be cut back? Should faculty salaries be cut? Should space be denied and accelerators shut down? Cost models do not answer these vital questions. Cutting back enrollment could adversely affect the nation's scientific progress a decade from now and it would take at least until the year 2000 to recapture momentum.

The prospect of a budget-ridden and economy-ridden future could discourage the entrance of bright young people to university teaching and research and thus impair the quality of higher education for a generation to come. Further erosion of faculty salaries could cause flight on the part of some of the most able members. It is not too far-fetched to imagine that, in an era already characterized by experts for export,

---

[27] "Graduates to Order," *Nature*, Vol. 220, November 23, 1968, p. 733.

they might seek foreign markets for their skills. In the current surplus of talent over availability of jobs in many countries, it appears that a nation less developed in science and technology could through this very means enter the "nuclear club." Scientists believe that the recent South African claim to the development of a new process for enriching uranium could only be substantiated on this basis.[28] Already there is evidence of a brain drain in reverse, as fewer scientists seek to enter the United States.[29]

Notwithstanding their limitations, cost models are being developed and used as a basis for education planning. The University of California's activities are typical.[30] There is the "student flow model," intended to indicate the university's "retention rate." It tells the number of students accepted, matriculated, and graduated. It counts the courses taken, the hours of credit. It tallies "dropouts." But, with all this intelligence, it does not indicate whether the latter really left college or merely transferred to another institution of higher learning, a crucial difference to anyone seeking to understand student needs and the educational process. The "faculty flow model" has as inputs the "economic" and "social" characteristics of the present academic staff. By whose judgment the latter are defined and by what reason the former are construed to be a university's business are not clear. What is definite is that the operation of the model is expected to yield "optimal hiring strategy." We need pause only briefly to wonder about the analysts' criteria for significant "social" characteristics (race? color? political affiliation? party behavior? conviviality?) and their consequent use in plotting "optimal hiring strategy."

Operation of the "optimum class scheduling model" calls for more intensive usage of plant. Cost considerations and plant utilization probably influenced the decision to institute a quarterly, four-term calendar, which is being abandoned — possibly an economic success but certainly a social failure, dissatisfaction having been evident on the part of students and faculty alike. The possibilities that compacting of courses into a quarterly system or holding evening classes might interfere with other activities of the student's life or adversely affect the teaching-learning process were not taken into account. If number of bodies processed in the academic mill is the prime consideration, then shorten-

[28] D. S. Greenberg, "South Africa: How Valid the Claim for a Uranium Process?" *Science*, Vol. 169, No. 3945, August 7, 1970, p. 563.

[29] Thomas P. Southwick, "Brain Drain: Fewer Scientists Enter U.S., More Seek to Leave," *Science*, Vol. 169, No. 3945, August 7, 1970, pp. 565–566.

[30] John E. Keller, formerly Director of the Office of Analytical Studies, University of California, remarks at meeting, "New Frontiers in Educational Program Planning and Budgeting and in Educational Cost-Benefit Analysis," Berkeley, California, January 15, 1968.

ing, hastening, and compressing the curriculum does wonders for the "productivity level." But such calculation disregards the dynamics of the learning-teaching process, its appropriate and meaningful objectives downgraded. Although not included, they are far from unaffected, however, for they may be violated by the distortions of resource ascription that occur.

There is evidence at all levels of education planning of a growing reliance on this lopsided approach to policy-making with respect to imposition or level of tuition fees, setting of requirements for matriculation and graduation, and funding special programs, in addition to the myriad matters already mentioned. Could it perhaps be that institutionalized misplacement of values is one of the factors contributing to student dissatisfaction? Planning through budgeting, for better or for worse, could remove decisions with far-reaching academic implications from faculty purlieu. For example, a directive curtailing funds for visiting scholars was issued as a kind of temporary economic expedient, but affects time-honored sabbatical privileges and indirectly increases teaching obligations substantially.[31] Although this step could be justified by some optimum faculty workload model, the question still remains as to whose judgment of optimality has been persuasive and is to be respected in future decisions of this kind.

Besides counting certificates of completion, diplomas, or degrees granted, how can one account for performance in program budgeting in education? How are benefits weighted, effectiveness measured? The ways are numerous and devious. They depend on an arbitrary definition of a here-and-now goal rather than on some firm long-living criterion. With the assumption of instant relevance occurs neglect of past lessons and nonsensical implications for the future. An institution of higher learning might attempt to justify its expenditure of federal funds by number of classrooms built. With the discovery that the total appears considerably under the original cost estimates, hastily-erected screens and temporary partitions have been known to raise the count impressively, although they reduced standard room-size to broom-closet dimensions. Physical plant for education lends itself to this type of manipulation and offers a splendid opportunity for cost-benefit juggling. Carried to its logical extreme, this approach could tie square footage to number of pupils, teachers, classes, or whatever. But with all the putting in of thumbs, pulling out of plums, and self-congratulation on the part of analysts, we would be little the wiser about the

[31] University of California (Berkeley), Office of the Chancellor, Memorandum to all Deans, "Budgetary Savings, 1970–71," October 28, 1970.
University of California (Berkeley), Office of the Dean, College of Letters and Science, Memorandum to Chairmen and Directors of College of Letters and Science Departments and Organized Research Units, October 30, 1970.

school's operation and achievements, except, perhaps, to be wary of the statistics it produced.

STUDENTS' GRADES AS INDICES

Traditionally, students' grades have been used as a measure of performance and as an index of a school's excellence. Certain institutions, like the Boston Latin Schools, established a national reputation on their graduates' records. Alumni were followed into Harvard and Radcliffe so that their stellar achievements would reflect glory on the *alma mater*. In lesser schools, performance may not have been so spectacular, but a similar pattern prevailed and the same yardstick was used. The meaning of grades seems, however, to be undergoing subtle change in the current ferment taking place in American education. New assessments are being made of the way in which ratings are earned, made, and interpreted.

Throughout his school career, the student is subjected to standardized tests of mental ability and accomplishment. The examinations, devised primarily as an aid to convenient classification by teachers, administrators, and college admissions deans, have exerted a feedback effect on curriculum planning and on the educational system. With the widespread emphasis and reliance on performance and achievement in these tests, "teaching to the test" has occurred to a greater or lesser degree in most American schools, particularly among the two million high school students who annually prepare for their College Entrance Board examinations. Recently, however, the College Board's Commission on Tests urged basic revision of the tests on the ground that they are insensitive, narrowly conceived, and inimical to the interests of many young people. Their indictment of the tests constitutes an oblique shaft at the American educational system itself, both for what it offers and what it rates as valuable through its system of weights and measures. Long accepted as the single index of undergraduate achievement and institutional excellence and used in the selection of students for graduate schools, Graduate Record Examination Tests are now coming under critical review because of their observed inadequacies.[32] Students, especially those who, through maturation as well as exposure to good instruction, have moved away from slavish, mechanical regurgitation to independent thinking, have been at a particular disadvantage with the Graduate Record Examination format.

A report on scholarship grades by the University of California's Of-

---

[32] Philip W. Anderson and John J. Hopfield, "Quality Education: Hanged Without a Trial." Letters to the Editor, *Science*, Vol. 162, November 8, 1968, p. 850.

fice of Institutional Research further illustrates the need for caution in relying on grades as indicators. The study revealed a steady rise in the percentage of A's and B's in both lower and upper division courses.[33] This finding could justifiably have been used by secondary schools as evidence of their excellence. It could and may have been used by analysts as the output for one of their models. It caused the Academic Senate's Committee on Educational Policy to raise a number of searching questions about the characteristics of the student body, grading policies of the faculty, and the tenuous relationship between grades and the quality of performance of those who teach and those who are taught. With respect to the students, it was readily apparent that increased screening and heightened competition occasioned by limited enrollment due to straitened budgets could have been a factor. The higher grades could, however, be attributed to changing faculty practices, the possibility being that the new breed of younger instructors, more sympathetic to the needs of the students than to the requirements of the system, treats grades more casually than did their senior colleagues.

TECHNOLOGICAL DEVICES AND EDUCATION

At the very time when thoughtful educators are pondering the shortcomings of tests and grades as measures of performance, a flotilla of latter-day Columbuses, some practicing program budgeting, some peddling "technological aids," has discovered education as a promising land for their wares. In Sacramento, California, "Space Age technology" has taken the form of a $10,000 alarm system, developed jointly by the Office of Advanced Research of the National Aeronautics and Space Administration and the Jet Propulsion Laboratory of California Institute of Technology. The device, described as "a spring-loaded striker and tuning fork about the size of a fountain pen," emits an ultrasonic signal which is picked up by a "network of microphones, amplifiers and relays." The gadget is intended to stop "potentially major disorders" in the seventy-six-classroom John F. Kennedy High School. A NASA spokesman reported on its usefulness in this way, "It has been used mostly when there have been fights but the officials feel it has probably prevented some major disorders." [34] As to what constitutes a "major disorder" and how such an event might be precipitated by the over-reaction of officials is, of course, never mentioned. The fact

[33] University of California, Office of Institutional Research, *A Report on Scholarship Grades — University of California, Berkeley*, Per Cent Distribution for Fall Terms 1961, 1963, 1965, 1967, 1969, October, 1970.
[34] "School Control, Statistical Aids Devised from Space Technology," *op.cit.*

that the alarm system has been used on an average of three times a week suggests that either the social situation of the school is in deep trouble or the staff is prone to push buttons instead of pressing for meaningful solutions to the problems. Applying the cost-benefit measure to the $10,000 expenditure, one is impelled to observe that such an amount would go far to provide recreational outlets, sports equipment, or subtle subsidy for a worthwhile cause.

A number of technological aids were paraded before a Joint Congressional Committee as adjuncts to the educational process.[35] The list included: ". . . educational television, both open and closed; video tape; computerized instruction; the use of computers for student testing, guidance and evaluation, and the storage, retrieval, and distribution of information; programed courses of instruction, teaching machines, particularly the 'talking typewriter'; the use of microfilm and microfilm viewing equipment; and language laboratories." The official report on this cornucopia also included "the 'system's' approach to the development and utilization of educational technology." This was described as "the creative combination of a variety of skills and devices to produce desired results, an approach that is proving highly successful in the military sphere,"[36] a statement which eloquently indicates and underscores the full extent of the gullibility and naïvete displayed by senators and congressmen and their consulting economists when their focus is technological advance and their forte is "economic progress" and not education.

Because purveyors of most of the items in the above array must justify and rationalize the virtuosity of their goods, they engage in fascinating exercises in the "costing out" of computerized instruction. Some make optimistic pie-in-the-sky statements about anticipated savings once equipment design becomes standardized and efficient production methods are brought into play. Per unit costs, we are assured, will some day be reduced.[37] Most estimates of cost savings turn out to be just another of the new myths discussed by Oettinger.[38]

Measures of effectiveness are harder to come by than cost items, but the technologist, steering clear of the substantive real-life concerns of educators, projects wishful thoughts to the day when, as there is now for cars rolling off the assembly line, there will be definition of some

[35] U.S. Eighty-ninth Congress, Second Session, A Report of the Subcommittee on Economic Progress of the Joint Economic Committee, *Automation and Technology in Education*, Washington, D.C.: U.S. Government Printing Office, August, 1966.

[36] *Ibid.*, p. 5.

[37] R. C. Atkinson and H. A. Wilson, "Computer-Assisted Instruction," *Science*, Vol. 162, October 4, 1968, pp. 73–77.

[38] Anthony G. Oettinger, *Run, Computer, Run*, Cambridge: Harvard University Press, 1969.

standard unit, some *erg* of learning and forgetting.[39] This type of output could be the inevitable result of the feedback mechanism built into automated, computerized systems that perforce teach to the test and in so doing perpetrate what has been called TV quiz teaching, the prime insult to the learning process. It works as follows:

> The first thing the student does is peck out his name on the typewriter. The computer then searches its memory to determine what the student did on his last lesson and what his lesson should be this time. If it is a reading drill, for example, the computer may display a word on the screen at the same time a recorded voice pronounces the word in the earphones. After several words are simultaneously displayed and pronounced, they are displayed on the screen and the recorded voice asks the student to pick out one. This can be done either on the typewriter or with the light pen. If the student selects the right answer, the recorded voice in his earphone says, "Yes, that's correct." [40]

The project described here is a joint effort, with the prestigious backing of the Carnegie Foundation, a sizeable grant from the U.S. Office of Education under Title IV of the Elementary and Secondary Education Act for the development and implementation of a computer-assisted instruction program in initial reading and mathematics for culturally disadvantaged children, and the participation of IBM in collaboration with a group from Stanford University. The whole exercise, now the model for many more, is a typical and far from isolated example of the exploitation of a worthwhile goal to justify certain means, no matter how inappropriate and possibly damaging. The effort to provide "culturally disadvantaged" children with reading and mathematics skills is commendable; but what wellspring of omniscience dictated that computer-assisted instruction be used? There is no evidence that the costly and cumbersome systems save money now nor that they ever will.

A two-year research program carried out at the Education Research Center of the Massachusetts Institute of Technology focused on the teaching-learning process at the university level. Decisively negating claims for any kind of specific techniques, the investigators offered the following concluding statement:

> The research provides little support for the view — still implicitly held — that there is a set of specifiable conditions for effective classroom teaching. It was clear that instruction was multidimensional, with different types of teaching fitting the needs and wishes of different students; and that learning was a markedly individualistic matter, strongly influenced by the student's interests, self-confidence, and willingness to "selectively neglect." *Ecological studies,*

---

[39] Atkinson and Wilson, *op.cit.*, p. 76.
[40] John Rhea, "1968 Seen Critical for Computer Education," *Aerospace Technology,* January 1, 1968, p. 20.

such as these, are therefore likely to increase, rather than diminish, the edu-
cator's sense of complexity and uncertainty about his methods of selection,
teaching, and assessment. Claims made for specific techniques — such as pro-
grammed learning and computer-assisted instruction — often underestimate
this complexity, and sometimes appear simplistic and misleading. (My italics.)[41]

There is certainly no shortage of teachers. In fact, with the current high rates of unemployment, the schools are experiencing an unprecedented buyers' market and can hire Ph.D.s and Ed.D.s for jobs at almost any level. There is even clear evidence that performance in reading and mathematics may have less to do with type and style of teaching than with factors outside the school system. In the Hunter's Point area of San Francisco, for example, the principal of the elementary school stated that the key factor in reading levels achieved by the children was simply poor attendance. He sought remedy in community health and welfare programs. But big business has "discovered" education and a gigantic sales campaign is underway. IBM has been joined by Xerox, RCA, General Learning Corporation, Raytheon, Westinghouse Learning Corporation, System Development Corporation, Lockheed Missiles & Space Company, and numerous other firms in the merchandising of educational software and hardware. Their particular brand of performance numerology practically assures proof of their products' "effectiveness," for, in the circular situation created by the canned curriculum, there is a nice correlation between input and output. What is taught gets tested.

Illustrative of this type of package with its self-bestowed seal of approval is the set of tapes and accompanying manual sold to and through public broadcasting stations, unions, and labor management groups as the quick-and-easy way to a high school equivalence diploma. Superficial in depth and limited in scope, the course of instruction teaches little and encourages no thought. The student parrots the words and passes the tests for which he has been primed. The certificate which he thus earns stands for nothing except the triumph of salesmanship. With the authentic high school diploma carrying little prestige in our society, widespread circulation of a sketchy facsimile thereof may only serve to devalue it further as currency in the job market to which it was purported to gain access.

Research into the results of computer-assisted instruction can be remarkably technical in emphasis and advocative in conclusion. Appraisals and evaluations come from persons whose professional background is in computer technology or who approach the teaching-learning process as one of "behavioral engineering." Some of the writing in

[41] Malcolm Parlett, "Undergraduate Teaching Observed," *Nature,* Vol. 223, September 13, 1969, pp. 1102–1104.

the field, to judge by the grammatical errors, would indicate that the authors may themselves be the products of a system of education in which essay writing has been sacrificed for sterile cafeteria-style tests that yield "always-never-sometimes" responses easily coded and graded by machine. Both the style and construction of the articles show that lessons in old-fashioned, pre-automated syntax would be extremely useful.[42] Some journal articles which are superficially analytical of results are in essence propaganda pieces, containing veiled kudos in the form of references to the "revolutionizing" of education. Their authors turn out to have a strong vested interest in the pre-packaged education business, in which they are consultants, advisers, or entrepreneurs.[43]

The "culturally disadvantaged" children, who are prime targets for the technological onslaught, probably need help. But the assumption that "computer-assisted instruction" is the best, or even a good, way to help them is presumptuous nonsense, the more dangerous because of its propensity for self-perpetuation through incestuous validation of "performance." Possibly the worst kind of approach to the special needs of poor children is a socially isolated, dehumanized learning experience. Perhaps their very cultural disadvantage can be attributed to the fact that an electronic box has been their mentor since birth. Surveys have shown that children under the age of six spend more than fifty-four hours per week in front of the illuminated box, their viewing time in inverse proportion to family income. By the time they reach school, they will have sat watching television more hours than they will spend in classrooms during their entire academic career.[44] The use of television by poor families living in substandard dwellings in the ghettos of our great cities has served as the basis on which "educational television programs" have been justified and handsomely funded by broadcasting companies, foundations, and government agencies. Thus, the addiction to television has been rationalized; no longer merely the baby sitter, it has now become the teacher.

Already conditioned at the preschool level to the one-way stimulus of the television set and subjected to programs contrived to make of

---

[42] Jack E. Bratten, "Educational Applications of Information Management Systems," presented to the Special Libraries Association Conference Session on Mechanized Information Systems in Educational Areas at the Statler-Hilton Hotel, Los Angeles, California, June 3, 1968, SP-3077/000/01, Santa Monica: System Development Corporation, June 6, 1968.

[43] Harvey J. Brudner, "Computer-Managed Instruction," *Science*, Vol. 162, November 29, 1968, pp. 970–976. The author, formerly dean of science and technology at the New York Institute of Technology, is vice president and director of research and development for the Westinghouse Learning Corporation in New York City.

[44] James S. Coleman, "Education in the Age of Computers and Mass Communication," lecture presented at the Johns Hopkins University — Brookings Institution Lecture Series, "Computers, Communications, and Public Interest," December 11, 1969.

education all play and no work, the disadvantaged children will come to school to sit in the solitary confinement of a booth, where the recorded voice in the earphones will say, "Yes, that's correct." Educators and psychologists have stressed that these children need, more than anything else, to be brought into a socializing learning experience, where their companions are real live children and not charming puppets and chattering animals, where their teacher is not a voice in a box nor a "television personality," but a flesh-and-blood person.

The possibility that "educational technology" may be violating basic psychological principles of learning was demonstrated long ago in an experiment conducted by Gordon W. Allport. He asked 250 college students to write down three vivid memories of their eighth grade school work and to indicate the kind and degree of their active participation in the recorded events. For example, were they reciting, playing, arguing, producing, talking? Or were they listening or watching passively without overt involvement? Allport found that three-quarters of the memories were for situations in which the subject himself was actively participating.[45]

The current multi-million dollar "educational television program" for preschoolers promises to add just another dimension to the cultural deprivation of the poor. Rationalization for this costly enterprise goes like this. About 5 million children, four years of age, are candidates for preschooling. Cost of teaching them in conventional school settings, exclusive of cost of buildings, is estimated at $2.75 billion. Therefore, great savings in money are to be realized by allocating resources to the television variety of teaching. The same argument for economic efficiency prevails with respect to computerized teaching. Perhaps there is a kind of hidden benefit in the retreat from humanistic into technological approaches.[46] Children trained by television and tape will not suffer too great cultural shock when they plod through the school system, where already their abilities are gauged by "objective," machine-readable tests, their reports come in the form of one-way, disposable IBM cards, their counseling a group affair conducted through tapes or closed circuit television.

Some social critics have warned that the aggressive invasion of education by technology will lead to an educational-industrial complex, in which large corporations will determine what children shall learn. Others have predicted that technological devices will create a generation of spectators imbued with and unable to challenge the prefabri-

[45] Gordon W. Allport, *Personality and Social Encounter*, Boston: Beacon Press, 1960, p. 185.
[46] Ida R. Hoos, "Technology and Morals — An Old Story," *World Future Society, Bulletin*, Vol. 2, No. 5, May, 1969.

cated clichés and stereotypes that in effect block development of the human thinking apparatus. From the psychological point of view, the one-way communication of a machine stunts the growth of skill in interpersonal relationships and denies the savoring of pleasure in them. Perhaps herein lies a clue to the immeasurable, unaccountable, but pervasive alienation of young adults. With vital and basic human needs long neglected, they have reacted by withdrawing from the society that failed them. Many "social dropouts" have banded into "communes" of one kind or another. Others participate earnestly in all sorts of personal encounter groups. The widespread phenomenon of new social arrangements, outside the traditional forms, marks, in essence, the emergence of *ersatz* primary groups, which may provide a clue to the way in which deficiencies within our educational and other systems right themselves through extreme and not always wholesome means.

Concomitant with the predilection to apply performance measures to school programs is the trend toward casting its pupils into the role of producers whose output constitutes the record on which the cost-benefit ratio is calculated. Administrators who have been beguiled into believing that they should or can make their accomplishments more visible to the public are eagerly at work from coast to coast, in city and hamlet, "implementing" program budgeting. Along with making themselves more vulnerable to the ploys of hard-selling salesmen of curriculum packages, they are encouraging emphasis in the classroom on "performance" to the detriment, perhaps, of the other, more important phases in the child's development. For example, "behavior modification" has come to be regarded as a legitimate activity of the school, and some 150,000 to 300,000 children who are considered "hyperkinetic"[47] are being dosed with amphetamines to calm them down. As the diagnosis of this ailment is far from certain, some educators have expressed fear that children whose inattention and inability to apply themselves may stem from hunger, overcrowded classrooms, or lack of understanding by family or teachers may be subjected to treatment by drugs, the long-term consequences of which are not adequately known. To justify the school's activities and, indeed, the lives of parents through the children's accomplishments puts the total burden on the youngsters without supplying them with creative avenues and outlets and guidance in their energetic and sometimes trying exploration. Instead, as was revealed in congressional hearings,[48] "chemical straitjackets" are

[47] Robert J. Bazell, "Panel Sanctions Amphetamines for Hyperkinetic Children," *Science*, Vol. 171, March 26, 1971, p. 1223.

[48] Subcommittee of the Committee on Government Operations, House of Representatives, Ninety-first Congress, Second Session, "Federal Involvement in the Use of Behavior Modification Drugs on Grammar School Children of the Right to Privacy

being used to induce conformity of behavior in the classroom and thus insure favorable "output" for teachers, programs, or whatever else is being weighed in the cost-benefit balance. Without moving closer to 1984, one can surmise that, with this kind of "production" philosophy dominating school planners, there may be an early resort, beyond behavior-modifying drugs, to the implantation of electrodes in the brains of recalcitrant students.[49] Found in experimentation on higher primates to guarantee prescribed behavior, this even more advanced Space Age innovation would seem to be the next logical step toward assuring high productivity in school children and favorable program performance in the most cost-effective way.

IMPLICATIONS OF PPBS IN EDUCATION

In California, criticisms of program budgeting and its techniques as conceived and applied have become the weapons in the campaign being waged by conservative Republican legislators and organizations against PPBS.[50] Convinced that these tools are a manifestation of internationalistic and nationalistic control that will wrest jurisdiction of schools from localities, alarmed over the subversion of U.S. education to collectivism,[51] with children indoctrinated into conforming to a socialist order, and incensed over the determined data acquisition that will lead to what is darkly referred to as "taxonomy," a manipulative device that they consider useful to malevolent "behavioral scientists,"[52] the United Republicans of California in early 1971 adopted by referendum the following resolution:

Subject: OPPOSE PPBS (Planning, Programming, Budgeting System) FOR THE CALIFORNIA PUBLIC SCHOOL SYSTEM

WHEREAS: The State Board of Education is considering adoption of a Planning, Programming, Budgeting System to answer a 1968 Legislative mandate to develop an accounting and evaluation system in the California Public School System, and

WHEREAS: PPBS "program" budgeting goes far beyond the scope of tradi-

---

Inquiry," September 29, 1970, Washington, D.C.: U.S. Government Printing Office, 1970.

[49] José Manuel R. Delgado, *Physical Control of the Mind*, New York: Harper & Row, 1969.

[50] Robert H. Burke, Assemblyman, seventieth district, California State Assembly, "Planned-Programed-Budgeting-Systems," *Reports from Sacramento*, February, 1971.

[51] Ruth Spencer, "PPBS — Tooling for '1984' through Budgeting," *Round-Up*, United Republicans of California, February, 1971.

[52] Statement by Mrs. Eleanor F. Forsyth, Agenda Item No. 6, Minutes, California Department of Education, Advisory Commission on School District Budgeting and Accounting, May 28, 1971, pp. 6–7.

tional budgeting procedures and involves policy "objectives" or changes in education and society over a span of years, allowing a great leeway of value judgment in projecting the "benefits" of those changes and providing funding therefor, and

WHEREAS: PPBS is a computer program based on a "conceptual" framework which is not limited to the procedures of only educational agencies but involves a total complex of goals, objectives and functions by government at all levels, culminating at federal level; in other words, the PPBS system could be said to be totalitarian, and

WHEREAS: PPBS designers, the RAND Corp. of Santa Monica, calls PPBS a "resource analysis system" and emphasizes that "the entire operation must be the personal responsibility of the *executive head* of the organization. *No one at a lower level* has the authority or the right or the ability to acquire the knowledge required to perform the necessary tasks of coordination" (RAND Corp. Memorandum RM-4271-RC, P. 41), and

WHEREAS: PPBS will be used not only for measuring and evaluating academic standards but will be concerned equally with attitudinal and behavioral objectives for both students and their families and this will *intrude into the private realm of the home,* and

WHEREAS: PPBS is a political hazard and could easily generate fatal change in the American political system, as such computerized system would *take control away from representative officials,*

NOW THEREFORE BE IT RESOLVED: That United Republicans of California strongly opposes the incorporation of PPBS into the California Public School System, and

BE IT FURTHER RESOLVED: That United Republicans of California seeks repeal of any legislation mandating the various elements thereof, and

BE IT FURTHER RESOLVED: That copies of this resolution be sent to all members of the California State Board of Education, to the bureau chiefs of the California State Department of Education, and to the Executive Board of the California School Boards Association.

The similarity of concerns voiced here with the objections raised on quite different methodological grounds and in an entirely different analytical perspective elsewhere in this chapter underscores the vulnerability of the techniques of program budgeting to ideological manipulation. Imposition of "value judgment" is suspect, not because the methods are purported to be value-free but because there is likely the inculcation of the wrong, that is, Socialist-Communist, values. The RAND imprint is questioned, not because it may be inappropriate but because of what it recommends, that is, stronger centralization.

PPBS is seen as a political hazard, not because of the methodological messes it could create but because it is a creature of computerization, an important factor in the possible overturn of the American political system.

Measuring the accomplishment of the American educational system, the impact of particular programs, and the achievement of schools, through the imposition of program budgeting, continues to be the national numbers game, supported by federal grants and aided by Presidential importunations for output measures.[53] Distorted and inadequate as these are acknowledged to be, they are certain to be exploited even more vigorously in the gathering battle over alternatives to traditional public education. An experiment, launched by the Office of Economic Opportunity,[54] calls for the use of vouchers, which parents may apply to a year's enrollment in any school, public or private, of their choice. Conceived as a means "for introducing free market competition into the elementary and secondary school system,"[55] the notion has become the subject of much controversy in which the dominant voices have been not those of educators, but of economists expounding and pontificating their views on schooling strategies for the poor. On the assumption that competition, healthy for business, must necessarily be good for society at large, these experts have come forward with proposals which, if taken seriously, could carry the whole educational system, public and private, for rich and poor, to its logical extreme of absurdity.

With schools vying for enrollment, there would at best be a reversion to the old European *Privatdozent* system, in which instructors were paid according to the number of students they attracted. At worst, curricula would be devised on the basis of instant relevance, merchandised like detergents, and market-tested like hair spray. The schools' performance would be rated like a television show. The products emerging from the school mart, unlike those of competitive industry, would not, however, have had even a modicum of consumer protection. Self-serving measurements of output would have carried the *caveat emptor* ethos into an area where professional standards and public service had once been valued. Public education, handled in this fashion, would provide a nice input-output exercise for the economist's tableau but would represent the final capitulation to technology and economics

[53] Message of the President on Educational Reform, March 3, 1970.

[54] "Education Vouchers," Center for the Study of Public Policy, Cambridge, Massachusetts, March, 1970.

[55] Report of the National Goals Research Staff, The White House, *Toward Balanced Growth: Quantity with Quality*, Washington, D.C.: U.S. Government Printing Office, July 4, 1970, p. 94.

working in tandem toward the devaluation of an important institution of a democratic society.

COSTS, BENEFITS, AND PERFORMANCE OF HEALTH PROGRAMS

In the dead and distant past, health was largely a private and personal matter. Only birth, death, and the occasional need to post a notice of quarantine brought officialdom into the medical affairs of the family. Life, health, and death were simpler in those days. But nostalgia for the era of the horse-and-buggy doctor should not obliterate the memory of attendant circumstances vis-à-vis health. The estival outbreaks of poliomyelitis, the hibernal scourge of diphtheria, and the perennial pneumonias left no household untouched. And even the most potent camphor worn in a little bag at the neck failed to ward off some of the diseases prevalent, dreaded, and scarcely understood. Medical services were more picaresque than professional. There was the corner druggist whose patent medicine practice flourished. In the towns across the country traveling medicine shows peddled all-purpose remedies. They probably set the stage for modern merchandising of pharmaceuticals through entertainment media. Today's constant television song-and-dance sales pitch that promises relaxation, regularity, and relief had its origins in the do-it-yourself dosing of a bygone era.

An exposition of the advances which have occurred in even a half century of medical science would necessarily be inadequate in this context. A historical account of a half century's changes in attitudes and expectations about health services would have to be so superficial as to negate any advantage to be derived from the effort. Suffice it for present purposes to say that the final third of the twentieth century finds medical knowledge in a period of continuing growth and specialization, the medical profession highly stratified and multi-faceted, and the delivery of health services a matter for private enterprise, public programs, and social concern. Comprehensive government programs, a series of legislative acts intended to ease the financial burdens of health care, and grants from foundations have contributed to making big business of the public's health and of its management a complicated matter calling for "scientific" tools and techniques.

Viewed as an ailing system, public health is an attractive patient for the ministrations of the experts in cost-benefit analysis, program budgeting, and other methodological niceties of the systems approach. And while in the field of education the technical solution carriers could attribute their ease of penetration to deep-seated and defensive inferiority feelings of the professionals, in medicine they have encountered no resistance for other reasons. Doctors know little and care less about and yet have a remarkable tendency to rely with unwarranted confidence on any clerical or record-keeping system that promises to take over tedious chores and details. Sophisticated though they may be as to the developments in their own field, they are notoriously naïve about the "business" aspects of their work. Consequently, the skillful merchandising of a "systematic approach" has found easy credence among the medical practitioners.

DOCTORS AND DATA SYSTEMS

Here, as in so many other fields, the sales campaign opens with a pitch for an information system which will provide efficient storage and access of information. Although the subject of management information systems in general will be discussed in detail in the next chapter, it is appropriate to consider here the peculiar characteristics and role of information in health services. The computerization of medical data exacerbates rather than solves the doctor's dilemma. Until recent years, the locked filing cabinet associated with his office practice kept his clinical findings confidential. In hospitals, the handwritten, and sometimes nearly illegible, charts ultimately stored in the records room were intrinsically safe if only because of the lack of systematic organization. The growth of health plans, both through public programs and private insurance arrangements, greatly increased the paper work in most doctors' offices. Record-keeping, reporting, and regulations are no longer perfunctory chores to be handled by the nurse in her spare moments. Instead, bookkeeping has become a major responsibility in the practice of medicine. The consensus of physicians at a meeting on the use of computers in clinical medicine seemed to be that the establishment of computerized data systems will be practically indispensable in the efficient and economical practice of medicine in the future.[56]

With data systems, however, has come the real possibility of the development of a health data bank, about which doctors have expressed considerable apprehension. Their main concern is over the maintenance of confidentiality and privacy because they recognize that medical information forms a crucial, perhaps damaging and possibly ominous, contribution to the dossier, to be discussed in the next chapter. On this matter computer scientists, concerned with the technical aspects of data security, can offer little reassurance. With release of medical information on specific individuals more a matter of system design

[56] E. R. Gabrieli, "Right of Privacy and Medical Computing," *Datamation*, Vol. 16, No. 4, April, 1970, pp. 173–178.

and program instruction than the decision of the doctor in the case, likelihood of unauthorized access is enhanced. How much and what kind of information should be made available to employers, credit agencies, insurance companies, police, or private investigators are questions which require medical knowledge, ethical sensitivity, and moral wisdom. Mr. William Holmes, director of the Computer Science Division of Cornell Aeronautical Laboratory, designated as "hazardous areas" the work of all programers, unauthorized inquiries, and release of data to other data centers. He also identified the various authorized users of the data as potential sources of leak of confidential information.[57]

As will be discussed in the next chapter, electronic data-processing methods are adopted for reasons of efficiency and economy. Efficiency implies ease of access, and economy means time and money saved. It is understandable, therefore, that information systems, hard and soft, are designed and merchandised on this brace of promises, however far short of the mark they actually perform. Security adds significantly to the costs, for there are expenses for a privacy administrator to insure that no invasions occur, special programing checks, the incremental cost in computer memory, additional operation expense owing to privacy programs, and the "nuisance cost" for identifying users. Actual dollar amounts can only be estimated,[58] but with efficiency and economy the prime desiderata for computerizing, in a cold-blooded cost/benefit analysis, the right to privacy is soon traded off.

To a great extent, these dangers are associated with all data banks. There are additional and special perils in computerizing medical information. There is, first of all, the possibility that where standardized, machine-readable medical records are used, self-evaluating feedback will occur and affect diagnosis and treatment. The assumptions will have been made that the information is complete and that it is accurate. A prominent surgeon warns against over-reliance on the first. He points out that the physician could passively withhold data and thus seriously damage the usefulness of the computer system.[59] A specialist in government information systems warns against the second. From among the many possible opportunities for erroneous input, she has focused on the one that has overriding importance in health information, viz., sure and certain identification of the individuals.[60] Unique identification of each individual so that relevant items of information refer to one and the same person is a problem for which

[57] Holmes, quoted in Gabrieli, op.cit., p. 173.
[58] Ibid., p. 176.
[59] Dr. G. E. Alfano, quoted in Gabrieli, op.cit., p. 173.
[60] Judith Moss, "Confidentiality and Identity," Socio-Economic Planning, Vol. 4, No. 1, March, 1970, pp. 17–25.

176 SYSTEMS ANALYSIS IN PUBLIC POLICY

current technology has no solution. There being no guarantee that actual data have not been attributed to the record of the wrong person or omitted from that of the right person, the whole concept of medical data storage deserves careful rethinking. While the technical aspects are challenging, the medical implications are chilling.

There is little demonstrable proof that doctors accomplish their professional mission more effectively with computerized files, that there even exists the technology for a hospital information system in its entirety, that institutions have come anywhere near successful management of their information.[61] In fact, an authoritative overview suggests that there has been "gross underestimation of the dimensions of the task at hand." [62] Nonetheless, public agencies charged with administering or implementing health programs are so overwhelmed by the burdens of bookkeeping that they are prone to interpret their whole mission as associated with the white plague to paper processing, and likely to succumb to the sales pressure and political propaganda that direct and exhaust their resources in costly and cumbersome information systems, sole justification for which is the busy work done.

Practical experience to the contrary notwithstanding, some public health officials continue to approach their administrative tasks as though primarily, if not simply, matters of information management. Faced with the ever-mounting complications and frustrations of all large-scale endeavors, they turn to "information experts." In so doing, they relinquish the opportunity to introduce drastic reform and abdicate the responsibility of planning to persons the state of whose art is neither ready nor necessarily appropriate. In California, for example, a request for a proposal "to aid the Office of Health Care Services in the efficient and effective management of the California Medical Assistance Program" [63] brought eighteen responses, mainly from aerospace companies, consulting groups, and accounting firms. Lockheed Missiles & Space Company won the quarter-million-dollar contract after having shrewdly and prudently completed what was curiously called "a progenitor overview cycle" as well as "a substantial part of the project preparation required." [64]

[61] Raymond R. Haggerty, "Organizing for the Computer," *Computers and Automation*, Vol. 20, No. 6, June, 1971, p. 8.

[62] J. H. U. Brown and James F. Dickson, III, "Instrumentation and the Delivery of Health Services," *Science*, Vol. 166, October 17, 1969, pp. 334–338. Dr. Brown is Associate Director for Scientific Programs and Dr. Dickson is Program Director for Engineering in Biology and Medicine, National Institute of General Medical Sciences, National Institutes of Health, Bethesda, Maryland.

[63] State of California, Office of Health Care Services, *Medi-Cal Total Management System Request for Proposal*, August 9, 1968, p. 6.

[64] Lockheed Missiles & Space Company, Proposal to California Department of Health Care Services, LMSC-DO80388, p. 6.

The Lockheed summary of the Medi-Cal Management System Design Project typifies the technical approach that confuses management of an enterprise with management of its record-keeping. Under the section called, "Purpose of the Project," the following was included:

The LMSC team will document and analyze present and future information requirements; it will develop preliminary design concepts for a more effective system. In addition, it will evaluate design concepts in terms of:
(a) benefits to the State and other participants and users of the system;
(b) effects of the system on participants;
(c) costs of development and implementation.
Finally, a recommendation will be drawn up representing a phased development and implementation plan of the selected Medi-Cal System design.

The plan will be system-oriented in the sense that it is concerned with all operations and information needed by the DHCS [Department of Health Care Services] to perform its function and satisfy the demands of local governments, the Federal government and other participants in the Medi-Cal Program.[65]

Beyond noting certain subtle normative presumptions, such as that a "more efficient system" would emerge from the Lockheed project, and after mentioning that the entire notion of the system design stemmed from the "total information myth," [66] we can achieve no useful purpose in analyzing the proposal. Field research, which included interviews with state and county health and welfare officials, provided interesting insights. To begin with, and not surprisingly, initiative for the Medi-Cal management information system study had come not from persons directly responsible for the program but from "management people upstairs." Aware that there were deficiences in the present system of handling claims and that there were information gaps, top administrators neither could pinpoint them nor believed that the Lockheed team, through interviews with them and their subordinates, could identify them. The only persons who looked for anything worthwhile to come out of this exercise were those whose primary responsibility was data processing and who had always the tail-wagging-the-dog view of the organization.[67]

The team of information experts, after the preliminary obeisance in the direction of information needs, proceeded to pull together the information already available with little attention to the total conceptualization and pruning that might more realistically have improved

[65] Summary of the Medi-Cal Management System Design Project, submitted by Lockheed Missiles & Space Company to State of California, October, 1968, p. 1.

[66] George J. Berkwitt, "The New Myths of Management," *Dun's Review*, Vol. 96, No. 3, September, 1970, pp. 25–27.

[67] Ida R. Hoos, "When the Computer Takes Over the Office," *Harvard Business Review*, Vol. 38, No. 4, July-August, 1960, pp. 105–106.

operation of Medi-Cal. With such an approach, the system failed to supply information where it was, perhaps, most needed — to the county medical societies that serve as the review agency for Medi-Cal. Lacking information and never having been included in the network, this vital decision point continued to be neglected. As a consequence, the fate of the Medi-Cal program rested in the hands of the elderly doctors, often former presidents of their local groups, for whom the post is a convenient sinecure. Interviews with some of them uncovered considerable hostility toward the program, their contention being that the Medi-Cal money should have gone to the patients themselves so that they could pay the doctors without having the government as middleman.

Because Medi-Cal is to a great extent a system of handling claims, eligibility having been established through regulation and statute, payment schedules are important. In California, procedures called for reporting to Washington on the basis of the *month of payment*. Because doctors have been notoriously laggard in doing their bookkeeping and submitting their bills on time, the delays, often the object of outraged editorials about inefficiency, unresponsive bureaucratic procedures, and the like, have been spectacular. The difficulty could have been overcome by the simple expedient of making *month of service* the date for reporting. And the whole transaction could have been speeded up by the mere introduction of forms that fit into the standard office typewriter. Those used at present require special equipment and king-size file drawers. Just whom the information system was supposed to serve was never satisfactorily clarified; just how the system could serve anyone became more dubious with each phase concluded. The determined reduction of the Medi-Cal program, regardless of its intrinsic merit, to its least common denominator, that is, the bits of information adhering to it, rendered it vulnerable to gubernatorial budget surgery. Without applying measures of cost-effectiveness to the sums spent on expensive systems studies and elaborate electronic data-processing arrangements, and without waiting to learn from the information experts what the objectives of the health program are or ought to be, an economy-minded state administration repeatedly ordered that services under Medi-Cal be cut to the bone.[68]

ANALYSIS OF COSTS AND
BENEFITS OF HEALTH CARE

Second only to the information system as the popular "technical" tool for improving health planning is cost-benefit analysis. The Nixon

[68] I am indebted to Mr. Wilbur L. Parker, former Chief of Research and Statistics in the California Department of Social Welfare, for many important insights into the administration of this and other public programs.

Administration, having built a case on its own campaign-made accusa-
tion that the nation's medical system is "cottage industry" and needs
major overhaul, urged coordinated planning and control. The macro-
approach calls for planning in the grand manner and assumes that a
macro-breakthrough must, therefore, follow. The systematic, comprehensive treatment is touted as the reasonable and rational antidote to
laissez-faire, patchwork, fragmented conceptions. But once the easy-
flowing and rapidly flipped charts have been exposed, the economists,
econometricians, operations researchers, information technologists, systems analysts, and others who have chosen health as the stamping
ground for their expertness, often lower their sights, narrow their focus,
and concentrate their activities on the bits and pieces that they can
count. All perform cost-benefit analyses, on the unarticulated premise
that out of the crazy quilt they produce there will emerge the ideal
system, its objectives clearly defined, its operations optimal, its methods
rational, its mission accomplished.

As between the cost and the benefit side of the ratio, figures for the
former seem to be more readily available. Even here, however, the possibilities for inaccuracy, error, miscalculation, poor estimates, and misleading conclusions have been almost limitless. Specific illness cost
studies have underscored the difficulties of obtaining reliable data.[69]
Empirical data are elusive and often contradictory.[70] Because of lack
of comparability in definitions, basic data, and methodology for individual studies, totals of individual illnesses do not anywhere near approximate the annual national outlays for health and medical care.[71]

Besides the fact that the various methods used are in conflict and the
data are both incomplete and unreliable, the difficulty of computing the
costs of illness is compounded by the fact that direct expenditures do
not measure even the full economic costs, to say nothing of many other
types of costs incurred. Calculation of the indirect costs, while necessary,
poses all the problems of coverage, compatibility, and consistency, and
then compounds them because of the nature of these costs. The National
Health Education Committee prepares annually a report which provides estimates of the costs of major and crippling diseases. Included
are estimates of wage losses resulting from days lost from work because
of acute and chronic conditions; earnings losses for those who died

[69] Anne A. Scitovsky, "Changes in the Costs of Treatment of Selected Illnesses,
1961–65," *American Economic Review*, Vol. LVII, No. 5, December, 1967, pp. 1182–
1195.

[70] William F. Berry and James C. Daugherty, "A Closer Look at Rising Medical
Costs," *The Monthly Labor Review*, Reprint No. 2590, November, 1968, p. 8.

[71] Dorothy P. Rice, *Estimating the Cost of Illness*, U.S. Department of Health,
Education, and Welfare, Public Health Service, Health Economics Series, No. 6,
Public Health Service Publication No. 947-6, Washington, D.C.: U.S. Government
Printing Office, May, 1966, p. 3.

from arteriosclerotic heart disease and cancer, and their tax revenue losses; annual indirect costs of heart disease, mental illness, arthritis and rheumatism, and cerebral palsy.[72] Gaps in the data and methodological matters render the estimates highly questionable. Even more troublesome is the omission of the intangible or psychic costs of disease. Pain and grief, for example, may not involve earnings or tax revenue loss; they certainly cannot be weighed and measured on the economist's scale. And yet, failure to include them may, according to some authorities, distort the overall economic and social costs because of the implicit assumption that the economic value of intangible losses is zero.[73]

Because the same data are used on both sides of the cost-benefit analysis to provide the measure of a man's worth, they deserve special scrutiny. On the cost side, loss of output to the economy in terms of earnings and taxes is calculated; on the benefit side, the life saved, the disability averted is computed on the same basis. Most of the economic calculations of the worth of the human life are attained by estimating the capitalized value of the average future stream of earnings of a person in a particular age group.[74] The use of such figures as an index has not undergone significant change since the pioneer work of Dublin and Lotka.[75] Lifetime earnings expectancy, as computed and used during the past decade, are shown in Table 9. Using human capital calculations as a basis for making decisions about health exceeds not only the economist's methodological competence but also the moral and ethical wisdom of any mortal man. The table shows, for example, that the life of a twenty-year-old man is worth the lives of two babies if they are boys and three if they are girls. Women's earnings place them in the category of second-class citizens vis-à-vis the benefits of education. They fare no better with respect to health. In fact, for the considerable proportion of women not in the labor force in 1963 (see Table 10), housewives' services had to be estimated. They were computed at the level of the average earnings of a domestic worker, with no credit allowed for longer daily hours, seven-day workweek, and full service rendered family and community as well. If the old lady has attained the seventy to seventy-four age bracket, she can now claim twice the earnings potential of the old man. Is this to imply that the geriatric problems of the female should be allocated

[72] The National Health Education Committee, *Facts on the Major Killing and Crippling Diseases in the U.S. Today*, New York: The National Health Education Committee, 1964.

[73] Dorothy P. Rice, *op.cit.*, p. 15.

[74] A. W. Marshall, *Cost-Benefit Analysis in Health*, Santa Monica: RAND Corporation, P-3274, p. 3.

[75] Louis I. Dublin and Alfred J. Lotka, *The Money Value of a Man*, New York: Ronald Press, 1946.

double the funds devoted to those of the male? For senior citizens as a group, the scale has ominous portent in an age when the youth culture prevails, *Lebensraum* disappears, and 1984-style euthanasia is an oft-repeated theme in avant-garde drama.

Despite warnings that the measurable is not necessarily the impor-tant,[76] and that cost-benefit analysis represents a kind of intellectual gadgetry in which self-deception is inherent,[77] the field of health con-

TABLE 9

Present Value of Lifetime Earnings, 1963
Amount Discounted at 4 Percent by Age and Sex

Age	Males	Females
	(in dollars)	
Under 1	59,063	34,622
1 to 4	64,989	37,938
5 to 9	79,333	46,289
10 to 14	96,736	56,422
15 to 19	114,613	64,936
20 to 24	126,688	67,960
25 to 29	128,698	66,826
30 to 34	122,904	64,389
35 to 39	111,956	60,998
40 to 44	97,301	56,608
45 to 49	80,325	50,896
50 to 54	63,027	44,371
55 to 59	45,948	37,467
60 to 64	28,387	30,164
65 to 69	15,043	23,579
70 to 74	9,264	18,118
75 to 79	5,344	12,888
80 to 84	2,935	6,916
85 and over	210	1,123

SOURCE: D. P. Rice, "The Direct and Indirect Cost of Ill-ness," Reprinted from subcommittee on Economic Progress, Joint Economic Committee, Congress of the United States, *Federal Program for the Development of Human Resources*, a Compendium of Papers, Vol. 2, Part IV. Health Care and Improvement (Washington, D.C.: Government Printing Of-fice, 1968), Table 10, p. 489.

[76] Herbert E. Klarman, *The Economics of Health*, New York: Columbia University Press, 1965.

[77] Harvey Leibenstein, "Pitfalls in Benefit-Cost Analysis of Birth Prevention," *Popu-lation Studies*, Vol. XXIII, No. 2, July, 1969, pp. 161–170.

TABLE 10
Women Not in Labor Force (1963)

Age group	Total number (000's)	Keeping house	
		Number (000's)	Percent of total
14–19	6,675	972	14.6
20–24	3,265	2,825	86.5
25–29	3,449	3,381	98.0
30–34	3,613	3,548	98.2
35–39	3,623	3,552	98.0
40–44	3,249	3,172	97.6
45–49	2,819	2,754	97.7
50–54	2,549	2,482	97.4
55–59	2,455	2,380	96.9
60–64	2,612	2,505	95.9
65 and over	8,514	7,613	89.4
Total	42,822	35,185	82.2

SOURCE: U.S. Department of Labor, Bureau of Labor Statistics, *Employment and Earnings*, February, 1964, Table A-16, p. 81.

tinues to be a fertile area for cost-benefit studies. In fact, authors of some of the critiques have themselves engaged in such attempts, perhaps to improve on the work of others, but invariably to founder on the same methodological rocks.[78] Besides being varied and numerous, cost-benefit studies in health are separate and dispersed. How they overcome the long-standing problem of piecemeal fragmentation is far from clear. While the individual exercises may be examples of methodological virtuosity, referred to and deferred to by the technical fraternity, they add up to little that is useful or even new.

HEALTH SERVICE EFFICIENCY IN BRITAIN

An example of cost-benefit at work is the study of health service efficiency in the British National Health Service by M. S. Feldstein. The very premises on which the methodology is adopted suggest that caution should be used in assessing the validity of the conclusions. Substantial progress has been achieved in developing a theory of cost-benefit analysis and applications have been made in a wide variety of

[78] Herbert E. Klarman,, "Syphilis Control Programs," in *Measuring the Benefits of Government Investments*, Robert Dorfman, ed., Washington, D.C.: The Brookings Institution, 1965, pp. 367–410.

fields: defense, water resource development, transportation, urban development, education, and health." [79] Our research finds no evidence of such "a theory of cost-benefit analysis"; moreover, close scrutiny of the applications cited indicate that such models as they provide are far from reliable planning instruments. Feldstein's unquestioning faith spills over to economic analysis, which, he states, "provides the framework for analyzing the use of scarce resources." The shortcomings of the strictly economic approach have already been stressed sufficiently to indicate temperance and caution on this point. Set forth as proof positive of the generalized platitude that "health care is an important area for the application of economic analysis" is the intelligence that "the health sector absorbs some five percent of gross national product of all western countries, is generally growing more rapidly than other forms of personal consumption, and lacks the usual market forces to promote efficiency." [80]

The study, concerned with "identifying and estimating relevant decision-making information and with applying optimizing methods to improve the efficiency of the British National Health Service," actually has two focuses of attention: the hospital as a "producing unit"; and the various factors, demographic, social, and environmental, affecting utilization of health services. The impressive bibliography of 243 entries includes references to everything from defense to rail passenger costs and gas supply and is probably intended to establish methodological respectability. The exercise, possibly a model of technical virtuosity, demonstrates again that (1) the measurable aspects of health services are subject to arbitrariness of definition and, hence, are a flimsy base for planning, as they can lead to totally erroneous conclusions; (2) omitting or ignoring the qualitative facets of health care merely because they are incalculable is truly to deny the value of the study's conclusions; and (3) the analyst's calculus of optimality as to size and "production" of hospitals may vitiate the vital realities of the real-life situation.

On the first point, a review of the study by an economist indicates that the outcome would be quite different if classifications were changed or "output" redefined.

. . . It seems quite possible that some of the major findings of the book would be *reversed* if a more complete adjustment for casemix differences could be made. . . . For example, the author examines the relationship between hospital size and adjusted costs per case, and concludes that there are slight diseconomies of scale beyond a size of 300 beds. But it could be plausibly argued that the largest hospitals have higher adjusted costs per case not because of

[79] Martin S. Feldstein, *Economic Analysis for Health Service Efficiency*, Amsterdam: North-Holland Publishing Co., 1967, p. 1.
[80] *Ibid.*

diseconomies but because they tend to handle the more elaborate and expensive cases within each of the nine categories.[81]

On the second point, the "dazzling array of weapons from his well stocked arsenal" [82] notwithstanding, if it is legitimate to leave out of consideration that which cannot be counted in, then, "hospital production," as measured by patient's length of stay, could logically ignore quality of care. This is precisely what was done. A Subject Index of five double-columned finely printed pages does not include the key word, *criterion*. But if number of bodies processed in a given period is a prime *desideratum*, what stops the superior logic from becoming supreme by merely dictating that hospital admission policy favor the moribund?

On the third point, a British journal has reported growing dissatisfaction with the design of hospitals,[83] which, the article contends, do not satisfy the real needs of patients but, rather, arise from consultants' conception of them. Sharply criticized is the "unsupported deduction" that general district hospitals should be units of 600 to 800 beds serving a population of 100,000 to 150,000. Although expert consultants have rationalized that this size would concentrate interesting cases and costly equipment in certain centralized locations, the actual results have been "unduly expensive buildings on so inhuman a scale that they defeat the broader purposes of health and welfare."

Another study of hospitals throughout Britain has underscored the salient point that, no matter how well designed, facilities are seldom used as planned. In fact, the report, issued by the King Edward's Hospital Fund (London) says, "In only one case was the building and equipment being used in exactly the way predicted by the skilled team which planned and designed it." Having discovered that most modern hospitals are too hot or too cold, too bright or too dark, and noisy at night, the authors of the study recommended evaluation and review conducted not by some central organization but by teams of planners, designers, and managers, responsible to the regional planning boards.[84]

The road to achievement of the symmetry, however short-lived, of cost and benefit, input and output, in health is full of conceptual, definitional, methodological, and operational pitfalls. In fact, the game second in popularity only to designing models micro and macro is method-

[81] Robin Barlow, Review of Martin S. Feldstein, *Economic Analysis for Health Service Efficiency, op.cit.*, in *The Economic Journal*, Vol. LXXVIII, No. 312, December, 1968, pp. 921–923.

[82] *Ibid.*, p. 922.

[83] John Weeks and Peter Cowan, "Health and Welfare," Letters to the Editor, *The Architectural Review*, Vol. CXLVIII, No. 881, July, 1970, pp. 63–64.

[84] Ken Baynes, Brian Langslow, and Courtenay Wade, *Evaluating New Hospital Buildings*, London: The King Edward's Hospital Fund, as cited in "Hospitals — Survival of the Unfit," *Nature*, Vol. 224, December 20, 1969, p. 1148.

ologically tearing down the models of others through exquisite and precise analysis of gaps and faults. But, once the caveats for other players have been stated, the game proceeds, the logic leading to results which, as Alice-in-Wonderland said, become "curiouser and curiouser."

EFFECTIVENESS OF DISEASE CONTROL
PROGRAMS IN THE U.S.

Perhaps most curious of all is the outcome of an analytical study undertaken by the Department of Health, Education, and Welfare (HEW) to compare the "effectiveness" of disease control programs. Selected for assessment of the "highest payoff in terms of lives saved and disability prevented per dollar spent" were tuberculosis, syphilis, cancer, arthritis, and motor vehicle accidents, the latter because "the results of motor vehicle accidents are the same as those of diseases — they kill, they maim, they disable." [85] By inference, the decision regarding seat belts was, according to the Assistant Secretary, a former RAND and Department of Defense analyst and later associated with an urban think tank with consulting services for hire, "illuminated by good analysis." In keeping with the oft criticized but never relinquished means of calculating the worth of a human life, aggregate future lifetime earnings discounted to present value was the sum used, even though the planners, recognizing it as a crude measure of productivity lost, accepted it merely because it was "better than nothing." [86] This excuse, often invoked as well for cost-benefit analysis, program budgeting, and systems analysis, reveals the state-of-the-art and the state of mind of practitioners. Possessed with the notion that they must quantify, they fail to take into account the possible damage and danger wrong or inadequate measures may cause.[87]

The economics of a human life, the roughness of the measures, and the foolishness that is imbedded in conclusions based on them should already be apparent. What need concern us now is the ingenuity that brought carnage on the highway into the calculations of a public health agency but failed to carry the argument to its logical extreme. The Health, Education, and Welfare cost-benefit study that made of motor vehicle and passenger injury the topmost social disease of the century

[85] Testimony of William Gorham, then Assistant Secretary (Program Coordination), Department of Health, Education, and Welfare, in *The Planning-Programming-Budgeting System: Progress and Potentials*. Hearings before the Subcommittee on Economy in Government of the Joint Economic Committee, Ninetieth Congress, First Session, September 18, 19, 20, and 21, 1967, Washington, D.C.: U.S. Government Printing Office, 1967, pp. 3–46.

[86] William Gorham, "Notes of a Practitioner," *The Public Interest*, No. 8, Summer, 1967, pp. 4–8.

[87] Harvey Leibenstein, *op.cit.*, p. 161.

was, obviously, inspired by sheer numbers. "Magnitude of numbers," the report stated enigmatically, "would indicate a major interest for all health agencies." [88] There is no gainsaying the seriousness of the problem, the figures showing that 10,000 persons are injured in motor vehicle accidents every day and 55,000 die every year. The argument based on size leaves one dubious about other possible large problems lurking in the shadows of our society. Will they similarly be discovered and given priority in our health agencies because their solution is quick, easy, and cheap?

As is evident in Table 11 seat belt use and restraint devices had spectacular payoffs. HEW's campaign, like those of the National Safety Council, public-service seeking advertising groups, and broadcasting corporations may have saved lives. But the question still remains as to whether highway safety is the business of HEW. If that were really the case, such an assignment should include careful analysis of the great number of factors contributing to the hazards of vehicular travel. Perhaps safety belts and other restraining and protective devices would not be needed if cars were designed for safety instead of speed, defects quickly rectified instead of challenged in the courts, and safety regulations on trucks, buses, and passenger cars properly policed and enforced. At present, regulations protect the industry rather than the public, with the Highway Safety Bureau failing to publicize trade names, lines, and sizes of tires that may be dangerous on the road. Last year, federal inspectors checked only 397 of the nation's more than 5,000 commercial buses used in legal, Interstate Commerce Commission-approved travel and none of the hundreds of "gypsy" buses, whose standards for equipment maintenance might reveal an even poorer record than the 300 defects discovered.

If HEW were truly committed to cutting down highway accidents, its analysts should have included more than "Reduce Driver Drinking," number six in the priority pay-off listing (see Table 11), and "Driver Licensing," item 12 on that scale. With drug abuse rampant in grade schools, colleges, service academies, among people of all ages and all classes, civilians and soldiers,[89] perhaps logic would dictate that attention could more meaningfully have been focused on the physical, mental, and emotional competence of the driver than on just the alcohol level of his blood or the fact that he once passed a *pro forma* test or even was exposed to a course in what is euphemistically called "driver education." Moreover, research has shown that the traffic phe-

[88] Elizabeth B. Drew, "HEW Grapples with PPBS," *The Public Interest*, No. 8, Summer, 1967, pp. 9–29.

[89] R. C. DeBold and R. C. Leaf, eds., *LSD, Man and Society*, Middletown, Connecticut: Wesleyan University Press, 1967.

TABLE 11
Benefit Cost Data
Selected Disease Control Programs
($ millions)[1]

Program	1968–1972 HEW Costs[1] (millions) 1	1968–1972 HEW & other direct costs[2] (millions) 2	1968–1972 Savings direct and indirect[2] (millions) 3	Benefit cost ratio 4
Selt belt use	$ 2.2	$ 2.0	$ 2,728	1,351.4
Restraint devices	0.7	0.6	681	1,117.1
Pedestrian injury	1.1	1.1	153	144.3
Motorcyclist helmets	8.0	7.4	413	55.6
Arthritis	37.6	35.0	1,489	42.5
Reduce driver drinking	31.1	28.5	613	21.5
Syphilis	55.0	179.3[3]	2,993	16.7
Uterine cervix cancer	73.7	118.7	1,071	9.0
Lung cancer	47.0	47.0[3]	268	5.7
Breast cancer	17.7	22.5	101	4.5
Tuberculosis	130.0	130.0	573	4.4
Driver licensing	6.6	6.1	23	3.8
Head and neck cancer	8.1	7.8	9	1.1
Colon-rectum cancer	7.7	7.3	4	0.5

SOURCE: Elizabeth B. Drew, "HEW Grapples with PPBS," The Public Interest, No. 8, Summer, 1967, p. 21.

NOTE: Numbers have been rounded to a single point from three decimal points; therefore the ratio may not be the exact result of dividing column 2 into column 3 as they appear here.

[1] Funding shown used as basis for analysis not necessarily funding to be supported by Administration.

[2] Discounted except where otherwise noted.

[3] Not discounted.

nomenon covers a multidimensional span, with physiological, psychiatric, medical, pharmacological, sociological, and legal facets.[90] An example of the multitude of facets of vehicular safety is a study by an Irish psychologist. She found that many road accidents involving children were related to upsets at home and the child's unconscious desire to punish harsh, unloving parents.[91] The point being made here is that if HEW's objectives were appropriate and legitimate, their adoption of

[90] H. J. Roberts, The Causes, Ecology, and Prevention of Traffic Accidents, Springfield, Illinois: Charles C Thomas, 1971.

[91] Lindy Burton, Vulnerable Children, London: Routledge & Kegan Paul, 1968.

the cheap pay-off diverted attention from the important aspects of the life and limb of a motorized society. HEW's contention that "the cost of saving a life with an effective seat belt program might be as little as $87" is not justification for subverting the purposes, however illusive of quantification, of a national health program.[92]

Setting aside this illustration of reduction to the least common denominator of absurdity of cost-benefit analysis and concentrating on the health of the nation, one need not look far to find fruitful avenues for thoughtful research and reform. Were one seeking the macro problem, the $35-billion per year cost of ill health due to man's misuse of the environment should prove interesting and worthwhile.[93] The cumulative impacts of pollutants have been shown to be prime health hazards for all age groups. For children under fifteen, asthma and eczema were seen as direct consequences; for adults, emphysema and even cancer of the stomach were possibly related to air pollution levels.[94] Some research has even indicated a connection between highway accidents and air pollution, as drivers' senses are dulled by the poisons they inhale. In view of the performance of a public health agency in allowing the knee-jerk action of cost-benefit analysis to propel it into a seat belt program at $87 per life, it may be expected, with rational justification based on observation, that its response would be mass-produced and distributed masks, a bargain at, perhaps, 87 cents apiece.

HEALTH PROGRAMS FOR THE POOR

Forsaking the formidable phalanx of cost-benefit analysts who have fragmented and fractionated health into useless bits, one RAND expert has taken a new tack. He answers the question, "How Much is Good Health Worth?" by a logic derived from his own orientation. The "think piece" is discussed in this context because it illustrates the shortcomings of quantitative analysis performed in unwonted places. The thesis is contained in the following abstract:

. . . A consumer-demand or subjective-value approach to valuing government health activities is recommended. The human-capital valuations generally used in cost/benefit analysis are unrelated to people's preferences and, therefore, irrelevant to political decisions. A number of policy conclusions emerge from

[92] William Gorham, Testimony at Hearings, *Planning-Programming-Budgeting System*, *op.cit.*, p. 6.

[93] Dr. Paul Kotin, Director, National Institute of Environmental Health Sciences, Address, Seventeenth General Assembly of the International Union of Biological Sciences, Washington, D.C., October 6, 1970.

[94] Dr. Harry A. Sultz, Mr. Joseph G. Feldman, Dr. William E. Mosher, Dr. Edward R. Schlesinger, "Epidemiology of Peptic Ulcer in Childhood," *American Journal of Public Health*, Vol. 60, No. 3, March, 1970, pp. 492–498.

applying the suggested principle that government activities be *valued on the basis of what people would be willing to pay for them*. Beyond programs to aid the poor, government health efforts should be restricted to overcoming deficiencies in the operations of the private marketplace; that is, to regulatory actions, control of infectious disease and environmental pollution, and aid to biomedical research. *Free services provided to the poor should be justified by the willingness of the nonpoor to pay for them. Thus, the preferences of the nonpoor are important in designing optimal poverty programs.* Under present circumstances, direct money transfers to the poor seem preferable to further increases in poverty medical programs. *The value of existing programs could be increased by giving more weight to what the poor want instead of what medical experts say is most important for their health.* (My italics.) [95]

The author credits several of his RAND associates, a colleague at the Institute for Defense, and an economist for "ideas, stimulation, and encouragement" in its preparation. However apportioned, their joint input provides a telling example of the outcome when technical experts apply their tools in a field where they lack substantive knowledge, theoretical framework, professional experience, and human understanding. The result, succinctly stated, is bad psychology, poor economics, and worthless social welfare policy.

Besides lacking even the usual pretension of methodological nicety sometimes displayed in this kind of exercise, the article is little more than an attempt to rationalize "systematically" a particular point of view. In harping on and pontificating about "the poor" but failing to articulate who they are, the author reveals a kind of elitist snobbery that assumes the poor to be a hodgepodge of hapless and helpless ne'er-do-wells. More perceptive research would have shown enormous differences among the nation's poor, with great variation over time. Among today's poor there are newcomers who, ten years ago, "never had it so good." These are the victims of retrenchment in aerospace and defense industries, institutions of higher and highest learning, and commercial enterprises suffering the "ripple effects" of unemployment. There are many families once solvent and now poor because spiraling costs and some financially crippling medical emergency drained their reserves. To lump together the diverse habits of "the poor" toward health care, their expectations of themselves as physical beings, and their conception of the good life and what it is worth is presumptuous and preposterous in the extreme.

The author argues that the preferences of the nonpoor should be taken into account in the design of "optimal" poverty programs.[96] "Opti-

---

[95] Vincent Taylor, "How Much is Good Health Worth?" *Policy Sciences*, Vol. 1, No. 1, Spring, 1970, pp. 49–72.

[96] *Ibid.*, p. 67.

mality" is not defined, but the implication becomes obvious. Optimality will be conceived from the point of view of the "haves" for the "have nots," a course that would lead back to a bygone era of sporadic and inadequate private philanthropy on the part of the rich and degradation and deprivation for the poor. The author anticipates and makes a feinting attack on critics of his position by a snide aspersion, unsupported by data derived from analysis of any kind:

. . . Only those who believe that taxpayers ought not to have so much money, that some of it ought to go to the poor, can object to giving the nonpoor a say in how government spends their money.[97]

Totally ignored in this display of ideological rhetoric is the fact that the poor pay taxes, too — probably more, in proportion to their income, than do the unpoor.

Paradoxically, the poor are given some decision-making power in the scheme presented here. They, it appears, should be able to specify their conception of their wants "instead of what medical experts say is important for their health." The argument goes as follows:

. . . The conflict between the criterion of maximizing subjective value and the judgment of health professionals is not surprising. Professionals in all fields believe that their assessment of "objective needs" should determine what is done, regardless of how the people affected feel about it. Professional educators, law enforcement officials, and military men all have strong views on what is required in their areas of specialization. Where these views conflict with the preferences of the nonprofessionals, the criterion of subjective value implies that the preferences of the nonprofessional consumers ought to dominate. *The conclusion that nonprofessional judgment ought to dominate professional judgment may seem peculiar, but it merely represents the application of the principle of consumer sovereignty to nonmarket areas.*[98] (My italics.)

This battle of words, in which the straw men of professional education, law enforcement, and the military are tumbled in a heap only serves to demonstrate the inappropriateness of assigning public welfare to the market area. Moreover, it reveals the glaring lack of sensitivity to the fundamental differences in the "professional" orientation of the three groups.

Peculiar, indeed, is a rank order of health planning that places the nonpoor on top, the poor in the middle, and the medical profession on the bottom. Doctors need no defense, but some poor people have serious need to be protected from themselves, and they need not "nonpoor" tacticians but competent medical experts to make the important decisions. Anyone who could propose that more weight be given to what the

[97] *Ibid.*, pp. 67–68.
[98] *Ibid.*, p. 67.

poor want than to what medical experts say is important for their health is unaware of the intensive and perceptive research into the lives and living habits of the poor as reported by Oscar Lewis in his studies of slum dwellers in this and other countries.[99] He observed that the long-time deprived tend to hedonistic behavior patterns. They live for today because they have no reason to hope for a better tomorrow. Obviously resigned to a harsh destiny, with pain and sorrow their heritage, they adopt a *carpe diem* philosophy which expresses itself in improvident spending habits both as to time and money.

As was noted in studies of retraining programs for welfare recipients, poor people are wont to display much the same kind of attitude toward their health. Ignorant of the long-term benefits of health care and unaware of the amelioration if not cure of their ailments, they respond only to the emergencies. They do not take care of health, but only of illness. Regular dental care is virtually unknown. Toothache is a frequent and common occurrence, with extraction and not treatment the usual procedure. Storefront, easy-credit dentists with their aggressive sales campaigns find ready prey among the unenlightened poor.

The designer of this "rational" health scheme apparently recognizes some of the implications of his logic, but, indicating his own subjective and normative interpretation, the conclusions are cavalier in the extreme:

. . . In terms of program content, responding to the desires of the poor will probably lead to *downgrading preventive care* and upgrading the convenience and pleasantness of acute care. The poor will gladly give up routine chest X-rays in order to reduce waiting times (which often exceed several hours) at public clinics. Prenatal and well-baby care may well be sacrificed to obtain more cosmetic surgery. *Such changes in program content are not likely to lead to an improvement in health indices, but this should not cause undue concern.* As pointed out earlier, health is only one facet of enjoyment in life, and people often sacrifice some health for other pleasures (over-eating, smoking, fast driving, skiing, etc.). *The poor as well as the nonpoor are entitled to such choices.* Further, as was also pointed out earlier, there are reasons for doubting the effectiveness of increased medical care; thus health levels may not differ all that much under the "best" health program and the one chosen by the recipients. *In any event, if the reasoning presented here is correct, permitting some sacrifice in health will produce benefits to both the poor and the nonpoor that far exceed the costs.* (My italics.) [100]

This RAND-Institute of Defense Analysis assessment of the worth of good health should serve as a prime example of the parody on planning that results when the wrong experts bring the tools of their trade into

[99] Oscar Lewis, *Study of Slum Culture*, New York: Random House, 1968.
[100] Taylor, *op.cit.*, pp. 70–71.

unwonted areas. The omniscience about "poor" people and their preferences, the specious economic arguments exploited, the sly preciosity of forensic — all help to obscure the gaps in knowledge, absence of wisdom, and lack of social responsibility which prevail when the technique of managing a program overrules professional appreciation of its substance and real-life dimensions.

Contrary to the presuppositions of "systematic" planners, public health is not virgin territory. Like education, it is an area of longtime concern to persons with professional competence and experience. The excuse that programs do not function as well as intended or that "delivery systems" are not as effective or efficient as might be hoped is not sufficient reason to bring in "technical experts" who mistake ignorance for objectivity and whose objectivity is suspect. Their technique serves as camouflage for normative judgments and subjective biases, dangerous because they are insidious and so embedded in the self-justifying rationality of the process. The cited examples in education and health should serve to alert public officials to the serious shortcomings of the techniques and the technicians. If the national commitment in health and education were to true improvement and not mere image-creation, administrators charged with the responsibility of implementing forthcoming legislation in these vital fields would be well advised to examine critically the stakes and the players before joining the popular national pastime of game-playing as a means to accomplishing their mission.

Instances of intentional or unintentional manipulating of facts and figures are duplicated wherever cost-effectiveness measures are being applied. If, as is likely, this has always been the case wherever decisions must be made in a political environment, we may expect an intensification and exacerbation of possible abuses because of the availability of larger amounts of information, the handling of which becomes an ever more complicated, technical matter. As has been seen in the numerous examples cited, the format of the systems approach and the orientation of its practitioners are determinative of objectives and of the path to achieve them. It must, therefore, be concluded that the systems approach in its various manifestations, especially program budgeting and cost-effectiveness measurement, may be less reliable and trustworthy as an instrument of public policy than was presumed before experience in the civilian sector became available as a gauge.

[7]

Management
Information Systems

MANAGEMENT OF INFORMATION

The introduction of computers for data-processing in the business world in the mid-1950s was accompanied by a fanfare of promises for faster record-keeping, better data flow, and reduction of clerical personnel and costs. Enthusiastic purveyors offered the new technology as the means by which to cope with the proliferation of paper generated by commercial intercourse. Fifteen years and two computer generations later, the promises are still illusory. To be sure records move faster, but their volume has increased exponentially. In quasi-Parkinsonian fashion, they have expanded to fill all the computer time; they have over-burdened transmission facilities and consumption capacity. Data flow has become a flood, requiring the services of technical specialists, who may know how to channel, but lack the wisdom to dam. As predicted, electronic data processing (EDP) has transformed the content and environment of office jobs.[1] Quite contrary to expectations, of both the optimists and the prophets of doom, EDP has not, however, cut down the number of workers nor has it lowered clerical costs. In fact, the price of processing paper has risen astronomically, and the public pays in every item purchased, every utility bill, and every government service.

Foretold early but discerned only dimly was the impact of EDP on organizational structure.[2] Information-processing, once regarded as an

[1] Ida R. Hoos, *Automation in the Office*, Washington, D.C.: Public Affairs Press, 1961.

[2] Ida R. Hoos, "When the Computer Takes Over the Office," *Harvard Business Review*, Vol. 38, No. 4, July-August, 1960.

adjunct to the organization, has become a function served by the organization, a factor in its structure, and even a prime criterion by which its overall efficiency is assessed. Armies of workers are employed in the preparation of data and cadres of information experts are required to maintain the system, that is, to keep it working and busy. The management of information has become equated with and is tantamount to the management of the enterprise. In fact, in a strange turnabout, management *of* information has receded from view and management *by* information has become the mode. The science of management is largely the science of managing information; it is also the science of managing by information. The metamorphosis from EDP, once deprecated as nothing more than a fast abacus, to MIS, the Management Information System, nerve center of the organization, is complete.

Representing a fusion between management science and computer technology, the information system has gained acceptance and acquired prestige beyond its accomplishments in the business world. One authority avers that far fewer systems than the sales and professional literature would have one believe have been put into operation and that, among those implemented, most have not performed as well as expected and some have been outright failures.[3] A number of surveys have uncovered growing disenchantment over the lack of demonstrable results.[4] Despite at least a billion dollars spent by U. S. industry, there is no proof that computers are helping managers make better decisions, nor can the heavy expenditure find corroboration through a discernible salubrious effect on profits. Herein exists a curious anomaly, in that the clever calculating capabilities of the computer, for all the alleged sophistication they bring to record-keeping, have not yet been able to provide a convincing accounting for themselves. With precise quantification the *raison d'être* of computerized systems, lack of identifiable performance is all the more noteworthy in view of the fact that such information would be extremely valuable not only to the organization paying for the system but also and especially to the computer industry and purveyors of software in substantiation for claims made for their products. And yet, an international conference on mechanized information storage and retrieval seeking clues to cost and effectiveness could find none.[5] The economics of computers have been explored and, at best, only subjective measures have emerged.[6]

[3] Russell L. Ackoff, "Management Misinformation Systems," *Management Science*, Vol. 14, No. 4, December, 1967, p. B-147.

[4] Arlene Hirshman, "A Mess in M.I.S.?" *Dun's Review*, Vol. 91, No. 1, January, 1968, pp. 26–27. Tom Alexander, "Computers Can't Solve Everything," *Fortune*, October, 1969, pp. 126–129, 168, 171.

[5] "Easing the Search," *Nature*, Vol. 223, September 20, 1969, p. 1205.

[6] William F. Sharpe, *The Economics of Computers*, New York: Columbia University Press, 1969.

Cost-cutting, having eluded capture through computerized quantification, cannot, therefore, legitimately occupy a place in the credit column. Neither can the claim of labor-saving, justified only by spurious comparisons with man-hours of manual work during the gaslight era. Ever since the introduction of EDP, the proclivity to sorceror's apprenticeship has been apparent. Indeed, the subtle sabotage took the form of deluging management with an overabundance of reports when automation first became a threat in the late 1950s.[7] Their responsibility being not to reason why, the office workers cheerfully "cooperated" with the foot-in-door experts lent by the vendors to expedite installation of the electronic system. The latter, trained to think not of *why* but rather of *how*, devised elaborate and cumbersome procedures for tasks that might have been relegated to less important status or even eliminated. The output of reports for management to digest was awesome. The outcome, more than a decade later, is not known. But it is a safe guess that the corporation, an oil company, is still hiring high-priced management consultants to deal with its information tangles.

In spite of the complaints of the dissatisfied and the caveats of the enlightened, management information systems as commodity and concept continue to be bought and sold extensively. Stock-in-trade of hardware and software merchants, epitome of management science to a generation of engineering and business school graduates, the MIS is now endemic in large organizations. Observed as common and erroneous assumptions underlying their design are several which deserve special mention: that lack of relevant information constitutes a critical deficiency for managers, and that more information will improve their decision-making.[8] Another might be added: that better management of the information means better management of the enterprise, that is, more efficient achievement of its organizational objectives.

The management syndrome pervading the public sector carries with it all the inherited myths of methodology. What is good for General Motors and General Dynamics is *ipso facto* good for the country; big government is big business, and, therefore, its operations will be run more efficiently by application of big business practices. Assumptions like these, even though questionable on their home ground, have become the rule for public planners: if administrators have more information, they will make better plans, perhaps arrive at better decisions; more and faster-moving information will improve government operations, that is, cut costs and provide better service; efficiency of operation is identical with service to community and society; this efficiency can best be achieved by more sophisticated accumulation and manipulation of

[7] Ida R. Hoos, *Automation in the Office, op.cit.*, p. 63.
[8] Russell L. Ackoff, *op.cit.*, p. B-147.

data; a technologically advanced information system is a highly technical matter calling for the specialized skills of an "information expert."

These apriorities, which have rationalized the MIS in the private sector, have been eagerly adopted by public officials who, in accepting their mandate to plan "rationally," have welcomed techniques, however untried and untrue. Information and the logistics of its aggregation and utilization appeal to them as an ideal starting point for bringing precision into public planning when they do not otherwise know how or where to proceed. The establishment of a data base early proved itself to be most useful not only as *sine qua non* for obtaining financial grants from foundations and federal agencies but also as manifestation of public concern without commitment, of activity without action.

Thanks to the enormous commercial and professional interests vested in management information systems, and in view of the self-perpetuating propensity of procedures once incorporated, it is likely that information and its management will remain central functions in the management of public affairs for many decades to come. With data gathering a key method in management science, political science, and urban planning curricula, and data management a primary activity of government, the tendency toward unquestioning faith in the information system has developed into a hard and fast rule of procedure. The main myths in the business world that most needed exploration and explosion have become doxology in government circles, with critical inquiry tantamount to heresy. Indeed, he who has the temerity to raise questions runs the risk of being considered not only anachronistically and iconoclastically unscientific but possibly a bit subversive and unAmerican as well.

INFORMATION SYSTEMS AS PART OF THE RATIONAL PLANNING PROCESS

Imposition of smart management techniques on government operations at all levels is largely a manifestation of the current ideology about "the powerful tools of technology." Adoption of the tools has been considerably hastened because of the prevailing tendency of civil servants and the public at large to consider the government laggard with respect to efficiency. The cliché, "If I ran my business that way," is well known and widespread. Overcome by "evidence" that sophisticated use of "management technology" has contributed to effective strategic planning in the defense establishment and persuaded that the computerized flow of information has enhanced efficiency in commercial and industrial enterprises, public officials have eagerly embraced the idea that rational planning can only be achieved through "advanced information technology." Receptivity thus assured, development of an information system to provide a data base has become the visible manifestation of innovativeness and the first step in the process of rational planning, associated with which is the implication that only a potential saboteur would question the wholly praiseworthy national effort to modernize public administration by the infusion of new methods. And herein lies one of its most serious dangers. Just because it may, indeed, become the basis for program formulation or evaluation, present and future, the information system, far from being a routine, mechanical matter, is crucial, its design demanding most searching inquiry.

The Matter of Facts

There appears to be widespread confusion as between *information*, *data*, and *facts*, all of which are used interchangeably and are somehow supposed to add up to knowledge. With computers to deliver quantity and speed, the predilection to gather and manipulate data grows and takes precedence as the primary approach to public decision-making. Crucial to the input-output models and cost-benefit ratios that characterize planning, the data bank has a solid sound and significance far exceeding its intrinsic worth, for somewhere in its generation, the items plugged in become "hard facts" and are accorded a reliability that is more wishful than actual.

On this matter, the thoughtful caveats of Oskar Morgenstern are pertinent.[9] What he perceives as likely areas for concern in the realm of economic statistics are not only applicable to but compounded by computerized information systems. He warns that information that is gathered must be fitted into a vast body of data which have been tested and retested and "into theories which have passed through the crucible of application." The level of precision and confidence in the information depends on the professional acumen of the persons doing the reporting. Knowledge of the composition, stages of classification, and all other characteristics of the data is essential but rarely available to users, likely to be "swamped with hosts of footnotes and explanations" but almost never enlightened. Deliberate lies, evasive falsification, and strategic silence affect the quality of the information which, good or bad, accurate or inaccurate, becomes incorporated into the system and forms the data base. Morgenstern stresses the point that all of these possible sources of error, already clearly evident in the physical sciences, become prevalent in the social fields, where nonmeasurable information and observations predominate. Honest error can occur, with far-reaching impact of its effect on the setting of policy. Such is the case of the Food

[9] Oskar Morgenstern, *On the Accuracy of Economic Observations*, Princeton University Press, 1963, second edition, pp. 17–70.

and Drug Administration's restrictions on the use of saccharin. The margin of safety imposed was grossly inconsistent with other additive regulations because the advisory committee of the National Academy of Science had based its calculations on data in which, it was later discovered, a misplaced decimal point had remained unnoticed. Differences of position become entrenched through selective use of information as in the Environmental Protection Agency's decision not to ban orange 2,4,5-T, a powerful herbicide used in Vietnam and suspected of having some linkage with South Vietnamese birth defects. Some scientists and consumer groups have criticized the report on which the EPA based its plan to permit widespread use of this weed killer as full of technical errors and omissions.

Implicit in the technical conception of the information system is the presupposition that facts, data, or information exist in pristine state and need only be captured as input. In the universal reverence for data that characterizes our computerized society, an interesting etymological anomaly exists. In its Latin origin, the word *datum* is something *given*. *Data*, the plural form currently used, is conceived as something *gotten* and, as such, must be divested of such attributes as accuracy and objectivity.[10] Who gathers the data and for what use are matters of considerable importance. The aggregation, selection, and organization of data are all part of a value-laden, mission-oriented process. Separated from source, the context in which they are used, and the conclusions derived from their manipulation, *data* would be an empty concept, probably so bereft of meaning as to be vacuous.

C. West Churchman suggests that there are no facts independent of the purposes of the user and that, moreover, there may be no such thing as accurate and objective information, especially in the context of social policy.[11] In similar vein, Abraham Kaplan reminds us that "how we conceptualize facts . . . depends on the theories that play a part in their cognition." [12] When, however, there are no theories to supply guiding principles, the neophyte in the given area shows a marked inclination to gather "facts" indiscriminately, irrespective of relevance, validity, or reliability. Information experts, for example, approach each task as though it were purely technical, with the data unequivocal, waiting to be gathered and processed, no matter what the field — education, crime, urban planning, or health. Their *summum bonum* is efficient

[10] Ida R. Hoos, "Information Systems and Public Planning," *Management Science* (Application Series), Vol. 17, No. 10, June, 1971, pp. B-658–672.

[11] C. West Churchman, "Real Times Systems and Public Information," Internal Working Paper No. 96, Space Sciences Laboratory, University of California, Berkeley, California, December, 1968, p. 3.

[12] Abraham Kaplan, *The Conduct of Inquiry*, San Francisco, California: Chandler, 1964, p. 313.

access and storage of data, the more the better. That such a system may not be sensitive and responsive to the needs of users is relatively unimportant in their schema.

But they should not be too severely castigated on this score. It may well be that there is no such thing as an information system which is sensitive and responsive to the needs of social planners. In all fairness to those of technocratic mind, it must be observed that omniscience does not reside conspicuously and exclusively on the bureaucratic side. Even if information experts were to abandon their customary avoidance procedures and, instead, try to establish liaison with professional planners, little would be changed or gained. The items which are crucial in planning may not be those amenable to processing. It is in the very nature of the computerized system to accept only quantified similarities, which may be far less important than the sensitively perceived nuances, the incommensurable factors, the individual differences. Consequently, no matter how earnest the effort at input by planners, the likelihood of development of a data system to meet current and future needs is highly nebulous. Government decision-makers attempting to articulate their data needs are particularly frustrated if these must be pre-cast in a form compatible with some larger system. Aware of the enormous complexity of their responsibilities, they are consequently and as a general rule petrified into a kind of inertia when faced with the opportunity or challenge to react to proposed information systems designers.

Something should also be mentioned in this context about "professional planning." Planning is an eclectic category, fast growing but lacking in discipline. Without a theoretical base, urban planning, for example, is a mixture of applied psychology, practical economics, political sophistication, horse sense and horse-trading.[13] The college curricula in the field reflect the amorphousness; the graduates demonstrate it when confronted with complex real-life problems. They learn early to resort to simulations and models as convenient abstractions which delay rather than clarify decisive planning. Overlooked is the fact that anything that can be simulated must be assumed to be reproducible. The vital circumstances surrounding social planning are largely irreproducible; whatever of them can be captured in simulation for repetition are likely to be the least critical aspects. Faced with life's complexities, the tyro planner turns gratefully to the information system as represented by the vendors, for it has been offered as a tool that will help in defining and structuring the problem and, thus, solving it.

In the absence of better conceptualization, planners, like information experts, subscribe to the notion that information is the root prob-

[13] Melville C. Branch, "Delusions and Diffusions of City Planning in the United States," *Management Science*, Vol. 16, No. 12, August, 1970, pp. B-714–732.

lem to many metropolitan development efforts. Their position is expressed in the following statement, which may be regarded as authoritative, because it occurs in a widely disseminated report: "Information (interpreted data) is the usual common denominator in metropolitan problem solution; it is the core of any metropolitan growth-management scheme, guidance mechanism, booster campaign, or research effort, both private and public. A tremendous range of metropolitan-oriented undertakings, private and public, operational *and* research-development oriented, founder for lack of data.[14]

The basic data identified as necessary to "increased community understanding" and "development of appropriate management tools" are then listed as: "people, automobiles, workers, levels of skills, housing available, number of unemployed, salaries, taxes, routes traveled, structures, land characteristics, utilities, *ad infinitum.*" [15] Noteworthy here is the casual lumping and dumping of poorly conceptualized items, like *structures*; overlapping categories, for example, *people, workers*; and downright nonsense, like *routes traveled*, a particular known to yield an avalanche of useless data. On the assumption that this authority in urban planning had transportation in mind when he included *routes traveled* in his shopping list, we might find it useful to mention that the "never-mind-the-why-and-wherefore" [16] approach to information gathering appears conspicuously in transportation planning.

An ambitious study in California under the Bay Area Transportation Study Commission (BATSC) resulted in a formidable accumulation of data on movements of people and cars, with destination, time, and speed faithfully recorded and physically stored on some 1100 reels of magnetic tape. BATSC reports earnestly recorded that information had been acquired from a multiplicity of sources and through a variety of techniques, aerial photography included. Using origin-and-destination Home Interview Survey, a method known to transportation planners, research personnel had covered a 5 percent sample of the Bay Area and collected about 10 million pieces of information at a cost of $1,500,000. Gathered were items on household characteristics, such as rent and income; individual members, such as education and employment; and data on each trip taken by members of the household, such as origin, destination, purpose, and mode of travel. The myriad of

---

[14] Richard D. Duke, "Urban Planning and Metropolitan Development — The Role of Technology," *Applying Technology to Unmet Needs*, Appendix V, *Technology and the American Economy*. Studies prepared for the National Commission on Technology, Automation, and Economic Progress, Washington, D.C.: U.S. Government Printing Office, February, 1966, p. V-8.

[15] *Ibid.*, p. V-9.

[16] W. S. Gilbert and Sir Arthur Sullivan, "Never Mind the Why and Wherefore," *H.M.S. Pinafore.*

items, included in elaborate questionnaires and garnered through field interviews, were then converted to punch cards, totalling some 1.5 million, which, in turn, were recorded on sixteen reels of magnetic tape. Despite the added intelligence that about one and one-half hours of IBM 7094 time are needed to reprocess the Home Interview file, interpretation of the three-million-dollar agglomeration has never been achieved; the raw data remain undigested and transportation remains the same hit-or-miss affair in the area studied as elsewhere.

The urban planner who finds comfort in the security blanket of information *pari passu* evinces enormous faith in the powers of technology. Excerpts from the article prepared for the National Commission on Technology, Automation, and Economic Progress provide evidence:

> Fortunately, the technology exists to quantify urban growth on a continuous basis for intra-metropolitan areas, to project urban data for various time periods with a reasonable degree of sophistication, and to simulate the effects of alternative courses of action and urban growth. In short, it is technologically feasible to develop an operational metropolitan management information system. This system could be designed to provide reliable information on many aspects of intra-metropolitan phenomena to all potential users, public and private, on a small-area basis (parcels, people, etc.); and to provide the inter-metropolitan information required for a proper regional and national perspective. . . .
>
> The technology for a working system — hardware, software, data sources, updating procedures, trained personnel — exists at some level. There is no question but that technological barriers could be overcome (*an industry that can launch astronauts or photograph Mars can most assuredly cope with these earth-bound problems*). (My italics)[17]

The position taken by some planners is, obviously, not much different from that of the information technologist. The important discrepancy appears to relate primarily to their expectations. The systems expert perceives his goal to be efficient storage and retrieval of data, and his conception of "efficiency" remains, until amended, one of quantity. The planner, however, hopes for a tool that will help him define objectives, assess alternatives, and otherwise deal rationally with the complex of political, economic, and social pressures that impinge on his task. Schooled to take refuge in a neat, well-ordered, and rational simulated world, he looks to the information system for guidance. And, cowed by the intricacies and technicalities of computerized systems, he abdicates the responsibility of articulating data needs to the systems experts. The resultant dilemma contributes to a stalemate in the state-

[17] Richard D. Duke, *op.cit.*, pp. V-9-10.

of-the-art of both planning and information systems design and explains why there is a plethora of burdensome, busy-working information systems on the flip charts of every organization that must plan. It also accounts for the fact that, in the public sector, there does not exist now an information system "sensitive and responsive to the needs of users." Whether there can or should be one so devised for the future depends less on technology than on social definition of "needs of users." Experience may yet teach us that the best data machine is the one which manufactures its own sabots to destroy itself. We may learn that social planning needs to be recognized openly as a primitive, experimental art, its resources too limited to be dissipated or squandered in pursuit of mechanistic devices that add weight but shed little light. As the mythology of the rational techniques spreads, the likelihood increases that quantifiable goals and factors will become predominant in the handling of public affairs. The very way of thinking about social problems may be preset, influenced, and determined by the methodology.

In the process of becoming accepted as a necessary step in rational planning, information systems have come to be regarded as a kind of problem-solving activity *per se* and, as such, entities in themselves. No longer the subsystem embedded in a larger system whose objectives and values should be realized, the gathering, processing, and manipulation of information have come to represent an end in itself. How "efficiently" this is accomplished is the norm for the entire endeavor.

Information Systems and Public Welfare

The extent to which preoccupation with records, forms, and data processing is being offered as substitute for, rather than an adjunct to, intelligent social problem solution becomes evident upon examination of specific cases. Public welfare has been a prime target for systems studies, which are intended to reduce rising costs of aid to the needy. On the assumption that more efficient management of paper-flow or of information will somehow reverse the trend toward higher welfare budgets, management-minded administrators have focused on reorganization of the information system. This, it must be conceded, is a politically palatable device, far preferable to overt acknowledgment of the handicapping economic and social factors making and keeping the poor poorer.

Asumption of the centrality of information as the crux of the welfare problem is illustrated in a proposed system for the Nassau County (New York) Department of Welfare. Its ultimate objective being "to aid the Welfare Department in optimizing programs, services, and resources to satisfy community needs," the projected information center was specifically intended to:

(1) establish Welfare Department goals and objectives;
(2) define information requirements and managerial techniques;
(3) establish information acquisition requirements;
(4) establish information distribution requirements;
(5) develop information feedback techniques;
(6) develop decision-making techniques;
(7) develop computerized information system.[18]

Notable here is the presupposition that the function of the *information center* can or should be to establish departmental goals, define data requirements, and prescribe managerial techniques. It implies that what is needed to improve the lot of Nassau County's citizens is a computerized information flow. In actual fact, its poor people are suffering not because their records do not move but because they cannot. A study shows recipients of public assistance, with annual incomes under $5,000, to be handicapped by poor health, lack of educational and vocational skills, deficiencies rendered virtually insurmountable because, trapped in pockets far from jobs, the poor had no access to adequate transportation facilities.[19]

In California, a consulting team of information experts selected the Aid to Families with Dependent Children program as its focus for a quarter-of-a-million-dollar study on the ground that "it offers some hope of reduction using the techniques of systems analysis."[20] The orientation was no more sound than the grammar; it ignored the factors which contribute to dependency as well as the statutes regulating eligibility for and amount of aid. As in so many other information systems designs, data-handling was allowed to occupy a key role in what was loosely referred to as "the welfare problem." Juxtaposed against a table of particular shortcomings of the current data-handling system was the following set of "design goals," as though the proposed information system could correct the failings, follies, and failures of the entire welfare system, and, somehow, reduce dependency, too:

(1) to increase the flow of information in order to promote better service and management control at all levels;
(2) to minimize administrative cost and improve efficiency;

[18] Sperry Gyroscope Company, *A Proposed Demonstration Project for a Nassau County Welfare Information Center*, Sperry Publication No. GJ-2232-1116, May, 1966, p. V.

[19] "Poverty in Spread City — Study of Constraints on the Poor of Nassau County." Study conducted in Nassau County Planning Commission under a grant from the U.S. Office of Economic Opportunity, November 19, 1969.

[20] Space-General Corporation, *Systems Management Analysis of the California Welfare System*, SCC 104SR9, March 15, 1967, p. 1.

(3) to provide research and statistical data for state planning and program evaluation purposes;

(4) to provide inquiry service for questions which cannot now be anticipated:

(5) to provide fiscal data for State planning and evaluation purposes;

(6) to provide a system sufficiently flexible to accommodate changes in needs, volume, policy, and/or data demands; and

(7) to reduce the cost of operations below that of the present information system.[21]

Even a casual review of this list shows it to be a stretched-out serialization of overlaps and contradictions rather than a thoughtful paradigm. Items (1) and (2) are variations on the same theme; the information system promised could not accomplish both of them and number (7) as well. Assuming, for the sake of argument, that the proposed system could achieve (1) and (2); it would fulfill (7) only if "cost of operations" were construed to mean unit cost, a figure which is nebulous at best. Even if one were to dignify as acceptable cost accounting the numerical sleight-of-hand that attaches a price tag to computerized bits, nothing of value could come of the exercise. Its result would be meaningless. Moreover, cost of present operations, while indubitably a matter of legitimate concern, is a norm of remarkable irrelevance.

Item (3) implies that the welfare system itself generates the information needed for planning and program evaluation. Actually, the "research and statistical data" crucial for planning and necessary in program evaluation should more properly be sought in areas other than the welfare system *per se*. For example, the state of the labor market may be the decisive factor in welfare planning in Seattle, as Boeing's cutbacks have their ripple effect on the total economy. A sharp rise in the cost of living in New York may topple marginal families onto the relief rolls. A change in legislation may redefine eligibility in Michigan and extend aid to a hitherto neglected category of poor people. By the same token, reference to factors outside welfare is crucial to "program evaluation," and the validity of the research and statistical data used in the assessment is far from an undisputed matter. Criteria for judging the efficacy of a particular welfare program are value-laden and reflect personal, social, and political bias. With many systems designers inclined to harbor a certain amount of contempt toward recipients, the "good" program would be the one that gets people off welfare, and "good" data would be those which prove a given course of action well chosen for this purpose. It is for this reason that the research function in some state welfare agencies has been subverted to the task of supplying unsympathetic legislators and administrators

[21] *Ibid.*, pp. 4–2, 4–3.

with the "facts" they need for cutting services for the dependent sectors of society.

Item (4) is presumptuous, for it ascribes to the information experts a clairvoyance denied professionals in the field. If, as the data architects state, "questions cannot now be anticipated," how can the answers be prescribed? Inquiry service for attainment of such information could not appropriately be confined to welfare alone. Does this mean that the experts have been able to encompass all other social institutions impinging on the status of individuals now and in the future? Item (5) is an extension of (3) and subject to the same critical questions. Item (6) incorporates many of the failings of (4). Its open-endedness is meant to suggest knowledge, whereas, actually, there is a void. Item (7) was discussed in connection with (1) and (2).

Generalized objectives like the seven listed above are frequently encountered in the information systems that are serving as placebos in welfare administration. Interesting to note, they appear in both original proposals and final reports, with attainment no closer in the latter than in the former. In either case, they have little merit, for they are based neither on professional experience in the field nor on technical analysis, but, instead, on stereotypes and clichés. The objectives, derived through a hasty review of current paper-flow and a swift "touching of bases" with welfare personnel, more to pick up the jargon than to gather knowledge, are conceived with an expertness directed only secondarily to understanding specific operations and purposes and primarily to capitalizing on customary bureaucratic complaints in a campaign to sell a new system.

The inevitable and universal result in public welfare agencies has not been "management information systems" of a type that could conceivably clarify objectives or improve operations or by any stretch of the imagination reduce welfare costs. Almost the exact opposite has occurred. Expensive and burdensome data-processing systems are factors in consuming resources already scarce. Moreover, the research function, which was supposed to be enhanced by the plenitude of information forthcoming, has actually been downgraded. Now in the hands of "technical experts," the tasks of research have become another of the popular management games of "playing around with a few programs." With the computer as a tool, enormous matrices are possible and certain patterns can be "teased out." In some studies, there is mere corroboration of long familiar relationships but no insights into causality. For example, without realizing that they were dealing with a well-known "poverty syndrome," a systems group "discovered" connections between low education, poor health, and unemployment. Interdependent rather than independent and moving in unison, each of these factors was treated as though an individual "predictor" of the others. To the professional researcher in the field, this kind of correlation is a useless belaboring of the commonplace, the inevitable outcome of the substitution of the indiscriminate pursuit and massage of data for thoughtful research design.

INFORMATION SYSTEMS AND LAND USE

Among the happiest of hunting grounds for information system vendors are the areas which are concerned with land usage. Attracted by large and numerous grants, mostly from the federal government, experts from computer manufacturing companies, accounting firms, aerospace and engineering companies, and think tanks of all stripe busily peddle their wares. And, it may be noted, they meet little sales resistance. Quite the contrary. Uncertain as to goals and defensive as to bailiwick, naïve about computer technology and oversold on Space Age management methods, anxious public planners have allowed themselves to be persuaded that a land data bank is a prime necessity for their and the community's greatest good. The feasibility study, performed by the potential recipient of a large follow-on contract, demonstrates not only feasibility but downright indispensability. Set forth as newly discovered are the bureaucratic overlaps, the jurisdictional duplication, the antediluvian procedures. In neat juxtaposition is the land use information system, which presumably will "facilitate effective sharing of land use data between departments within a jurisdiction and between jurisdictions." [22]

The California Regional Land Use Information System Project, referred to as CRLUISP in the official documents, was conceived as a demonstration of "the sophisticated techniques of systems analysis" and methodology applied in such manner as to "provide a solution to problems in governmental information systems." [23] The major objective of the pilot project, for which a $225,000 contract was awarded to TRW Systems, was to develop the system that would "facilitate effective sharing of land use data between departments" [24] within and between jurisdictions. Almost two years later, the final summary report emerged, its format and appearance more that of a sales brochure than a professional document. [25] Consisting of about twenty-three unnumbered

[22] *Scope*, State Office of Planning, Department of Finance, State of California, Third Quarter, 1966, p. 1.

[23] State Office of Planning, Department of Finance, State of California, *California Regional Land Use Information System Project*, Urban Planning Assistance Grant Application, November 3, 1965, p. 2.

[24] *Scope, op.cit.*

[25] TRW Systems Group, *California Regional Land Use Information System*, no date.

pages, the pamphlet contained at most eleven pages of text, much of which was an agglomeration of platitudes, for example, "Information about land is collected and used by many different organizations at many different levels, *i.e.*: major agencies of the federal government within the state; major agencies of the state government; counties; cities; industrial and commercial businesses; special intergovernmental organizations and districts." [26] This insight accounted for four-fifths of the text on the page. The rest of the printed matter conveyed information of similar depth. Half of the page was devoted to a pictorialized map, with delicate tracery, black dotted lines, cryptic markings, and no explanatory legend. Diagrams and drawings, sample displays and printouts occupied considerable space in the booklet. Three and one-half pages were photographs, neither illustrative nor enlightening. The equivalent of more than one page was given over to decorative but not especially relevant drawings, and a full page exhibited a gallimaufry of items — a clock face with hands at noon; a field; a freeway; a female fiddling with a dial; a fisherman in a canoe; a family picnicking on a beach; a stylized cow sculpture; an elongated raccoon; assorted sky-scrapers and industrial sites — all pictured on a globe. Accompanying this fanciful display were the numerals, *1973*, probably meant to be portentous, although the arcane symbolism eludes the observer.

Somewhat in contrast to these vagaries, the report offered "hard" facts as evidence of scientific precision at work. A page of tables showing "basic characteristics of the land data environment" pinpointed in percentages the unfulfilled data needs of agencies:

Jurisdiction	Unfulfilled Data Needs (in percent)
Federal	5
State	20
County	15
City	8
District	1
Private	25

Another surprisingly precise display provided a summary of "tangible cost savings"; $803,000 in 1970, for example. Such nicety can impress only persons totally unfamiliar with bookkeeping practices, in the public or private sector. Actually, one of the most serious deficiencies of the project was its neglect of the costing aspects, both as to realistic estimates and allocation. Nonetheless, even the contingencies were made to sound as though exactly computed instead of the possibly erroneous platitudes they were: "If participation and services rendered exceed the estimates used in this analysis, the operation costs will be

[26] *Ibid.* No page number cited here because pages of the report were not numbered.

correspondingly higher; however, the benefits will increase with stronger participation." Further to demonstrate the exactness of the system team's operations and to allay any notion that the work of information-gathering was not busily done, a full page, over 4 percent of the total report, was devoted to a reproduction of the survey questionnaire used, with half of another page to the following "Survey Facts":

> Each questionnaire contained 412 data elements — with 10 questions about each element.
> A total of 844 questionnaires were sent to agencies in state.
> A total of 554 questionnaires were completed and returned.
> The resulting information amounted to 35,000 records and about 10 million characters.

The rest of the half-page, some 2 percent of the total space used in reporting this quarter-of-a-million-dollar investment of public funds, was left blank. Listed *verbatim* and *in toto* are the "Principal Conclusions":

> There is a heavy traffic in the exchange of land-related data.
> Significant benefits are possible from the solution of identified data problems.
> Data users are aware of the needs and are highly cooperative.
> A statewide land data system should be implemented.
> *The index and additional key functions should be centralized.
> *Data collection, storage, and retrieval should remain the responsibility of the cognizant organizations within the individual data centers.
> An operating statewide system is possible in five years, with partial services available in three years.
> Five-year development and operational costs will be $2.9 million.
> Net savings of $1.6 million over costs are estimated for the same period.
> The development and operational effort should be under the direction of an interorganizational Policy and Plans Group.

There were two interim reports before the grand finale, but they contained little worthwhile substance and many rationalizations for the team's failure to fulfill its promises. The Project Steering Committee, made up of a state-level executive, a county planner, a bank economist, and a university professor of agricultural economics, were pragmatic in their orientation and wanted a workable system. Their communication with the engineers was generally unsatisfactory, and the necessary second-level liaison groups were never formed. As a result, the team went its own way, one which did not necessarily correspond to a planned highway to efficiency in government.

Notwithstanding the project's shortcomings, rendered invisible by a change in state administration, TRW claimed that it cost them twice as much to carry out the work they had done than the $225,000 they received. Santa Clara County, used as pilot, got a classification system to help in coding, but this was nowhere near a working model for analysis, retrieval, and exchange of data, despite the 10 million characters gathered by the team. Moreover, the prime accomplishment, a comprehensive index file, serving as a catalogue of individuals, agencies, and organizations that collect, store, process, and utilize land-related information, was destined for a short life. Prospects for financing continued maintenance, a *sine qua non* in assuring its usefulness, were not bright at the state level and nebulous at the federal level once the original, demonstration phase was over.

In land use information systems, compatibility of classification is vital to computerization. But a workable set of definitions has never been achieved. Moreover, the requirement that the data fit or be forced into fixed categories obscures differences, deviations, and divergencies that may be more important to planners than the similarities. Selected as items for the typical data base are those which are visible and machine-processable. Then they are homogenized into a state of isomorphism. Land use information systems leave much to be desired and yet to be realized most of the promises of better resource allocation and improved efficiency in land usage. As to the former, an experienced government official observed that the really crucial decisions occur at the ballot box.[27] As to the latter, "efficiency" is a value-laden term, the very conception of which reflects fundamental matters of choice. According to one authority, preoccupation with the analytical or managerial tools distracts attention from the basic issues and policies which deserve study before we concern ourselves with "efficiency." The problem is not absence of knowledge; it is rather that appropriate actions are constrained by political factors reflecting the anticipated reactions of various interest groups.[28]

INFORMATION SYSTEMS AND CRIME

A prime example of information systems that stand on their own ends is to be found in the current, nationwide war on crime. The term applied to these efforts usually includes "criminal justice," words that conjure up all good things, *viz.*, apprehension of criminals, deterrence of crime, the meting out of punishment that fits the crime, wise administration and direction of police work, intelligent ordering of

[27] Howard E. Ball (Bureau of Outdoor Recreation, U.S. Department of the Interior), comments on Ruth P. Mack and Sumner Myers, "Outdoor Recreation," in *Measuring Benefits of Government Investments*, Robert Dorfman, ed., Washington, D.C.: The Brookings Institution, 1965, p. 101.

[28] James R. Schlesinger, *Systems Analysis and the Political Process*, Santa Monica: RAND Paper, P-3464, June, 1967, p. 26.

procedures for bail, probation, and parole, court calendars which are
consonant with the needs, jails which are institutions for correctional
rehabilitation. These elements, all essential to the design of a system
of criminal justice, appear, in boxes, or in bubbles with arrows between,
on many flow charts. But, more often than not, what starts out to be a
"system of criminal justice" ends as little more than a technological
game of cops-and-robbers, with the information system the key
instrument.

"The development of an information system linking together various
agencies of criminal justice and being capable of evaluating program
and system effectiveness through collection, storage, and processing of
appropriate data" [29] was, for example, the crucial item in a system of
criminal justice proposed for the State of California. The engineers who
won the contract based their calculations on statistics of convicted offenders and in so doing disclosed the simple-minded belief that crime is
that which gets punished. Forgotten was the truism proclaimed by the
Sergeant in his little song:

> When a felon's not engaged in his employment, his employment,
> Or maturing his felonious little plans, little plans,
> His capacity for innocent enjoyment, 'cent enjoyment,
> Is just as great as any honest man's.[30]

Culling records of arrests, the team of information experts devised a
neo-Lombrosian [31] taxonomy, in which the crucial factors were sex, age,
ethnicity, education, employment status, and geographical location.
When commitments to California penal institutions were scrutinized,
the major portion of offenders was found to be male, between 14 and
29 years of age, Negro or Mexican-American, poorly educated, unemployed, and from heavily-populated, low income geographic areas. Analyzing the statistics, the analysts thought they had discovered "criminal
characteristics" that set the offenders apart from the population at large.
In actual fact, experienced criminologists contend that persons behind
bars bear greater resemblance to those outside than to their fellow in-
mates. Really identified in their study was the shared haplessness that
renders certain groups, under certain conditions, more susceptible to
the embrace of law than others. Ironically, the system of criminal justice

[29] Space-General Corporation, *Prevention and Control of Crime and Delinquency
in California*, Final Report, PCCD-7, July 29, 1965, p. 4.
[30] W. S. Gilbert and Sir Arthur Sullivan, "When a Felon's Not Engaged," *The
Pirates of Penzance*.
[31] Cesare Lombroso, a nineteenth century criminologist, expounded the theory that
criminality was a kind of atavism, a throwback to ancestors, and that the inherited
traits were identifiable and distinguishable. Recognition of them was, to him, a central factor in controlling crime.

which was designed on this shaky basis caught those sectors of the society which were least protected and most needed protection from and by law. The poverty syndrome — poor education, lack of employment, a slum address, a dark skin — became, within the system engineers' conception of that term, the accepted "indicators" of propensity for a life of crime.

As further evidence that arrest and conviction records are a poor index to crime in our society, authoritative estimates place figures on offenders, that is, persons known arrested, at 25 percent of total crimes known to have been committed. Crime in ghetto areas is under-reported, much that occurs going unrecorded. Certain classes of "crime" in upper class white neighborhoods is dismissed as "reprimand and release," while other types, such as burglary and rape, barely noted in the slums, are meticulously recorded because of the insurance aspects. Statistics show concentration of law enforcement activity rather than incidence of lawbreaking. A police "crackdown" can, on any given day, net hundreds of prostitutes, but advance warning of such an event can cause a swift, albeit temporary disappearance of such persons from the local scene. Events like these have high visibility on the record but little long-run effect in the streets. Much of the distinction between that which is taken to be a criminal offense and that which passes for legitimate activity depends on the level of community tolerance. The same noisy demonstrations that excite extreme reaction from sheriff and police at one time and place are allowed to occur without interference and event at another. The rock music festival that has, with its devotees, metamorphized a sleepy village into a midsummer nightmare of crowding and general disruption could result in mass arrests, for marijuana smoking, if not for other infractions. Yet, such happenings have occurred without much official notice or interference and, hence, without leaving substantial mark on the police blotter. Much depends on the discriminatory enforcement of law, which, in itself, is a manifestation of community tolerance. The enforceability of laws, rather than their intrinsic intent, also influences policing. Many laws, for example those governing deployment of pickets during labor disputes, are disregarded with impunity when the arrest and prosecution of all offenders seem unlikely. "Failure to provide" could, for any given month, initiate at least 5,000 warrants for arrest in California, but there are simply not enough courts to process them.

The urgent question that must be faced when trying to identify *the criminal* is: What is crime? Rates are meaningless. Although crime rates have been used as the data base for programs of control, there has been little attention paid to the factors which have placed certain illegal acts in the official ledger and ignored others. Actually, the situational conditions under which policemen write crime reports may determine the outcome of the incident. An empirical study derived from a three-city observation of routine police encounters isolated the following conditions relating to the production of official crime reports: legal seriousness of the complaint; the complainant's observable preference for police action; the relational distance between the complainant and the suspect; the complainant's degree of deference toward the police; and the complainant's social class status.[32]

As more and more persons, disenchanted with conventional and institutionalized ways of achieving change, express their frustrations through civil disobedience in the form of marches and street demonstrations, they will become known to the law. Counting them like burglars will add little to an understanding of and coping with crime. Codes relating to civil disobedience, drugs like marijuana, and sexual activity between consenting adults are undergoing revision, and it is apparent that an activity listed as criminal today may be outside the proper reach of the law tomorrow. Consequently, it should be obvious that the concept of crime is one of definition, institutional, cultural, legal, political, and social, and subject to enormous latitude and vicissitude as to interpretation.

If, for the sake of pursuing an argument, one still insisted on harboring the simplistic notion that crime is that which gets punished and the criminal is the person who was or should be caught and punished, one could then more comfortably accept the next "logical" step in the development of "criminal information systems." This is the automated file, set up to implement the capture of criminals. It has high priority in every town and county, city and state budget and appears in federal appropriations as well. Indeed, so persuasive is the idea that crime can be controlled through application of information technology that large portions of the money made available through Safe Streets legislation have been subverted to data-gathering about people who might be interesting to law enforcers. Criminal justice information systems, intended to help "control crime" through rapid apprehension, have received enormous impetus and are in various stages of development and implementation throughout the country. They deserve close scrutiny, for their implications for the continuance of a democratic society are far-reaching.

Proponents of the allocation of up to $350,000 for the design of a system of criminal justice information in California derived much support from two earlier systems studies. The report by Space-General Cor-

---

[32] Donald J. Black, "Production of Crime Rates," *American Sociological Review*, Vol. 35, No. 4, August, 1970, pp. 733–748.

poration, *Prevention and Control of Crime and Delinquency in California*,[33] and one by Lockheed Missiles & Space Company called the *California Statewide Information System Study*[34] were cited as concluding, to the surprise of no one, that "an integrated information system for the effective management of public data is necessary and feasible. These reports, prepared by outstanding scientific industrial research organizations, point out that acceptance and utilization of modern systems analysis technology are essential if public agencies are to respond adequately to current service demands. *Specific reference was made to the administration of criminal justice as an area that would benefit particularly by the application of scientific analysis and organization.*"[35]

Although this expression of unquestioning faith revealed the prefabricated approval of the architects of the project, other items in the Request for Proposal indicated oblique criticism. Possibly to circumvent the usual extensive sales campaign, rendered somewhat redundant anyway by the obvious enchantment of the California Department of Justice with the notion of a criminal justice information system, the condition was set forth that:

The proposal format should be relatively austere and without fancy or expensive art work, unusual printing or use of materials that are not essential to the utility and clarity of the finished product. The written proposal must stand alone as no films, exhibits, or briefings will be accepted with the proposal.[36]

The Request for Proposal was a detailed statement, underlining the gaps and lags in the present data systems; it articulated the objectives of the project:

The purposes of the project are to develop a functional design and prepare an implementation plan for an advance statewide integrated information system which will serve each state and local criminal justice agency in its operations, administration, and decision making as well as provide for the timely sharing of available information to assist the participating agencies in the performance of their respective responsibility. The success of this project will be determined by the improvement attained in the processes of criminal justice that result from the advance information system design. *An auxiliary benefit will be the establishment of the means for a systematic accumulation of data which can be utilized for the control and prevention of crime, the development of more effective programs for the treatment of offenders, and a data-*

[33] *Op.cit.*

[34] Lockheed Missiles & Space Company, *California Statewide Information System Study*, Y-82-65-5, July 30, 1965.

[35] Department of Justice, State of California, *Criminal Justice Information System Design Study Project, Request for Proposal*, December 22, 1966, p. 25.

[36] *Ibid.*, pp. 25–26.

base for research by behavioral scientists, police administrators, jurists, penologists, and criminalists.[37] (My italics.)

Noteworthy here, as in other instances of information system development, is the notion that the "advance information system design" is the vital factor in criminal justice (undefined) and that "systematic accumulation of data" is the *ne plus ultra* for the "control and prevention of crime" (undefined). For proponents of the project to insert in the Request for Proposal the idea that the data base would implement "development of more effective programs for the treatment of offenders" was extraneous embellishment, not taken seriously in the responding proposals nor in the ultimate system recommendations. Such information as the planned system would generate could only serve to divert and subvert whatever efforts are being made to achieve reform in treatment of offenders. Further glutting an already overloaded system holds little promise for amelioration of already thoroughly documented and explored problems connected with handling and rehabilitation of criminals. Promising the data base for research was a poor sop, serving at best as a built-in defense for the indiscriminate gathering of all kinds of information with the idea that out of this heterogeneous morass, professional research people could or should make some sense *ex post facto*.

The most significant, but least regarded, of the tasks to be performed was described thus:

Project and assess the probable trends in the social order during the next ten years insofar as they will relate to demands upon the administration of criminal justice. The criminal justice system does not operate in a void. The daily functions within the system are responsive to current events that impinge upon society and result in economic, political, technical and philosophical adjustments. This assessment shall serve as a setting for the information system design proposal.[38]

This obeisance in the direction of social responsibility was well-intentioned but without visible effect. Far from serving as the "setting" for the design proposal, social factors were relegated to a lonely box on the flow chart and treated as a separate entity with no relevance to the rest of the endeavor. The information technologists working up the information system neither knew nor cared about the Social Trends Study. There was no interaction between them and the consultant hired to provide social dimensions to the comprehensive information network.

The Request for Proposal elicited responses from a variegated array of contenders — aerospace companies like Lockheed Missiles & Space

[37] *Ibid.*
[38] *Ibid.*, p. 16.

Company, Space-General Corporation, and North American Aviation; well-known "think tanks," like Systems Development Corporation and Stanford Research Institute, and less well-known "associates" selling management methods and systems designing; and accounting firms like Price-Waterhouse and Touche, Ross, Bailey, and Smart. The fourteen proposals were reviewed by a committee which included the sheriff of Riverside County, an official of the California Highway Patrol, an administrator in the Los Angeles Police Department, and a representative of the State Department of Finance. Chairman of the advisory group was a member of the operations research group at Systems Development Corporation.

The contract was awarded Lockheed Missiles & Space Company, whose winning proposal set forth the objectives for the Criminal Justice Information System as follows:

(1) Prevention of crime;

(2) Crime investigation and apprehension of offenders;

(3) Rapid and positive identification of those with whom the agencies come in contact;

(4) Interagency sharing of current factual information regarding those individuals being processed through the criminal justice system;

(5) Knowledge and control of the major instruments of crime, such as narcotics and weapons;

(6) Identification and retrieval of stolen property.[39]

During the eighteen-months study period, the Lockheed engineers established the parameters for the criminal justice information system of their design. (1) The program was "conceived primarily with the identification and ordering of information flows between criminal justice agencies to assist them in fulfilling their responsibilities." (2) It was "directed toward effective and feasible use of advanced information management analysis and automation technology to provide assistance to criminal justice agencies." [40] To judge from the engineers' analysis of the benefits forthcoming from the system they had devised, the rapid gathering and movement of information was the crux of the major problems adhering to the state of crime in California:

(1) One of the major benefits from CJIS will be the improvement in the apprehension of criminals at large. There is almost no question that arrests will increase as soon as law enforcement officials are armed with the computer in the conduct of their normal operation. The experience obtained through

[39] Lockheed Missiles & Space Company, *A Proposal for a California Criminal Justice Information System*, LMSC-699401, January 30, 1967, p. 4.

[40] Lockheed Missiles & Space Company, *California Criminal Justice Information System, Preliminary System Recommendations*, T-29-68-8, April 29, 1968, p. i.

the use of the two well-known automated information systems used in law enforcement, PIN and AUTO-STATIS, both confirm this generalization. Estimating the monetized value of this increased apprehension factor is difficult. It represents the cost to society of allowing those offenders to remain at large which the system would either remove from society or put under supervision.[41]

This particular "benefit," even more shortsighted than ungrammatical, betrayed the current, technologically inspired preoccupation with a particular subsystem, that of information, as though it were the be-all and end-all of criminal justice. Emphasis on "improvement in apprehensions" and increase of arrests indicated the "police" mentality of the system's designers. Using number of arrests as the measure of the success of the system was a manifestation of a state of extreme naïvete or ignorance either residing in the technologists or imputed by them to the public at large. There was no consideration in the proposed California system for rampant and documented procedural abuses, archaic laws relating to civil commitments, narcotics, alcoholism, and sexual offenses, or the state of the court calendar, clogged as much by deliberate delaying tactics of attorneys as by the shortage of judges and overload of prisoners.

The information system designed for the State of California's pursuit of criminals in the name of justice by Lockheed Missiles & Space Company can best be described as an on-line accumulation of baseline data about individuals known to the law or, by some stretch of someone's imagination, likely to become so known. This liberal interpretation of its mandate by the project team encouraged them to gather whatever they conceivably could and produced virtually the same items of information about potential jurors as potential criminals. Although some of the most doughty and sanguine law enforcers experienced temporary discomfiture about the health of a society with freedom from crime so insured, the notion of the police information system thrives and is being implemented through generous funding. Some of the wider implications of the technologically designed information system as a tool of social control will be discussed in "Information Systems and the Invasion of Privacy."

The account of the California Criminal Information System would not be complete without describing in greater detail the Social Trends Study mentioned earlier. This was to be a ten-year projection of possible trends in the social order insofar as they would impinge on the administration of criminal justice.[42] The research was to be carried out simultaneously with, but independently of, the work of the Lockheed team.

[41] Lockheed Missiles & Space Company, *California Criminal Justice Information System, op.cit.,* pp. 6-2, 6-3.

[42] Department of Justice, State of California, *Criminal Justice Information System Design Study Project, Request for Proposal, op.cit.,* p. 16.

Instead of serving as a setting for the information system design proposal, however, it was treated as so distinct an entity that the lawyer hired especially to do the study had no contact with the engineers and had no idea what they were doing. *The Social Trends Study* appeared at the end of the project, hardly in time to serve as a "setting for the information system design proposal." Standing by itself, the study is nonetheless a remarkable document, with its insights leading to the conclusion that crime can only be reduced by fundamental social changes. For the planners of the project to have recognized the importance of the social dimensions of crime was truly commendable. For them to have presumed that anyone, no matter how well intentioned, could ascertain or predict social conditions ten years hence was a manifestation of ignorance. Sociologists still grope for explanations of events of the decade just past and have neither crystal balls nor techniques to make accurate forecasts for the future. To expect systems designers to program future social conditions betrayed naïvete about the state-of-the-art of information technology and the state of the artists developing the system.

Although the California experience has been singled out for critical review, it is not an isolated instance but, in fact, just one of a countrywide network that links into similar systems developing from coast to coast. They all will no doubt have direct connection with the FBI's National Crime Center.[43] These information systems are guilty of the same myopia of view and misconception of mission as California's and, therefore, subject to the same criticism. Structurally resistant to factors outside the system, even though they may actually bear more weight on the problem than those captured inside it, functionally deterministic to the point of making a criminal of the hapless person who is trapped, perhaps by mistaken identity, by the system,[44] the criminal justice information system is a prime example of the boomerang effect on the larger society when a subsystem is taken as an end in itself.

INFORMATION SYSTEMS AND THE INVASION OF PRIVACY

With benefits calculated in terms of efficient operation and costs so submerged as to evade proper calculation, information systems con-

---

[43] Robert R. J. Gallati, "The New York State Identification and Intelligence System," in *Information Technology in a Democracy*, Alan F. Westin, editor, Cambridge: Harvard University Press, 1971, pp. 40–47. Stanley Robinson, "The National Crime Information Center (NCIC) of the FBI: Do We Want It?" *Computers and Automation*, June, 1971, pp. 16–19.

[44] In a municipal court faced with twenty pages of calendar, it is likely that neither judge nor clerk takes time to indicate that the prosecutor dismissed a case because of proven mistaken identity. The only notification on the person's record will be *case dismissed*, an entry which could forever cast suspicion on him.

cerning everything from the scatological to the eschatological have become indispensable to management, public and private. Storage of records for rapid interrogation, search, and retrieval has, through constantly advancing mechanization and computerization, developed its own image, that of the "data bank." The very concept is imbued with virtue, for, associated with the values of the Protestant Ethic, it not only conjures up the bright, lively, and good things associated with banking generally — saving, interest, and the like — but it replaces the dreary and dusty archive. To the government agency and the private organization, the one in discharge of its duty, the other, in pursuit of its business, the data bank has become a reality and all of them are busily gathering all types of information about people. With "management science" rationalizing the data base and technology facilitating its growth and development, it is reasonable to imagine a state of Big Brotherhood unprecedented in a democratic society.

Government means regulation, and, in order to regulate, the government needs to know. As the administration of public affairs becomes more encompassing and more complicated, the areas in which controls may properly be exercised expand. So also do the opportunities for improper gathering and use. The government itself, in its personnel practices and other procedures, has been criticized for perpetrating "one of the most subtle invasions of privacy" through its information on American citizens.[45] An investigation conducted by the Senate Subcommittee on Administrative Practice and Procedure probed the inventory of information maintained by the U. S. government. The inquiry into the practices of the federal departments, independent agencies, and selected boards, committees, and commissions resulted in a report, titled *Government Dossier*,[46] and summarized as follows:

(1) Government contractors, consultants, and their employees are required to submit such information as the birthplace of parents, name, legal, investigational, and health data as a condition to securing a potential job and, in some cases, no confidentiality is extended on this data.

(2) The Selective Service System requires all registrants under the Universal Military Training and Service Act to supply legal and investigational information such as police records, security or other investigative reports, and any involvement in civil and criminal court action. All additional information such

[45] Edward V. Long (Chairman, Subcommittee on Administrative Practice and Procedure, Committee on the Judiciary), Foreword to *Government Dossier (Survey of Information Contained in Government Files)*, Subcommittee on Administrative Practice and Procedure, Committee on the Judiciary, U.S. Senate, Ninetieth Congress, First Session, Washington, D.C.: U.S. Government Printing Office, November, 1967.

[46] *Government Dossier (Survey of Information Contained in Government Files)*, Subcommittee on Administrative Practice and Procedure, Committee on the Judiciary, U.S. Senate, Ninetieth Congress, First Session, Washington, D.C.: U.S. Government Printing Office, November, 1967.

as religious or financial information is only required from those registrants seeking a deferment for such a reason.

(3) Certain agencies require their top or key employees to furnish certain financial information on a "Statement of Employment and Financial Interest."

(4) Form 57, credit reports, and agency personnel files contain an excessive amount of information about an individual such as the birthplace of his parents, his income and assets, and certain health information such as a personality inventory and alcoholism or drug addiction traits.

(5) Most medical and police forms require the individual to list his race. This would be permissible if it is used for statistical purposes only.

(6) Security clearance tends to require the individual to list most of the information cited in the questionnaire. However, since the individuals securing a clearance will have access to classified records, it is essential that this detailed information be obtained.

(7) Applicants for the Government's various grants and fellowships are required to usually divulge their police record, security, or other investigative reports, and any involvement in civil or criminal court action. This information appears to be excessive and nonessential as long as all academic requirements are fulfilled.[47]

The report called attention not only to the government's accumulation of nonessential or too detailed information but also to the possibility that current statutes and regulations were not providing adequate safeguards against misuse. The report could have been more emphatic in view of the fact that some agencies actually make a practice of selling lists of names and addresses. The California Department of Motor Vehicles, which keeps files on every driver, his license, vehicle registration, violations, court convictions, and accident reports, provides this information to insurance companies and other customers for a nominal fee.[48] The Federal Communications System, charged with licensing ham radio operators, sells their names to radio equipment companies for $55 per reel of computer tape. The Coast Guard sells names of its licensees to the boating industry; the Atomic Energy Commission, the Railroad Retirement Board, and the Department of Commerce are engaged in similar business. The Internal Revenue Service, withholding the names, supplies data indicating comparative income areas by zip codes. Aggressive merchants would find here ideal marketing information for bulk mailing addressed to "Occupant." More determined salesmen would not be daunted by the absence of names. Available to them through a software company is SAMS (Street Address Matching System), which can match and merge any two files whose common element is street address,[49] thus delivering precise identification of individuals. Technology has

[47] *Ibid.*, pp. 7–8.
[48] R. E. Montijo, "California DMV Goes On-Line," *Datamation*, May, 1967, pp. 31–36.
[49] Advertised in *Computers and Automation*, Vol. 19, No. 8, August, 1970, p. 65.

advanced even beyond this point. For a purchase price of $2,800, a Los Angeles company will deliver a system that can search a name file to locate persons of a particular ethnic group. ENID (Ethnic Name Identification System) is a ready-to-use program, purported to have greater efficiency than those written in FORTRAN and already at work.[50] In the face of such technological miracles, one cannot but shudder at how much more "efficient" Hitler and his evil henchmen would have been in their inhumanity toward a minority people.

The better to discharge their duties and in the name of achieving "efficiency of operation," all the agencies of government at every level are busily engaged in the collecting and storing of data. Some of it is positive, as, for example, the type collected by the Bureau of the Census. But even here, the resistance threshold is rising as the public and Congress become more sensitive about the limits of the government's right to know. Some of it is negative, as, for example, the kind gathered by the U. S. Army through surveillance of certain political activities. Exposed in hearings before the Senate Constitutional Rights Subcommittee [51] was the existence of Defense Department data banks in which the Army stores dossiers on 25 million American civilians who have expressed dissent in speech, writing, or by association and assembly. These persons are considered by the Army to "constitute a threat to security and defense" and included among those on the target list are Senator Adlai E. Stevenson 3rd and former Governor Otto Kerner of Illinois, as well as a host of state and local officials. Military justification for the Army's domestic intelligence gathering is that in the event of large-scale civil disorders, in which the military might be called upon to control the situation, information of this kind would be useful. The Senate Committee also learned that the U. S. Passport Office maintains a secret, computerized file of 243,135 Americans whose applications may be of interest to it or to other law enforcement agencies. Listed as items of such interest are the following categories:

(1) Individual's actions do not reflect to the credit of the U. S. abroad.
(2) Defectors, expatriates, and repatriates whose background demands further inquiry prior to issuance of a passport.
(3) Persons wanted by a law enforcement agency for criminal activity.
(4) Individuals involved in a child custody or desertion case.
(5) Delinquents or suspected delinquents in military service.
(6) Known or suspected Communists or subversives.

Since the State Department's primary function in issuing a passport is to verify American citizenship, the extra-curricular activities were re-

[50] Advertised in *Datamation*, Vol. 16, No. 11, September 15, 1970, p. 115.
[51] Senate Subcommittee on Constitutional Rights. Hearings on computers, data banks, and the Bill of Rights, February 23, 1971 to March 17, 1971.

garded by Senator Sam J. Ervin, Jr., chairman of the Senate Subcommittee and former judge on the North Carolina Supreme Court, as "beyond any reason whatsoever."

Another security data bank has come about through recommendations of the Warren Commission investigating the assassination of President Kennedy. The Commission Report suggested that the Secret Service be authorized to amass and digest information on who might threaten the President, members of his family, or high officials. On this basis, the Secret Service issued guidelines to federal and local law enforcement agencies with requests for this kind of information and more, as, for example, items about attempts to embarrass high officials; participation in civil disturbances; individuals seeking "redress of imaginary grievances, etc."; persons making "irrational" or "abusive statements" about high government officials; activities in connection with anti-American or anti-government demonstrations.

Not with the intention of mongering a scare but to protect borrowers from unwanted intrusion into their reading preferences, the American Library Association officially and publicly resisted attempts by agents of the Internal Revenue Service to gain access to circulation records in several large cities. The rationale for this monitoring was to search out the names of persons who had taken out books on explosives. Information was sought because of the proliferation of bombings across the country. The professional librarians, aware that police may have neither time nor talent for discrimination, realized that a roster of suspects could easily be expanded, especially in a climate of political suspicion, to such a degree that the public would feel uneasy about surveillance of its borrowing habits. Not only would they certainly eschew Karl Marx and others who might be considered revolutionary but, with Winnie-the-Pooh regarded as having psychiatric overtones, Madeline as indicating latent Lesbianism, and that once revered classic *Uncle Tom's Cabin* as an expression of rampant racism, their paranoia might be justified. It would all depend on *who* has "got a little list."

Police information networks stretch across the land; welfare information systems proliferate and, with the wider coverage resulting from such programs as distribution of food stamps and medical insurance coverage, will continue to draw even larger portions of population into their purlieu. Educational institutions have become counting-houses, with numbers of pupils processed, number of I.Q. tests administered, and number of teacher hours saved by automated devices the criteria for planning. That the quest for knowledge may have been lost in the pursuit of information is relatively less important than the fact that the school system maintains an up-to-date electronic data-processing setup that is a strong link in the cradle-to-grave records being accumulated on every individual in the country. The health of the nation presumably depends on nothing so much as facts and figures about everybody from birth to death and at all in-between stages. Although public programs, such as Medicare and Medicaid, have cost much and been of benefit to relatively few,[52] they have succeeded in one respect, *viz.*, the generation of vast files of information about people. Huge and complicated systems are being operated almost irrespective of the delivery of health services to the individuals about whom so much is known and so little done.

Just as every military and civilian agency, every official bureau at every level, is busily gathering and manipulating information about people, so also is every religious, social, and fraternal organization in the land. Information about people is big business, too. The Associated Credit Bureaus of America, for example, maintain credit files on more than 110 million individuals. The security and accuracy of these reports have become a matter of official concern for they contain "a volatile mixture of personal, sensitive, and public record information." Typically included are items of personal identification, employment, and personal history, such public records as arrests, lawsuits filed, judgments, marriages, divorces, and bankruptcies; and credit history showing size of accounts, slow payments, and defaults. In addition, special credit investigations through interviews with the employer, banker, landlord, neighbor, and fellow workers yield information about personal character, habits, and reputation.[53]

The publisher of 1,400 different city directories advertises that for almost 100 years it has been "in the business of keeping track of people — who and how many they are, where and how they live, where they work and what they do." [54] This big brotherly concern takes the form of city-wide, door-to-door canvasses in about 7,000 American communities. The materials gathered in this unofficial census then become the source record for printing the directories-for-sale and for preparing what is called "The Urban Information System." This, too, is for sale, eligible for federal funding, and available on tape for local processing or ready for merging, or cross-referencing with other data, stored in the company's files [55] or elsewhere, if such systems as the previously noted SAMS (Street Address Matching System) are used. H. and R. Block, Inc., a commercial income tax service which operates 4,000 offices and franchises

[52] Joel R. Kramer, "Medical Care: As Costs Soar, Support Grows for Major Reform," *Science*, Vol. 166, No. 3909, November 28, 1969, p. 1126–1129.
[53] Alan F. Westin, Prepared Statement for *Commercial Credit Bureaus.* Hearings before a Subcommittee of the Committee on Government Operations, U.S. House of Representatives, Ninetieth Congress, Second Session, March 12, 13, and 14, 1968, Washington, D.C.: U.S. Government Printing Office, 1968, pp. 16–17.
[54] R. L. Polk and Co., *Computerized Urban Information System*, a Presentation of the Urban Statistical Division, January 15, 1968, p. 25.
[55] *Ibid.*, p. 3.

and claims to prepare the returns for some eight million Americans annually, has been formally accused by the Federal Trade Commission of using illegally confidential information supplied by its customers in compiling lists of persons to be solicited for other business.

Information systems planned and in operation are capable of providing a full dossier on any individual. The table of particulars already looks something like this:

Birth	Date, place, name, age, legitimacy, country of origin, citizenship, and religion of parents.
Education	Schools attended, courses taken, grades, problems relating to attendance, performance, adjustment, and behavior.
Employment	Jobs held, when, where, how long; salaries; security clearance; official reason for termination.
Health	Immunizations, operations, hospitalizations, venereal disease, births, miscarriages, abortions (legal), prescription drugs regularly used; psychiatric care, public and/or private, commitments for institutional care; status vis-à-vis public health programs, e.g., Medicare, Medicaid; involvement with private group health programs, e.g., Blue Cross.
Crime	Traffic violations, misdemeanors, felonies, sexual offenses, drug abuses, alcoholism.
Military Record	Induction data, assignments, performance ratings, combat record, disciplinary actions taken, conditions of discharge from service.
Finances	Valuation of property owned, federal, state, and local tax data; credit history and rating; information on all types of insurance, health, accident, life, and automobile.
Affiliations	Professional, social, religious, fraternal.
Miscellaneous	Marital status; number of offspring; location, size, type, and condition of dwelling; foreign travel — visas held, countries visited, etc.[56]

Concern that such an accumulation of data might be more harmful than beneficial has been dismissed by information experts as sheer paranoia. One of the most revered of their number derided critics as afraid; he implied that perhaps they had something to hide. As proof of the self-satisfying virtues of probity, he boasted of having been investigated and cleared a number of times by the Federal Bureau of Investigation. For the population at large, however, such euphoric complaisance does not seem justified because of the properties of the input information and the possible abuses and misuses of the storehouse of data.

If one were to examine closely the categories listed above in the dos-

---

[56] The format used and many of the items included were suggested by M. E. Maron, "Large Scale Data Banks: Will People Be Treated as Machines?" *Special Libraries*, January, 1969, p. 5.

sier, one would find that there exists in each of them the likelihood of inclusion of information which is erroneous, inaccurate, incomplete, and outdated. Moreover, the reliability of some of the data might be subject to doubt because of the possibility of bias in its selection and interpretation. The occurrence of errors in dates, spelling, and simple fact is commonplace and widespread, likely to be compounded the farther the information moves from its source and the more times it is reprocessed and manipulated. Inaccuracies are made permanent, nuances and modifications obscured. Less obvious, more elusive of detection, and, therefore, more damaging are entries derived from questionable procedures or far from unequivocal personal judgments.

Under the category of *Education*, for example, it is customary to include teacher evaluations which, if not hasty and perfunctory, are likely to be projections of personal bias. Of more serious, long-run consequences are the I.Q. and personality test results frozen into the permanent record. Used as the basis by which students are classified for purposes of assignment to classes and courses of instruction, performance on Stanford-Binet and Wechsler has been for several generations of school children the crucial and determining factor in their educational, and, hence, their whole life, pattern. Only recently have the sensitivity of the tests, their appropriateness, and the competence of school psychologists to administer and interpret them been challenged. A suit was filed in the United States District Court in Boston on September 14, 1970, on behalf of a number of students and also as a class action in behalf of all children who might suffer from the alleged misclassification. Named as defendants in the suit, handled by staff attorneys of the Boston Legal Assistance Project and the Harvard Center for Law and Education, are city and state school officials. It charged that the Boston school system, through a faulty method of testing and classification, had mistakenly shunted large numbers of poor but normally intelligent children into special classes for the mentally retarded, thus causing irreparable harm because they could not receive the education they needed. Insensitive and narrowly-based diagnostic instruments have been shown to fail to take into account cultural differences and lack of facility in English; they do not distinguish between mental retardation and perceptual handicap or emotional disturbance. However the Boston lawsuit comes out, the information generated by such tests will lie heavy in the memory file.

If, for example, test results indicate learning disability or behavior problems, will the children become the target for the "new wave" approach to public education, in which amphetamines are used? With experimental school drug programs reported to be underway in Omaha, Nebraska, and Little Rock, Arkansas, a congressional investigation into the use of these dangerous narcotics on elementary school children has heard testimony from representatives of the National Education Association, the National Institute of Mental Health, and the Food and Drug Administration.[57] A number of moral and ethical, as well as medical and educational, issues emerged. Besides those dealing with the possible impact of such programs on the nation-wide effort to curb the use of narcotics, there are those concerning the harmful long-range effects on the youngsters themselves. Important in the context of our discussion in this chapter is the reliability of the information used to select the subjects for this experiment. By what norms or tests do the experimenters distinguish between "hyperactivity" and the mere over-activity of bright but bored children? How much weight is given to the evaluation by the overworked teacher who appreciates conformity rather than creativity and who would rather tranquillize than cope? What kind of follow-up tests will be used to ascertain the true results of this biochemical intrusion into the educational process and how will they be incorporated in the permanent record? Will the child, at age six, be tabbed as a drug user?

The category of *Crime* offers all kinds of opportunity for inclusion of mistaken, misinterpreted, and misleading information. In addition to the specific instances discussed earlier, we might mention that the maintenance of a life-long record on every individual would reverse the philosophy of the juvenile court. At present, because the primary goal is to protect the juvenile (and not society), certain records of offenses perpetrated by youngsters are expunged. Computerized maintenance of the life-long *vita* would make such selective obliteration of youthful misdeeds impossible, and offenders would carry and pay for the rest of their lives for peccadilloes better forgotten. Some of the consequences come readily to mind. Young lawyers about to face the bar have to certify that they have never been arrested; they would not be allowed to practice their profession, because of a youthful encounter with the law. Some young men, eager to enlist in the armed forces, have concealed a police record and been court-martialed for the attempt.

Many people have become known to the law through arbitrary police action enabled by statutes. Until very recently, for example, a regulation in New York State allowed the arrest of any person who "loiters, remains, or wanders in or about a place without apparent reason and under circumstances which justify suspicion that he may be engaged or about to be engaged in crime." The statute, used by police to ar-

[57] House of Representatives, Ninety-first Congress, Second Session, Subcommittee of the Committee on Government Operations, "Federal Involvement in the Use of Behavior Modification Drugs on Grammar School Children of the Right to Privacy Inquiry," September 29, 1970.

rest persons they suspected of criminal acts or of plans for such behavior, was declared unconstitutional in September, 1970, by a criminal court judge, who called it a subterfuge by which police could arrest
and search people without probable cause. A good law to have on the
books when police want to conduct a roundup, the regulation of loiter-
ing no doubt added many items to individual dossiers before it was
overturned. New and stringent federal legislation, enacted in mid-1970
by Congress, included features that are bound to bring many more
persons into the system and add entries into their dossiers. First, there
was authorization for "no-knock" search, in which a police officer with
a warrant can enter a home or building without knocking or identifying himself if he believes that evidence may be destroyed. Second, there
was preventive or pre-trial detention which allowed for the incarcera-
tion of criminal suspects up to sixty days, if on the basis of their record
the judge deemed them likely to commit other crimes while awaiting
trial. Third, there were sections under which juveniles under sixteen
could be tried in the regular courts, would have no right to trial by
jury, and could be found delinquent on the basis of "a preponderance
of evidence." That changing legislation affects the dossiers of untold
thousands of persons is portentously clear.

Questions regarding the uses and users of all this information have
yet to be answered satisfactorily. It is already apparent that data sup-
lied and gathered for one purpose and in one context frequently appear in another, where they may be inappropriate or improper. Used
as a basis for projection and planning, they may be misleading; used
as an instrument of coercion and control, they may be downright dangerous. One merely has to turn back a page or two in time or move the
pointer on the globe to realize how powerful a weapon such an accumulation of information could have been to Hitler and how it could
be used by those who, like him, would govern by repression, retribu-
tion, and reprisal. Under certain circumstances, no one is safe. With
technology as the potent aid, selection for control could be based on
such conventional characteristics as race, color, age, sex, income, religion, or political posture. With advances in medical and psychological
technology, genetic, behavioral, and cerebral processes could be subject to modification through drugs if not by even more sophisticated,
post-1984 devices, such as implanted electrodes and remote computer
control, already successfully achieved by Professor Delgado in his experiments with higher primates.[58] Even under the most benevolent
regime the possibilities for misuse, through intent or sheer ignorance,
are enormous. Nor are the potentialities for abuse limited to the po-

[58] José Manuel R. Delgado, *Physical Control of the Mind*, New York: Harper &
Row, 1969.

litical arena. Drawn by piles of raw data and enchanted by what they regard as an exciting new research tool, social and behavioral scientists are busily and determinedly engaged in the massing and manipulation of information about people and their private lives. In the name of science they are exhibiting a greed far in excess of their need or capacity for meaningful absorption of data.

THE NATIONAL DATA BANK

To discuss the Federal Data Center is not to beat a dead horse. Although squelched in capital letter form by lack of congressional approval several years ago, the concept of a federal data center in another, lower, case is far from defunct. With the information systems associated with the government's regular order of business and those being developed for its extraordinary activities growing inordinately, the issues are still alive, the more so because linkage between and among them is a simple technical matter. The federal data bank, irrespective of its formal capitalization, poses problems of great public concern.

The engineers who design information systems might, in the name of efficiency, be expected to demonstrate preoccupation with the technical aspects of storing and retrieving data and insensitivity to the wider consequences and implications. But such trained incapacity is not appropriate for social scientists and suggests that perhaps they have been seeing the mote in their brother's eye while neglecting the beam in their own.[59] For the "soft" scientist, the temptations of technology are, apparently, as irresistible as to his "hard" brothers. It was a group of highly respected economists, econometricians, political scientists, and such who deliberately promoted the development of a National Data Center, which the Bureau of the Budget proposed, in 1961, as the way to centralize and computerize the numerous personal records now scattered throughout various federal agencies. Known as the Kaysen Committee, the Task Force was asked to consider measures which should be taken to improve the storage of and access to U.S. Government statistics.

After reviewing the shortcomings of the present statistical system and itemizing its inadequacies and inefficiencies, the committee strongly recommended creation of a National Data Center with responsibility for the following:

(1) Assembling in a single facility all large-scale systematic bodies of demographic, economic, and social data generated by the present data-collection or administrative processes of the Federal Government;

(2) Integrating the data to the maximum feasible extent, and in such a way

[59] Matthew VII: 3, 4, 5.

as to preserve as much as possible of the original information content of the whole body of records;

(3) Providing ready access to the information, within the laws governing disclosure, to all users in the Government and, where appropriate, *to qualified users outside the Government on suitably compensatory terms*. (My italics.) The Center would be further charged with cooperation with state and local government agencies to assist in providing uniformity in their data bases, and to receive from them, integrate into the federally generated data stock, store, and make accessible, the further information these agencies generate. The funding and staffing of the Center should recognize both these functions.[60]

Architects and proponents of the proposed National Data Center saw in it a harnessing of a technology which offered "a new kind of capability in servicing the requirements of public policy and public management for statistical information"; they thought that this capability was "an order-of-magnitude different from any capability in the past"; they were convinced that it promised a "major 'pay off' in improving the public and private decision process, and in improving research aimed at improving our understanding of the social process." [61] In their enthusiasm for the proposed system, they failed to recognize its implications, both with respect to an assured cradle-to-grave surveillance and for further erosion of personal privacy. They also made a number of assumptions: that the Center would improve the quantity, quality, or availability of reliable data; that functioning of and decision-making in government agencies supplying and being supplied by the Center would be improved by the centralization and integration of information-gathering and processing; that the Center would be a cornucopia of worthwhile social and economic data for research purposes.

Congressional hearings [62] and a subsequent investigation sponsored by the Computer Science and Engineering Board of the National Academy of Sciences [63] indicated that the Task Force's complacency over privacy

[60] Carl Kaysen, Chairman
    Institute for Advanced Study
Charles C. Holt
    University of Wisconsin
Richard Holton
    University of California (Berkeley)

George Kozmetsky
    University of Texas
H. Russell Morrison
    Standard Statistics Company
Richard Ruggles
    Yale University

"Report of the Task Force on the Storage of and Access to Government Statistics," *The American Statistician*, Vol. 23, No. 3, June, 1969, pp. 15–16.

[61] Edgar S. Dunn, Jr., "The Idea of a National Data Center and the Issue of Personal Privacy," *The American Statistician*, Vol. 21, No. 1, February, 1967, p. 21.

[62] *Privacy and the National Data Bank Concept*, Thirty-fifth Report by the Committee on Government Operations, Ninetieth Congress, Second Session, August 2, 1968, Union Calendar No. 746, House Report No. 1842, Washington, D.C.: U.S. Government Printing Office, 1968.

[63] This two-and-a-half year study, initiated in early 1970, is directed by Alan F. Westin, Professor of Public Law and Government at Columbia University.

was not universally shared. Explored and exploded were the myths of technological security and procedural sacrosanctity. Computer experts testified that there were no foolproof locks and that, moreover, ease of access, and not the opposite, was the benchmark of the efficient system. Legal authorities could offer little hope of protection, for the law is known to be a notorious laggard with respect to technology, with no redress forthcoming until after damage is claimed and proven. Privacy, it seems, is still a nonlegal concept, much of the history of privacy in the law still being ahead of us, according to one opinion.[64] Protective legislation would be long in coming, for the legislative process needs a great deal of lead time while technological development occurs rapidly. Westin has indicated, nonetheless, that, ultimately, the safeguards will have to be of a legal nature, with an independent regulatory agency to enforce proper controls.[65] Suggested as necessary precautions were "reasonably precise standards," legislated by Congress, reinforced by statutory civil remedies and penal sanctions.[66]

Articulated as guidelines were: limitations on the information which can be extracted from private citizens by federal agencies; prohibitions against recording any information without specific authorization from Congress; opportunity for individuals to review and challenge entries; and storage of information according to "sensitivity" or "accessibility," with access keys assigned to government officials so that they can reach only those portions of the center's files that are relevant to their particular function. That which is done properly, that is, within the limits of existing laws, is not necessarily identical with that which is right, a moral matter, nor with that which is done right, a procedural matter. For all his faith and trust in the law, Westin made a plea for socially conscious information-keepers and a code of ethics for the computer profession.[67] Concerned with human rights throughout the world, the United Nations issued a statement, prompted by the proposed National Data Center, but worth pondering in connection with all information systems, large and small:[68]

One of the important features of a democratic government is the doctrine of the separation of powers which makes it difficult for any branch of the government to jeopardize the fundamental rights of the individuals. Certainly, at present, the multiplicity of agencies and procedures and the resulting red

[64] Clark C. Havighurst, Foreword, *Law and Contemporary Problems*, Vol. 31, No. 2, Spring, 1966, p. 251.

[65] Alan F. Westin, *Privacy and Freedom*, New York: Atheneum, 1967.

[66] Arthur R. Miller (Professor of Law, University of Michigan), "The National Data Center and Personal Privacy," *Atlantic*, CCXX, November, 1967.

[67] Alan F. Westin, *op.cit.*, p. 326.

[68] Commission to Study the Organization of Peace, *The United Nations and Human Rights*, Eighteenth Report, August, 1967, pp. 42-43.

tape protect the individual against undue invasion of privacy by making it more difficult for various government officials to know enough to cause real trouble. But if all the available data are integrated and stored in a computer in a way permitting instantaneous access to the record of each person, a sword of Damocles is going to hang all the time over the head of everybody. Even the best of us have done something which can be easily blown up out of proportion, or have offended somebody who would be glad to deposit a little misinformation in our file. In addition, there is always the possibility of misfiling, of mistaken identities, or pure spite and vindictiveness of casual acquaintances with warped personalities. On the other hand, it seems quite impossible to envisage a process which would purify the data in the computer through properly protected legal proceedings. Considering the effort required to check the incomplete data which are now available to various agencies, when they have to decide on the employment of persons in positions which are sensitive from the point of view of national security, we can easily see that there are not enough investigators, funds, and, in case of dispute, judges to deal even with one-hundredth of the problem. It is, therefore, doubly important to consider the advisability of the whole scheme and, in case of its execution, to provide sufficient safeguards with respect to the maximum accuracy of the data, their confidentiality, access to them, and the permissibility of their use in situations involving an invasion of individual privacy.

Conclusion of the discussion on the privacy issue in the Federal Data Center will also serve as a fitting finale to considerations earlier in this chapter of that aspect of other information systems. Although Congress ruled against creation of the proposed center, society at large and the individual in particular can derive little comfort from the gesture. Hundreds of data banks at the various levels are bound to be linked with one another; the result will be both statistical and regulatory federal data centers. With information and its gathering, processing, and dissemination a profitable industry and a promising governmental activity, we may expect even greater commitment of public resources to information systems. A dénouement of the Federal Data Center should, therefore, serve as a useful reservoir of caveats about all information systems, for it exposes preconceptions and misconceptions rarely challenged and, hence, foreordained to be repeated.

The first item in the post-mortem has to do with the preservation of human rights and individual freedom. If a committee of such professional stature could have perpetrated "a gigantic oversight" by assuming that "protection of personal privacy was a given condition," [69] then society must be prepared for the worst from the hordes of unprofessional but technical information experts who design systems. Does the chairman of the Task Force differ to any reassuring degree from the

[69] Edgar S. Dunn, Jr., "The Idea of a National Data Center and the Issue of Personal Privacy," *The American Statistician*, Vol. 21, No. 1, February, 1967, p. 23.

sanguine computer designer who scoffed at "paranoia" when he dismissed as "the stuff of right wing ideology" [70] the possibility of oppression through invasion of privacy? Are the articles of faith expressed in a paper rationalizing the Task Force's recommendations sufficiently convincing and well-founded to merit adoption by our society?

Without decisively choosing one over the other of these ideological stances, and with full recognition that a government too feeble for the welfare of its citizens in some matters may be too strong for their comfort or even liberty in others, it is possible to believe, as I do, that the present balance of forces in our political machinery tends to the side of healthy restraint in matters such as these. After all, the very course of discussion on these problems, since the Center was first considered, supports this view. Accordingly, I conclude that the risky potentials which might be inherent in a data center are sufficiently unlikely to materialize so that they are outweighed, on balance, by the real improvement in understanding of our economic and social processes this enterprise would make possible, with all the concomitant gains in intelligent and effective public policy that such understanding could lead to.[71]

Even if we can all maintain calm confidence that "the present balance of forces in our political machinery tends to the side of healthy restraint," can we assume that the present balance will remain constant? Perhaps more to the point in the short run is the economic aspect. Item Three of the Task Force's recommendations promised to make available, "on suitably compensatory terms," ready access to the data. With records a lucrative business and information a valuable commodity, the ethics of the marketplace would prevail over "healthy restraint" in this as in all other matters in which public responsibility and private gain have been pitted against each other. Assuming that one were willing to accept the "risky potentials," is there any assurance that the proposed centralization of information will bring about "real improvement in understanding of our economic and social processes," "with all the concomitant gains in intelligent and effective public policy that such understanding could lead to"? An answer to this question can best be found by critical review of the previously-mentioned assumptions underlying the notion of the Federal Data Center.

To begin with, there was the preconception that the Center would improve the quantity, quality, or availability of reliable data. Actually, the Report assumed improvement without paying attention to quality control. Nowhere mentioned were the statistical techniques needed if data are to be of acceptable quality and properly analyzed. Without specific attention to the frame, the meaning of terms, the sampling variations, and the major sources and amounts of bias, the mass of

[70] Carl Kaysen, "Data Banks and Dossiers," *The Public Interest*, Spring, 1967, p. 60.
[71] *Ibid.*

data has dubious value. According to R. A. Fisher, an authority in the field, the interpretation of data must be made in terms of the physical arrangements under which they were generated and gathered. If, for example, the theory of random sampling was not applied during the collection stage, then the theory of probability and statistics cannot be applied to their interpretation. Divorcing the interpretation of data from the explanation of how they were gathered and processed has been seen as a "fatal defect" of computerized systems to date.[72] The plan for a Federal Data Center made no mention of the quality of the data at source and as output. Nothing was said of the need for scrutiny of such data-gathering instruments as questionnaires and fact sheets, often so poor in design and fuzzy in conception that they defy honest, unambiguous response. No thought was given to the technical excellence of the sampling plans. Perhaps this was simply assumed as were the professional qualifications of the persons who would collect, process, and interpret the data. Professionally competent though the members of the Task Force were, they neglected or took for granted these aspects of quality. These are fundamental, for they relate to the uncertainties in the data, to accuracy, precision, and validity, and to whether their quality is such that they can serve as a reliable basis for estimates, interferences, and decisions.

Secondly, there was the presupposition that integration of information gathering and processing would improve efficiency in the functioning and decision-making of the participating agencies. Actually, decentralization is being prescribed as a promising antidote to growing unwieldiness of government. It is difficult, therefore, to accept as persuasive the argument in favor of centralization. Forgotten in the enthusiasm for "efficiency" is the fact that a sound statistical program is intrinsic and vital to the workings of any agency. Separation of this function from the agency would not only deprive officials of an essential tool in their decision-making but even divert resources perhaps better used for maintenance, control, and meaningful utilization of data at home base.

The important point has been made that Congress created the existing agencies for specific purposes and empowered them to collect the data needed to achieve those objectives.[73] As agencies differ in function and mission so also do their data needs and their data collection intricacies. There is nothing to support the contention that compatibility

[72] This and many of the points of incisive criticism are suggested by A. C. Rosander, "Analysis of the Kaysen Committee Report," *The American Statistician*, Vol. 24, No. 1, February, 1970, pp. 20–25. Dr. Rosander was for thirty years a supervisory mathematical statistician in the Bureau of Labor Statistics, the War Production Board, the Internal Revenue Service, and the Interstate Commerce Commission.

[73] *Ibid.*, p. 21.

of the data or coordination of the statistical function is necessary or even desirable. In addition to the attenuation of quality control, an increase in expense and in delays would be likely as centralization and reconciliation of non-compatible systems occurs. Far from reducing total processing costs and streamlining operations, the establishment of a center would necessitate preparation and storage of twice as much tape as before as well as a system of liaison for communication and feedback.

The assurance of eradication of duplication always receives a ready welcome in the political and bureaucratic environment. Efficiency of operation is an attribute highly prized by any administration and goes hand-in-hand with the current popular trend toward "rational planning" through management science. Major reorganizations in government structure have been instituted as a remedy for duplication, redundancy, and overlap. Similarly, redistribution of function may expect the same kind of ready support, so universally accepted have become the favorable stereotypes about streamlining, so convincing the singularity of purpose achieved through efficiency. That redundancy may actually contribute reliability of performance to a system and enhance its adaptability rarely enters into the calculations of planners. This insight, developed in a thoughtful article,[74] may well be the crucial fork in the road where rational planners and realistic social scientists part, with the former building their models of perfect systems for perfect men and the latter recognizing that beyond the simulation lie the humans, fallible, capricious, and unpredictable. The crux of Landau's argument provides a fitting cap to the discussion concerning the streamlining of functions in general and the prospective contribution to that end by the Federal Data Center in particular:

At one and the same time, redundancy serves many vital functions in the conduct of public administration. It provides safety factors, permits flexible responses to anomalous situations and provides a creative potential for those who are able to see it. If there is no duplication, if there is no overlap, if there is no ambiguity, an organization will neither be able to suppress error nor generate alternate routes of action. In short, it will be most unreliable and least flexible, sluggish, as we now say.

"Streamlining an agency," "consolidating similar functions," "eliminating duplication," and "commonality" are powerful slogans which possess an obvious appeal. But it is just possible that their achievement would deprive an agency of the properties it needs most — those which allow rules to be broken and units to operate defectively without doing critical damage to the agency as a whole. Accordingly, it would be far more constructive, even under condi-

---

[74] Martin Landau, "Redundancy, Rationality, and the Problem of Duplication and Overlap," *Public Administration Review*, July/August, 1969, pp. 346–358.

tions of scarcity, to lay aside easy slogans and turn attention to a principle which lessens risks without foreclosing opportunity.[75]

The third presupposition about the Federal Data Center was that it would provide a reservoir of worthwhile social and economic data for research. This enticement appeals to those whose research appetite is whetted by profusion. On second thought, even the most quantitatively oriented of them would agree that, without a carefully conceptualized design, mere availability of a storehouse of data is almost worthless for careful research purposes. The analysis and the interpretation of statistical data cannot be divorced from their collection without sacrificing the essential quality controls. R. A. Fisher's strictures about the handling of data are more applicable today, in an era when matrices are huge and standard tests of significance anachronisms, than thirty-five years ago. To assume, therefore, that the mere aggregation of quantities of data would serve research purposes was a manifestation of wishful thinking if not disingenuousness. In extolling the Elysian prospect, the chairman of the Task Force, it may be recalled, went so far as to list as a certain beneficial outcome "the real improvement in understanding of our economic and social processes this enterprise would make possible, with all the concomitant gains in intelligent and effective public policy that such an understanding could lead to." [76] Inherent in this statement are the apriorisms that such information as that residing in the Federal Data Center, or in almost any data bank for that matter, can automatically be translated into significant research materials, that the missing ingredient for "improvement of our economic and social processes" is more information, and that, once an understanding of those processes is achieved, "concomitant gains in intelligent and effective public policy" will follow. This scenario fits better the simulated, optimized world of the formal model-maker. The stuff and substance of intelligent and effective public policy demand far more than a data-juggling approach. Wise humanitarian planners have much to reckon with: the economic and political balances of power at home and abroad; shifting sources of pressure as public concern is aroused over specific international, national, and local issues; rapid and profound changes in attitudes and expectations of the citizenry vis-à-vis government; growing self-determination on the part of certain minorities, demanding recognition and rights; the incalculable, immeasurable, and unpredictable social values which are so elusive of identification and definition and yet which must play the decisive role in intelligent and effective public policy now and in the future.

[75] *Ibid.*, p. 356.
[76] Carl Kaysen, *op.cit.*

[8]

Futurology and the Future of Systems Analysis

FORECASTING THE FUTURE
THROUGH SYSTEMS TECHNIQUES

Applied in the future tense, systems analysis takes on new and portentous proportions. When used as the methodology by which to "study," "design," or "forecast" the future, its techniques carry with them all the pitfalls and shortcomings of their applications in the present and the added difficulties attendant on "studying" something that has not yet happened. Lacking knowledge of what is yet to come, social forecasters attempt to achieve a future perfect state by devising a "rational" plan even though, as we have seen, their methods have not contributed demonstrably to a better present. In their endeavor they are, nonetheless, encouraged and abetted by all those who yearn for the orderly future as relief from the chaotic present. For the systems entrepreneur in search of new markets for his reservoir of restless talents, futurism invites unfettered play of imagination.

Just as systems analysis of the conventional type offered an enticing grab bag to practitioners with wide diversity and background, the art of designing the future has attracted an even greater heterogeneity. Arrogating to themselves the task of creating a better world, philosophers, urban planners, sociologists, economists, engineers, and many others have banded together in societies of which the leaders, prone to quote one another reverentially, bask in the glow of mutual adulation. With their conferences proceeding in cybernetic fashion, each one's result causing another to occur, futurists engage in solemn methodological discourse. Uninhibited by time or space, they indulge in simulations that range from the presumptuous to the ludicrous, a description the more apt when one recalls its derivation from Latin, *ludi*, meaning *public games and spectacles*. They posit a supranational model in which nations will behave more rationally than the people who populate them. They blithely overlook the eternal struggle for existence that makes coexistence a chimera. The design of the future "one world" demonstrates even more glaringly the gap between the perfection of the system dreamed up by the international jet set intellectuals and the imperfections which are the down-to-earth realities.

The more ambitious the model, the more likely is the fraternity of futurists to ignore fatal flaws and defer to it as a landmark. Such, for example, has been Forrester's computerized simulation of a city.[1] Demonstrated here was the fact that only the most arbitrary assumptions, for example, unchanging environment, no suburbs, and external funding, could make the model "work." The procedures used by Forrester to compare alternative policies were, contrary to the systematic and methodological pretensions of the exercise, intuitive, policy being adjudged desirable or undesirable without elucidation as to the basis for such evaluations. In his comment on the role of computer simulation models in the design and testing of alternative urban policies, one reviewer of Forrester's work observed that

there are risks in the extension of "systems analysis" to social problems: it requires both extrapolation of inadequate behavioral theories and assumptions about subjective values. The impressive combination of confident technician and massive IBM computer must not be allowed to obscure those risks.[2]

THE STATE-OF-THE-ART OF FUTUROLOGY

In view of the limitations with respect to one simulated city, extension of the technique — in space, to include all cities, the nation, the world, or the universe; and in time, to encompass the rest of this century and part of the next — might seem ill-advised. And yet this is the determined activity of a number of organizations. One of them, the Club of Rome, is attempting to "simulate the reality of the world through mathematical insight." Funded by the Volkswagen Foundation, the group uses the Forrester model as its prototype. Its computer technologists having arbitrarily selected five main values as the ones important in the whole world, interlinkage is made by some eighty nonlinear equations "devised from the best information available in the international organization." The ultimate objective of this ambi-

---

[1] Jay W. Forrester, *Urban Dynamics*, Cambridge: MIT Press, 1969.
[2] James Hester, Jr., "Systems Analysis for Social Policies." Review of Jay W. Forrester's *Urban Dynamics*, *Science*, Vol. 168, No. 3932, May 8, 1970, p. 694.

tious undertaking is "to find ways to project which institutions and which processes will be necessary if we are to reach the point where there is some global management of the whole world."[3] Presumably, management is the *summum bonum*, and everyone on the face of the globe will live happily ever after in the computerized paradise engineered with benevolence aforethought.

The systems approach attacks the future in much the same way as it deals with the present. There is the same pseudo-serendipity that "discovers" paths long trodden; there are the same tools and techniques, used now, however, without the few constraints imposed by real-life tests in the present. There are the data banks, which, according to the futurist's handbook, must be appropriately stocked and organized and related to formal models of important dynamics. The fancy guesswork, with all its technological embellishment, of simulation and gaming, Delphi techniques and scenario construction, will serve to "invent credible paths between present conditions and hypothetical future states."[4] Embedded in this bill of particulars are many normative, methodological, and unsupported presuppositions. The assumptions are also made that information in data banks is, or can be, appropriate to needs not yet defined and organized according to specifications not yet delineated; and there are formal models both adequate and so future oriented that they anticipate what may at some later point in time prove to be important dynamics. As in the case of conventional applications of systems analysis techniques, where the more the critical observer knows of the specific field, the less convincing he is likely to find the "technically" contrived solution to its problems, so with the assessment of the art of the futurist, the farther away in time and the more widespread the uncertainty, the greater is the ease of acceptance of the grand plan.

Notwithstanding professionalization of the soothsayers' and seers' auguries in the form of games and other Delphian devices, or even R. Buckminster Fuller's "comprehensive anticipatory design science," the design of the future is little more than an image projection, more revealing of its creator's *Weltanschauung* than of the form and direction of social changes ahead. The model he devises, whether he knows it or not, epitomizes the basic philosophical conflict between free will and determinism. The will exercised is, of course, his, for he has made

[3] Aurelio Peccei (Managing Director, Italconsult), "Models and World Systems," Berkeley, California, University of California, Institute of International Studies, Guest Lecture Series, *Prospects for a Future "Whole World,"* April 1, 1971 (mimeo).

[4] Marvin Adelson, "The Technology of Forecasting and the Forecasting of Technology," Santa Monica: Systems Development Corporation, SP-3151/000/01, April, 1968, p. 19.

a number of important value-laden judgments and choices. Determinism is displayed in the very conception and operation of the model. Based on and extrapolated from a view, however eclectic, of the known present, it has certain "logical" and, therefore, unavoidable conclusions, which, moreover, are in the nature of the closed loop of a servomechanism. The whole process of systems analysis, or social engineering, takes on a decidedly architectonic thrust when applied to the future. Because of the likelihood of prediction feedback and the opportunity for advocacy, open or covert, of a particular course of action, the methodology provides the makings of a self-fulfilling prophecy. Popper reminds us of the influence that prediction may have on the predicted event and calls it the "Oedipus effect." [5]

Bertrand de Jouvenal describes the process as follows:

Any so-called "prediction" is always a starting point for examination of what *should be done on the assumption that it is true*, but always also *an outcome of assumptions concerning what will have to be done to make it come true*.[6] (My italics.)

Self-fulfillment is bound to come about when the essential components that are selected are organized in such fashion as to make the prediction come true.

Systems analysts and other futurists who have taken upon themselves the task of designing a better future seem to regard the undertaking as their private Promethean burden. Bauer, for example, describes the problem of foreseeing the future as among the most difficult and unsolved as any with which man is confronted. "Yet it is a problem which is inescapable," he avers without, however, supplying the reason for having assumed a task so thankless and hopeless. His exposition comes to the conclusion that a possible solution must be attempted "no matter how poor the result." [7] The assumptions built into the logic here and elsewhere in the futurists' approach are that the future can be "studied" or "foreseen"; that there are methods by which to predict social change; that social change should be planned and controlled, even though the techniques are admittedly crude and the results "poor"; that application of their "rational" procedures will guarantee a better future than some other, perhaps less "rationally" devised.

Unravelling the mystery of the future was once the bailiwick of sooth-

[5] Karl R. Popper, *The Poverty of Historicism*, London: Routledge & Kegan Paul, 1957, p. 13. In the legend, Oedipus killed his father, whom he had never seen; this was the direct result of the prophecy that had caused his father to abandon him.

[6] Bertrand de Jouvenal, "Notes on Social Forecasting," in *Forecasting and the Social Sciences*, Michael Young, ed., London: Heinemann, 1968, p. 120.

[7] Raymond A. Bauer, "Detection and Anticipation of Impact: The Nature of the Task," in *Social Indicators*, Raymond A. Bauer, ed., Cambridge, Massachusetts: MIT Press, p. 17.

sayers with omens to scrutinize, seers with crystal balls, and astrologers with their charts. The Cumaean Sybil and the Delphian Oracle of antiquity are the old mythology. The new mythology has developed its own shibboleths. The mystique of futurism purports to study the future scientifically, explore alternative futures rationally, and thus design the best of all possible futures. In assuming that that which has not yet happened can be studied, the futurists proceed without acknowledging their intellectual indebtedness. Actually, they follow the footsteps of philosophers of history, especially those historiographers who have tried to discern and analyze recurring patterns of the past as referents for the pattern of the future.

Oswald Spengler traced the decline of many civilizations and foresaw decay and ruin as inevitable.[8] Toynbee's hypothesis [9] was that civilizations crumbled when they failed to meet certain challenges. The ray of hope that would save twentieth century Western man was the salvation to be achieved through religious penitence. For Sorokin,[10] whose cultural dynamics were derived from a kind of Hegelian dialectic, religion itself was a manifestation of the prevailing social and cultural *Zeitgeist*, and neither extraneous to nor exerting influence on it. As a result of the inexorable "law of immanent causation," religion and all other manifestations of experience in the Sensate period, which Sorokin designated as ours, are sensual, secular, and non-transcendental.

That no one true pattern of social change has emerged from attempts at systematic study of the past is manifest in the internal inconsistencies within the divergent theories, the contradictions among the theorists, and the generally Procrustean treatment of intractable events of history resistant to the pre-set mold into which the historiographers tried to cast them.[11] Hindsight seems to suggest that the clue to predicting most accurately the shape of things to come lies in the rare and brilliant intuition that identifies a key dynamic aspect of the social order and perceives its potential developmental significance. James Bryce [12] for his time, Gunnar Myrdahl [13] for our time, and Alexis de Tocqueville [14] for all time exemplify the durability, if not permanent verity, of forecasting based on the combination of social insight, experience, and judgment. Their approach may not have been necessarily right, but because it made no pretensions to "rational," "scientific," or "logical" methodology, it

[8] Oswald Spengler, *Decline of the West*, New York: Knopf, 1929.

[9] Arnold J. Toynbee, *Civilization on Trial*, London: Oxford University Press, 1946.

[10] P. A. Sorokin, *Social and Cultural Dynamics*, Boston: Porter Sargent, 1957.

[11] Karl R. Popper, *The Poverty of Historicism*.

[12] James B. Bryce, *The American Commonwealth*, London and New York: Macmillan, 1888.

[13] Gunnar Myrdahl, *An American Dilemma*, New York: Harper and Brothers, 1944.

[14] Alexis de Tocqueville, *Democracy in America*, Henry Reeve text, revised by Phillips Bradley, New York: Alfred A. Knopf, 1963.

could be readily evaluated and assessed, accepted or refuted, whichever seemed reasonable.

Such is not the case with the social forecasting performed by today's futurists whose expertness has not been demonstrated convincingly with respect to understanding the past or present. Their scholarly conferences and compendia of papers having bravely thrashed the straw man of conventional statistics for being unreliable and inadequate, they try to develop "social indicators," which will somehow provide macro-insights into the multiplicity of changes still to come. Ignoring the perils of linear curve extrapolations, they repeat old mistakes by establishing their conception of a firm and reliable data base which then becomes their springboard into the future. Their literature stoutly affirms that the indicators need not necessarily be quantitative, and, in fact, that it is desirable that the qualitative be considered. But their focus and emphasis belie their heroic assertions. They start ambitiously with the universe or Planet Earth but soon whittle out a few variables which they and their computers can handle comfortably.

The mythology of systems analysis accompanies its forward march into the future. Presented as though it had accomplished wonders and taken the guesswork out of planning, the technique is represented as the key and clue to the salvation of mankind on this planet. Those who sell this notion believe their own sales story and they are finding buyers among decision-makers in the far flung corners of the earth. What is new and portentous here is that invocation of "scientific" tools and techniques, which provide a dutiful and convenient rationale for whatever cause of action seems politically expedient, may stifle thoughtful research and experimentation. Heady with heterogeneous facts and shy of theory, the futurists may be directly or indirectly abetting the anti-intellectualism that has already gained considerable momentum in this country and abroad.

Through propagandistic promotion, iteration, and reiteration, the tools borrowed from technology and the techniques derived from a heterogeny of disciplines are not precasting the shaping of the future. As the accepted means for controlling and directing social change, they have transformed futurism from the cynical game of the men under the Iron Mountain,[15] and others in "think tanks" secret and not-so-secret, into a game plan for the social order to come. The players are experts, entrepreneurs, and social engineering buffs who have persuaded themselves and a gullible public into believing that the future can be studied, that their methods should be used even though "crude" and leading to

[15] *Report from Iron Mountain on the Possibility and Desirability of Peace*, New York: Dial Press, 1967.

"poor results," [16] and that the future designed through "rational" procedures will be better than its much maligned, disorderly, democratic alternative, arrived at through the presumed anarchy of social forces without vector.

SYSTEMS ANALYSIS IN SOCIAL PERSPECTIVE

It is important that we concern ourselves with systems analysis as it appears in the future tense; it is imperative that we keep our focus on the self-fulfilling prophetic propensities implicit in its present usage. We first must recognize systems analysis as more than an assemblage of techniques and methods but rather as a social phenomenon fraught with social significance, perhaps all the more because it is characterized by contradictions, internal and external. Even though its assumptions and presumptions lack empirical confirmation, it has, within a remarkably short time, developed into a pervasive methodological ideology. The state of its art paradoxically less advanced than that of many intellectual streams from which it has derived form but neither content nor discipline, it has been accorded a prestige not earned and a respect not demonstrably deserved. Its mentors the military and its models econometric, its credibility has somehow managed to survive the defrocking of McNamara and the plunge of his methods to the nadir of their popularity in the Pentagon as well as the disenchantment among economists over preoccupation with the technique that has won international kudos for their professional brethren. The very durability and resilience of the systems approach is a factor worthy of note in a review of its phenomenology.

Supposed to overcome the piece-meal fragmentation of other, more specialized approaches, the systems approach has provided a language that talks of total embrace of social processes and dynamics but delivers methods that reduce wholes to their arbitrary and often least important common denominators. Supposed to solve social problems, it has merely served to redefine them in a way amenable to the technical treatment. If, as we have observed in so many cases, an initial error was attributing to certain categories of events more precision than was warranted by their nature, then a cardinal sin was committed in the case of events that were human and social. Experience has shown that the orderly and predictable factors may, in the final analysis, be those of least importance in the dynamics and direction of social change.

Carried to logical extremes, emphasis on quantification could so limit and bias perspectives as either to distort and violate the essential nature of social problems by forcing them into a tractable soluble state or to

---

[16] Bauer, *op.cit.*

institutionalize and legitimize neglect of them or their vital parts. All but forgotten in the methodological game-playing is the fact that the systems approach was supposed to encompass in its comprehensive grasp all facets and not a limited aspect of the matter under consideration. Merchandised as a Space Age specialty, a precise and sophisticated set of tools, systems analysis has become the stock-in-trade of practically any individual or organization seeking a government grant or contract or engaged in a project. Its language is the life line of everyone who aspires to make his work appear systematic or technically sophisticated. Deeper probe reveals how thin lies the veneer of glossolalia over fuzzy conceptualization and hyperkinetic data accumulation. With emphasis of both buyers and sellers of systems on quantity, qualifications are nebulous and quality control of output nonexistent.

As an instrument of public policy making, techniques of systems analysis have encouraged emphasis on the wrong questions and provided answers the more dangerous for having been achieved through a "scientific" or "rational" means. The ultimate result is a systematic foreclosing of promising avenues toward possible improvement and reform. Contrary to being an instrument of innovation, the systems approach is essentially reactionary. By defining problems in terms accessible to the tools, systems analysis has encouraged systematic neglect of facets and variables which could be crucial in both their generation and amelioration. In most social problems, even those attributable in large part to technology, aspects amenable to technical treatment are likely to be less important than those which are culture-bound, value-laden, and honeycombed with a political power network.

Cost-benefit ratios, program budgeting, and other procedures have forced preoccupation with only limited and arbitrarily delineated facets of public affairs, with the objective more likely to be bureaucratic self-justification than the general social welfare. Supposed to produce economies in cost of government and efficiency in operation, the technology of systems analysis with its hardware and software has burdened government decision-makers with elaborate mechanisms which use vast resources of money, time, and energy without demonstrably cutting costs or improving efficiency. Despite the exquisite calculating capabilities of computerized accounting, there has been no serious attempt at a cost-benefit study of systems analyses conducted at government expense. No one in government can tell how much is being spent on information systems and cost-benefit studies nor how much is involved in the frenetic nationwide switch to often unworkable and possibly already obsolescent program budgeting. And even if the costs could be enumerated, the benefits would be nebulous.

The application of the techniques may yet result in game-plan government relevant primarily to its simulated and skewed model but unresponsive to a fast-changing society. While administrators may have become peculiarly susceptible to and satisfied with symbolic solutions, the public at large is becoming more acutely aware of its rights and could demand more tangible evidence of concern for its welfare. Perhaps herein lie the seeds of a coming social revolution, one in which the technologically contrived and perfected image of a well-being never experienced will be the prime target.

Dazzled by the panoply of "Space Age tools" and overcome by the panegyrics of systems analysis enthusiasts who have made public problem solving their business, administrators have been put on the defensive vis-à-vis their managerial efficiency. They have been captivated by the sophisticated techniques touted to be so potent elsewhere and try to improve performance, however ill-defined, by hiring outside experts as consultants. While use of outsiders to perform specialized tasks is not new, what is noteworthy here is the growing incidence of government-by-contract that removes from public officials responsibility of the decisions made. Because consultants are never held accountable for bad advice, the arrangement shields everyone from criticism. There is already substantial evidence of dependence on the strategem of hiring outside experts to perform systems studies as a political ploy to convey the notion of official attention even when action is not politically feasible or desirable. Moreover, because of the way in which systems analysis can be crafted to suit the occasion, the use of hired specialists may serve the politically useful purposes of masking bureaucratic ineptness and inadequacy, of providing support for a course of action already decided upon, or of working as a red-herring, diversionary tactic. Whatever else it accomplishes, the team of outside systems analysts, pre-empts function and funds which might otherwise have enabled professional research. "Captive by contract" research blunts the edge of justifiable inquiry and criticism and militates against exercise of intellectual autonomy that should be encouraged to make and keep government responsive to social and human needs. What is ominous is that there will always be willing mercenaries, some of them academic and all with an entrepreneurial bent interested in using closed-book, mission-directed analysis as a vehicle for personal fame and fortune. That this is happening at the very time that universities and institutions of higher learning are feeling the backlash of public disaffection may have significance the full dimensions of which are not immediately discernible.

The trend at all levels of government toward increasing involvement with private consultants has deeper implications than the sometimes mentioned threat to the Civil Service posed by circumvention of regulations through occasional hire of an outside specialist. Emerging as a factor in policy-making processes are the constituency of research institutes and corporations which, individually or in tandem, are becoming a kind of shadow government. Allocated contracts to execute the planning, design, implementing, and even evaluation of projects costing millions of dollars and thousands of lives, these techno-corporate entities have been seen as a force undermining the very form of government prescribed by the Constitution. Ready with a façade and made-to-order proposals designed to infuse confidence in their "systems capability," far-ranging consortia sometimes compete for and sometimes cooperate in transportation systems in the Northeast, low cost housing in St. Louis, rural development in Uruguay, and agricultural reform in Nigeria. Hired by and under the mission direction of regulatory agencies, consultive experts are in a position to perpetrate a kind of advocacy planning that has stunning potential for circumventing the checks and balances protective of the democratic process and influencing the shape and direction of domestic and foreign affairs. The selective examination and evaluation they perform lend the authority of technico-logical justification to regulations which may serve certain industries better than the commonweal. As adjuncts to advisory bodies, they are likely to be called on even more frequently in the future as public issues encompass considerations which are increasingly technological in nature. As they apply their skills in such situations, outside experts bring their own prejudices and predilections. In areas of social policy planning, consultants chosen for their "systems competence" could prescribe courses of action which could lead to a certain, but democratically unsafe and unsound, social order.

The game of musical chairs has long been played in government circles. Admirals and generals retire to become top potentates in industries that advise and sell their wares to the military. With every change in administration, the top echelons of appointees move out in a body. In recent years, many have joined research institutes, where they accept the commission to take on tasks which, as bureaucrats, they proclaimed were impossible. The advantage they distinctly enjoy in the new location is the freedom from the responsibility to provide workable, implementable, and realistic plans. As civil servants they had to fulfill certain obligations and meet some expectations; as freelance operators they have no such constraints and their output is subject not even to the modicum of quality control that may have been applied in the bureaucratic setting.

With the exodus to the consulting sidelines, there is the periodic influx of industry's best, armed with the latest tools and techniques for ensuring efficiency of operation. But, in the resulting blurring of lines between the public and private interest, the public's welfare receives low priority. The coalition of special interest and corporate power can influence decisions of far-reaching importance, with the pertinent considerations tailored to fit better the needs of certain select groups than the public at large. The role and function of government to protect the interests of the public become more and more attenuated as the key points in the decision-making apparatus are relinquished. Many regulations which should be enforced for the social good may be clearly uneconomical and not good business. But, when government accepts business as its model and economics as its decision-making means, and depends for guidelines on experts whose techniques have a strong bias, its goals are calculated with measuring devices of limited scope. In accepting and applying systems techniques, government planners have allowed the medium to become the message. The technique dictates the desiderata and assigns the priorities according to the pre-fabricated scenario.

While remarkably successful in becoming entrenched as the Space Age nostrum for society's ailments, systems analysis has not served as a likely cure for the aerospace industry's failing health. Having recognized its failure as a diversification tactic to supply job opportunities for the thousands of displaced workers, at least one representative has acknowledged that the systems management developed to such a high degree of sophistication in his business has little relevance in social concerns.[17] To suggest that systems analysis should not be hailed as the prime spinoff of the national space endeavor is not to belittle the accomplishments of the National Aeronautics and Space Administration nor any other bodies, public and private, that have engaged in the gigantic undertaking of getting men and instruments to the moon and beyond. Systems techniques, in myriad forms, may have played an important part in these activities. Certainly, the organizational skills displayed have been spectacular. But experience has shown that the methods are not universally applicable. Systems management, as applied in the Department of Defense and National Aeronautics and Space Administration, has little direct relevance in the social arena; social systems resist management. Social systems, as Lockheed's engineers discovered, are "complex, conflicting, and indefinable." [18] Their components cannot be treated like little black boxes and their goals are prismatic — a shifting mosaic of the society's values.

The variegated experts who have chosen to invade the market for systems studies and designs have been slower to acknowledge the inade-

[17] Dean S. Warren (Manager of Market Planning and Research for the Missiles System Division of Lockheed Missiles & Space Company), as quoted in "Humans vs. Hardware — A Critical Look at Aerospace as an Urban Problem Solver," *Aviation Week & Space Technology*, June 7, 1971, pp. 62–63.
[18] *Ibid.*

quacy of their tools for the job to be done. With technique their sole repertory, they ply their trade wherever there is a willing customer. And there still will be many. In the move into the systems field they have come from a heterogeny of intellectual backgrounds, in all of which certain bodies of theory and reservoirs of accumulated knowledge kept them within bounds. The farther from home base the experts have roved, the more attenuated has become the discipline. In fact, the less acquainted they were with the problem areas, the louder have been the pronouncements of the value of objectivity, the quality they were substituting for substantive knowledge. On this point, Popper's wisdom is especially cogent. He stresses the fact that scientific objectivity is not a product of the individual scientist's impartiality but rather an outcome of participation in a particular scholarly community based on the inculcation of standards of discourse and investigation as well as the public disclosure of methods and results.[19] So far as an individual scientist's objectivity can exist, it is not the source but the result of social or institutional arrangements governing the discipline. What passes, in the systems approach, for interdisciplinary effort turns out to be undisciplined activity, a game almost anyone can play. Nonetheless its advocacy assured through interest now vested, systems analysis and its surrounding methodology have become the prevailing style in public and private affairs. Even though fulfillment lags far behind iterated promise, proponents will entertain only those questions having to do with technical niceties.

Adherents of the approach usually counter critical review with an offensive: "What technique would *you* propose as an alternative to systems analysis?" "How would *you* improve systems to accomplish socially worthwhile purposes?" "To what better uses would you put systems analysis?" These questions, like the logic that prompts the technique, are inappropriate in the context in which they appear. The fact that they are raised at all indicates the extent to which the technological imperative enters into the phenomenology of the systems approach. They might appropriately be countered with, "Why should we use systems analysis in these matters at all?" "Why not explore means and methods better suited to the problem at hand instead of slavishly invoking techniques just because they are available?" Muddling through is probably safer in the long run than the wrong cure. Just because we have an arsenal of hydrogen bombs and powerful delivery systems need not mean that we search out a potential enemy to eradicate from the face of the earth. Similarly, we need not feel impelled to provide *ex post facto* justification through utilization of every technological device and development that springs from Aladdin's lamp. A technical

---

[19] Karl Popper, *The Open Society and Its Enemies*, pp. 405–406.

approach that may have served a useful purpose in one context may not be viable in another and may actually be detrimental.

The question we have asked in this research study is, "Are the techniques of systems analysis appropriate when we are dealing with problems which are essentially human and social?" The findings indicate that in their present condition they are not. And the direction in which they are developing promises little improvement. Refinement of methodology has led only to greater preoccupation with abstraction while the mythology that social problems can be solved remains unchallenged. In fact, this false assumption plays an important part in the perpetuation of the magic spell which promises a technology to solve social problems.

This is not to say that systematic approaches do not have a contribution to make to the understanding of social process and improvement of the social condition. The problems besetting mankind are plentiful, complex, and multi-faceted enough to provide challenge to and invite the commitment of professionals from a variety of disciplines. The clearly non-linear, normative, and value-laden dimensions of these problems need deter the efforts of only those experts who approach with predetermined solutions. The systems approach, if it is ever to become conceptually sound, must be a genuine multi-disciplined endeavor, in which contributions from the pertinent fields of knowledge are meaningfully synthesized, and not merely homogenized into a synthetic and symbolic language.

Based with some degree of confidence on the empirical evidence, the rebuttal to assertions of defensive support for current systems analysis as the answer to society's problems could state the known truth that, despite the methodological, systematic, and systemic pretensions of systems analysis and systems analysts, there is no single method for all problems for all people at all times. There is no cosmic scale solution. The appropriate approach is a function of the particular problem, the particular researcher, and the attendant circumstances. Each analyst must seek out, develop, and apply the particular set of tools required for the task at hand. The outcome of his work will probably not be perfect, but he will not feel called upon to rationalize his results or justify his course of action through manipulation of technicalities. Amendments and improvements will occur, if ever, on the real-life scene and not on the shadow screen reflecting the playing out of a scenario. To the oft-iterated counter argument that one should not criticize systems analysis unless one can supply something better, there is an answer — competent research and experimentation, with conceptualization first, technique last, and professional judgment always.

[9]

Imprint and Implications
of Systems Methodology

INTRODUCTION

There are good reasons to discuss so seemingly disparate an array of subjects as education, health, nuclear safety, and information technology contextually in this chapter. To begin with, and if for no other reason, they all represent prime targets for systems analysis in forms familiar in times past and in such future-oriented mutations as risk analysis and technology assessment. Moreover, some of the subject areas are foundation stones so basic to the social structure that anything affecting one has profound effect on the whole. More than contiguous, these areas are functionally related in ways that are vital to the working of society. But while each has its own, intrinsically different, characteristics, they all have been subjected to the same methodological treatment and by the same type, if not body, of experts. An apt description of this approach to problem-solving comes from A. Maslow:[1] if the only tool you have is a hammer, you tend to treat everything as though it were a nail. The task before us is to ascertain the effects of this hammering. What has happened seriously influences every facet of life on this planet and perhaps beyond and certainly for this and generations still to come.

Without belaboring points made in earlier chapters, we might do well to keep in mind some of the salient features of systems methodology in theory and practice: (a) it is intolerant of and even antagonistic to unquantifiable variables; (b) it contains a bias against social and human factors; (c) its ethic is that of the marketplace; (d) it is driven by technical optimism. Nonetheless, so firmly have the tech-

---

[1] Abraham Maslow, *The Psychology of Science: A Reconnaissance*, New York: Harper & Row, 1966.

248

niques established their synonymity with *rationality* that to criticize them is to condone the antonym, *irrationality*. Thus, not only have other approaches been delegitimized but a *cordon sanitaire*, setting off the area of concern as technical, has isolated the debate within arbitrary confines of a certain limited model. Quarantined in this way, the problem becomes the bailiwick of "technical" experts.

COST/EFFECTIVENESS IN EDUCATION

Perhaps nowhere are the effects of the dominant paradigm more socially significant than in the field of education, which is interactively cause and consequence of its temporal, spatial, and intellectual environment. Not unexpectedly, then, school administrations, anxious to achieve accountability and productivity as demanded by the prevailing industrial model, have applied the principle of cost/effectiveness to planning and operations at all levels. In this, they are not only abetted by the expert consultants to whom they have turned for advice, they are actually mandated by the agencies and organizations to which they look for support. With the ghost of PPBS (Planning-Programming-Budgeting System) still hanging over the budgeting process, education, competing against other services for state and local tax dollars, must perforce justify costs by displaying benefits. A multitude of management specialists has been engaged in this task, the technical knowhow generally taking the form of quantitative analysis. But while costs, like salaries, supplies, and overhead, are fairly easy to identify, opportunity costs are not. "Benefits" become more difficult to define and even harder to quantify in a society where the time-honored equation between schooling and success has been toppled by countervailing forces. Nonetheless, on the basis of calculations about cost/effectiveness, a case has almost always been made for some kind of technical fix, which could and did take any number of forms. This should come as no surprise. Daniel Bell, a Harvard professor known for his views on the post industrial society, has gone so far as to say that technology is "the instrumental mode of rational action,"[2] a position that paves the way for the introduction of television and computers in the schools, and microelectronics into every phase of our lives.

Paradoxical though it may seem, we are unable to ascertain precisely how the application of cost/effectiveness measures has affected the American public school system. Even though much of the money spent on education goes into record-keeping, data-gathering, and analysis of

[2] Daniel Bell, "The Social Framework of the Information Society," in *The Computer Age: A Twenty-Year View*, editors, Michael L. Dertouzos and Joel Moses, Cambridge, Massachusetts: The MIT Press, 1980, p. 167.

analyses, we still lack useful information with which to make sensible judgments. This deficiency may be attributed in large part to the funding practices of such government agencies as the National Science Foundation and the evanescent Department of Education. Themselves at the mercy of the Office of Management and Budget, they have tended to request and reward proposals for the development of methodologies for evaluating programs rather than direct evaluation of programs themselves. The focus has been deflected to *how to measure* rather than *what is being accomplished.* For the funding agencies, this kind of research lends itself more readily to inhouse processing procedures than does study of a type more innovative and less structured. Hence, the predilection for proposals dealing more with technique and less with substance. In this way agencies facilitate their own management of research, raise their own productivity and performance, and improve their own cost/effectiveness ratio. Providing useful information has no place on their list of priorities.

A National Academy of Sciences report,[3] largely ignored by the profession, actually pinpointed reliance on quantitative methodology as a problem and recommended qualitative techniques akin to those used by clinicians and historians in educing theory by observation, interviewing, and review. While these approaches might not establish clear-cut cause-and-effect relationships, they could, according to the report, aid appreciably in understanding impacts of various programs in real-life terms and would be "preferable to Procrustean distortion of phenomena to fit preferred methods in pursuit of spurious rigor." Unfortunately, the report has received scant recognition, probably because it does not conform to the popular model. It certainly has not attracted the support of professional schools of education, which, bent on improving their somewhat déclassé image, long ago adopted systems analysis techniques as part of their core curriculum. They thereby perpetuated the paradigm with all its limitations, for their students carry forth the message of the methodology as though it were gospel. By the same token, if ever we could have looked to the faculties of our institutions of higher learning for a broader, independent view, that likelihood has been diminished by cost/effective budgeting practices that rate courses by popularity and professors by "productivity." Ability to attract funds is not a minor consideration in some fields, and research institutes on and off campus are attuned to the marketplace. Academics, like all competi-

---

[3] Jeffrey R. Travers and Richard J. Light, eds., *Learning from Experience: Evaluating Early Childhood Demonstration Programs* (Panel on Outcome Measurement in Early Childhood Demonstration Programs), Committee on Child Development Research and Public Policy; Assembly of Behavorial and Social Sciences, National Research Council, Washington, D.C.: National Academy Press, 1982.

tors for dwindling research dollars, must abide by the rules of grants-manship. Put simply, the theme is, "Whose bread I eat, his song I sing." The fact that academic integrity is losing its meaning and is becoming little more than a negotiable anachronism has serious significance in situations, ever more numerous, where academics are called upon to serve as experts in such matters as risk analysis and technology assess-ment, for example.

At this point in the chapter we must still concern ourselves with the way cost/effectiveness measures have affected public school education, from kindergarten to college. On the one side, it imposed the "no frills budget"; on the other, emphasis on performance. These notions, cal-culated to save tax dollars by eliminating the waste, inefficiency, and featherbedding presumed to pad public payrolls, are consistent with the demand for accountability in schools. In some cities, budget re-duction has taken the form of eliminating elementary reading teachers, cutting library staff, curtailing book orders, dropping instrumental music instruction, and decimating psychological services as well as speech and hearing therapy, to mention only some of the items dubbed "expendable frills." While benefits to the budget may be palpable, costs to the community are incalculable. Deprived of art, music, books, per-sonal instruction, and after-school activities, schools in financially-pressed districts could revert to the status of "poor schools," as they were called before the advent of universal access to public education. They would also be the schools for the poor.

TECHNOLOGY AS "OPEN SESAME" TO EFFICIENCY IN EDUCATION

Costs having been cut, the effectiveness side of the ratio must be bolstered, and, for this, productivity is all-important. *Productivity* on the part of the school spells *performance* on the part of the students, with reading scores the prime indicator. Note that we do not mention ability to read or comprehend, nor do we refer to reading and writing habits. The national obsession with reading scores has yielded bizarre and unanticipated consequences. With due allowance for the vagaries of tests, reading scores, even when appearing to indicate some improve-ment, bear little relationship to ability to comprehend or interpret beyond a superficial level. A 1981 National Assessment of Education Programs[4] found that overall "inferential reasoning ability" of 13 to 17-year olds had declined in the 1970s. Countless school districts across the country have been forced to lower the reading requirement for high school graduation to junior high school levels to save their own and

[4] U.S. Department of Education, *Reading, Thinking, and Writing*, Washington, D.C., November 11, 1981.

their students' face. An eighteen-year deterioration in academic achievement as shown in statistics released by the College Entrance Examination Board strengthens the ominous signs of growing functional illiteracy. The National Assessment report declared, "A society in which habits of disciplined reading, analysis, interpretation and discourse are not sufficiently cultivated has much to fear." Also issued was the not too subtle warning that "in a world overloaded with information, personal and business advantage will go to the individual who can sort the wheat from the chaff, the important information from the trivial."

After eighteen consecutive years of no change or of decline, average Scholastic Aptitude Test scores did rise two points on the verbal and one on the mathematics segments. Hailed by some as a hopeful sign or even a turning point, the increase was deplored by William J. Bennett, chairman of the National Foundation for the Humanities. He saw in it an erosion of interest in the humanities, already evidenced in the spread of narrow notions of careerism and in the surge of experimental courses that catered to what Daniel J. Boorstin, the Librarian of Congress, has labelled "presentism." To counteract these trends, the National Endowment for the Humanities funded a $1.5 million "children's media" program, radio and television presentations of the classics "to put worthwhile materials in the marketplace of ideas to attract children's minds." Widespread aliteracy, i.e., the non-reading proclivity of the American public, indicates a change in attitude toward reading and a decline in the value of reading as a way to get information. How aliteracy affects the nation and what diminished reading skills mean cannot be accurately nor fully predicted, but there are signs. A study by the Comptroller General's Office[5] attributes the failure of millions of car owners to respond to offers of recall and free repair to their low reading proficiency. With nearly 128 million vehicles, tires, and related items known to be defective, the potential safety hazard is enormous. The Johnny who cannot read cannot drive safely either! The General Accounting Office has recommended lowering the reading level of the recall letters in the hope of increasing owner response rates.

The Library of Congress' Center for the Book is trying to promote books by disseminating reading lists on various topics. Television is the medium that carries that message. But here we see the principle of iatrogenesis in operation. The cure itself causes the disease. Television, introduced benignly as the technical fix to remedy the ailments of reading instruction, may not only have had deep-seated and far-reaching effects on learning behavior in and out of school but may also have

5 General Accounting Office, *Changes in the Motor Vehicle Recall Program Could Reduce Potential Safety Hazards*, Washington, D.C. GAO/CED–82–99, August 24, 1982.

paved the way for the technological invasion that was to follow. Despite, or perhaps because of, the plethora of studies and reports, we do not yet understand learning-teaching mechanisms, nor do we know the precise causal relationships among the factors involved. So preoccupied are we with quantifying causal relationships that we fail to acknowledge the reality, i.e., that television-watching can and often does interfere with school performance. Dr. Wilson Riles, State Superintendent of Schools in California, saw some connections, however. A survey of 500,000 students in the sixth and twelfth grades showed that the more a student watched television, the worse he did in school.[6] Dr. Riles observed that no matter how much homework the students did, how intelligent they were, nor how much their parents earned, the relationship between television and test scores was practically identical. He concluded that "for educational purposes, television is not an asset and it ought to be turned off."

An updated study commissioned by the Surgeon General corroborates the inverse relationship between education and television-watching among the American population-at-large. While statistics are subject to diverse interpretation and manipulation, there is no gainsaying the fact that television has become "the most important external factor in American life." The Surgeon General's report cited a survey showing that for large numbers of people television ranks third among all activities, after sleep and work, in hours spent watching.[7] It is almost inevitable then that television would not only influence opinions about almost everything but also eating patterns, buying practices, attitudes toward policemen, doctors, lawyers, behavior as to racial, sexual and family relations, and stands on public issues, national and international. Television has even created a curious inversion in our consciousness. Its reality becomes ours. What is presented on the screen becomes so real, in fact, that criminal justice is Kojak at work; the practice of medicine is encapsulated in "General Hospital," and even science is "show biz," only remotely related to the actual classroom or laboratory. This technical takeover is particularly ominous when we consider the warning by the National Assessment of Educational Progress of the dangers of information overload. Information technology, still in its infancy, has already ensnared large sectors of the population. The video screen is their main source of information about international events and national issues and their sole source of diversion and entertain-

6 *The New York Times*, "Coast Survey of Students Links Rise in TV Use to Poor Grades," November 9, 1980.

7 U.S. Department of Health and Human Services, National Institute of Mental Health, *Television and Behavior, Ten Years of Scientific Progress and Implications for the Eighties*, Vol. I, Summary Report, 1982, pp. 7–8.

ment. The Surgeon General proposes education as the last line of defense and, in resigned capitulation, recommends "television literacy" as the way "to counteract the possible deleterious effects of television and also to enhance its many benefits." Suggested are lessons on all facets of television technology and programming, such as camera techniques, format, narratives, commercials, and discussion about reality, fantasy, and television's effects. But this is quixotic, since it unwittingly furthers the cooptation of education by the media. Considering the nature of technology, and the technocratic predilection of "experts" inside and outside the school system, one cannot but regard these antidotes with skepticism. Designed as intervention procedures, they are actually conduits for easier penetration by more technology.

All in the name of "computer literacy," much effort and money are going into bringing electronics into the classrooms of America. The National Science Foundation, aggressively promoting its "Development in Science Education" programs, which reflect the exclusively technical orientation of its Division of Information Science and Technology, solicited donations of microcomputers from several manufacturers. The objective was to foster the use of computers in science education; the donors would enjoy certain tax benefits. Radio Shack, Atari, Inc., Digital Equipment Corporation, IBM, and the Apple Education Foundation promptly agreed to donate about $850,000 worth of equipment and materials. But that was only the beginning of the electronic penetration. Thanks to legislation officially entitled The Technology Education Act of 1982 but soon, and for obvious reasons, to be known as the Apple Bill, a plan was devised to put an Apple computer system in every elementary and secondary school in the United States. The legislation would allow manufacturers to deduct the market value, twice the production cost, of donated computers. As a result of this Act, the Treasury would lose about $15 million in tax revenues in one year, according to Congressional Budget Office estimates. The total donation would be valued at $200 to $300 million at retail prices. This gift would result in a tax saving to the company of somewhere between $35 and $75 million, depending on whether Apple paid at the maximum corporate tax rate of 46 percent. Beyond the advantages to the company of a tax saving, a major publicity coup and perpetual brand-name promotion, a move of this kind would have enormous societal significance. It would insure that a whole generation would be indoctrinated with the computer cult. Anyone familiar with B. F. Skinner's operant conditioning[8] cannot fail to see herein the makings of a reinforced control process passing for education.

[8] B. F. Skinner, *Beyond Freedom and Dignity.* New York: Alfred A. Knopf, 1971.

Are we overlooking the obvious when we fail to see that what is welcomed as an aid to public education may ultimately deprive us of an educated public? Experimenters at the Children's Learning Center at MIT have developed a computer language, LOGO, and provide a "computer-based learning environment" that they already see as obviating the need for teachers. With their view that the computer serves as "an agent for exposing the child to a set of possibilities for acculturation, whether in mathematics, in science, or in language itself," they raise the question whether "such demarcated institutions as schools make any sense." Seymour A. Papert, who heads the LOGO project, writes:

The presence of the computer is what will make a deschooled society possible and even necessary, because if my vision of the way computers will be used is realized, it will come into conflict with the rational structure of schools on every level, from the epistemological to the social.

Papert backs his prevision by a prediction:

The next few years will see an explosion in the number of privately-owned computers. Much more significantly, they are about to cross a power threshold that will support the LOGO-like use of them. When this happens, there will be for the first time, *a viable alternative to schools* and the possibility that education will once more become a private act.[9] [Emphasis added]

Swaddled in the polemic against public education as we now know it is a subtle *argumentum ad hominem* that ends in a *reductio ad absurdum*. Johnny can't read, spell, calculate? Thanks to the wonders of microcomputers, he doesn't have to. It's all in the black box. The technocrats who are planning to "bring sophisticated forms of computer power to hundreds of millions of illiterate people by leaping beyond the conventional possibilities of education"[10] seem to be unaware that these underprivileged people will become further deprived—hostages to a future forecast in the hyperbole of technical optimists. Papert acknowledges the sinister potential for a kind of elitism and the possibility of troublesome class issues but expresses the hope that educational technology will not amplify inequality. At the same time that we note the social naivete that would harbor so unrealistic a hope, we should remind ourselves of the reason put forward to introduce computers: to overcome the deficiencies that made for inequality!

[9] Seymour A. Papert, "Computers and Learning," in *The Computer Age: A Twenty-Year View*, Michael L. Dertouzos and Joel Moses, eds., Cambridge, Massachusetts: The MIT Press, 1980, p. 85.
[10] Jean-Jacques Servan-Schreiber, *The World Challenge*, New York: Simon and Schuster, 1980, pp. 214–215.

TECHNOLOGY AS MODEL-MAKER

Notwithstanding the rather surprising sparcity of reliable data about the relationship between television and education *per se*, useful inferences can be drawn from studies on television and violence, a subject that has direct bearing on the social milieu of which schools are a part and with which schools must cope. Unmistakable connections have been established by considerable research. Television having been dubbed by the Surgeon-General "a violent form of entertainment," the link to aggressive behavior in children and teen-agers has been made in a number of studies. This conclusion is corroborated by field research in other countries, but disputed by researchers funded by the National Broadcasting Company. Consensus does exist among content analyses showing violence, along with obscenity and sexual provocativeness, as predominantly popular themes at all hours. Even two-year-olds find television available and absorbing. Moreover, everyone, regardless of age, watches the same programs. That children commit such adult crimes as armed robbery and murder, that alcoholism, abortion, drug addiction, and suicide have become children's issues are the inevitable consequence. There are many more, more subtle, consequences—all facts of social life which affect schools and schooling.

Concerned that television programs constituted a social threat to the country, the American Medical Association asked advertisers to reduce the amount of violence in them. Consumer groups and parent organizations enlisted the cooperation of the Federal Communications Commission in designating family hours for early evening viewing. The response of the producers and writers was a court challenge on grounds of violation of the First Amendment and infringement on the right of trade. The matter was rendered moot by further advance in technology: cable television has brought pre-packaged pleasure into the home. Tailored to suit the fancy of subscribers, such highly lucrative operations as Escapade, Cable Scope, et al., provide prurience at the push of a button. Pornography is a popular item. Salaciousness sells via ultra-high-frequency cable. Another technical gadget, the cassette, is readily available for rent or for sale, with estimated sales of X-rated video-cassette tapes at $60 million last year. Its catalogue, like that of Nanki-Poo, the wandering minstrel in Gilbert and Sullivan's *Mikado*, is "long, through every passion ranging, and to your humours changing." With sales figures showing the enormous market and preference for hard-core pornography and explicit sex, the "humours" can only be described as base. And every man is his own impresario; the First Amendment will not interfere with his fun.

STAR WARS AND SPACE WARS: GAME AND REALITY

Not to be omitted from the electronic march on education is the onslaught of "video games." Their appeal far surpassing that of the simple pin-ball machine to which they are deprecatingly likened by an industry determined to develop a benign image, the games have swept the country. The business, starting in the early 1970s with "Pong," an electronic table tennis game, burgeoned into one estimated at $5 billion per year. In every city, town, and hamlet, coin-operated games appeared wherever there was a shopping mall, pizza parlor, or store. An increase in truancy was an immediately apparent symptom of this social epidemic. A survey by the New York State Division of Substance Abuse Services of 102 business establishments housing video games showed that illicit drugs were available or being sold at 66 of them. Some municipalities tried to restrict access to the games by young people, especially during school hours, but their efforts were thwarted by court action. In the case of *Aladdin's Castle, Inc. vs. the City of Mesquite, Texas,* where truancy and drug-dealing had caused alarm, the U.S. Federal Appeals Court for the Fifth Circuit in New Orleans ruled that playing video games is an activity protected by the First Amendment. While zoning ordinances or stiff licensing requirements restricted public game-playing somewhat, technology made the ban irrelevant by bringing the game into the home. Cartridges, selling for $20 and up, are already the fastest-growing item in consumer electronics. Sales in 1981 totalled an estimated $1.2 billion and this was seen by financial analysts as only the beginning. The Consumer Electronics Group, an industry association, estimated that the eight million video game modules and 55 million game cartridges sold in 1982 approximately double the number sold during the previous year. Profits from these new forms of recreational technology may be great, but physiological and psychological costs may be higher than we care to calculate. Computer trade journals have reported that a screen flicker rate of sixty frames per second affects the sensory nervous system. Workers assigned to video display terminals complain of specific maladies, stemming from photooptic irritability and stress. Already reported by the Mayo Clinic are several cases of epilepsy brought on by playing video games.

There is a famous saying by the Duke of Wellington that the Battle of Waterloo was won on the playing fields of Eton. Can it be said, similarly, that space wars of the future are being played at the shopping malls of America today? Already bored with Pac Man, who does nothing more exciting than devour dots in a maze, youngsters have fought Space Invaders, Space Raiders, Space Wars, Space Battle, Spacechase, Space

Fury, Space Cavern, Space Hawk, Space Vultures, and even Communist Mutants from Space. The next generation of games promises to be more realistic, more complex, and more frightening. Against this background in fantasy looms the reality. In an unclassified digest of a secret report to Congress,[11] the General Accounting Office urges the Pentagon to hasten the development of laser battle stations in space, so as "to provide a credible air and ballistic missile defense system for the United States."

Thus have death and destruction been transmuted into screen play. Reality has become fantasy and fantasy has become real. Playing war games via computer and waging war via microchip are nearly identical. It is the tidy, abstract character of such war scenarios that appeals to the gamesmen who are the strategic analysts and to their back-up teams of computer specialists, whose life work will be dealing out death and destruction unemotionally, dispassionately, and efficiently. Perhaps by way of countering this sinister affinity, a group, Computer Professionals for Social Responsibility, announced its nascent existence with the following statement: "We deplore the squandering of our knowledge in the pursuit of greater military power that contributes not to our security but to our common peril."[12] Noble intent notwithstanding, General William Westmoreland, former Chief of Staff of the U.S. Army, is quoted[13] as predicting that

on the battlefield of the future, enemy forces will be located, tracked, and targeted almost instantaneously through the use of data links, computer-assisted intelligence evaluation, and automated fire control.

In preparation for this day, the booming military simulator industry utilizes the sophisticated computer graphics imagery that is rapidly advancing the state-of-the-art of video games. Already, electronic weaponry has changed the face of warfare.

The free Apple for every teacher may seem far from the electronic battlefield, but is it? They are both way stations on the "rational" road to cost/effectiveness. First, we are beguiled into accepting computers as teachers' aides, all in the name of efficiency. Then, fun and games become the learning process. From there it is only a short step to making war out of games and a game out of war, where the logic of cost/effectiveness is applied. General Westmoreland tells how:

[11] General Accounting Office, *DOD's Space-Based Laser Program: Potential Progress and Problems*, Washington, D.C., C–MASAD–82–10, February 26, 1982.

[12] Marguerite Zientara, "D Pers Form Group to Block High Tech for Military Uses," *Computerworld*, November 8, 1982.

[13] Frank Barnaby, "Microelectronics in War," in *Microelectronics and Society*, Gunter Friedrichs and Adam Schaff, eds., A Report to the Club of Rome, Oxford, New York: Pergamon Press, 1982, pp. 254–5.

With first-round kill probabilities approaching certainty, and with surveillance devices that can continually track the enemy, *the need for larger forces to fix the opposition physically will be less important.* [Emphasis added]

Electronic weaponry brings good business to the powerful multi-national electronics industry and may thus be a factor in the state of the economy. Perhaps we are witnessing a new and ominous afterword to *The Report from Iron Mountain on the Possibility and Desirability of Peace.*[14] Its message was that peace does not pay.

General Dwight D. Eisenhower must have sensed this danger when he uttered his famous warning about the role of the military-industrial complex in world affairs. That two-party relationship long ago became a triumvirate, with academe a symbiotic third party. Since World War II, the Defense Department in particular has been a major sponsor of and influence in the growth and development of science and technology. The universities' constant need for money was always reason enough for seeking and welcoming this financial aid. Mounting pressures to demonstrate cost/effective operation made the urgency even greater. The changing character of science, with equipment and experimentation becoming ever more expensive and esoteric, certainly made outside funding a vital necessity. Dependency was the inevitable price that academe had to pay. Universities learned how the bountiful flow of dollars from Washington could be transformed into a trickle as politics dictated policy. Clashes occur between government and universities over national security considerations in research on very high-speed integrated circuits. Differences have arisen over restrictions on research in cryptography, on control of technical information in areas deemed sensitive. Microelectronics is an area of special concern to the Department of Defense, one of the universities' primary sources of funding for work with computers, lasers, and the like.

The lessening of the bonds between two of the partners in the tri-lateral liaison may have contributed to catapulting academe into the arms of big business in a multi-million-dollar affair. The Massachusetts Institute of Technology embraced the Whitehead Foundation's offer of $20 million for building and an eventual endowment of $100 million to cover operating costs of a center to pursue research into the applications of molecular genetics to developmental biology. Harvard is peripherally involved in a $70-million-dollar contract between its affiliated Massachusetts General Hospital and Hoechst A.G., a West German pharmaceutical company, which will create a new department of molecular biology there. Washington University and the Monsanto

[14] *The Report from Iron Mountain on the Possibility and Desirability of Peace, op. cit.*

Company, neighbors in St. Louis, Missouri, will collaborate in a $23.5 million, 5-year biomedical research project. Yale University will conduct basic research on enzymes, particularly those useful to chemical and fabric production, for Celanese Corporation under a 3-year, $1.1-million contract. And this is only the beginning of many university-industry connections now taking innovative organizational forms.

The commercialization of academic research is fraught with danger, as much for society-at-large as for the institutions and for the disciplines affected. Support from industry is usually directed toward specific fields of potential commercial interest to the donor. These understandably become the magnet to which are drawn the activities of professors. If faculty members pursue fundable projects, at the possible expense of necessary basic research, however, the industry connection could cause considerable strain. The Whitehead arrangement at MIT, for example, has aroused concern on the part of faculty members that the new center's staff will be selected for their potential contribution to its aims rather than those of MIT, that the new set-up will create an imbalance in the biology department since it will provide one third of the full professors, and that there will be a lack of symmetry in the voting power of the scientists over the activities of the rest of the department. The possibility that the quality of teaching and research is being compromised by the growing commercialization of scientific research is already in evidence. There is fear among academics that colleagues whose work is financed by corporations will treat their discoveries as trade secrets. Others believe that professors involved in such mission-directed activity will eschew basic research in favor of profitable projects. Some faculty members, especially in what promises to be the lucrative field of genetic research, have actually relinquished tenured university positions in favor of commercial enterprise. It is reported that intense rivalries have sprung up at laboratories working on competing programs led by faculty allied to different companies. Researchers are in some cases sworn to secrecy about the nature of their work. Whether these objections are valid or only the bitter dregs of sour grapes is purely academic. Whatever the situation, scientists use rising costs, diminishing support, and the threat of competition from business or from other countries as arguments justifying the new alliances.

Jacques Barzun,[15] the eminent educator, regards these developments in academic life as a flight from teaching that began during the Roosevelt administration, when Washington drew on the universities for help in designing the New Deal. His views on the beginning of the trend

[15] Jacques Barzun, "The Wasteland of American Education," *The New York Review*, November 5, 1981, p. 34.

are germane now as it comes into full flower. He sees in the alliances a kind of colonialism in which outsiders establish spheres of influence and exert control. Their favor sought and cherished, they obviously divert professional allegiance from the university to some outside, monied power. Using the campus as a convenient base for far-flung excursions, with leave of absence a prestige symbol, flying faculty deprive universities of what Barzun thinks is most needed—good teaching. He laments the deplorable loss of integrity in academic life. Perhaps Barzun and those inclined to agree with him are indulging in sentimental nostalgia for good old days that never were. Perhaps the academic life has never been wholly pure. After all, even the noble Newton is known to have fudged figures in order to fit a hypothesis. And the saga of science has never presumed to be above mercenary inducement, whether for prize or for profit. Dalliance with the truth for the sake of capturing the Nobel or other prizes has a long history.

The linkage between today's universities and big business appears to be growing in strength and importance. Our concern in this chapter being the latter-day forms of systems analysis techniques, *viz.* risk analysis and technology assessment, it is vital that we remain alert to who the "experts" are and the centrality of their role. It is they who generate, gather, and interpret the data; it is they who guide the regulators; it is their conception and their calculation of the costs and benefits that will, in the final analysis, prevail. Now that universities are developing quasi-commercial institutions to patent and exploit new products using the technology of gene-splicing, for example, academic scientists will have forfeited the role of independent advisor, for they will find it virtually impossible to take a critical position about a matter in which they or the university has invested name and capital. Government agencies which rely on outside specialists in regulations and licensing decisions may have even more difficulty locating disinterested consultants. When the experts are themselves the entrepreneurs, technology assessment, thanks to methodology now in general use, becomes a kind of self-validating process. If ever we could have looked to the university for a balanced perspective, for impartial experts, that day is gone.

STATE OF THE NATION'S HEALTH

The nation's health can be seen as a crossroads of many disciplines. The physical sciences, medicine, policy analysis, management science, psychology, sociology—all converge. Little of the activity deserves the label *interdisciplinary*. Instead, there is a kind of *e pluribus unum*, the unifying point being that of emphasis on what may be variously defined as their *technical* aspects. Within each of them, the impulse toward developing a methodology has pushed concentration toward quantifiable variables, with "rational trade off" the basis for decisions. It is clear in the case of health, as it was with education, that this approach allows only certain kinds of options and favors only certain courses of actions. Interesting to note, the same model prevails, with the same assumptions, the same formalized procedures, and even, to a remarkable extent, the same language. The same tripartite transection of problems occurs here as we will note again later when we discuss technology assessment and risk analysis—government, industry, and academia assiduously applying the principles of cost/benefit analysis and curiously achieving results not necessarily or demonstrably beneficial to the public's health.

Cost/Effectiveness in the Delivery of Health Care

During the past decade, with cost/effectiveness of health services a central issue in government funding, the concept of the health maintenance organization (HMO) gained widespread support. The objective, according to Joseph A. Califano, Jr., then Secretary of Health, Education, and Welfare, was to improve access to care by injecting competition, presumably to lower costs already boosted by the third-party reimbursement system. The model looked fine but it did not work. The doctors, hospitals, and health insurers who had once opposed the HMO concept because it smacked of socialized medicine found in it and in Medicare and Medicaid programs that channeled vast sums of federal money into HMO's a new and fruitful coalescence. Califano's *ex post facto* comment is eloquent:

In our rush to provide access, the Great Society had let the health industry set the prices, and had acquiesced in its reimbursed systems. Over the intervening decade the industry had used America's quest for broad access to quality health care *to protect and enhance its financial interest and solidify its legislative and regulatory position.* The health industry was seated comfortably at a groaning table set by the taxpayers.[16] [Emphasis added]

The nation's health is big business. Our second largest employer, our third largest industry (after food and housing) in consumer spending, the health sector is growing faster than any other. In 1965, it accounted for $39 billion, or 5.9 percent of gross national product; by 1980, $230 billion, or over 9 percent. Califano estimated that by the year 2000, Americans would be spending at least $1 trillion annually, or some 12

---

[16] Joseph A. Califano, Jr., *Governing America*, New York: Simon and Schuster, 1980, p. 142.

per cent of gross national product, on health. However calculated, these figures represent indisputable trends and an irresistible target of opportunity for profit-seeking entrepreneurs. Health care is now being provided by a large and growing network of private corporations which control lucrative hospital chains. Dr. Arnold S. Relman, in a seminal article, describes the phenomenon which he calls "the new medical-industrial complex"[17] as the network of proprietary hospitals and nursing homes, diagnostic laboratories, homecare and emergency-room services, hemodialysis, and a wide variety of other services. Dr. Relman calculates that between $35 billion and $40 billion, about one-fourth of the total expended on personal health care in 1979, went to investor-owned businesses supplying health services for profit. And this calculation, he points out, does not comprise the "old" medical-industrial complex, i.e., the one which included the manufacture and sale of drugs, medical supplies, and equipment. Together, the old and new form a formidable lobby, well-financed and well-prepared to act when their vested interest is at stake.

What, then, are the implications for the health and well-being of society when the market-place model has been imposed on them? We pointed out in earlier pages the pitfalls of relying on cost/benefit analysis as a means to planning public health programs; we saw the limitations of cost/effectiveness as the measure for evaluating health services and facilities. With the take-over of health by big business, we are now seeing the principles of cost/effectiveness put into practice with results different but no less deleterious here in the health industry than those, discussed earlier, in the automotive industry; the same formula applies: $C/E = ce$. Cost/Effectiveness equals *caveat emptor*.

At present, large corporations supply emergency care packages; diagnostic and laboratory services, including mobile CAT scanning and cardiopulmonary testing, are provided by profit-making companies; corporate-owned, multi-institutional chains operate hospitals and nursing homes; and often, physicians derive pecuniary benefit from all of the activities. But benefit to the public is another matter. In theory, large corporations, through exercise of superior management, economies of scale, and greater incentive to control costs, should be able to deliver better and lower-priced products and services than can public or voluntary organizations. But the public does not receive quality service at lower fees. Despite the frenetic "research studies" of the hundreds of think tanks now specializing in health care systems, definitive comparative data are lacking. There is, however, empirical evidence to suggest that the free market model which rationalizes the commerciali-

[17] Arnold S. Relman, M.D., "The New Medical-Industrial Complex," *The New England Journal of Medicine*, October 23, 1980, pp. 963–970.

zation of health services in effect may be not only inappropriate but pernicious.

The coalition of corporations constitutes an influential lobby whose voice is heard by an Administration committed to the simplistic notion of revitalizing the economy by freeing big business of regulation. In early 1982, for example, the Secretary of Health and Human Services drafted proposals to relax a number of the Federal standards for nursing homes. Later, disregarding what was already an appalling state of affairs, he issued rules that would permit less frequent inspections of nursing homes. In September, 1982, the Department of Health and Human Services approved and sent to the Office of Management and Budget a proposal to relax or repeal many of the regulations affecting 1500 hospitals. The legislation was drafted to provide hospital operators with "more flexibility" and to reduce the costs of meeting Federal health and safety regulations. In effect, it was a blatant boost to their profits. To qualify for Federal funding, hospitals would only have to establish "quality assurance" programs, internally validated. Specifically excised by the legislation were regulations that protected patients from unnecessary surgery. It being a well-documented fact that an excess of surgery seems to be attributable not to the physical needs of the patients but to the financial needs of hospitals and doctors, here is an area where better enforcement and not abandonment is called for. Evidence of needless and/or poorly done surgery would be buried with the dropping of the requirement for routine pathology examination of all tissue removed in surgery. The Administration identified the American Hospital Association and the American Medical Association as "interested parties," expected to react favorably. No mention was made of the elderly, the poor, or any other of the patients who were the truly interested parties.

Because of the scandal-ridden history of the health industry, especially the nursing home sector, because of the fact that half of its multi-billion-dollar revenue is derived from public programs such as Medicare, and because its clientele are mainly the hapless and helpless, this rationale for deregulation is a travesty only to be explained, albeit not condoned, by the way cost/benefit analysis works. In the topsy-turvy world of health care systems analysis, the approach may make sense. But in the real world, the advantages accruing to the business investors may be costing the public dear. On every issue that pits the economic interest of a powerful special group against the public interest, the odds are stacked in favor of the former. Not only does quality of health service suffer, but there seems to be little likelihood for improvement so long as national health policy is orchestrated by private business. The merchandizing of health care on a franchise basis virtually dictates institutional care and rules out any viable, less costly arrangements that might otherwise be devised. It is estimated that present residency in nursing homes could be halved if supportive services were available in communities. "Cream-skimming," long recognized as a troublesome practice in connection with proprietary hospitals, has now become an acute problem. Profit-seekers exclude the "unprofitable" patients, i.e., those who are uninsured, on welfare, and/or suffering from complex or chronic illnesses. At the same time, persons who need round-the-clock care must at present wait for openings. Low-frequency service, no matter how necessary, just does not pay.

Preoccupation with cost/effective management has devalued the common-sense objectives of health care to such an extent that qualitative aspects such as patient comfort are simply omitted from the calculations. The likelihood of neglect and abuse is, however, real and the nefarious outcome of misplaced priorities is revealed in a recent study reported in the *New England Journal of Medicine*.[18] Of the 7.5 million Americans who undergo bladder catheterization annually, a half-million will suffer urinary tract infections. These victims are three times more likely to die than are catheterized hospital patients who do not develop infections of this kind. Interesting to note, this finding, dubbed "provocative" by the director of the Hospital Infections Program of the Centers for Disease Control, merely stimulated questions about the measurement of causal factors and interpretation of the data. No mention was made of indifferent nurses, hired like Kelly Girls on a daily basis, undersupervised technicians, and the army of aides and orderlies, at the bottom of the pay scale and the skill hierarchy, performing procedures such as catheterizing routinely and, perhaps, not always with the professional dedication called for in the Hippocratic Oath.

INFORMATION TECHNOLOGY AND HEALTH

Where profits are involved, productivity is prized. So easily justified on this basis is technology in various forms that any questions raised have only to do with *how much* and not *whether*. Commonplace and already taken for granted, for example, are the applications of computer technology coming under the heading of medical information systems. Indeed, an "assessment," performed by the Office of Technology Assessment at the request of the Senate Committee on Human Re-

---

[18] Richard Platt, B. Frank Polk, Bridget Murdock, and Bernard Rosner, "Mortality Associated with Nosocomial Urinary-Tract Infection," *The New England Journal of Medicine*, September 9, 1982, pp. 637–642.

sources,[19] is not an assessment at all, but merely a statement based more on technical optimism than observation, that medical information systems *could*, if developed and utilized properly, perform a number of useful services. This is a platitude that no one would deny. What was called for and should have been performed was a critical examination of what is expected of the systems, how they are working, and how they are affecting the delivery of medical care.

At the time the Office of Technology Assessment performed the study, some 90 percent of the hospitals in the United States were using electronic data-processing, mainly for such business and administrative functions as posting charges, preparing bills, and the like. One might reasonably expect that automation had been introduced to perform those functions more cost/effectively, regardless of whether any savings ever reach the public. But more searching inquiry has shown that with computerization has come a proliferation of billing protocols and a mushrooming of items for which an individual physician or hospital can bill. Associated with the need for precise definition of services, especially where third-party, fee-for-service arrangements are involved, is an unmistakable tendency, propelled by electronic data-processing, to disaggregate procedures into finer, step-by-step components. If the sum of reimbursements is greater for the many than the one global procedure, herein lies an incentive for the multi-item bill.[20]

The trend manifests itself in the subdividing of a service or procedure into several layers of complexity and then billing them separately. Showstack et al. illustrate this practice by tracing the upward shift in terminology and fees.[21] In 1956, the California Relative Value Studies, a compilation of medical sources developed by the California Medical Association, listed two types of visit: "Office Visit" (first call—routine history and necessary examination) and "Follow-up Office Visit." By 1974, there were 15 different ways to charge for an office visit. The authors cite evidence to support the contention that the change from one system of nomenclature caused a 15 percent increase in the average charge for a physician visit. Besides contributing to the rising costs of services, the mechanics by which bills are processed can have substantial

[19] Congress of the United States, Office of Technology Assessment, *Policy Implications of Medical Information Systems*, Washington, D.C., November, 1977.

[20] Stanton A. Glantz, "Microprocessors to Improve Physician Productivity: Economic and Manpower Issues," in *Microprocessors in Patient Care*, Henry S. Eden and Murray Eden, editors, Parkridge, New Jersey: Noyes Medical Publications, 1981, pp. 114–120.

[21] J.A. Showstack, B.D. Blumberg, J. Schwartz, and S.A. Shroeder, "Fee-for-Service Physician Payment: "Analysis of Current Methods and their Development," *Inquiry*, 1979, *16*, p. 242.

impact on the institutional structure through which medical service is delivered.

Technology assessments of medical information systems, of which the one dutifully performed by the Office of Technology Assessment is exemplar, proceed on the assumption that the technology under scrutiny is good and necessary. Thus, their report is a rosy filter through which the medical information system is viewed. Its potential boundless, its progress hindered only by the recalcitrance of people or bureaucracy, the technology is described and even promoted, but never assessed. Perhaps we are already too late to expect a balanced appraisal of the costs and benefits. If some of the effects are less than salutary, they have been screened out in calculations that focus on physician productivity, quite irrespective of whether an increase is necessary and of what that implies for patient-care.[22] As to the first point, Glantz underscores the fallacy of assuming that there is a shortage of doctors. He cites current manpower studies to show that the supply is adequate and growing. Given the ability of medical professionals to generate a demand for their own services, Glantz sees the benefits of heightened productivity accruing to the physician in the form of increased income or leisure, with little advantage to patients or public.

Microprocessor-based technologies for capturing patient data are regarded with favor because they relieve medical professionals of paperwork and free physicians from burdensome tasks. But taking the family history as part of the medical record is known to be a most valuable diagnostic procedure. Glantz reminds us that the time invested by physician and patient in a history and personal interview plays an important role in the development of a positive therapeutic relationship. As more is learned about the hereditary nature of many disorders and as new therapies for them become available, detailed information about familial occurrence of diseases and ailments becomes essential. Feinstein[23] discusses the place of medical records in the care of patients; he deplores the "Bethesda transformation," in which the electronic medium now virtually dictates the message. In his analysis, he finds only illusory advantages and contends that the quality of health care generally suffers.

This critical stance gains credibility as we inquire further into the expanding role of computerized medical information systems. Lincoln and Korpman[24] take the clinical laboratory as a microcosm of the health

22 Glantz, *op. cit.*

23 Alvan R. Feinstein, "The Problems of the Problem-Oriented Medical Record," *Annals of Internal Medicine*, Vol. 78, No. 5, May 1973, pp. 751–762.

24 Thomas I. Lincoln and Ralph A. Korpman, "Computers, Health Care, and Medical Information Science," *Science*, 17 October 1980, pp. 257–263.

care system and find that many tasks that appear to be suitable for automation may actually present such severe operational problems as to cause serious errors. The technology introduced to cure the ills of data management only makes them worse. Glantz directs his questions to computer-based medical decision-making systems. He points out that the algorithms embodied in such systems are incapable of including many subjective elements, such as definition of diseases and syndromes, preferences of patient and family, and participation of medical care providers. Moreover, submerged in the program are the programmer's values, often determinative of the course of action that will follow. Even medical professionals are inclined to accept the computer as omniscient and might not understand the branching logic of the program. Nor would they be likely to know that certain branches that they might have chosen to consider were not even in the program.

Glantz gives us even more serious matters to ponder when he turns his attention to the quality of the data base that eventually gets locked into the code of decision-making programs. Such programs are usually a compilation of the medical literature, taken at face value by programmers. His considerable research into the statistical methodology underlying many of the studies incorporated in this body of literature leads him to conclude that

the literature, unfortunately, is notoriously unreliable in its handling of quantitative issues, especially those related to probability and statistics, the very topics that sit at the core of the branching probablistic trees that make up these programs. *Often, the programmer does not even have these data to work from and is reduced to buttonholing experts to force them to estimate the likelihood of the various events of interest* and the possible interconnections.[25] [Emphasis added]

Glantz bolsters his point about errors in statistical methodology residing unchallenged in the literature by citing studies of articles published over a period of time in the most prestigious journals. Three independent reviews, one in 1964, one in 1976, and one in 1977, all different in approach, reached almost the same conclusion—that nearly half of the papers examined contained ambiguous or erroneous use of biostatistics.[26]

It is to the "clinical disasters produced by an idolatrous worship of mathematical strategies and models" that Dr. Alvan R. Feinstein (professor of Medicine and Epidemiology at the Yale University School of

[25] Stanton A. Glantz, "Microprocessors to Improve Physician Productivity," *op. cit.*
[26] Stanton A. Glantz, *Primer of Biostatistics*, New York: McGraw-Hill Book Company, 1981, pp. 6–7.

Medicine) directs his inquiry.[27] A great appeal of mathematical approaches, he says, is that

they have seldom been adversely criticized, mainly because they could seldom receive a thoroughly critical evaluation. Most clinicians either would not understand them or would be too awed or flustered to raise probing doubts about them.

This point, like the one made by Glantz should serve to remind us that the updated version of GIGO (Garbage In, Garbage Out) is Garbage In, Gospel Out. It should serve as warning that medical information systems may be dangerous to our health.

In earlier chapters, our discussion of computerized medical information systems stressed the issue of privacy. The state-of-the-art has advanced considerably during the past decade and so have the incursions into personal privacy via electronics. The proliferation of data banks in the insurance and health industries, the linkage between computing and communications technology, and increasing sophistication in computer matching are potent factors in making a myth of confidentiality. The computerized medical record is a useful addendum indeed to the dossier about which we seem to have become complacent but which has powerful potential to make every life an open book. Robert Ellis Smith (publisher of *Privacy Journal* and member of the American Bar Association Privacy Committee)[28] warns that all of the elements of an Orwellian society are in place. "Just about every salient fact about an individual is in a computer file somewhere." No aspect of the private life is more vulnerable, and more subject to electronic prying, than that having to do with one's health—physical, emotional, or psychological. Nonetheless, the issue of confidentiality, an item for sober contemplation, is treated with cavalier disregard for its implications in the conventional technology assessment of medical information systems. Standard procedure is to refer to the legal and technical safeguards, although these offer little succor to the long-suffering public.

PUBLIC HEALTH POLICY ADMINISTRATION AND ANALYSIS

If the prescription for public health policy is cost/benefit analysis, as is generally the case, then presumptions are always the same and procedures identical whatever the special area of concern—administration of hospitals, delivery of services, regulation of additives in foods, de-

[27] Alvan R. Feinstein, "The Haze of Bayes, the aerial palaces of decision analysis and the computerized Ouija board," *Clinical Pharmacology and Therapeutics*, Vol. 21, Number 4, April, 1977, p. 483.
[28] Robert Ellis Smith, "Privacy: Still Threatened," *Datamation*, September, 1982, p. 306.

velopment of new drugs, or setting and enforcement of standards for clean air, clean water, and safety at work. This point, already made in foregoing pages, is amplified in a compendium of papers derived from a 1979 Brookings Research Institution conference on health and safety regulation.[29] For each of five topics—passive restraint devices for automobiles, occupational exposure to cotton dust, sulfur oxide air pollution standards, saccharin as a food additive, and waterborne carcinogens—scientists, economists, and regulators were called on, respectively, to summarize evidence on the nature of the risks and examine the costs and benefits of proposed regulations.

Implicit in the format of the book and the conference proceedings on which it is based is a model of the policy at the crucial point of which consensus exists. Such a felicitous assumption is patently fallacious, as is evident throughout but exemplified especially in the chapter on saccharin. A subject of controversy as long ago as 1911, saccharin still remains a debatable issue. During the past half century, almost every administration has funded studies, appointed committees, or turned to the National Academy of Sciences for elucidation. Despite over fifty years of inquiry, the question of saccharin's carcinogenicity has not been settled. Each generation earnestly recommends long-term studies but resorts to short-term trade-offs dictated by the exigencies of the times, such as sugar shortage during war or economic woes claimed by the affected industries, such as the food-processors or soft-drink manufacturers.

With respect to sweeteners and other food additives, Congress has passed a number of Food, Drug, and Cosmetic Acts, each reflecting the wishful but unwarranted notion that precise tolerances can be established for "added poisonous or deleterious substances" whose occurrence in food "cannot be avoided" or whose use is "required" to produce the food. With some 2700 food additives and 33 color additives now regulated by the Food and Drug Administration, the "zero-risk" concept embodied in what is called the Delaney Clause has become virtually unenforceable. There is rarely agreement among experts as to whether and in what amount a known carcinogen poses a "significant" risk to human health and there is always the ready argument that some are worth the risks because of the benefits derived from them. Thus, the use of furazolidone and diethylstilbestrol (DES) is condoned because, when given to poultry, cattle, and swine, they promote weight gain, prevent disease, increase feed efficiency, and thus increase the most yield per pound of feed use. For the past decade, American farmers and chemical manufacturers have lobbied assiduously and successfully to

29 Robert W. Crandall and Lester B. Lave, editors, *The Scientific Basis of Health and Safety Regulations*, Washington, D.C.: The Brookings Institution, 1981.

prevent the Food and Drug Administration from restricting the use of tetracyclines, penicillins, and other antibiotics in animal feed. The argument is that the F.D.A. can do little to reduce the health risk but could greatly reduce the farmer's ability to put weight on their livestock. Increase in consumer prices is always the *coup de grâce* in the argumentation favoring such additives.

There are, however, dangers in using low levels of antibiotics in the barnyard, which thereby becomes an incubator for breeding antibiotic-resistant strains of bacteria. According to one source,[30]

Even though a certain strain of bacteria may not infect man, it can pass on acquired resistance through genetic transfer to another type of bacteria that does infect humans. . . . Loss of effectiveness of the most widely used anti-bacterials (i.e. tetracyclines and penicillins) poses risks to both human and animal health. *Therapeutic failure with these antibacterials would lead to large but presently unquantifiable morbidity and mortality in humans and animals . . . . Once significant effects on human and animal health do become widely observable and quantifiable, it may be too late to address the problem.* [Emphasis added]

RISK AND BENEFIT IN PUBLIC HEALTH POLICY

The pattern is repetitive to the point of monotony: pesticides, fungicides, additives, and preservatives, suspect as to toxicity or carcinogenicity, are rarely banned outright. Battle over the "scientific data" serves as a convenient staying action with experts ranged on opposing sides to contest the "facts," modes of experimentation, and interpretation of findings. Uncertainty is, curiously, an argument favoring use, especially at a time when "regulatory relief" to food, drug, and chemical companies appears to be the prime objective in public health policy. Where the premise is "what you don't know won't hurt you," logic dictates that further inquiry be stifled. Dilemma turns to disaster, however, because dangers ultimately make themselves known, as has been the case with DES and thalidomides. Here is an instance of the inverse relationship, often overlooked, between time and truth.

The point is tellingly illustrated in the Food and Drug Administration's revival of irradiation as a way of preserving foods. Irradiation technology uses high doses of radiation to sterilize beef, pork, and poultry products. As long ago as the 1920s the Army began experiments with irradiating bacon. Studies sponsored jointly by the Department of Defense and Atomic Energy Commission have been strongly biased in favor of the technology. Hence, all of the cost/benefit calculations look

[30] Congress of the United States, Office of Technology Assessment, *Drugs in Livestock Feed*, Washington, D.C., June, 1979.

good. According to them, the process could virtually eliminate salmonella contamination and drastically reduce the need for nitrates to destroy botulinus toxin. Packing, storing, and shipping would be simplified and enormous savings realized from lowered need for refrigeration. Irradiation was also deemed a boon to developing nations unable to afford refrigeration. Ironically, the very food treated by this cost/effective process to provide nutrition to hungry nations and to offer variety to Spam-sated soldiers could bring about their demise by cancer. It is known that the food thus treated is radioactive, and we have no firm facts about safe lower limits, long a bone of contention.[31] Because irradiation alters the character of food, it was explicitly classified as an additive, subject to the Delaney Amendment of 1958. Nonetheless, in March, 1982, discounting any possible ill effects or inconclusive results of much-disputed studies, the F.D.A. prepared a proposal to permit the preservation of fruits, vegetables, and spices by irradiation. If the present predilection for speedy review continues, we can predict the outcome. The process hailed as efficient because it extends shelf life in stores and warehouses, lengthens storage time at home, and increases the distance that fresh food can be transported will receive the endorsement of producers and the approval of the government.

Counteracting any temptation toward complacency, however, is a General Accounting Office report[32] which states that at least 80,000 articles have been published internationally on the health effects of ionizing radiation. It is said that there is no other issue about which there is so much information. It can also be said with equal validity that there is no other issue about which there is so much controversy. Basic disagreement over the interpretation of data among the 22 members of the National Academy's Committee on the Biological Effects of Ionizing Radiation (BEIR) was so intense as to have delayed a long-awaited report,[33] which appeared with a dissenting statement. The controversy centered on the "linear hypothesis," which some of the members criticized as exaggerating the risks of low-level radiation and thereby exacerbating "excessive and detrimental apprehension" over hazards. Not to join the argument but merely to underscore the impasse that occurs and the confusion that results in situations of this kind,

[31] Ida R. Hoos, "Risk Assessment in Social Perspective," in *Perceptions of Risk*, Proceedings of the Fifteenth Annual Meeting of the National Council on Radiation Protection and Measurements, Washington, D.C., March 14–15, 1979, pp. 57–85.

[32] U.S. General Accounting Office, *Problems in Assessing the Cancer Risks of Low-Level Ionizing Radiation Exposure*, 2 Volumes, Washington, D.C., January 2, 1981, EMD–81–7, Volume 1, p. 7.

[33] National Academy of Sciences/National Research Council, Report of the Committee on the Biological Effects of Ionizing Radiation, *The Effects on Populations of Exposure to Low Levels of Ionizing Radiation*, Washington, D.C., 1980.

resort to technical battle draws us inevitably into the highly critical matter of ascribing expertness. This occurs in a process that is an amalgam of perception, prejudice and preference. Once the credibility of the expert has been accepted, then his data, his methodology, and his pronouncements support and are supported by the belief system.[34] Since there exists only a fine line between information and propaganda, much of risk analysis is tantamount to assessment with a purpose, and here public perception of risk has become a ploy. The trick is to get the public to accept a particular risk by altering its perception of it. The skill of psychologists, sociologists, and anthropologists have been marshalled in the task of drawing lines between actual and perceived risk. The premise is that a public persuaded that their perception of a risk is "all in the head" may be more receptive to accepting exposure of one kind or another to radiation. The fallacy here is, of course, that the risk exists, whether and how it may be perceived. These are matters still to be addressed in the section on risk analysis. At present we need only return to the Academy's basic conclusions that there is no threshold below which exposure to low-level radiation is safe, that there is no dose below which radiation entails no risk of damage, and there appears to be evidence that the relationship between dose and damage is not linear, but rather quadratic, at least where the induction of some kinds of cancers is involved. Only ignorance prevails insofar as genetic extrapolation is concerned.

The canons of cost/effectiveness can be counted on to override considerations of health and safety. We can, therefore, expect that irradiated foods will be added to the long list of substances bearing the familiar label, "May be dangerous to your health." By the same token and identical calculus, they will join the flood of known hazardous chemicals, pesticides, drugs, and devices manufactured in the United States, perhaps even banned in industrialized countries, but shipped to developing countries. A report prepared under then Secretary of State Alexander M. Haig, Jr. and Secretary of Commerce Malcolm Baldridge perceived curtailment of this traffic as adversely affecting the U.S. balance of trade, encouraging the shift of manufacturing to overseas locations, and reducing the sales of individual firms without beneficial effect on recipients who could obtain the products from other sources. Buried by this marketing strategy is the irony that the products are being distributed for the recipients' benefit! The fact that the govern-

[34] Ida R. Hoos, "The Credibility Issue," pp. 20–31 and "Assessment of Methodologies for Radioactive Waste Management," pp. 31–47, in *Essays on Issues Relevant to the Regulation of Radioactive Waste Management*, Washington, D.C.: U.S. Nuclear Regulatory Commission, Office of Nuclear Material Safety and Safeguards, NUREG–0412, May, 1978.

ment of Bangladesh in August, 1982, outlawed 237 products already banned in industrialized countries and ordered multi-national drug manufacturers to halt distribution of nearly 2,000 more during the next nine months suggests that U.S. export policy is not achieving notably salubrious international relations.

As with public health at home and abroad, so with safety at work, policy is being made with profit given highest priority. Here as in the instances discussed above it is the economic condition of the affected industry that outweighs those affecting life and limb of workers. Whose interest will be served is, despite all the methodological macramé, a matter of power and politics. Management techniques such as cost/ benefit and risk analysis are merely vehicles serving the strong master, just as Robert S. McNamara long ago said they would. In light of this quarter century of experience, a tremor of trepidation might be warranted as we ponder the words of the present director of the Occupational Safety and Health Administration, Thorne Auchter:

Our approach is one of intensive management. I think that's the reason I'm here. *I'm a believer and a creator and an implementor of management systems.*[35] [Emphasis added]

The portent of this message was quickly felt. The Reagan Administration abandoned standing policy of viewing cancer-causing substances at any level of exposure as a risk to human health. Changes promptly proposed included (1) assuming risks at varying "thresholds"; (2) differentiating between cancer-causing substances that change genetic properties of the cell and those with different effect so as to alter regulations accordingly; (3) relying less on laboratory tests on animals and waiting instead for epidemiological studies of illness and death before acting on chemicals and carcinogens; (4) placing more emphasis on voluntary "life-style" causes of cancer, such as smoking, and less on environmental sources, such as carcinogens in air, food, water, and at the workplace; (5) giving increased weight to the costs as well as to the benefits of regulatory decisions. This last item must be taken as a particularly serious caveat because of the prevailing propensity on the part of policy-makers to rationalize bad decisions on the basis of investment already made. This toe-in-the-door approach is used to advantage in the cost/benefit analysis. Thus, millions spent on a badly designed nuclear plant are rationalization enough for its continued operation. Return-on-investment and point-of-no-return have a peculiar affinity for each other in the business of allocating the costs and benefits of risks. The full meaning of the new policy on regulating cancer-causing agents

[35] Quoted in R. Jeffrey Smith, "OSHA Shifts Direction on Health Standards," *Science*, 26 June, 1981, p. 1482.

can better be understood when one takes into account the government's pro-industry bias. Up front and clearly visible are moves to lower protective standards, ease enforcement, and relax regulations. More subtle but ultimately more potent, perhaps, are the actions taken to curtail the flow and reduce the amount of information available to the public. Always in the name of cutting expenses and insuring cost/effective operation, the Administration cut back statistics-collection and report-publication. Items dealing with "social issues" are prominent among the latter slated for elimination. Selected to be withdrawn from circulation, with warehoused stocks destroyed because "it no longer represents agency policy" is a notable entry: "Cotton Dust: Worker Health Alert, Cotton Dust Standard: Management's Role, and Cotton Dust Can Destroy Your Lungs—poster."[36]

RISK ANALYSIS

In a society beset with all kinds of risks, and at a time when there are techniques purported to analyze them "rationally," it is to be expected that risk analysis would become a matter for official concern. There is no gainsaying the urgency. The U.S. House Committee on Science and Technology in its 1979 Authorization Report asked the National Science Foundation to develop a program of systematic research on comparative risk analysis:

One of the most critical problems faced by health, safety, and environmental decision-makers is how to assess and balance risks and benefits.[37]

But a proper assessment of risk, in which costs are to be balanced against benefits, must start with clear articulation of the risk under consideration. And, interesting to note, even this step, rudimentary in any analysis, is hard to achieve because it, in itself, is freighted with value judgments. Whether a risk exists at all, whether it is *significant,* whether it is *acceptable*—these are matters which depend on the point of view, which will govern the choice of experts, the selection of data and the trade-off to be made in the final analysis. How difficult, indeed, is the task is exemplified in the work done by the National Science Foundation/ National Academy of Sciences Committee on Risk and Decision Making. They attempted to compile a classification scheme on the generation of risk and finally produced the following:[38]

36 David Burnham, "Government Restricting Flow of Information to the Public," *The New York Times*, November 15, 1982.
37 National Academy of Sciences, Committee on Risk and Decision-Making, Assembly of Behavorial and Social Sciences, *Risk and Decision Making*, Washington, D.C.: National Academy Press, 1982.
38 *Ibid.*

The Generation of Risks: A Simple Classification Scheme

Self-Hazardous Behavior: Situations in which an individual creates and incurs the same risk. Illustrative examples: smoking, alcohol abuse, not using seat belts, or hang gliding.

Co-generation of Risks: When the combined actions of two or more parties impose a risk on one of the parties. Illustrative examples: risks imposed on a worker resulting from combined actions of worker and employer or risks imposed on consumers by the combined actions of producer and consumer.

Risks Generated by Production Externalities: When productive enterprises generate risks that are incurred by people not directly involved in the production or consumption of a good. Illustrative examples: air and water pollution, nuclear accidents, and hazardous wastes.

Risks Imposed by Particular Individuals on Others: When individuals generate risks that are imposed on others. Illustrative examples: crime, speeding, drunken driving, child abuse, and smoking in public places.

Risks Generated by Nature: A category including natural hazards such as earthquakes, droughts, and floods as well as certain physical conditions generated by nature (e.g., diseases of old age, genetic mutations, and disease from natural ionizing radiation). Of course, the degree of possible risk can be tempered by individual or social actions: deciding to live near a fault zone, earthquake resistant design or construction, construction of dams, and so on.

Risks Generated by Economic Conditions: Individuals and communities create and incur risks due to various economic conditions. Financial insecurity itself is a risk that also creates risk for health and safety. Illustrative examples: Poverty-induced disease and unemployment-induced stress.

Risks Generated by Government Policies: Public policies sometimes subsidize, encourage, or force individuals or organizations to create risks. For example, some national energy policies create risks to human health, safety, and the environment as well as to national security and the likelihood of war.

The exercise by the Academy Risk Committee ended in a meaningless taxonomy which strengthened the sophistic and curiously defeatist position that everything has its risks; all living is fraught with danger. Classifications of this kind are commonly found in analyses. Perhaps they are part of the reductionist approach that assumes that through classification will come clarification. This is not necessarily so. Most frequently, it is a diversionary tactic that keeps analysts assigned to such tasks as, for example, the disposition of fissionable wastes busily engaged for contract after contract without ever addressing fundamental issues. In the National Academy analysis, categories were fuzzy and crossovers unavoidable. The proverbial apples and oranges in the various bins lost their generic identity. With staff time wasted on this fruitless activity, the Committee slighted the questions set forth as basic by the National Science Foundation.[39] Some of them bear iteration here as

[39] National Science Foundation, *Addendum to the PRA Program Announcement for Extramural Research* (NSF 78–78).

we review critically the methodology of risk assessment, for the National Academy/National Science Foundation activity is prototypical of the current scene.

The Foundation's first question, "How do we determine how safe is safe enough?" goes beyond casuistry. It actually encourages the feckless pursuit of a technique to measure the immeasurable. If the question is not mere logomachy, it is dangerously loaded, for it baits the credibility trap into which such matters are inevitably drawn. How safe is safe "enough" depends on *who* is determining *what* and by what *standards*. The point is tellingly illustrated in an article[40] promulgating the notion that nuclear power is "even safer than engineers had presumed" prior to the accident at Three Mile Island. Such presumption was based on what the author of the article called "the concept and criteria behind the design safety of nuclear reactors." These, he averred, resided in the "defense in depth philosophy" which implied (a) the best quality assurance; (b) highly redundant and protective systems; and (c) engineered safety systems. Experience has shown that such paper-drawn Maginot lines do not stand up well under the pressure of reality.

The second question, "How adequate are the data on which we depend for estimates of the risks associated with different technologies?" brings to the fore many of the problems already known to be associated with the gathering, processing, and interpreting of information. They demand thoughtful reconsideration now as we ponder the validity, reliability, and longevity of the data on which judgments about risk are based. The very ascription of credibility to the experts is, in itself, crucial when one assesses adequacy of data.

Difficulties are compounded in matters such as nuclear safety because positions are polarized. Hence, we find the executive director of an organization named "Scientists and Engineers for Secure Energy" calling critics of nuclear safety "unfit," because "they are not able to compute risks."[41] In other words, his is the old argument that this is a technical matter for which only scientists and engineers are fit authority. It is this contention, as we pointed out earlier, that shields the problem from debate but sheds no enlightenment. Moreover, implicit in this frequently-repeated assertion is the notion that technical experts know and agree. This is patent nonsense and refuted by reality, as exemplified in an important and ongoing controversy over the use of potassium iodide (KI) to block thyroidal uptake of radiodides downwind from a nuclear accident releasing a large amount of such isotopes to the

[40] Jon Gilbertson, "Nuclear: The Safest Energy Around," *Fusion*, September, 1980, pp. 18 ff.
[41] Miro Todorovick, "Nuclear Safety: Critics, Unfit to Cry 'Wolf,' " Letters to the Editor, *The New York Times*, September 25, 1982.

atmosphere. This eventuality having been acknowledged by the Nuclear Regulatory Commission in a technical report buried among many of its kind,[42] Rosalyn S. Yalow, a Nobel Laureate, criticized the Food and Drug Administration's risk/benefit conclusions that recommended that the drug be administered to the affected populace.[43] Her facts and figures were promptly challenged by another eminent scientist on grounds of what he called her "incorrect linear extrapolation." Many of the estimates of incidence of thyroid tumors following radiation exposure were drawn from the so-called Rasmussen Safety Study,[44] itself a notable example of the fallacy of figures. Perhaps the most telling commentary on this battle between the experts is couched in the following observation:

If the lineup at the hearing is any indication, it would appear that the main opponents of general distribution of KI are also the stringent nuclear power enthusiasts.[45]

The Food and Drug Administration and the Federal Emergency Management Agency favor using KI for the general population. The members of the Nuclear Regulatory Commission, leery about admitting publicly that there are dangers associated with nuclear power or that such an accident might occur, oppose. As will be seen when we discuss further the assessment of nuclear risk, not only are the technical data at issue, but, even more important, the position of the experts with respect to nuclear energy. "Facts" to believers are "fallacies" to skeptics and *vice versa*.

Three of the remaining six questions on NSF's agenda dwell on the perception and, relatedly, acceptance of risk. Emphasis on these aspects has added a new twist to analytic techniques and calls upon psychologists, sociologists, anthropologists, and others willing to cooperate in or be coopted by the game, the name of which is public acceptance. The object is, of course, to get the public to accept a nuclear plant or a waste dump by altering the perception of risks associated with it. With the underlying premise being "it's all in your head," these experts make a distinction between "actual" and "perceived" risk and trivialize dangers by comparing them with risks which the society seems to suffer

[42] Nuclear Regulatory Commission, *Technical Bases for Estimating Fission Product Behavior During LWR Accidents*, Washington, D.C., 1981.
[43] Rosalyn S. Yalow, "Potassium Iodide Effectiveness After Nuclear Accidents," Letters, *Science*, 19 November, 1982, p. 742.
[44] Nuclear Regulatory Commission, *Reactor Safety Study: An Assessment of Accident Risks on U.S. Commercial Nuclear Power Plants*, Washington, D.C.: Report Wash. 1400, 1975.
[45] Constance Holden, in "News and Comment," *Science*, 19 March, 1982, p. 1485.

willingly.[46] This pooh-pooh logic has been applied frequently in the case of everything from the siting of MX missile siloes to the disposal of radioactive materials. Alteration of perception is achieved through contrived games and exercises, propaganda masquerading as "public education," and other forms of artful suasion. In this way, risk analysis becomes a process with a purpose, a tool for subtle coercion, to make some one believe something. Thus, an American public which smokes billions of cigarettes per year is told that it has forfeited the right to be worried about having nuclear waste buried in its backyard.

Among the ploys used to manipulate attitudes about nuclear energy is the cost/benefit notion, insinuated into the process of trade-off so that radiation risks will be accepted. Slid with subtlety into the cost/benefit equation is the debt owed the piper. Through invocation of the inexorable truth that there is no such thing as a free lunch, the public is reminded that it has enjoyed the "advantages" of nuclear power and, therefore, must face the costs. This is the rationale that has been used to counter citizens' protests over having radioactive shipments transported through their streets or their objections to having waste repositories built near their homes. New York City, which tried to ban shipments of spent fuels, and California, which objected to off-site storage of wastes, were accused of selfishness for refusing to assume their "share" of "national responsibility." More often than not, the strategy of transforming benefit into a kind of guilt and imbuing it with a moral obligation is utilized when disposition of radioactive wastes from laboratories and hospitals is at issue. Deflected by the spurious argumentation is attention to the fact that the amounts, while substantial, are insignificant compared to those generated by commercial and miliary reactors, the quantity generated by the latter being a matter of secrecy, of course. Their "low-level" classification should not, however, divert from their toxicity. Their length of lethal life may not be as great as that of transuranics but the damage they can do to humans may be greater than many calculations show. Moreover, the moralistic argument may serve to divert attention from some known vital facts of life, such as that the amount of such low-level wastes is growing in proportion to the expanding use of radioactive materials in laboratories and hospitals, and that with familiarity there has been increasing complacency. Failures to package properly, to label correctly, and to adhere to safety regulations are commonplace. The possibility of over-use of radioactive materials has been all but obscured in the pious assumptions about its benefits, which, ultimately, add on to the debt society is expected to pay.

[46] Aaron Wildavsky, "No Risk is the Highest Risk of All," *American Scientist*, January–February, 1979, pp. 32–37.

Can we miss the parallel here with the situation in Seveso, Italy, where the inhabitants, exposed to dioxin from an explosion in a nearby factory, were faced with terrible illnesses? Forced to evacuate their homes and flee the contaminated countryside, these people were burdened with the realization that they had once been willing beneficiaries of the plant's operations. Not only had it provided jobs and a payroll with all the advantageous ripple effects throughout the community, it had also been the source of a kind of back-door bounty to which the residents had been party and had thus been made partners in the poisoning. For years, the people of Seveso had brought their sick and dead chickens to the factory and had been paid off in thousands of lire, many times the worth of the poultry.[47] The message is always the same: prosperity is dear. We all enjoy it. Some one has to pay.

ASSESSMENT OF NUCLEAR RISKS

A proper assessment of the risks of radiation calls for a firm comprehensive data base specifying sources, extent, intensity, and effects of radiation exposure. Nothing of the kind exists and it is patently impossible, despite attempts at encyclopedic inventory, to develop one. Consequently, despite pretentions to the contrary, the numerous assessments are, at best, partial, and at the worst, misleading. Official interest in the biological effects of ionizing radiation has changed over time and has migrated considerably. Before the late 1960s, empowered by the Atomic Energy Act of 1954, the Atomic Energy Commission (AEC) was the lead agency. Under its aegis, the National Laboratories[48] were established to carry out all research and development programs related to atomic energy for civilian and military purposes.

The principal provision of the 1954 Act was an instruction to the AEC to issue licenses to private companies to build and operate commercial nuclear power stations. A corollary provision directed the agency to adopt whatever regulations it deemed necessary to protect the health and safety of the public. Harold Green, a former AEC attorney and a recognized authority on atomic energy law, had this comment:[49]

There are about 31 references in the law to the "health and safety of the public." I counted them once. But there is not a single reference in the legis-

[47] Thomas Whiteside, *The Pendulum and The Toxic Cloud: The Course of Dioxin Contamination*, New Haven, Connecticut: Yale University Press, 1979.

[48] Lawrence Berkeley Laboratory, Lawrence Livermore National Laboratory, Los Alamos National Scientific Laboratory, Oak Ridge National Laboratory, Fermi National Accelerator Laboratory, Sandia National Laboratories, Argonne National Laboratory and Pacific Northwest Laboratory.

[49] Cited in Daniel Ford, *The Cult of the Atom*, New York: Simon and Schuster, 1982.

lative history (4,000 pages of reports, debates, and Congressional testimony) as to what those health and safety considerations really were. *Nobody really ever thought that safety was a problem. They assumed that if you just wrote the requirement into the Act that it be done properly, that it could be done properly.* [Emphasis added]

In 1974 Congress divided the AEC into the Energy Research and Development Administration (ERDA) and the Nuclear Regulatory Commission (NRC) in response to the possible conflict of interest involved when authority to regulate nuclear power was exercised by the same agency that promoted and developed it. ERDA became the Department of Energy (DOE) in 1977 and absorbed ERDA's authority to assure compliance with government standards for exposure in its own facilities. The NRC retained regulatory control over private industry. Responsibility was further dispersed, when, as a result of atomic bomb testing, radiation levels in air, water, milk, and food became a matter for public concern. The Health Education and Welfare (HEW) agencies were given new authorities and additional agencies were created. The roster became a confusing welter; responsibility was dissipated to the vanishing point. An effort by the Carter Administration to coordinate activity resulted in a task force as evanescent as all such bodies tend to be. No formal report is available. With prevailing political winds favoring industry, agencies once charged with environmental protection and public health and safety were soon to be sapped through budget cuts.

Meanwhile, sources of ionizing radiation are numberless and the list grows. Radiation pathways in the environment, bio-medical effects of exposure and thresholds for radiation are all matters about which there is little agreement among experts. One existing dogma has been that since mankind has, from time immemorial, been exposed to ionizing radiation, an additional dose need not cause concern. This argument presumes that natural radiation does no harm, a contention long disputed by Gofman and Tamplin.[50] At present, there is a strong inclination toward *ignotum per ignotius* (literally, "the unknown through the more unknown") Thus, "options," like the one to dispose of nuclear wastes in space, are based on a few known facts derived from laboratory-scale experiments and superordinate assumptions. Apropos here but unheeded are the warning words spoken by Banquo as he listened to the runic incantations of the witches:[51]

[50] John W. Gofman and Arthur R. Tamplin, "Federal Radiation Council Guidelines for Radiation Exposure of the Population-at-Large—Protection or Disaster?" Testimony before the Subcommittee on Air and Water Pollution, Committee on Public Works, U.S. Senate, Ninety-first Congress, November 18, 1969.
[51] William Shakespeare, *Macbeth*, Act 1, Scene III.

> And oftentimes, to win us to our harm,
> The instruments of darkness tell us truths,
> Win us with honest trifles, to betray's
> In deepest consequence.

Methods of monitoring and measuring radiation are manifestations of the drunkard's search. Known trivia are gathered to fit models from which sanguine extrapolation is made to order, while vast unknowns are deliberately ignored. Advocacy parades in the trappings of analysis in studies contracted to substantiate stands already taken. Thus, the Department of Energy, bent on "solving" the nuclear waste problem, marshals its army of retainers as authority for recommendations contained in a document remarkably subtitled *Waste Confidence Rulemaking* and purporting to be the "Statement of Position of the United States Department of Energy."[52] This position of euphoria apparently emanates from some 700 references, the huge preponderance of which are to studies performed dutifully by the National Laboratories, think tanks unlikely to kill a goose that lays golden eggs for them, and consultants ever ready to paint the bull's eye on the target after the arrow has been shot.[53]

The analytical methods used in nuclear risk assessment seem to lend themselves to the tasks assigned to and accepted by the Department of Energy's "hired guns." That agency's excessive use of contractors has been the subject of investigation by the Comptroller General,[54] and of a joint Congressional inquiry,[55] where Senator David Pryor revealed that over $9.6 billion of its FY1980 budget was allocated to contracts, many among which amounted to millions of dollars. For example, Booz Allen and Hamilton had a $2.3 million contract "to support" the Office of Administration; PRC (Planning Research Corporation) had a $7.8 million contract to "support" the Office of Solar Applications. According to Senator Pryor, the contractors were "not merely the invisible hands behind DOE's basic plans and programs, but the hands that

[52] U.S. Department of Energy, *In the Matter of Proposal Rulemaking on the Storage and Disposal of Nuclear Waste (Waste Confidence Rulemaking), Statement of Position of the United States Department of Energy*, PR–50, 51; USNRC; DOE/NE–0007, 15 April, 1980.

[53] U.S. House of Representatives, Subcommittee on Human Resources of the Committee on Post Office and Civil Service, *Contracting Out*, Hearings, Ninety-sixth Congress, September 7, 11, 20, and October 4, 1979.

[54] General Accounting Office, *Government Earns Low Marks on Proper Use of Consultants*, Washington, D.C., FPCD–80–48, June 6, 1980.

[55] U.S. Senate Subcommittee on Civil Service and General Services and U.S. House Subcommittee on Human Resources, *Federal Government's Use of Consultants*, Washington, D.C., June 24 and July 22, 1980.

literally produced the final version of [the] "documents," even though they bore the label of the Department and "betrayed no hint of private involvement." How deeply embedded was vested interest and how rife was conflict of interest are evident in the introductory statement by Pryor:

We found that contractors are the hidden mainsprings behind DOE's early dealings with the public. We found contractors employed to prepare advertising campaigns, to respond to mail and answer phone calls, to perform searches in response to Freedom of Information requests, and to manage public hearings.[56]

For all the determined data-gathering and sophisticated modeling therewith, we are dealing with the very small known rabbit in Anthony Down's famous horse-and-rabbit stew recipe.[57] The horse has huge proportions, unknown. With respect to nuclear wastes, for example, most of the calculations are based on known, albeit disputed quantities. Main preoccupation has been with disposition of spent fuels as capacity of on-site storage space nears exhaustion. Amounts are calculable as to volume, weight, and even radioactivity. Estimate of effects, on environment and people, is highly controversial. High-level attention has been paid to low-level wastes, defined by Nuclear Regulatory Commission standards as those which are not high-level, not a by-product of the mining and milling of uranium, nor of reprocessing nuclear fuel, nor containing transuranic elements at more than 10 nanocuries per gram. Statistics show that out of the 79,000 cubic meters generated in 1979, some 20 to 25 percent came from biomedical uses.

In the inventory of high-level wastes, there can of course be no accounting for those associated with weapons research and development. Yet, this is where the preponderance lies—out of reach for security reasons, unknown and therefore uncounted. Vastly underestimated until recently was the toxicity of another source of wastes—*viz.*, nuclear reactors which, due to malfunction or old age, can no longer operate safely. Conventional wisdom had been that their levels of radiation would decline to insignificance after several decades. Contrary evidence was brought to light in 1976 by Marvin Resnikoff, then a physicist with the New York Public Interest Research Group. He revealed that some components will remain radioactive for thousands of years after a plant is shut down. The isotopes of nickel and niobium had been overlooked by the nuclear industry and now must be reckoned with as reactors, built in the 1960s, approach their end in the 1990s. It has

[56] *Ibid.*, Opening Statement, June 24, 1980.
[57] Anthony Downs, *op. cit.*

been claimed that rubble containing radioactive nickel may remain hazardous for up to 1.5 million years.[58] The utilities have had no experience in taking down and disposing of a large radioactive reactor. Basic information on factors central to a determination of costs has been adjudged inadequate and unreliable since all studies were prepared by sources affiliated with the nuclear power industry.[59] While dollar costs are already calculated to be mounting, the costs in terms of public health and safety are incalculable and largely ignored..

And what of untold environmental assaults as yet untallied? What count, for example, is there of fallout from nuclear power in space? We know of the high-level concern over contamination from the breakup of a Soviet nuclear satellite over Canada in 1978; much is made of another Soviet satellite's demise in 1983. But the U.S. space nuclear power program, i.e., the Department of Defense's plan to build a new generation of compact nuclear reactors to power laser battle stations and its other military satellites, already has a history of failures unpublicized and of plutonium releases. The health effects were officially pronounced to be "minor," although they were never studied in depth. The sanguine assumption was made, anent the plutonium fuel pack aboard the aborted Apollo 13 moon-landing mission, that the container would remain intact for about 860 years. Such neat certitude, designed to give assurance, can only be attributed to self-validating models built on artificially-hardened data.

Similar complacency is evident in the plans being developed by the U.S. Navy for sea disposal of up to 100 nuclear submarines scheduled for retirement during the coming three decades. Known is the fact that each decommissioned vessel would contain up to 50,000 curies, more than all the radioactivity already in materials dumped in either the Atlantic or Pacific. Unknown, and perhaps to be learned only when irreversible effects are evident, are the impacts on human health. We do not yet know precisely what quantity of radioactive waste has been dumped in our oceans, let alone the effects of this accumulation on the food chain from plankton to man.[60]

---

[58] Colin Norman, "A Long-Term Problem for the Nuclear Industry," *Science*, 22 January, 1982, pp. 376–379.

[59] *Initial Brief of the Resale Customer Group, United States of America before the Federal Energy Regulatory Commission, Connecticut Yankee Atomic Power Company, Docket No. ER78–360,* June 22, 1979. I am indebted to Daniel Guttman, Esq. for this document and much helpful guidance in research on the reliance on consultants.

[60] *Dumping of Radioactive Waste off the Pacific Coast,* Subcommittee of the Committee on Government Operations, U.S. House of Representatives, Ninety-sixth Congress, Second Session, October 7, 1980.

SAFE RADIATION STANDARDS

Figuring large in radiation risk analysis is the concept of the "safe standard," historical review of which reveals how greatly old verities can undergo change with experience and over time. (Need we remind ourselves that x-ray technology was once considered so benign that early British radiologists "magically" counted the pence in the pockets of little boys' breeches as a parlor trick?) Twenty-five years ago, there was widespread acceptance of the theory that so long as an individual's dosage did not exceed a certain threshold, no radiation damage would occur. This rather comforting conviction was not substantiated by subsequent research, and by 1965 the International Commission on Radiological Protection (ICRP) recommended that *any* exposure to radiation be considered potentially harmful to man. The position taken earlier by Lauriston S. Taylor, then Chief, Atomic and Radiation Physics Division, National Bureau of Standards, was that "aside from medical applications, no radiation is good for man." [61] Even this hallowed beneficium was ultimately to be withdrawn.

Over the years, serious controversy has arisen over methods of calculating the effects of radiation exposure. Once acceptable maximum permissable exposures based on linear extrapolation were deemed by the National Academy of Sciences' Committee on the Biological Effects of Ionizing Radiation (BEIR), revising its 1972 estimates, to require a tenfold reduction. But there was no unanimity among epidemiologists as to validity of data, design of studies, or the analyses performed. Among the assumptions proven erroneous over time were those relating to risk from low-level radiation exposure. Singled out as "the real culprit for unnecessary population dose" were the uses once officially condoned because they were either assumed to be salutary or could be rationalized on the cost/benefit basis. Professor Karl Z. Morgan[62] contends that the medical profession, exempt from the ICRP's recommended maximum permissable exposure, is responsible for 90 per cent of man-made radiation to which the public is exposed. He deplores the misuse and overuse of diagnostic x-rays. With ever more powerful scanners, and hospitals' determination to make them operate cost-effectively, "benefits" to patients are, indeed, dubious. With nuclear medicine still in its infancy, whose are the costs and whose the benefits are matters for grave concern.

[61] Lauriston S. Taylor, "Radiation Exposure as a Reasonable Calculable Risk," *Health Physics*, Vol. I, 1958, p. 63.
[62] Karl Z. Morgan, "How Dangerous is Low-Level Radiation?" *New Scientist*, 5 April, 1979, pp. 18–21.

The Safety Image

The supposition, then, that all sources of radiation are known and can be accounted for in the risk analysis models has no foundation. Faith in that assumption is likely to go hand-in-hand with belief that there is a safe standard. This, for all its propensity to shift, has become reified and deified because it suited so well the mission of the Atomic Energy Commission; this was to promote and preserve the *image* of the safety of the silent-atom-peacefully-at-work. The game plan of the AEC and its lineal descendants, ERDA, DOE, and NRC, has been to shield the public, purportedly, from anxiety by withholding and distorting information and even tampering with perceptions. Familiar, indeed, are the official first and last words on any incident involving radioactivity, whether A-bomb testing at Yucca Flat, waste seepage at West Valley, or accident at Three Mile Island: "The levels did not exceed safety standards." Because much damaging information has been withheld from public view, optimism about the safety of nuclear power plant design and operation is suspect if it is based on officially-released facts and figures. Important technical and institutional weaknesses were revealed when the Union of Concerned Scientists requested, under the Freedom of Information Act, access to Nuclear Regulatory Commission documents. Among them was a special, internal log, called "The Nugget File"[63] on some ten years of serious accidents and safety deficiencies.

The Nugget File is a collection of short reports, averaging perhaps 2–3 pages in length, about a wide variety of astonishing safety deficiences at U.S. nuclear power plants. It casts light on both the technical and institutional aspects of nuclear power reactor safety and shows how seriously the image of safety in the nuclear program is blemished by simple and widespread carelessness. For want of fuses, key nuclear safety equipment is rendered inoperative. Electrical relays fail because they are painted over or welded together or disconnected. Valves in safety equipment are destroyed because switches on their motors are incorrectly adjusted. A 3000-gallon radioactive waste tank is found in an operating plant to be connected with the plant's drinking water system. Emergency power sources fail routinely; bizarre equipment failure modes are a common occurrence and operator errors are an endemic feature of the U.S. nuclear program. Simple maintenance operations disrupt established safety precautions, as when valves that affect the water level in the reactor were accidentally shut off during the repair of a leaky faucet in a plant laboratory. Sensitive pieces of safety equipment malfunction because they are frozen or burned or flooded or dirty or corroded or bumped or dropped or overpressurized or unhinged

---

[63] Robert D. Pollard, ed., *The Nugget File*, Cambridge, Massachusetts: Union of Concerned Scientists, January, 1979, pp. 2–3.

or miscalibrated or miswired; they are also known, to cite one of Hanauer's [Dr. Stephen H. Hanauer, the Nuclear Regulatory Official who kept the file] marginal comments, to be "guaranteed not to work" because of bad initial designs.

Perhaps most shattering to the contrived image of safety have been disclosures about the AEC's deliberate deception, as was exemplified in the reopening of a case, *Bulloch et al. v. The United States*, originally tried in 1956. At issue was whether Utah sheep ranchers were entitled to government compensation for the 4,390 sheep alleged to have been poisoned by fallout from A-bomb testing in Nevada. U.S. District Civil Judge, A. Sherman Christensen, declared that

agents of the government had made false and misleading representations, that witnesses were improperly pressured, that crucial information was intentionally withheld or unrepresented, and that "by these convoluted actions and in related ways the processes of the court were manipulated to the government's advantage."[64]

Damning evidence, not about sheep and their lambs, but about residents and their babies, showed up in a landmark civil damages trial in which 1,192 plaintiffs accused the United States of negligence in the conduct of atmospheric nuclear testing. The government's claim remained essentially the same as it had been during the 1950's, i.e., that radiation exposure from fallout did not exceed the "federal safety standard" of five rads for workers in the nuclear industry. The suit filed on behalf of 460 victims of leukemia, Hodgkin's Disease, and other forms of cancer uncovered evidence that the government's estimates failed to note that "safe" radiation readings had been taken 25 or 26 days after the explosion of "Dirty Harry," a 32.4 kiloton bomb. An official monitor, whose personal badge registered 1,720 milirems, almost six times as much radiation as conceded in his report, admitted that he had failed to record unusually high levels that "didn't enforce my natural prejudices."[65] Further to underscore the folly of accepting the figures on which nuclear safety analysis confidently relies is the mounting case material amassed by the National Association of Atomic Veterans. Their files contain the history of Van R. Brandon, once member of a medical team charged with monitoring the exposure of soldiers at the Yucca Flat Nevada test site during four atomic tests in 1956 and 1957. Brandon kept silent because he had been warned in the mustering-out interview in 1961 that he could be charged with treason under

[64] R. Jeffrey Smith, "Atom Bomb Tests Leave Infamous Legacy," *Science*, 15 October, 1982, p. 266.

[65] Testimony of Frank Butrico, cited by R. Jeffrey Smith, "Atom Bomb Tests Leave Infamous Legacy," *op. cit.*, p. 268.

the National Security Act if he disclosed the nature of his duty. Now eager to help other atomic veterans receive compensation, he revealed that he himself had been denied benefits because the Army refused to acknowledge that the top secret unit in which he had served had ever existed. Two sets of ledgers had been kept to record the levels of radiation shown on the badges of the exposed soldiers. One set was to show that no one had received an exposure above the approved dosimeter reading. "The other set of books was to show what the actual reading was. That set of books was brought in in a locked briefcase attached to a man's wrist by a set of handcuffs every morning."[66]

It would be an injustice to attribute this long-standing policy of fabrication to engineered tunnel vision alone. An adamant image of safety had to be defended at all costs, even that of truthfulness, because by dint of some machinated calculations, it provided a protective shield in the face of liability and, hence, was cost/effective. Through litigation there were bound to be established precedents as to the government's liability vis-a-vis not only radiation from various sources but also a multiplicity of other carcinogenic and toxic substances. In addition, national security considerations always serve as a convenient rationale for the analyst who conceives of his task as making nuclear energy acceptable. It could be argued that the country's well-being would be endangered if the so-called "option" of nuclear energy were adversely affected by public anxiety over radiation exposure. Since demonstration, disruption, and civil disobedience could be construed as a source of aid and comfort to the enemy, suppression of any intelligence would appear justified. Many agencies, including the Nuclear Regulatory Commission, have filed appeals on grounds of national security for exemption from the Freedom of Information Act.

METHODOLOGY OF RISK ANALYSIS

The methodology used in the analysis of nuclear reactor safety is grafted from military and space roots. Called fault-tree analysis because of the tree-like schematic design used to depict relationships within the system, the technique became the cynosure when Professor Norman Rasmussen of MIT and his team of experts applied it in estimating the probability of a core meltdown.[67] According to their diagram, at every branch point along the path of the reactor's operation, there would be a safety system, either responding or failing to respond. The "safety

66 "Ex-Medic Says Army Kept False Records on Radiation," *The New York Times*, February 8, 1982.

67 U.S. Nuclear Regulatory Commission, *Reactor Safety Study*, WASH–1400 (or NUREG–75–014), Washington, D.C., 1975.

system fails" branch might then lead to a branch point for "Plant evacu-ation alarm," which would or would not sound. The probability of a "pathway to disaster," i.e., the chain of events in which everything goes wrong, is computed by considering the probability of each of its constituents' failures. The risk associated with a pathway is then de-termined by multiplying its probability of occurrence by the magni-tude of its consequences. The sum of the risks associated with each pathway represents an estimate of the total for the system. Based on judgment of risk at every step of a specific sequence of events leading to an accident, the conclusions were that "the actuarial risks (sums of the probabilities of consequences multiplied by the severity of conse-quences) are very small" and that "the chances of severe accidents that would cause large numbers of casualties are extremely small—so small as to be within the range of risks we hardly deign to consider."[68] Ex-perts applying this method of calculation to health risks associated with the accident of the Three Mile Island reactor in Pennsylvania on March 28, 1979, found them to be "negligible." In their view, "a single automobile accident during the evacuation would have done more damage." Even though subsequent review[69] found the WASH-1400 probability estimate low, perhaps by a factor of as much as 500, and the expected number of cancers for a given accident several times higher, the methodology emerged unscathed.

What should concern us as we review the continued and unshaken faith in the techniques of calculation of risk is the certainty of the con-clusions it offers about uncertain questions. More than a function of style or volume, this is a matter of methodology and one that must be assessed critically because, just as in the case of the parent methodology of systems analysis, the mythology of the emperor's new clothes persists. Of overarching importance is the fact that the honest use of the tech-niques is as dangerous as their abuse, what with their potential for incorporating and obscuring bias and for providing validation for pre-determined conclusions. A nice bit of irony resides in the claim that theirs are the conclusions that are "scientific" and "rational," while others, which do not fit the model, are "emotional" and "irrational." The latter are, according to official policy, impediments to achieving "rational energy policy" and must, therefore, be overcome. It is by this calculus that hazards at the Three Mile Island Plant have been dis-

---

[68] National Academy of Sciences, National Research Council, *Energy in Transition 1985–2010, Final Report of the Committee on Nuclear and Alternative Energy Systems*, San Francisco, California: W. H. Freeman and Company, 1979, p. 461.

[69] W.K.H. Panofsky (Director, Stanford Linear Accelerator Center), Testimony be-fore Subcommittee on Energy and the Environment, Committee on Interior and In-sular Affairs, Washington, D.C., June 11, 1976.

missed as trivial, *even though the full extent of the danger to human beings is not yet known.*

Underlying the fault-tree approach is an abstract mathematical theorem, facetiously called the "Bayesian haze."[70] First reported in 1763 and set aside by its creator, the Reverend Mr. Thomas Bayes (because he had doubts about the validity of his logic), the Bayesian principle was resurrected in recent years because it was found useful in statistical inference. Methodological superstructure has obscured the essential subjectivity of the Bayesian premise, which is one of "equi-probability of the unknown criterion." This means that one man's guess work is as good as another's, that the probabilities across the range are *all* equal and, thus, that *any* starting point for the analysis is allowable.

If, then, one were to accept the assumptions of the Reactor Safety Study, one would have to conclude that the accident at Three Mile Island never occurred. What happened was simply outside the realm of probabilities as calculated on the premises. Indeed, this is the gist of the argument put forward by Babcock & Wilcox Company in the $4 billion law suit brought against them by the General Public Utilities Corporation, whose subsidiary, Metropolitan Edison Company of Reading, Pennsylvania, operated Three Mile Island. The case was settled out of court for $37 million after a three-month trial. Babcock & Wilcox' claim was that if mechanical procedures had been continued without operator intervention, the core of the reactor would not have been uncovered, and the incident would have been relatively minor. If this were to be the case, problems of estimating nuclear safety would not be lessened. There is more, much more, to safe operation than what is included in a particular fault/event tree diagram. Besides design features, *engineered* to be safe but not necessarily *executed* that way, there are the many problems associated with safe operation over time. Embrittlement of vessel walls is occurring sooner than expected; corrosion and vibration are causing tube failures, which along with the system woes they precipitate also add significantly to worker radiation exposure.

In contradistinction to the Reactor Safety Study's starting point on the Bayesian array that "normal" operation has extremely low probability of accident is the one that starts from the premise that accidents are bound to occur, that by their very complexity systems will run into trouble because parts are highly interactive and the tight coupling amplifies the effects of equipment, design, or operator errors in incom-

---

[70] Alvan R. Feinstein, "The Haze of Bayes, the Aerial Palaces of Decision Analysis, and the Computerized Ouija Board," *Clinical Pharmacology and Therapeutics*, Vol. 21, Number 4, April, 1977, pp. 482–496.

prehensible and unpredictable ways. By this reckoning, Three Mile Island was a normal accident.[71] Another starting point, mentioned only *sotto voce* because of its fearful implications, is the deliberately-induced accident. Other scenarios have treated the nuclear reactor as though it were a neutral object. But to do so is to deny the reality. There are many persons, inside and outside the heavily-guarded walls of a nuclear reactor, who would, for one reason or another, like to have a catastrophe happen. Sabotage and terrorism could be nightmarishly effective if directed to many of the phases in the nuclear cycle including, most ominously, the plutonium produced in the breeder. The tree branching sequences that have led to reassuring risk calculations may have been correct; they started from the wrong place on the tree-trunk.

The perilous fallacy in fault/event tree methodology as applied to reactor safety lies in overlooking the socially significant point that *for every variable* there is a *distribution* and every distribution has *extreme values*. We do not, we cannot, know which one of these extremes should receive serious weight. But to ignore any is to court disaster. Perhaps we should acknowledge that the question is not which of the points along the Bayesian scale we should start with but, rather, whether we should, as a matter of public policy, base safety regulations and enforcement practices on the institutionalized iffiness of statistical probabilities. The cozy cocoon of figures protects no one and deflects from the common sense, Murphy's Law principle that anything that can go wrong will.

The range of probabilities covered by a given fault tree is necessarily and arbitrarily limited. This means that there is a strong likelihood that other paths have been bypassed. The Rasmussen fault tree, for example, rested on only those mechanical events that could lead to reactor core meltdown. From that premise, the task was logically delineated as one of identifying all accident sequences in the operation that could cause this disaster, and, by assigning probabilities to each event in each chain, to calculate probabilities for the main categories of serious accidents. But is this conceptual model adequate to produce reliable predictions of systems failure probability? At even so early a stage as comments on the draft of WASH-1400, reviewers expressed doubts. These views were buried in the appendices. Characteristically and consistent with the *argumentum ad nominem* that surfaces in every aspect, even the technical, of the debate over nuclear safety, the official response of the Nuclear Regulatory Commission at that time and subsequently was to turn to those Nobel Laureates who agreed with them and to their

[71] Charles Perrow, "Normal Accident at Three Mile Island," *Society*, 18:5, July/August, 1981, pp. 17–26.

own cadre of experts for the "balanced perspective." The Rasmussen Report left us with the statistically-contrived certainty that (a) no serious nuclear accident would occur and (b) the radioactivity released would be of little concern. Necromantic use of data is calculated to convey the idea that nuclear power is safe compared to coal with its mining disasters, particulate emissions, and radioactive smokestacks, less harmful than the diagnostic x-rays to which one routinely submits without protest, and much less risky than travel by air or car, or the myriad "normal" activities associated with living in today's world. And so we come full circle back to the "it's-all-in-the-head" starting point.

Probablistic calculations are only as credible as the facts that go into them. The less we knew, the more sure we were. A fool's paradise of ignorance once preserved the image of the atom as the cheap, clean, safe source of energy. Time and events have brought intelligence that makes old certainty foolhardy. There is mounting evidence, for example, that there is little relationship between official book rules and regulations on design, construction, and operation of nuclear reactors and inspection and enforcement. The files of the regulatory agencies show that the government's inspection policy is one of almost exclusive reliance on assurances provided by the regulated industry.[72] The records kept by both have, in the words of a former construction inspector, "a very poor confidence level."[73] One revelation after another underscores the instability of the factual base on which probablistic safety calculations rest. Perhaps most damaging is evidence related to design errors and to faulty construction. As to the former, there is the case of the Diablo Canyon reactor, built in proximity to a known earthquake fault. Pacific Gas & Electric Company, the utility involved, had survived challenges by scientific and public groups for its ignorance or deliberate ignoring of a fault, named Hosgri, but on September 28, 1981, notified the Nuclear Regulatory Commission that the blueprints for constructing the reactor had been reversed. The design charts had been so transposed that some structural supports intended to help withstand potential earthquake were in the wrong place; pipes carrying nuclear fuel, radioactive wastes, and a coolant were insufficiently buttressed; others had been given needless protection.[74]

[72] General Accounting Office, *Reporting Unscheduled Events at Commercial Nuclear Facilities: Opportunities to Improve Regulatory Commission Oversight*, Washington, D.C., EMD–79–16, January 26, 1979.

[73] Joseph M. Varela in February 12, 1976, letter of William Anders, Chairman, Nuclear Regulatory Commission, quoted in Lawrence S. Tye, *Looking but not Seeing*, Cambridge, Massachusetts: Union of Concerned Scientists, 1978, p. 1.

[74] R. Jeffrey Smith, "A Seismological Shoot-Out at Diablo Canyon," *Science*, 30 October, 1981, pp. 528–529.

One Congressional investigation after another has found that the existing federal inspection system is not capable of offering genuine assurance that the nuclear power industry is being operated safely. Theory about safe design and operation does not jibe with experience. Quite apart from records deliberately doctored to look good and occurrences purposely downplayed so as not to arouse public anxiety, technical difficulties resulting from normal operation are coming into view. These have not entered into or as yet altered the safety calculations although they are beginning to cause concern here and abroad. Pressurized thermal shock caused by embrittlement of the welded steel plates on the older reactors is a danger now acknowledged by the U.S., West Germany, and Finland, although the Atomic Industrial Forum maintains the position of "no near-term safety concern." (In its review of actual records, the Nuclear Regulatory Commission found that the scenario for vessel cracking as steel lost its toughness and flexibility was not only plausible; it had actually happened.) If, as common sense would suggest, a case can be made for greater vigilance on the part of the government regulatory agency, then it is all the more regrettable that current economic ideology condones NRC budget cuts, ordains earlier licensing of light water reactors and fewer obstructions in the path of the controversial breeder, and takes deliberate steps to prevent information from leaking to the public, affected whether it does or does not perceive the dangers.

First and last, the questions of safety become battles between the experts. With respect to the accident at Three Mile Island, General Public Utilities, the parent company of Metropolitan Edison, charged Babcock & Wilcox, designer of Three Mile Island, with $4 billion in corporate misconduct and reckless indifference for neglecting to keep the utility informed of problems in the reactor's design. General Public Utilities had a similar lawsuit pending against the U.S. government, the charge being that the Nuclear Regulatory Commission was negligent in its duty to regulate the utility. Babcock & Wilcox mounted a countersuit, charging the utility with "negligence and recklessness and, in certain respects, deliberate and willful misconduct that overwhelm any possible finding of failure" on their part. We may be sure that in any case fact and fiction will blend in proportions varying with the self interest of the parties and not that of the public. In litigation of this kind, *who* is at fault is the issue and *not* nuclear safety. Absolution for one or the other side, or even invocation of the statute of limitations, serves as a screen to shield the industry or the government from financial liability and in so doing deflects focus from the damage being done regardless of where responsibility for it lies.

TECHNOLOGY ASSESSMENT

The techniques of systems analysis have, over time, found many uses and have appeared in many guises and contexts. Cost/benefit analysis, risk assessment, risk analysis, and even the ubiquitous Environmental Impact Statement all belong to the same family. Technology assessment, serving as a kind of umbrella for all of them in a variety of manifestations, is, therefore, largely déjà vu. To judge from the accepted definitions, there have been no methodological refinements and the mythology remains the same. According to Hetman,[75] for example:

Technology assessment is a *systems analysis* approach to providing a whole conceptual framework, complete both in *scope and time*, for decisions about the appropriate utilization of technology for *social purposes.* [Emphasis added]

Note that Hetman's definition makes a point of tying technology utilization with *social* purpose. This is a significant dimension, reflected also in the definition offered by the Congressional Research Service of the Library of Congress.[76] Here we find articulated the connections among the various techniques, identification of cost/benefit analysis as a component, centrality of information, future orientation, and the wedding to social purpose, broadly conceived:

Technology assessment is the process of taking a purposeful look at the consequences of technological change. It includes the primary cost/benefit balance of short-term localized marketplace economics, but particularly goes beyond these to identify affected parties and unanticipated impacts on as broad and long fashion as is possible. It is neutral and objective, seeking to enrich the information for management decisions. Both "good" and "bad" side effects are investigated since a missed opportunity for benefit may be detrimental to society just as is an unexpected hazard.

These definitions are worthy but not workable in that both are imbued with the same kind of idealism that once made the concept of a systems analysis approach attractive. With what we now know as the characteristics of the methodology that has evolved, both statements are contradicted by reality. Hetman calls for a *whole conceptual framework,* complete in *scope and time,* for decisions about the *appropriate* utilization of technology for *social purposes.* Systems analysis as we have seen it applied would not provide a "whole conceptual frame-

75 Francois Hetman, *Society and the Assessment of Technology*, Paris, Organisation for Economic Co-operation and Development, 1973, p. 56.

76 Richard A. Carpenter, "The Scope and Limits of Technology Assessment," *OECD Seminar on Technology Assessment*, Paris, January 26–28, 1972, pp. 1–2.

work" but accommodates only that part that would fit the technical model. The introduction of the *time* factor implies that future impacts can be anticipated, accounted for, and measured. In reality they are often not only unknown but unknowable. *Appropriate* utilization is nicely eudaemonic, and *social purposes* add an idyllic touch. What Hetman outlines may be right, good, and necessary but it is patently impossible to achieve, because the parameters lie outside the scope of systems techniques. Similarly, the Congressional Research Service statement, more idealistic than realistic, contains many contradictions. It would be quixotic in the extreme to assume that an assessment that is "purposeful" is also "neutral" and "objective." Precisely because of the "primary cost/benefit balance of short-term localized market-place economics," the impacts on "affected parties" will be rationalized in one way or another. Risk analyses performed with preciosity will conjure away the need for concern over "unanticipated impacts," which can be contrived to seem unlikely and/or insignificant. The inverse time-to-veracity relationship is nowhere more evident. "Good" and "bad" side-effects are, in essence, judgments imposed by history, often not recognized in their time, and usually not agreed upon even centuries later. Bagdikian[77] reminds us that it has taken two hundred years of the Industrial Revolution for men to realize that they are very good at predicting the consequences of their inventions.

In view of the state-of-the-art, we would be disingenuous to the point of dishonesty to proceed as though technology assessment were any more objective, any less value-laden than its antecedents and constituents. Difficulties are compounded by the very elements of uncertainty and risk that the methodology, its orientation now mainly toward the future, is purported to handle. Technologies advance, effects ripple, and time-bombs make their presence known in ways that elude futurologists, forecasters, and technology assessors. To be sure, Space Age electronics has given impetus to the pursuit of analytic techniques and provided the capability for sophisticated modeling. It is all the more ironic, therefore, that the methodology of assessment founders on the threshold of the very technology that has made it all possible. We refer, of course, to information technology (IT) in its rapidly-changing and burgeoning forms and manifestations.

ASSESSMENT OF INFORMATION TECHNOLOGY

Interdependent and indistinguishable in their convergence into IT are three components, each with its own developmental history—

[77] Ben H. Bagdikian, *The Information Machines*, New York: Harper & Row, Publishers, p. 1.

computers, microelectronics, and telecommunications. Whether IT heralds a second Industrial Revolution or is just another, albeit giant, step in an evolutionary process need not concern us here, although, like the advent of automation decades ago, it is the subject of much debate. What is important is whether technology assessments, of which there is already a plethora, are instructive as to the impacts.

To begin with, we find emphasis almost exclusively on hardware and software capability and then only on the limitless possibilities. In making much of the marvels ahead for mankind, such studies convey the message that society's shortsighted resistance to change and recalcitrance in the face of technological advance are the impediments to realizing wondrous benefits. Slavish adherence to the techniques of assessment inevitably produces the canard that society is reprehensibly laggard and must adapt in order to survive and prosper. Cited as the model for emulation is Japan, which leads the world in innovation, enjoys prosperity, a favorable trade-balance, and, presumably, an economically secure future. Assessments of IT contain a built-in favorable bias, since their focal point is cost/effectiveness in a specific application. Not to be overlooked here is the incestuous, self-validating utilization of the information system to prove the point.

Longer-term and wider-ranging impacts, because they lie outside the purlieu of "analysis," are relegated to a kind of *obiter dicta* category and given short shrift. Thus, we find a special issue of *Science*[78] devoted to "an assessment of the revolution in computers and electronics." Twenty invited papers, replete with details and diagrams, describe the hardware and software, outline uses, and discuss prospects. The editor's blanket introduction acknowledges the deliberate omission of military applications, "a topic that is not readily portrayed," and also his reason for failure to include the societal impacts:[79]

I sought the counsel of a number of experts whose responsibility it is to be future-oriented in such matters. They were all hesitant about making specific predictions. The consensus was that the impact will be very great.

The editors of a compendium of papers published by the Club of Rome[80] regard microelectronics-based technologies as a phenomenon already having profound effect on our lives and likely to have an even greater impact on the future.

Microelectronics, through miniaturization, automation, computerization, and robotization, will fundamentally transform our lives and impinge on most of its facets: at work, at home, in politics, on science, at war and at peace.

[78] *Science*, 12 February, 1982.
[79] Philip H. Abelson, "The Revolution in Computers and Electronics," *Ibid.*, p. 753.
[80] Gunter Friedrichs and Adam Schaff, *Microelectronics and Society*, Oxford, New York, and elsewhere: Pergamon Press, 1982, p. v.

This is a trenchant statement, worthy of note because of its explicit acknowledgement that the manifestations of IT are multiple and the range of their consequences far-reaching. Regrettably, interest ceases with this lip-service and the theme pervading this volume as well as many others on the subject echoes the old refrain—that ultimately IT will have beneficial effects and that it behooves mankind to forsake benighted apprehensions and ride the wave of high technology to the brave new post-industrial world. The pattern is monotonous. Assessments of IT are determinedly positive—predeterminedly positive if we are to judge from the following:[81]

Some of (the) developments are already further advanced than many realize—indeed, many companies are loath to trumpet their new systems for fear of encouraging hostile trade union reaction.

One cannot but wonder at the bravura that inspires such confident optimism, even in the face of ignorance, about the technology and, at the same time, the modest reticence of "experts," so designated by *Science* by virtue of their "responsibility to be future-oriented." (This curious attribution of "expertness," which would include seers, astrologers, and tea-leaves-readers, is a subtle manifestation of the second-class status accorded any but the "hard" disciplines.) Abelson found them "hesitant about making specific predictions."

The point that should be made is not that we do not know enough to make specific predictions but that we know better than to do so. Far more eloquent than a table of numbers showing the growth or decline of office jobs since the introduction of electronic data-processing—a matter about which there still exists disagreement despite years of statistics-gathering and analysis—is Abelson's own paragraph in summation of societal impacts as he sees them:

While bringing many benefits to society, the revolution will also bring problems, tension, and disbenefits. Changes in employment carry with them trauma for those displaced. To the ancient tension between rich and poor will be added tensions between those with high intellectual capacity and the less gifted, and between the well educated and the untrained. Problems will develop with fixation on entertainment and possible misdirection of computer systems for antisocial purposes.

This statement is useful for two reasons. First, and of passing interest, it contains tacit refutation of a position often taken by technical optimists. This equates interest in social impacts with what Florman[82]

[81] Tom Forester, editor, *The Microelectronics Revolution*, Cambridge, Massachusetts: The MIT Press, 1981, p. xvi.
[82] Samuel C. Florman, *Blaming Technology: The Irrational Search for Scapegoats*, New York: St. Martin's Press, 1982.

calls "an irrational search for scapegoats" by making a spurious straw-man of technology. Such argumentation carries the sly intimation that attention to consequences is somehow tantamount to subversion. Flor-man therefore feels called upon to "demolish the myth of technological determinism." Abelson's paragraph suggests that there is no need to tilt at this windmill. To try to assess the impacts and implications of IT is not to demonize technology. It is, rather, to appreciate it, but not from the ostrich's stance that sees only benefits and makes us vulnerable to potentially enormous repercussions because of ignored negative im-pacts. Further giving the lie to a journalistically-popular but misin-formed notion, *viz.*, that persons questioning the effects of technology are automatically opposed to technology or prone to attribute *deus ex machina* status to it, or both, is the irrefutable fact of life that how far and fast IT advances is in the main a social matter, a manifestation of what Sorokin labelled the *Zeitgeist*.[83] What this implies is that technology is an intrinsic part of the social fabric at any given time. Social cognoscenti know, without further disputation about "blame" or whether technology is an autonomous force, that in our society the requirement for more information, coupled with accelerating costs of processing it, complements the advance of microelectronics and is heightened by it. This cybernetic relationship describes the dynamic. It does not, however, encompass the larger social dynamic that makes for change in a society. Here, Sorokin's "law of immanent causation," like Hegel's dialectic, serves a useful purpose in that it reminds us that every period, even the Age of the Computer that is ours, bears the seeds of revolt, sometimes even revolution. When, how, and in what forms the reactions world wide to the global impacts of microelectronics will manifest themselves depend on how IT affects the social order.

Abelson's brief commentary serves also as a convenient trajectory for a discussion of the "problems, tensions, and disbenefits" that, in our paradigm, might cause the seeds of disenchantment to grow. His "future-oriented experts" who eschewed "specific predictions" were right, but for the wrong reasons. Their kind of analysis would compartmentalize effects and thus invite the customary let-them-eat-cake placebos. Work-ers displaced by robots? let them become computer technicians. Elec-tronic systems intruding on privacy? let the marketplace protect, if it pays. Students can't spell? get them word processors.

Using a widened lens and cognizant of their synergistic nature, we now turn to those areas most often mentioned in the compendia of concerns but slighted in information technology assessments. For pur-poses of our discussion, we have designated three broad categories: work life, private life, and quality of life. Necessarily overlapping, sometimes

---

[83] P. A. Sorokin, *op. cit.*

concentric, often intersecting, they are all disdainful of international borders and, indeed, have global repercussions. Of special significance are the differential impacts within the categories, since information technology will have varying effects on certain sectors of national and international economies and will create new divisions as to the have's and the have not's within and between them.

Our first category deals with the nature of jobs in post-industrial society and with the meaning of joblessness. Worklife cannot, of course, be separated from personal life, for the changing content and structure of jobs, the stresses and strains related to work or the lack thereof, manifest themselves in ways which might also fit appropriately into our quality-of-life category. We next focus on IT's role in transforming private life into a goldfish bowl existence. The information systems and data banks discussed in early sections of this book have proliferated and prospered. They have become so much a part of the apparatus of the "information society" that we scarcely notice their existence. Certainly, their intrusions do not figure as costs in information technology assessments. Deemed particularly cost/effective for purposes of law enforcement, for example, electronic communications systems could serve as instantaneous connection for tens of thousands of criminal justice systems, now being linked to the Federal Bureau of Investigation's center, one of the largest, most complicated data banks in the world. What this means for justice, civil liberties, and personal freedom is a matter for grave concern, already far beyond conjecture.[84]

The multitude of computer-based record-keeping systems has been multiplied by the burgeoning use of microcomputers. So cheap and accessible as to have become a household adjunct, the personal computer hastens the day when privacy will become an anachronism. The microcomputer is a key ingredient in electronic funds transfers, electronic mail, and the like. Access to information is facilitated through linkage of the home computer to any number of data bases, less immune to tapping than is generally acknowledged. Whatever line may once have existed between private and public information has disappeared, erased by a technology that makes Little-Brother-Next-Door a threat more uncontrollable than Orwell's Big Brother.

Dare we overlook, in our overview of the capability of IT to intrude in people's lives, its potential as the *idée-force* that makes dogma of current political idealogy and curtains minds against social injustice? Here, the synergism is unmistakable. Suppose, for example, that widespread unemployment were to breed the kind of unrest feared by French authorities and already evident in Germany. Large sectors of the popu-

---

[84] David Burnham, *The Rise of the Computer State*, New York: Random House, 1983.

lation dispossessed of jobs and devoid of hope for gainful employment make for wholesale disenchantment that does not contribute to a state of domestic peace and tranquillity. To maintain order, the powers that be, whoever they are, will be armed not only with such means of coercion as stored data on potential "trouble makers" and dissidents but also, more ominously, with the mind-shaping mechanism for brainwashing the public-at-large as to what is the "right" attitude toward elements deemed disruptive. Hitler succeeded in indoctrinating a whole generation. We cannot know who the next Hitler will be nor where he will surface. We do know that he will climb to power over the bodies of media-made scapegoats, every last one the object of collective and choreographed hate and all the more vulnerable thanks to IT's relentless capability for personal surveillance. There can be no doubt that new rivalries for employment will make for new confrontations—class warfare on the home front and trade wars on a global scale. Herein, according to two French finance officials, lies a potent "moving force of history."[85]

The admittedly generic quality-of-life heading cannot be treated as an entity apart from the above considerations, for they are all part of a larger pattern. Which is warp and which is woof matters less than the recognition that they are all interwoven. Accordingly, when we explore the implications of the information society, it is incumbent on us to ponder the challenge to and meaning of education, the changing structure, content, and value of information, and the outlook for a society in danger of forgetting human values and how to value humans. Far from frivolous is the question: How will the 21st century work?

WORKLIFE—EMPLOYMENT, UNEMPLOYMENT, AND EMPLOYABILITY

Statistics tell little about the impacts of IT on employment. To begin with, the grids in classification systems are not fine enough to capture changes as they occur. Even the gross picture is distorted by the government's definitions and ways of acquiring data. Official employment rates lack credibility because of who is and who is not included in the employed category. Underemployed persons such as those working part-time are counted. The nearly one million discouraged workers who have abandoned the search are not, nor are the untold thousands of "undocumented" aliens huddled in the ethnic anonymity of slums throughout the country.

Included, clearly as a ploy on the part of the Administration to boost the overall rates, are persons working for the military. The decision, in

---

[85] Simon Nora and Alain Minc, *The Computerization of Society*, Cambridge, Massachusetts: The MIT Press, 1980.

February, 1983, to count them among the employed was unprecedented and obvious. It caused the unemployment rate to drop even though it changed the employment picture not one iota. The Bureau of Labor Statistics gets its numbers from a monthly household survey sample taken by the Census Bureau, mainly through telephone interview. The information thus gleaned is a poor indicator of the true situation even though it is the basis for all kinds of rate-calculation. Data derived in this way fail to reflect the extent of joblessness, especially among minority youth and others who have left their family home and neighborhood. Above all, statistics do not show the devastating difference between unemployment and leisure. All too often, technical enthusiasts make much of the pie-in-the-sky, freedom-from-work aspects of electronics, without realizing the myriad deprivations associated with being without work and without a paycheck.

For clues as to how IT is affecting the labor market, historical reference to the Industrial Revolution or even to more recent technological innovation is irrelevant. In the past, new fields replaced some affected by automation. And, in periods of expansion, farm workers could move into industry; there was room in offices for some of the factory workers. Moreover, during times of economic prosperity, firms could afford a policy of humane retrenchment with incentives for early retirement, attrition rather than lay-off, and so on. The redundant worker of today is not kept on the payroll. Efficient operation dictates otherwise, and he has nowhere to turn. His experience and skill are obsolete. IT progresses rapidly on all fronts, in manufacturing, in processing, in all branches of office work, and in many kinds of service work at a time when the world economy is in a state of decline. And everywhere the jobs lost are gone forever, not only from the grasp of the current employee but from the ladder onto which another generation might have hoped to climb.

The all-pervasive nature of IT, which has already eliminated thousands of jobs, some even in such "high-technology" industries as telecommunications, makes a mockery of the whistling-in-the-dark compensation theory, viz., that growth in some other sector will somehow offset the losses. There are a number of attendant and attenuating circumstances mitigating against this happy solution. To be reckoned with are such matters as price trends, market saturation, and the state of the world economy in general. Also, there is the iron law of cost/effectiveness which, when applied as a measure of and for productivity, makes labor-saving desirable no matter what the state of the labor market happens to be. Not to be ignored is the world-wide excess supply of labor in both the industrialized and the developing countries, all with serious unemployment especially among their youth. For decades, the displacement-without-replacement trend realized through mechanization, then automation, and now robotization has spelled serious foreclosure of job opportunity. There is still work to be done, a great deal of it, but it is not valued or rewarded in the current market. While experience teaches that the greater the reliance on mechanical systems, the greater is the need for human and social services, the cost/effective ratio mandates substitution and, ultimately, elimination of the latter. Ultimately, the society pays the costs, but rarely are they linked to the causes. The manifestations are already visible, however—in racial strife in Great Britain and riots in Berlin. Perhaps what is called for in assessing the impacts of IT is the sociological equivalent of Bentham's moral thermometer.[86]

To be perennially unemployed is to be virtually unemployable. Two decades ago, we saw the ranks of the hard-core unemployed visibly increased by minority youth for whom there were no jobs. They, smarter than the welfare workers paid to motivate them, teach them Good Grooming and Job Decorum, and drill them in simple reading and arithmetic, knew that it was all a useless charade.[87] There simply were no jobs. J. Raga,[88] in a report for the International Labor Office, sees the outlook in many countries as grim:

To absorb the net increase in the labor force in the 1980s, 11 million jobs will need to be created in the United States on the assumption that the decade begins with an unemployment level of six million. In the United Kingdom as many additional jobs will need to be created as are already needed for the number of people currently unemployed; and France, starting the decade with an unemployment figure of about one million, will have to at least double the number of jobs that were created in the past 20 years. The Federal Republic of Germany entered the 1980s with about one million unemployed, and nearly two million jobs will need to be created during the decade to absorb the labor force increase.

At the threshold of the third year into the decade, official figures for the U.S. show over twelve million jobless—the highest number since 1933 and twice the starting level posited by Raga in setting the estimated need for new jobs at 11 million. Current unemployment statistics tell only part of the story. The tables do not show that the periods without a job are lasting longer and that workers are willingly down-grading themselves in desperation. Moreover, the takeover by IT puts a serious dent in the payrolls needed as a cushion, such as Social Security, to

[86] Jeremy Bentham, *Introduction to Principles of Morals and Legislation*, 1789.

[87] Ida R. Hoos, *Retraining the Workforce*, Berkeley, California: University of California Press, 1967, see especially Chapter 6.

[88] J. Raga, *The Impact of Microelectronics*, Geneva, Switzerland: International Labor Office, 1980, pp. 76–77.

ameliorate the impacts of job loss. The ripple effects on the business community are deepseated and widespread, as are the consequences for the life of a community.[89]

Much has been written about the devastating human costs of unemployment. The films, novels, and plays about the Great Depression of the 1930s, the social programs rising from its ravages—all are part of a historical record that should sensitize us to the pathological consequences of joblessness. Medical researchers of today are finding that many problems of physical and mental health are directly attributable to the stresses created or aggravated by unemployment. Dr. Harvey Brenner[90] of Johns Hopkins University designated as indices of pathology rates of age and sex-specific mortality, cardio-vascular-renal disease mortality, suicide mortality, homicide mortality, mental hospital admission, imprisonment, and cirrhosis of the liver mortality. Using correlation and regression analysis and data for a period from 1940 to 1973, Dr. Brenner found that the linkage to unemployment was statistically significant. Specifically, for every one percent increase in the unemployment rate sustained for six years 920 individuals commit suicide and 620 homicide. There are 37,000 total deaths, 20,000 of them due to cardiovascular causes. Cirrhosis of the liver, a disease due to heavy drinking, claims some 500 lives. Admissions to state mental and penal institutions are increased by 4,000 and 3,300 respectively. These findings are noteworthy in that Dr. Brenner has succeeded in expressing in statistical terms relationships previously reported in descriptive terms and thus not accorded scientific credibility. His conclusions are supported by a growing body of medical research. They show up obliquely in such findings as the potentially lethal combination of such widely-used tranquillizers as valium and automobile accidents, for example. The emotional strains caused by job loss manifest themselves in myriad ways, not yet amenable to statistical analysis but nonetheless discernible in statistics—on abuse of alcohol, drugs, spouses, and children. The psychic scars are indelible on individuals, families, and their communities.

Along with the health, physical and mental, of persons without work, there is also the health, physical and mental, of those at work that must be taken into account in an assessment of information technology. The application of microelectronics affects all aspects of work. Through years of research it is known that the main determinants of job satisfac-

[89] Barry Bluestone and Bennett Harrison, *The Deindustrialization of America*, New York: Basic Books, Inc. Publishers, 1982.

[90] M. Harvey Brenner, "Estimating the Social Costs of Natural Economic Policy: Implications for Mental and Physical Health and Clinical Aggression," testimony prepared for Joint Economic Committee, U.S. Congress, Washington, D.C., 1976.

tion are content and meaningfulness of the work; opportunites for learning; environment and social climate of the work place; job security and rewards. Identified among the factors affecting job content are skill requirements, responsibility, and autonomy, i.e., freedom from close supervision, all of which are directly affected by changes in IT.

Already apparent is the down-grading of skills while standardization of previously skilled jobs prepares them for robotization. In the printing industry, for example, typesetters, once the elite of the trade, have been replaced by visual display unit operators for whom typing is the sole requirement. Similarly, word-processing systems are usurping the formerly sacrosanct preserve of the secretary. Not only does IT lower that status, it also exerts a subtle and degrading effect on the executive, now often expected to perform his own letter and report-writing. Moreover, thanks to IT in the form of "teleconferencing," he too must sit in front of a screen instead of enjoying the respite of a trip to far-off meetings. One cannot fail to see that older workers, women in particular, are especially vulnerable as microelectronics advances the control of the system over clerical workers, with every transaction minutely clocked and every finger stroke counted. Significant in this respect are the results of a study showing that female office workers developed coronary problems at nearly twice the rate of other employed women.[91]

Heightened work intensity, coupled with growing social isolation at work, makes for increases in stress, a condition long recognized as a serious deterrent to healthful well-being. Interesting to note, the medical information system known as MEDLARS (Medical Literature Analysis and Retrieval System) contains over 500 entries under the heading of *stress*, with nearly 90,000 technical articles in the past 30 years. MEDLARS' collection defies summary but even superficial scan is instructive as evidence of the impact of job-related anxieties on health.

These problems show up in statistics on alcoholism and drug abuse at every level of the workforce. Of special interest in this context, however, is a study undertaken in 1974 by the National Institute on Drug Abuse (NIDA), which found a clear correlation between job pressure and drug use. High technology, computer-related companies in the vicinity of Boston's Route 128 were accorded special attention in that "their labor force represents an important sector of American workers from the standpoint of drug consumption—young, mobile, well-educated, highly paid.[92] An increase in their numbers, with the exponential

[91] S. G. Haynes and Manning Feinleib, "Women, Work, and Coronary Heart Disease: Prospective Findings from the Framington Heart Study," *American Journal of Public Health*, Vol. 70, No. 2, February, 1980.

[92] Marvin Grosswirth, "Stoned at the Office," *Datamation*, February, 1983, pp. 30–36.

growth of the electronics industry over the subsequent eight years, coupled with evidence on drug abuse, has ominous portent. Dr. Stephen C. Duvall, long associated with Control Data Corporation's Employee Assistance Program, commented on the computer and data-processing personnel:

> Some people use drugs to alleviate boredom. Many of the jobs are structured in ways that are repetitive and are not particularly creative or challenging. . . . Keypunchers basically are just sitting there checking in data eight hours a day. Programmers and systems analysts do work that can be aggravating or exhausting. It takes forever to find the flaws in the program and the frustration factor is severe and real. Sometimes drink or drug use is a real way to alleviate tension, or to relax, or to get away from it for a bit—or just to "space out" intentionally.

IT adds another category of stress-laden occupations not yet specifically identified as such in conventional surveys. Included here are the jobs performed by "interfacers," those persons who must face the public and simultaneously cope with systems recalcitrant in operation, prone to break down, irritating in their autocratic intractability. The vagaries of computerized systems which, paradoxically, countenance no such frailties on the part of the client seeking help or, perhaps, an exceptional favor, frustrate clerk and customer alike. But the airlines agent, bank teller, or credit clerk, caught between the computer and the often-irate public, is the interfacer whose own "productivity" is all the while closely watched and recorded.

Another group, perhaps less visible but no less vulnerable to IT-induced stress, occupy certain management positions. Cognizant that computers are the very heart of their business but that they are not conversant with their intricacies, such persons sense a loss of control. They do so with good reason. In the first place they must rely on technical specialists who may or may not share their knowledge of or devotion to the particular organization. Indeed, where the software is concerned, the volatility of personnel is notorious. "Head hunting" by competitors, the lure of greener pastures in other companies or in personal entrepreneurial ventures contribute to high turnover and to headaches for the manager. Moreover, when changes are called for, as would be the case of an accounting program in the face of new tax laws, difficulties are encountered if the original programmer has departed the scene. Managers also know and worry about the fact that no system of software is error-free. Frequently mistakes are not discovered until great damage is done. Nor are computerized systems tamper-proof. Take, for example, the case of J. Walter Thompson, the advertising agency, where $24.5 million in nonexistent revenues were logged into the computers over a four-year period. Discovery of the "cooked books" forced the company to lower its net income for 1978–81 by $12 million and resulted in a 21 percent drop in the company's stock.

Occurrences like these give managers cause for high anxiety. Systems that do not function as planned cause stress in abundance, and there seem to be more of both in evidence as computers shrink in price and size and become the nerve center of millions of businesses large and small. A growing number of cases, often settled out of court, testifies to the kind of problem created by systems which do not work or which work erroneously. A company critically dependent on its electronic system for billing and accounting can go bankrupt without realizing that it has been getting misinformation from its own records.[93]

There are some executives who are so enamored of personal computers that they use them to circumvent the company's data-processing departments, if they find them slow or inflexible. At the present, early stages of this trend, these "information guerrillas" pose problems to managers of data-processing departments because of the proliferation of data bases, which could possibly lead to conflicting decisions within the organization. One can predict that over the longer term IT will eliminate certain cadres of middle management and continue to undermine executive status in a trend long ago foreseen.[94]

Private Life—Information Technology as Intruder

Most of the ways in which IT intrudes on privacy would, paradoxically, appear on the benefit side of the conventional technology assessment. The computer matching that would bring together all kinds of personal information residing in thousands of data banks would, presumably, increase efficiency in government or business operations. Electronic links between police files and the Federal Bureau of Investigation would lengthen the arm of the law, and therefore, control crime more effectively. Electronic banking would speed financial transactions, all in the name of "full service to the public." Electronic mail would expedite communications. Telecommunications would upgrade, expand, and enhance them. Interactive systems connecting home computer, video screen, and related equipment would establish instantaneous contact and feedback.

This is, of course, the bright side of the coin. The darker side, if acknowledged at all, inspires admonitory pronouncements and edi-

---

[93] "Why Computers Don't Work," *The MacNeil-Lehrer Report*, New York, N.Y.: Educational Broadcasting Corporation and GWETA, November 26, 1981.

[94] Ida R. Hoos, "When the Computer Takes Over the Office," *Harvard Business Review*, July–August, 1960, pp. 102–113.

torials about the need for safeguards to ensure privacy. However, review of technical journals and papers offers little assurance that there exists now or in the future any feasible technical fix. The contrary may, in fact, be more likely, as advances in telecommunications facilitate entry into every facet of personal life. There is no longer a need, for example, to use a wiretap to eavesdrop. Recording and listening to the business of others have become so simple that they will happen unless specific technical steps are taken to prevent them. As we move into the information society, more information will be kept, more will be retrieved, and the opportunities for use, misuse, and abuse will multiply.

Electronic banking opens a large and lucrative field for personal information mining, with the implosion of financial transactions into memory banks. Seen from the legal point of view, the portent is serious:[95]

On the one hand, the privacy issue is usually treated as one concerned with the need to protect confidential information because of the potential embarrassment which disclosure would bring or because of the commercial value of the confidentially-held information. These values are important and deserve protection at least on a par with the legal protection given tortiously-induced emotional trauma or tortiously-appropriated business secrets. [Here the original cites Tort Law] But *of greater concern is the potential for political control which the recording of every financial transaction would bring.* [Emphasis added]

Justice Douglas' dissenting opinion in a case involving access to information serves as a useful corollary:[96]

In a sense a person is defined by the checks he writes. By examining them the [government] agents get to know his doctors, lawyers, creditors, political allies, social connections, religious affiliations, educational interests, the papers and magazines he reads, and so on *ad infinitum.* . . . These other items will enrich that storehouse and make it possible for a bureaucrat—by pushing one button— to get in an instant the names of the 190 million Americans who are subversives or potential and likely candidates.

The full-service automatic teller machine enables customers to withdraw cash and make deposits to both their checking and savings accounts, as well as to transfer funds between accounts and to make balance inquiries. New electronic hookups will include electronic funds transfers from home and retail point-of-sale terminals. The "full-service" concept, dangled to bedazzle the consumer will, however, cost him some of the benefits of careful money management. Gone will be the "float" that he enjoyed while checks cleared and purchases on

95 Stephen M. Ege, "Electronic Funds Transfer: A Survey of Problems and Prospects in 1975," *Maryland Law Review,* Vol. 35, No. 1, 1975, p. 54–55.
96 *California Bankers Association v. Schultz,* 416 U.S. at 85.

credit cards were being processed. That advantage will, in fact, not only be taken away but a penalty will be imposed on users who cling to paper-based transactions. In the past four years, banks have doubled the average charge for checking, raised the amount on deposit required to avoid the fee, and now talk of billing customers who insist on receiving their cancelled checks. Ironically, here, as in many other instances of advancing IT, "full service" is synonymous with an increase in costs, in money and convenience, for the customer. Forfeiture of float, charges for banking once free, deprivation of the cancelled checks by which to conduct private business, all are disbenefits, part of the growing loss of control over one's own fiscal affairs. A further step in this growing usurpation of control, the so-called service of having bills paid through point-of-sale transfer of funds, deprives the customer of the opportunity to check the accuracy of the transaction that will tap his bank account directly but burdens him with the maddening task of coping with the arcane world of computerized systems if something is amiss or goes astray.

These fringe disbenefits are minor, however, when considered in the light of the larger issues associated with privacy. In this respect IT solves none of the problems discussed in an earlier chapter on information systems; it merely adds acute proportions and compounds them. We once might have raised questions about who is gathering information about us, where the sources are, about timeliness and accuracy of the data, who may have access, who is responsible for and who owns the information. The numbing penumbra of the cost/effectiveness justification for everything IT does has so dulled our perceptions and lulled our sensibilities that these questions no longer seem to demand urgent attention. In fact, anyone brash enough to go against the tidal wave of rationalized acceptance is likely to evoke a question more dulling in its portent than any of the above. Simply stated it is: who cares?

Computer specialists, the very professionals designated as experts in assessments of the technology, apparently do not. When Dr. Willis Ware, an authority on computer crime, warned his colleagues that the profusion of electronic mail and business-to-business computer linkages constituted a threat to individual privacy, he could arouse little interest.[97] Perhaps an explanation for this indifference lies in the intensively trained incapacity of computer professionals. The following excerpts from what purports to be the printout of an exchange among "hackers" (computer addicts) corroborates a great deal that has been said on the subject but is rarely documented, even fictionally:[98]

[97] Paul Gillin, "Little Interest Greets Ware's Call to Study Electronic Mail, Linkage Security Problems," *Computerworld*, October 4, 1982.

[98] "The Hacker Papers," *Psychology Today*, August 1980, p. 63.

There is no one field in particular in academia that has a monopoly on production of single-interest people. . . . But there is one field that seems to be
more consistent in this practice . . . This essay, rooted in personal and pain-
ful experience, is about the people in computer science . . . These are people
who spend their lives with computers and fellow "hackers." These are the
members of a subculture so foreign to most outsiders that it not only walls itself
off but is walled off, in turn, by those who cannot understand it. The wall is
built from both sides at once. These people deserve a description. In very few
ways do they seem average. First, they are all bright, so bright, in fact, that they
experienced social problems even before they became interested in computers.
Second, they are self-contained. Their entire social existence usually centers
around one another. Very, very few remain close to their families. Very, very
few associate much with anyone who is not at least partially a member of the
hacking group. . . . Third, all aspects of their existence reinforce one another.
They go to school in order to learn about computers, they work in jobs in
programming and computer maintenance, and they lead their social lives with
hackers . . . In creating a subculture and isolating it, we are destroying the
chance that computers might be used wisely as an integral part of our society.
We are precluding the human values so necessary for the wise application of
this technological achievement.

Indifference to IT's incursions into personal freedom may be attributable to the "hacker mentality." It is nonetheless, or perhaps even more,
deplorable because while the specialists do not care, persons outside
their closed circle of expertness do not dare. Lack of technical credentials not only drains their concerns of credibility, it also, as we noted
earlier, serves as reinforcement of the barrier preventing assessment
from becoming anything but a purely technical matter. We have already
reached a situation in which, while those persons who know IT do not
care and those who care not do know IT, the fragile framework of rules
once conceived as protection against invasion of freedom has buckled
under if not knuckled down to intertwined technological and political
pressure. Surveillance, long known to be an effective instrument for control, is intrinsic in and justified by totalitarianism. Advances in IT increases that capability which is in a sort of reflex way propelled by public
concern, warranted and unwarranted, about crime, terrorism, and the
like. To this state of what Bertram Gross[99] has affixed the oxymoronic
label, friendly fascism, IT brings a potent tool.

It is in the domestication of the computer that IT takes over the last
vestige of the personal domain and, ironically, without resistance because the electronic penetration is perpetrated in the name of partici-
pative democracy. Already an unlimited medium of intercommunica-
tion, the home computer, endowed with interactive capability, becomes
the two-way electronic highway bringing in pre-packaged ideology and

[99] Bertram Gross, *Friendly Fascism*, New York: M. Evans, 1980.

carrying out the individual's views and opinions, which could, depending on the prevailing political definition, be considered dissident, subversive, and potentially disruptive. Enthusiasts rhapsodize the computer's potential for involving the private citizen in the decision-making process. The instantaneous referendum on controversial issues is made to sound like utopian democracy: the citizens' voice would be heard. But whether this would ring out throughout the land as liberation from the convolutions of representative government or strengthen the tyranny of a new form of functional feudalism over the minds and lives of citizens is a matter of dire social consequence. The pervervid optimism of technical apologists finds little substantiation in current or past political process. Power and control go hand-in-hand and IT, for all its benign potential, is a juggernaut of pragmatism.

QUALITY OF LIFE

Whatever we might now say about information technology as it affects quality of life would be, in essence, a summation and, perhaps, synthesis of much that we discussed in earlier pages. Even so, we are caught between the Scylla of trivializing the effects by dwelling on petty personal irritants and the Charybdis of polemicizing about the Faustian bargain that ultimately has done nobody good. While instances of the former multiply, implications of the latter abound. But the jeremiad that would inevitably result is not the conclusion intended for this book. We might usefully remind ourselves that the focus of our research has been the methodology by which society runs its affairs. And we necessarily repeat the crucial point that predilection for the quantitative techniques whose development we have traced is consonant with our *Zeitgeist*. This removes us from tendentious debate about technology-as-driver and debarrasses us of the need for further rumination about IT's autonomy or culpability. There exists a technological imperative in which IT, for all its revolutionary potential, is actually part, in an evolutionary process. This is in no way to underrate its potency but rather to underscore its portent.

A study performed by the Institute of the Future at the behest of the National Science Foundation[100] speculates that by the end of the century IT will have transformed home, business, manufacturing, school, family, and political life. Even before the fateful 1984, that transformation has already advanced significantly in all these sectors. For all practical purposes, the electronic future is here. If there seems to be an insensitivity to the changes which are occurring and apathy as

---

[100] Institute for the Future, *Teletex and Videotex in the United States*, New York: McGraw Hill Publications, 1982.

to likely consequences, it is because for decades our thinking has been dominated by the means-end relationship intrinsic to cost/benefit calculations. Each incremental change in IT has found justification in its promise of payoff. Thus, automation in office, field, and factory, computers in hospitals, schools, and laboratories—each advance has been rationalized by its potential to reduce costs, increase efficiency, and improve productivity. In each instance, a worthy end could be evoked to justify the means. We have seen this line of argument advance from simple office automation[101] to "smart" nuclear bombs.

The ratiocination that had ends justifying means in a long history of incremental developments provides ready approval for the quantum leap. For example, over the years, the speed and power of computers have grown steadily. For every advance, there was a reason; for every improvement, a purpose. The fact that promise did not correspond to outcome seemed hardly to matter, so great has been the rise in our tolerance for incongruity. We hardly took note of the discrepancy between promise and consequence. The escalation seemed natural as systems and dependence on them grew interactively. IT's momentum *sui generis* constituted its justification.

Computers introduced to make our jobs easier took them away from us. Systems designed to provide us with information created such an overload we can no longer distinguish trash from treasure. Technology purported to extend our capabilities has dulled our capacity: it can provide all the answers but we lack the will or wisdom to ask good questions. The machines introduced as an aid to pedagogy are depriving that process of its primary essence—the joy of learning. Good writing has gone the way of the word-processor. The machine designed to help us think well now thinks for us. And if it is programmed to seek only half the truth, another generation, bred to be "hackers," will be none the wiser. Systems purported to promote international amity have created suspicious animosity. Systems intended to strengthen national economic stability have weakened us by making us instantaneously dependent on global insecurities. Systems designed to protect us from terrorism or enemy attack make us ever more vulnerable to it.

Now we enter the era of the supercomputer, estimated by American engineers to have the capability for performing one billion operations per second and planned by the Japanese to do ten. The new hardware is being promoted for the building of "better" weapons, breaking codes, and advancing military research. A notable design feature is the dense packing of microelectronic chips; this raises the speed by lowering the signal and reducing to the greatest degree the time taken to move the

---

[101] Ida R. Hoos, *Automation in the Office*, Washington, D.C.: Public Affairs Press, 1961.

electric pulses among the chips. Whereas earlier computers used sequential processing, this generation performs parallel processing in which many computations are performed simultaneously. The assumptions are, of course, that design is perfect, execution will be impeccable, and performance will live up to expectation. Caution and common sense based on the record suggest a different view. Recollection of misplaced objectives, mistakes in calculations, overlooked defects, and unexplained glitches in simpler and slower systems could be construed as useful warning signals. The crowning blow to complacency comes from advancing technology itself.

The technical justification that has parlayed us into ever more complicated computerized systems for defense has betrayed us into a position of consummate vulnerability. The computer, at the heart of the defense system, is its Achilles' heel, the supercomputer all the more so because of its susceptability to the disturbance that an electromagnetic pulse (EMP) would create. This, in fact, has been viewed as the ultimate chaos, in that a single nuclear blast in outer space could completely disrupt telecommunications on earth. Defense strategists claim[102] that a single warhead detonated 200 miles above Nebraska would blanket the United States with an EMP of 50,000 volts per meter. Instant pandemonium would result. EMP would shut down the power grid and "perform an electronic lobotomy" on computer memories. The chaos produced by EMP would make it difficult if not impossible for the President to direct and communicate with the U.S. strategic nuclear forces. The ultimate irony is that systems analysis techniques, transplanted from outer space and the military to improve man's management of his earthly affairs, should be the factor rationally leading him and his planet to disaster.

[102] William J. Broad, "Nuclear Pulse (I): Awakening to the Chaos Factor," *Science*, 29 May, 1981, pp. 1009–1012; "Nuclear Pulse (II): Ensuring Delivery of the Doomsday Signal," *Science*, 5 June 1981, pp. 1116–1120; "Nuclear Pulse (III): Playing a Wild Card," *Science*, 12 June, 1981, pp. 1248–1251.

Index